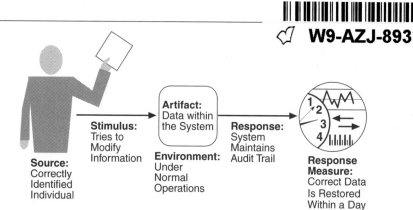

Sample security scenario. A correctly identified individual tries to modify system data from an external site; system maintains an audit trail and the correct data is restored within one day.

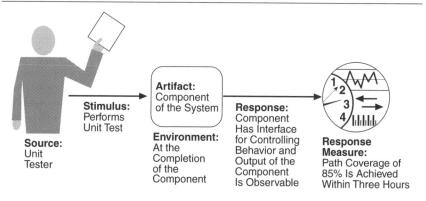

Sample testability scenario. A unit tester performs a unit test on a completed system component that provides an interface for controlling its behavior and observing its output; 85% path coverage is achieved within three hours.

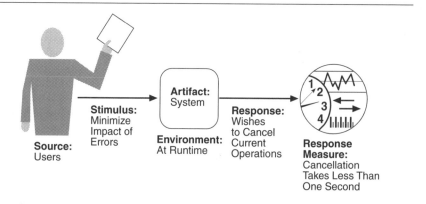

Sample usability scenario. A user, wanting to minimize the impact of an error, wishes to cancel a system operation at runtime; cancellation takes place in less than one second.

Software Architecture in Practice

Second Edition

Software Architecture in Practice

Second Edition

Len Bass
Paul Clements
Rick Kazman

✦✦Addison-Wesley

Boston • San Francisco • New York • Toronto • Montreal
London • Munich • Paris • Madrid
Capetown • Sydney • Tokyo • Singapore • Mexico City

Carnegie Mellon
Software Engineering Institute

The SEI Series in Software Engineering

Library of Congress Cataloging-in-Publication Data
Bass, Len.
    Software architecture in practice / Len Bass, Paul Clements, Rick Kazman—2nd ed.
        p.   cm.
    Includes bibliographical references and index.
    ISBN 0-321-15495-9 (alk. paper)
    1. Computer software. 2. Computer architecture. 3. System design I. Clements, Paul.
II. Kazman, Rick. III. Title.

    QA76.754.B37 2003
    005.1--dc21

                                              2003045300

ISBN 0321154959

5 6 7 8 9 10 CRW 07 06 05 04

5th Printing   January 2005

Contents

Preface

Software architecture is an important field of study that is becoming more important and more talked about with every passing day. Nevertheless, to our knowledge, there exists little practical guidance on managing software architecture in a real software development organization, from both technical and managerial perspectives. This book has emerged from our belief that the coupling of a system's software architecture and its business and organizational context has not been well explored.

Our experience with designing and analyzing large and complex software-intensive systems has led us to recognize the role of business and organization in the design of the system and in its ultimate success or failure. Systems are built to satisfy an organization's requirements (or assumed requirements in the case of shrink-wrapped products). These requirements dictate the system's performance, availability, security, compatibility with other systems, and the ability to accommodate change over its lifetime. The desire to satisfy these goals with software that has the requisite properties influences the design choices made by a software architect.

In this book we demonstrate this coupling of software architecture and corporate context through the use of case studies drawn from real systems. Our examples include the following situations:

- The desire to share documents quickly and easily within an organization, with a minimum of centralized control, led to the software architecture of the World Wide Web.
- The extreme safety requirements of air traffic control led one company to build a system around an architecture for achieving ultra-high availability.
- The distribution of the subsystems of a flight simulator to remotely located developers led to an architecture geared to enable smooth integration of these subsystems.
- The need to satisfy simultaneous product deliveries led (in fact, forced) one company to adopt an architecture that enabled the company to build a set of complex related software systems as a product line.
- The need to standardize architectural approaches across organizations and in the community at large led to infrastructures such as J2EE and EJB.

These and other case studies show that software architectures flow from the requirements of organizations and their business models, from the experience of the organization's architects, as well as from the prevailing design climate.

In addition, we show how architectures themselves can be powerful vehicles for influencing all of the preceding. A successful product or set of products can influence the way other products are built. Certainly the case study about the software underlying the World Wide Web is a good example of this. Before this system existed, there was far less network awareness, less thought was given to accessibility of data, and security was the concern of only a few organizations, typically financial institutions and government agencies.

Our book is aimed at software professionals—the people who design and implement large software-intensive systems, the managers of software professionals, and the students who are hoping to become software professionals.

We believe that a software architecture is the development product that gives the highest return on investment with respect to quality, schedule, and cost. Because its architecture appears early in a product's lifetime, getting it right sets the stage for everything to come—the system's development, integration, testing, and modification. Getting it wrong means that the fabric of the system is wrong, and it cannot be fixed by weaving in a few new threads or pulling out a few existing ones, which often causes the entire fabric to unravel. Also, compared to other development activities, analyzing architectures is inexpensive. Thus, architectures give a high return on investment because decisions made for the architecture have substantial downstream consequences and because checking and fixing an architecture is relatively inexpensive.

We also believe that re-use is achieved best within an architectural context. But components are not the only artifacts that can be re-used. Re-use of an architecture leads to the creation of families of systems, which in turn leads to new organizational structures and new business opportunities.

We devote a large percentage of this book to presenting real architectures that were designed to solve the real problems of real organizations. We chose the cases presented here to illuminate the types of choices that architects must make to achieve their quality goals and to illuminate how organizational goals affect the final systems.

In addition to the case studies, this book offers a set of techniques for designing, building, and evaluating software architectures. We look at techniques for understanding quality requirements in the context of an architecture, and for building architectures that meet these quality requirements. We look at architecture representation and reconstruction techniques as a means of describing and validating software architectures. We look at techniques for analyzing and evaluating an architecture's fitness for its purpose. Each of these techniques is derived from our experience, and the experience of our colleagues at the Software Engineering Institute, with a variety of software systems. These systems range up to millions of lines of code and are large-team, multi-year development efforts.

Although we discuss business issues throughout the book (for example, an architecture's effects on an organization's ability to compete in a market or a product family's time-to-market), we present this material without going into great depth on the business issues, and without business jargon. We are, after all, software engineers. We present the technical sections of our book in more depth. These sections represent current work in the field of software architecture—the point where research meets practice. The case studies illuminate these technical foundations, and show how they are realized in practice. To benefit from the lessons illuminated by the case studies, you will need a reasonable background in computer science, software engineering, or a related discipline. However, we have written them in such a way that you will not need expertise in the application domain from which the case study was drawn. For example, you do need not be a pilot to understand either the air traffic control system or the flight simulation case studies.

WHAT'S NEW IN THE SECOND EDITION

Our goals for this second edition are the same as they were for the first, but the passage of time since the writing of the first edition has brought new developments in the field and new understanding of the important underpinnings of software architecture. We reflect the new developments with new case studies and our new understanding both through new chapters and through strengthening the existing chapters. Also, the writing of this second edition has been strongly influenced by several other books that we have collectively authored since the publication of the first edition—*Documenting Software Architectures*, *Evaluating Software Architectures: Methods and Case Studies*, and *Software Product Lines: Principles and Practice*. The creation of these books, along with other technical and research activities, has greatly influenced us in developing this book. This second edition reflects the fact that architecture analysis, design, reconstruction, and documentation have all had major developments since the first edition.

Architecture analysis has developed into a mature field with industrial-strength methods—reflected here by a new chapter in Part Three about the Architecture Tradeoff Analysis Method (ATAM^{SM}). Many industrial organizations have adopted the ATAM as a technique for evaluating software architectures.

Architecture design has also had major developments since the first edition. The capturing of quality requirements, their achievement through small-scale and large-scale architectural approaches (tactics and patterns, respectively), and a design method that reflects knowledge of how to achieve them are all discussed in various chapters. Three new chapters treat understanding quality requirements, achieving qualities, and the Attribute Driven Design Method (ADD).

Architecture reconstruction, or reverse engineering, is an essential activity for capturing undocumented architectures. It can be used as a portion of a design project or as an analysis project, or as input into a decision regarding what to use as a basis for reconstructing a system. In the first edition, we briefly mentioned a tool set (Dali) and its uses in the re-engineering context, but in this edition the topic merits its own chapter.

Documenting software architectures is another topic that has matured considerably in the recent past. When the first edition was published, the Unified

Modeling Language (UML) was just arriving on the scene. Now it is firmly entrenched, a reality reflected here with all-new diagrams. More important, an understanding of the kind of information to capture about an architecture, beyond which notation to use, has emerged. A new chapter covers architecture documentation.

The application of software architecture to enable organizations to efficiently produce a variety of systems based on a single architecture is summarized in a totally rewritten chapter on software product lines. This chapter reinforces the link between architecture and an organization's business goals, in view of the fact that product lines (based around a software architecture) can enable order-of-magnitude improvements in cost, quality, and time-to-market.

In addition to the architectural developments, the technology for constructing distributed and Web-based systems has become prominent in today's economy. We reflect this trend in our updated chapter on the World Wide Web by using Web-based examples in the chapter on the ATAM and the chapter on building systems from components, by replacing the case study on Common Object Request Broker Architecture (CORBA) with one on Enterprise JavaBeans (EJBs), and by introducing a case study on a wireless EJB system designed to support wearable computers for maintenance technicians.

Finally, we have added a chapter that looks more closely at the financial aspects of architectures. In this chapter, we introduce a method—the Cost Benefit Analysis Method (CBAM)—for basing architectural decisions on economic criteria, in addition to the technical criteria that we discussed previously.

As in the first edition, we use the Architecture Business Cycle (ABC) as a unifying motif. All of the case studies are described in terms of the quality goals that motivated the system's design and how the system's architecture achieves those goals.

In writing the second edition, as with the first, we were very aware that our primary audience is practitioners, and so we have focused on material that has been found useful in many industrial applications as well as what we expect practice to be in the near future.

We hope that you enjoy reading this second edition at least as much as we enjoyed writing it.

Acknowledgments

Without the first edition of this book, there would not be a second edition, and so we are pleased to continue to acknowledge the people who helped with the earlier version. Coauthors of chapters were Gregory Abowd, Lisa Brownsword, Jeromy Carrière, Linda Northrop, Patricia Oberndorf, Mary Shaw, Rob Veltre, Kurt Wallnau, Nelson Weiderman, and Amy Moormann Zaremski. The many people at the Software Engineering Institute who helped to make the first edition happen through their support and encouragement include Linda Northrop, Sholom Cohen, Lisa Lane, Bill Pollak, Barbara Tomchik, and Barbara White.

We owe a debt of gratitude to our many reviewers, including Felix Bachmann, John Bennett, Sonia Bot, Lisa Brownsword, Bob Ellison, Larry Howard, Richard Juren, Philippe Kruchten, Chung-Horng Lung, Joaquin Miller, Linda Northrop, David Notkin, Patricia Oberndorf, Jan Pachl, Lui Sha, Nelson Weiderman, Amy Moormann Zaremski, and several anonymous Addison-Wesley reviewers. Commander Rob Madson of the U.S. Navy provided partial support for the development of graphics. Peter Gordon of Addison-Wesley kept us grounded in reality.

For this second edition, we owe many thanks to the chapter co-authors: Linda Northrop, Felix Bachmann, Mark Klein, Bill Wood, David Garlan, James Ivers, Reed Little, Robert Nord, Judith Stafford, Jeromy Carrière, Liam O'Brien, Chris Verhoef, Jai Asundi, Hong-Mei Chen, Lisa Brownsword, Anna Liu, Tanya Bass, James Beck, Kelly Dolan, Cuiwei Li, Andreas Löhr, Richard Martin, William Ross, Tobias Weishäupl, Gregory Zelesnik, Robert Seacord, and Matthew Bass. As always, our reviewers deserve much credit for helping us make this book better. We thank Alexander Ran, Paulo Merson, Matt Bass, Tony Lattanze, Liam O'Brien, and Robert Nord.

Many people contributed to the body of work related to the characterization and achievement of software quality attributes. We are indebted to John McGregor, Bob Ellison, Andy Moore, Scott Hissam, Chuck Weinstock, Mario Barbacci, Heather Oppenheimer, Felix Bachmann, Stefen Kowalewski, and Marko Auerswald.

Special thanks to Mike Moore of NASA's Goddard Space Flight Center for providing the ECS system that was the subject of the CBAM case study in Chapter 12.

At the SEI, we are indebted to Linda Northrop for her management, commitment, and contributions to this work; to Bob Fantazier for steadfastly producing the book's graphics; to Sheila Rosenthal for her research assistance; and to Laura Novacic, Carolyn Kernan, and Barbara Tomchik for their support.

At Addison-Wesley, Peter Gordon continues to be the taskmaster with the velvet whip. We thank him and all of the people involved in this book's production.

Len Bass did some of the production work on this book while visiting at the Commonwealth Scientific Industrial Research Organization in Australia. He would like to thank them for their support.

And finally, we would like to thank the special people in our lives for their endurance and encouragement throughout this process.

Reader's Guide

AUDIENCE

This book is for software professionals, or students who have knowledge and experience in software engineering. We anticipate three classes of reader:

- Practicing software engineers who wish to understand both the technical basis of software architecture and the business and organizational forces that are acting on them.
- Technical managers who wish to understand how software architecture can help them to supervise the construction of systems more effectively and improve their organizations.
- Students of computer science or software engineering who might use this book as supplemental reading in a first or second software engineering course.

PARTS AND CHAPTERS

The book is divided into four parts, roughly following a life-cycle perspective, which we call the *Architecture Business Cycle*, of how architectures fit into a business:

- Envisioning Architecture—Chapters 1–3
- Creating an Architecture—Chapters 4–10
- Analyzing an Architecture—Chapters 11–13
- Moving from One System to Many—Chapters 14–19

The case studies are in Chapters 3, 6, 8, 13, 15, 16, and 17, and are clearly noted in the chapter titles.

In detail, the parts and chapters cover the following ground.

PART ONE: ENVISIONING AN ARCHITECTURE

Chapter 1 – The Architecture Business Cycle. The theme that weaves through this book is that architectures do not exist by themselves, but are part of a cycle. Architecture is a means toward an end. It is influenced by the functional and quality goals of both the customer and the developing organization. It is also influenced by the architect's background and experiences and by the technical environment. Architecture in turn influences the system being developed, and it may be a core asset that influences the developing organization. The system also has an effect on the developing organization; the architecture; and, potentially, the technical environment. This effect affects the future goals for the system and its organization. The influences and feedback loops that surround an architecture form the ABC.

Chapter 2 – What Is Software Architecture?   An architecture is a description of system structures, of which there are several (module decomposition, process, deployment, layered, etc.). Architecture is the first artifact that can be analyzed to determine how well its quality attributes are being achieved, and it also serves as the project blueprint. An architecture serves as the vehicle for communication, is the manifestation of the earliest design decisions, and is a re-usable abstraction that can be transferred to new systems. These are the things we mean when we use the word *architecture*.

Chapter 3 – A-7E Avionics System: A Case Study in Utilizing Architectural Structures.   The A-7E Avionics System was a project that paid special attention to the engineering and specification of three distinct architectural structures to achieve developmental simplicity and modifiability. The chapter shows how (and why) the structures were designed and documented.

PART TWO: CREATING AN ARCHITECTURE

Chapter 4 – Understanding Quality Attributes.   A motivating factor for all architectures is the desire to achieve particular software qualities. This chapter discusses software qualities and their implications. It presents a method for understanding qualities in architectural terms, by characterizing the stimuli that we apply to systems in order to observe their qualities, and by characterizing the systems' responses in measurable, observable ways when manifesting those qualities.

Chapter 5 – Achieving Qualities.   Once the desired qualities of a system are known, the problem of designing an architecture to achieve these qualities remains. This chapter describes a number of techniques used to achieve development- and runtime qualities. The primary mechanisms are *tactics*, which are design decisions that influence the control of a quality attribute. Tactics can be grouped into architectural strategies and architectural patterns.

Chapter 6 – Air Traffic Control: A Case Study in Designing for High Availability.
A system designed for air traffic control had the quality goal of extremely high availability. This goal motivated a number of architectural decisions, which are discussed in this chapter. In addition, this case study emphasizes the interplay of

architectural structures and views (as discussed in Chapter 2) and architectural tactics (as discussed in Chapter 5), and it shows how they work in concert to achieve qualities.

Chapter 7 – Creating the Architecture. With the foundational tools in hand (architectural views and structures, expressing quality attributes, tactics and patterns for achieving them), we are ready to address creating the architecture. This chapter discusses the role of architecture from the perspective of a system's overall life cycle. It presents a design method for producing an early architecture that can be refined and can evolve. Once the architecture is sketched, it can be used to form the project's team structure and to create a skeletal system as the basis for incremental development.

Chapter 8 – Flight Simulation: A Case Study in Architecture for Integrability. This chapter describes an architecture for flight simulation. It shows how careful attention to the software architecture in a complex domain enabled the construction of a set of large systems that met their stringent functional and fidelity requirements, could be understood by a variety of software engineers, were easy to integrate, and were amenable to downstream modifications.

Chapter 9 – Documenting Software Architectures. An architecture is only as good as its ability to be communicated to and understood by its stakeholders. This chapter lays out an approach to documenting a software architecture. Documenting an architecture is a matter of recording the relevant views and then recording the information that applies across the views. The chapter provides templates for a view, for cross-view information, and for software interfaces.

Chapter 10 – Reconstructing Software Architectures. Suppose we have a system but we don't know its architecture. Perhaps the architecture was never recorded, or was lost, or the system diverged from the architecture through evolution. How do we maintain such a system? How do we manage its evolution to maintain the quality attributes that its architecture has provided for us? Architecture reconstruction is the process where the "as-built" architecture of an implemented system is obtained from an existing system. This chapter presents an approach to architecture reconstruction and an example of its application.

PART THREE: ANALYZING AN ARCHITECTURE

Chapter 11 – The ATAM: A Comprehensive Method for Architecture Evaluation. The Architecture Tradeoff Analysis Method is a way to evaluate architectural decisions in light of specific behavioral and quality attribute requirements. This chapter describes the ATAM and walks through a comprehensive example of its application.

Chapter 12 – The CBAM: A Quantitative Approach to Architecture Design Decision Making. The software architect or project decision maker wishes to maximize the difference between the benefit derived from a system and the cost of implementing the design. The Cost Benefit Analysis Method addresses this need for economic decision making centered on an analysis of architecture. The CBAM builds on the ATAM to model the costs and the benefits of architectural design decisions and provides a means of optimizing such decisions. This chapter presents the CBAM and a case where it was applied.

Chapter 13 – The World Wide Web: A Case Study in Interoperability. The World Wide Web was created out of a single organization's desire to exchange information among its researchers, but it has far outgrown those original goals. This chapter describes the architecture of the software underlying the Web, how this architecture has changed to allow the Web to grow, and how that growth, in turn, has influenced the organizations that use it.

PART FOUR: MOVING FROM ONE SYSTEM TO MANY

Chapter 14 – Product Lines: Re-using Architectural Assets within an Organization. One of the most powerful applications of software architecture is its use as the foundation of a software product line. This chapter presents the basics of software product line production, highlighting architecture as the keystone for achieving large improvements in productivity, time-to-market, quality, and cost. The chapter explores in detail a few of the software engineering development and management activities that take on a special dimension in a product line context.

Chapter 15 – CelsiusTech: A Case Study in Product Line Development. CelsiusTech is an organization that successfully implemented a product line based on an architecture. This chapter describes the architecture of the product line and shows why this architecture was crucial to CelsiusTech's success. Without this approach, it would not have been able to build these systems—it simply did not have adequate personnel. The product line approach brought consequent changes to the organizational structure and the manner in which it both solicits and contracts for business.

Chapter 16 – J2EE/EJB: A Case Study of an Industry-Standard Computing Infrastructure. This chapter presents an overview of Sun Microsystems's Java 2 Enterprise Edition (J2EE) architecture specification, as well as an important portion of that specification, the Enterprise JavaBeans (EJBs) architecture specification. The J2EE specification provides a standard description of how distributed object-oriented programs written in Java should be designed and developed. The chapter examines the business drivers that led to the creation of such an industry standard architecture for building distributed systems, and shows how the J2EE/EJB architecture addresses such needs.

Chapter 17 – The Luther Architecture: A Case Study in Mobile Applications Using J2EE. The Luther architecture was designed to provide a general framework to provide customized solutions in the domain of maintenance or operation of large vehicles or industrial infrastructure. It is based on J2EE, and so this chapter becomes an application of the general J2EE/EJB framework discussed in Chapter 16. This case deals with an environment where the end user is connected over a wireless network and has a device with limited input/output capabilities, limited computational capabilities, or both.

Chapter 18 – Building Systems from Off-the-Shelf Components. Systems are being constructed with more and more off-the-shelf components. The use of such components changes the design process because the components can constrain the architecture. Typically, components are chosen to achieve some set of functionality, but they also embody architectural (and hence quality) assumptions. This chapter describes a lightweight process to guide an architect in choosing components that will work well in concert. The chapter includes a demonstration of the process applied to a recently fielded system.

Chapter 19 – Software Architecture in the Future. We look at the Architecture Business Cycle again and identify some of the yet to be solved problems associated with software architecture and discuss why more research is needed.

CASE STUDY ORGANIZATION

We realize that different readers of the book will want to mine different information from it, and that most of them will want to read the book at various levels of detail. To address this need, we have organized the case studies in a consistent fashion around the following sections:

- A brief description of the study, the problems it was solving, and the points about software architecture it illustrates
- A description of how the ABC was realized (or partially realized) in this study
- The requirements and qualities that propelled the design
- The architectural solution: a detailed discussion that comprises the bulk of many of the case studies
- A summary of the important points made in the chapter

The architectural solution contains most of the detail in the case studies. If you are interested only in the technical and business environment and a high-level description of the architectural approach, you can get the gist of a case study by reading the brief description of it, its requirements and quality goals, and the summary. For a fuller discussion, you can also read the architectural solution section of each case.

THREADS THROUGH THE BOOK

While the ABC is the primary theme of the book, other conceptual threads run through it. A reader interested in pursuing a particular aspect of architecture may wish to concentrate on the chapters that carry one or more of the following threads:

- Where do architectures come from?—Chapters 1, 2, 4, 7, 11, and 12
- Business issues—Chapters 1, 4, 7, 11, 12, 14, 15, and 18
- How qualities derive from architectures—Chapters 4, 5, 11, and 12 and the case studies
- Case studies of qualities deriving from architecture—Chapters 3, 6, 8, 13, 15, 16, and 17
- Architecture as a re-usable asset—Chapters 14, 15, 16, 17, and 18
- Component-based systems and commercial infrastructures—Chapters 13, 16, 17, and 18
- Architectures for real-time systems—Chapters 3, 5, 6, 8, and 15
- Architectures for information systems—Chapters 13, 16, 17, and 18

SIDEBARS

Throughout the book we have located short, signed, visually separated sidebars written by only one of us. These features are intended to give background or perspective that is outside the normal flow of the text.

PART ONE

ENVISIONING ARCHITECTURE

Where do architectures come from? They spring from the minds of architects, of course, but how? What must go *into* the mind of an architect for an architecture to come *out?* For that matter, what *is* a software architecture? Is it the same as design? If so, what's the fuss? If it's different, how so and why is it important?

In Part One, we focus on the forces and influences that are at work as the architect begins creating—*envisioning*—the central artifact of a system whose influences persist beyond the lifetime of the system. Whereas we often think of design as taking the right steps to ensure that the system will perform as expected—produce the correct answer or provide the expected functionality—architecture is additionally concerned with much longer-range issues. The architect is faced with a swarm of competing, if not conflicting, influences and demands, surprisingly few of which are concerned with getting the system to work correctly. The organizational and technical environment brings to bear a weighty set of sometimes implicit demands, and in practice these are as important as any of the explicit requirements for the software even though they are almost never written down.

Also surprising are the ways in which the architecture produces a deep influence on the organization that spawned it. It is decidedly not the case that the organization produces the architecture, ties it to the system for which it was developed, and locks it away in that compartment. Instead, architectures and their developing organizations dance an intricate waltz of influence and counterinfluence, helping each other to grow, evolve, and take on larger roles.

1

The Architecture Business Cycle (ABC) is the name we give to this waltz, and it is the theme of this book and the focus of Chapter 1. Chapter 2 lays the foundations for the study of software architecture, defines it, places it in the context of software engineering, and provides some conceptual tools for its consideration. Chief among the concepts is the notion that architectures consist of separate coordinated structures and that each structure provides an engineering leverage point in system development.

Chapter 3 is the first case study in the book. It illustrates how a particular architecture solved a unique set of requirements—in this case, a real-time embedded avionics system whose focus was on long-term modifiability—but also brings home the conceptual points made earlier. Three separate architectural structures—module decomposition, uses, and process structures—came together to provide the architectural solution for this system.

With this introduction, we begin our tour of the Architecture Business Cycle.

1

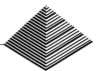

The Architecture
Business Cycle

> *Simply stated, competitive success flows to the company*
> *that manages to establish proprietary architectural control*
> *over a broad, fast-moving, competitive space.*
> — C. Morris and C. Ferguson [Morris 93]

For decades, software designers have been taught to build systems based exclusively on the technical requirements. Conceptually, the requirements document is tossed over the wall into the designer's cubicle, and the designer must come forth with a satisfactory design. Requirements beget design, which begets system. Of course, modern software development methods recognize the naïveté of this model and provide all sorts of feedback loops from designer to analyst. But they still make the implicit assumption that design is a product of the system's technical requirements, period.

Architecture has emerged as a crucial part of the design process and is the subject of this book. *Software architecture* encompasses the structures of large software systems. The architectural view of a system is abstract, distilling away details of implementation, algorithm, and data representation and concentrating on the behavior and interaction of "black box" elements. A software architecture is developed as the first step toward designing a system that has a collection of desired properties. We will discuss software architecture in detail in Chapter 2. For now we provide, without comment, the following definition:

> The software architecture of a program or computing system is the structure
> or structures of the system, which comprise software elements, the externally
> visible properties of those elements, and the relationships among them.

Chapter 2 will provide our working definitions and distinguish between architecture and other forms of design. For reasons we will see throughout, architecture serves as an important communication, reasoning, analysis, and growth tool for systems. Until now, however, architectural design has been discussed in the

The Swedish Ship *Vasa*

In the 1620s, Sweden and Poland were at war. The king of Sweden, Gustavus Adolphus, was determined to put a swift end to it and commissioned a new warship the likes of which had never been seen before. The *Vasa*, shown in Figure 1.1, was to be the world's most formidable instrument of war: 70 meters long, able to carry 300 soldiers, and with an astonishing 64 heavy guns mounted on two gun decks. Seeking to add overwhelming firepower to his navy to strike a decisive blow, the king insisted on stretching the *Vasa*'s armaments to the limits. Her architect, Henrik Hybertsson, was a seasoned Dutch shipbuilder with an impeccable reputation, but the *Vasa* was beyond even his broad experience. Two-gun-deck ships were rare, and none had been built of the *Vasa*'s size and armament.

Like all architects of systems that push the envelope of experience, Hybertsson had to balance many concerns. Swift time to deployment was critical, but so were performance, functionality, safety, reliability, and cost. He was also responsible to a variety of stakeholders. In this case, the primary customer was the king, but Hybertsson also was responsible to the crew that would sail his creation. Also like all architects, Hybertsson brought his experience with him to the task. In this case, his experience told him to design the *Vasa* as though it were a single-gun-deck ship and then extrapolate, which was in accordance with the technical environment of the day. Faced with an impossible task, Hybertsson had the good sense to die about a year before the ship was finished.

The project was completed to his specifications, however, and on Sunday morning, August 10, 1628, the mighty ship was ready. She set her sails, waddled out into Stockholm's deep-water harbor, fired her guns in salute, and

FIGURE 1.1 The warship *Vasa*.   Used with permission of The Vasa Museum, Stockholm, Sweden.

promptly rolled over. Water poured in through the open gun ports, and the *Vasa* plummeted. A few minutes later her first and only voyage ended 30 meters beneath the surface. Dozens among her 150-man crew drowned.

Inquiries followed, which concluded that the ship was well built but "badly proportioned." In other words, its architecture was flawed. Today we know that Hybertsson did a poor job of balancing all of the conflicting constraints levied on him. In particular, he did a poor job of risk management and a poor job of customer management (not that anyone could have fared better). He simply acquiesced in the face of impossible requirements.

The story of the *Vasa*, although more than 375 years old, well illustrates the Architecture Business Cycle: organization goals beget requirements, which beget an architecture, which begets a system. The architecture flows from the architect's experience and the technical environment of the day. Hybertsson suffered from the fact that neither of those were up to the task before him.

In this book, we provide three things that Hybertsson could have used:

1. Case studies of successful architectures crafted to satisfy demanding requirements, so as to help set the technical playing field of the day.
2. Methods to assess an architecture before any system is built from it, so as to mitigate the risks associated with launching unprecedented designs.
3. Techniques for incremental architecture-based development, so as to uncover design flaws before it is too late to correct them.

Our goal is to give architects another way out of their design dilemmas than the one that befell the ill-fated Dutch ship designer. Death before deployment is not nearly so admired these days.

— PCC

light that, if you know the requirements for a system, you can build the architecture for it.

This is short-sighted (see the sidebar The Swedish Ship *Vasa*) and fails to tell the whole story. What do you suppose would happen if two different architects, working in two different organizations, were given the same requirements specification for a system? Do you think they would produce the same architecture or different ones?

The answer is that, in general, they would produce different ones, which immediately belies the notion that requirements determine architecture. Other factors are at work, and to fail to recognize them is to continue working in the dark.

The focusing question is this: What is the relationship of a system's software architecture to the environment in which the system will be constructed and exist? The answer to this question is the organizing motif of this book. Software architecture is a result of *technical, business,* and *social* influences. Its existence in turn affects the technical, business, and social environments that subsequently influence future architectures. We call this cycle of influences, from the environment to the architecture and back to the environment, the *Architecture Business Cycle* (ABC).

This chapter introduces the ABC in detail and sets the stage for the remainder of the book. The major parts of the book tour the cycle by examining the following:

- How organizational goals influence requirements and development strategy.
- How requirements lead to an architecture.
- How architectures are analyzed.
- How architectures yield systems that suggest new organizational capabilities and requirements.

1.1   Where Do Architectures Come From?

An architecture is the result of a set of business and technical decisions. There are many influences at work in its design, and the realization of these influences will change depending on the environment in which the architecture is required to perform. An architect designing a system for which the real-time deadlines are believed to be tight will make one set of design choices; the same architect, designing a similar system in which the deadlines can be easily satisfied, will make different choices. And the same architect, designing a non-real-time system, is likely to make quite different choices still. Even with the same requirements, hardware, support software, and human resources available, an architect designing a system today is likely to design a different system than might have been designed five years ago.

In any development effort, the requirements make explicit some—but only some—of the desired properties of the final system. Not all requirements are concerned directly with those properties; a development process or the use of a particular tool may be mandated by them. But the requirements specification only begins to tell the story. Failure to satisfy other constraints may render the system just as problematic as if it functioned poorly.

We begin building the ABC by identifying the influences to and from architectures.

ARCHITECTURES ARE INFLUENCED
BY SYSTEM STAKEHOLDERS

Many people and organizations are interested in the construction of a software system. We call these *stakeholders*: The customer, the end users, the developers, the project manager, the maintainers, and even those who market the system are a few examples. Stakeholders have different concerns that they wish the system to guarantee or optimize, including things as diverse as providing a certain behavior at runtime, performing well on a particular piece of hardware, being easy to customize, achieving short time to market or low cost of development, gainfully employing programmers who have a particular specialty, or providing a broad

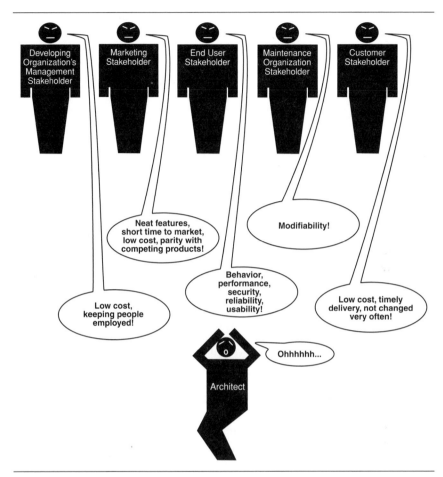

FIGURE 1.2   Influence of stakeholders on the architect

range of functions. Figure 1.2 shows the architect receiving helpful stakeholder "suggestions."

Having an acceptable system involves properties such as performance, reliability, availability, platform compatibility, memory utilization, network usage, security, modifiability, usability, and interoperability with other systems as well as behavior. Indeed, we will see that these properties determine the overall design of the architecture. All of them, and others, affect how the delivered system is viewed by its eventual recipients, and so they find a voice in one or more of the system's stakeholders.

The underlying problem, of course, is that each stakeholder has different concerns and goals, some of which may be contradictory. Properties can be listed and discussed, of course, in an artifact such as a requirements document. But it is a rare requirements document that does a good job of capturing all of a system's quality requirements in testable detail. The reality is that the architect often has to fill in the blanks and mediate the conflicts.

ARCHITECTURES ARE INFLUENCED BY THE DEVELOPING ORGANIZATION

In addition to the organizational goals expressed through requirements, an architecture is influenced by the structure or nature of the development organization. For example, if the organization has an abundance of idle programmers skilled in client-server communications, then a client-server architecture might be the approach supported by management. If not, it may well be rejected. Staff skills are one additional influence, but so are the development schedule and budget.

There are three classes of influence that come from the developing organization: immediate business, long-term business, and organizational structure.

- An organization may have an immediate business investment in certain assets, such as existing architectures and the products based on them. The foundation of a development project may be that the proposed system is the next in a sequence of similar systems, and the cost estimates assume a high degree of asset re-use.
- An organization may wish to make a long-term business investment in an infrastructure to pursue strategic goals and may view the proposed system as one means of financing and extending that infrastructure.
- The organizational structure can shape the software architecture. In the case study in Chapter 8 (Flight Simulation: A Case Study in Architecture for Integrability), the development of some of the subsystems was subcontracted because the subcontractors provided specialized expertise. This was made possible by a division of functionality in the architecture that allowed isolation of the specialities.

ARCHITECTURES ARE INFLUENCED BY THE BACKGROUND AND EXPERIENCE OF THE ARCHITECTS

If the architects for a system have had good results using a particular architectural approach, such as distributed objects or implicit invocation, chances are that they will try that same approach on a new development effort. Conversely, if their prior experience with this approach was disastrous, the architects may be reluctant to try it again. Architectural choices may also come from an architect's education and training, exposure to successful architectural patterns, or exposure to systems that have worked particularly poorly or particularly well. The architects may also wish to experiment with an architectural pattern or technique learned from a book (such as this one) or a course.

ARCHITECTURES ARE INFLUENCED
BY THE TECHNICAL ENVIRONMENT

A special case of the architect's background and experience is reflected by the *technical environment*. The environment that is current when an architecture is designed will influence that architecture. It might include standard industry practices or software engineering techniques prevalent in the architect's professional community. It is a brave architect who, in today's environment, does not at least consider a Web-based, object-oriented, middleware-supported design for an information system.

RAMIFICATIONS OF INFLUENCES ON AN ARCHITECTURE

Influences on an architecture come from a wide variety of sources. Some are only implied, while others are explicitly in conflict.

Almost never are the properties required by the business and organizational goals consciously understood, let alone fully articulated. Indeed, even customer requirements are seldom documented completely, which means that the inevitable conflict among different stakeholders' goals has not been resolved.

However, architects need to know and understand the nature, source, and priority of constraints on the project as early as possible. Therefore, *they must identify and actively engage the stakeholders to solicit their needs and expectations*. Without such engagement, the stakeholders will, at some point, demand that the architects explain why each proposed architecture is unacceptable, thus delaying the project and idling workers. Early engagement of stakeholders allows the architects to understand the constraints of the task, manage expectations, negotiate priorities, and make tradeoffs. Architecture reviews (covered in Part Three) and iterative prototyping are two means for achieving it.

It should be apparent that the architects need more than just technical skills. Explanations to one stakeholder or another will be required regarding the chosen priorities of different properties and why particular stakeholders are not having all of their expectations satisfied. For an effective architect, then, diplomacy, negotiation, and communication skills are essential.

The influences on the architect, and hence on the architecture, are shown in Figure 1.3. Architects are influenced by the requirements for the product as derived from its stakeholders, the structure and goals of the developing organization, the available technical environment, and their own background and experience.

THE ARCHITECTURES AFFECT THE FACTORS
THAT INFLUENCE THEM

The main message of this book is that the relationships among business goals, product requirements, architects' experience, architectures, and fielded systems form a cycle with feedback loops that a business can manage. A business manages this cycle to handle growth, to expand its enterprise area, and to take advantage of

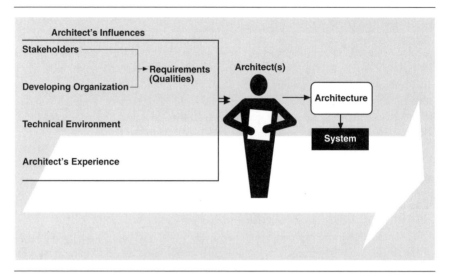

FIGURE 1.3   Influences on the architecture

previous investments in architecture and system building. Figure 1.4 shows the feedback loops. Some of the feedback comes from the architecture itself, and some comes from the system built from it.

Here is how the cycle works:

1. The architecture affects the structure of the developing organization. An architecture prescribes a structure for a system; as we will see, it particularly pre-scribes the units of software that must be implemented (or otherwise obtained) and integrated to form the system. These units are the basis for the development project's structure. Teams are formed for individual software units; and the devel-opment, test, and integration activities all revolve around the units. Likewise, schedules and budgets allocate resources in chunks corresponding to the units. If a company becomes adept at building families of similar systems, it will tend to invest in each team by nurturing each area of expertise. Teams become embedded in the organization's structure. This is feedback from the architecture to the developing organization.

In the software product line case study in Chapter 15, separate groups were given responsibility for building and maintaining individual portions of the orga-nization's architecture for a family of products. In any design undertaken by the organization at large, these groups have a strong voice in the system's decompo-sition, pressuring for the continued existence of the portions they control.

2. The architecture can affect the goals of the developing organization. A successful system built from it can enable a company to establish a foothold in a particular market area. The architecture can provide opportunities for the efficient production and deployment of similar systems, and the organization may adjust

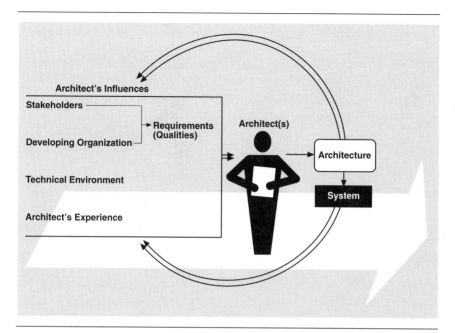

FIGURE 1.4   The Architecture Business Cycle

its goals to take advantage of its newfound expertise to plumb the market. This is feedback from the system to the developing organization and the systems it builds.

3. The architecture can affect customer requirements for the next system by giving the customer the opportunity to receive a system (based on the same architecture) in a more reliable, timely, and economical manner than if the subsequent system were to be built from scratch. The customer may be willing to relax some requirements to gain these economies. Shrink-wrapped software has clearly affected people's requirements by providing solutions that are not tailored to their precise needs but are instead inexpensive and (in the best of all possible worlds) of high quality. Product lines have the same effect on customers who cannot be so flexible with their requirements. In Chapter 15 (CelsuisTech, A Case Study in Product Line Development), we will show how a product line architecture caused customers to happily compromise their requirements because they could get high-quality software that fit their basic needs quickly, reliably, and at lower cost.

4. The process of system building will affect the architect's experience with subsequent systems by adding to the corporate experience base. A system that was successfully built around a tool bus or .NET or encapsulated finite-state machines will engender similar systems built the same way in the future. On the other hand, architectures that fail are less likely to be chosen for future projects.

5. A few systems will influence and actually change the software engineering culture, that is, the technical environment in which system builders operate and learn. The first relational databases, compiler generators, and table-driven operating systems had this effect in the 1960s and early 1970s; the first spread-sheets and windowing systems, in the 1980s. The World Wide Web is the example for the 1990s, as we will suggest in its case study in Chapter 13. J2EE may be the example for the first decade of the twenty-first century, as we will discuss in Chapter 16. When such pathfinder systems are constructed, subsequent systems are affected by their legacy.

These and other feedback mechanisms form what we call the ABC, illustrated in Figure 1.4, which depicts the influences of the culture and business of the development organization on the software architecture. That architecture is, in turn, a primary determinant of the properties of the developed system or systems. But the ABC is also based on a recognition that shrewd organizations can take advantage of the organizational and experiential effects of developing an architecture and can use those effects to position their business strategically for future projects.

1.2   Software Processes and the Architecture Business Cycle

Software process is the term given to the organization, ritualization, and management of software development activities. What activities are involved in creating a software architecture, using that architecture to realize a design, and then implementing or managing the evolution of a target system or application? These activities include the following:

- Creating the business case for the system
- Understanding the requirements
- Creating or selecting the architecture
- Documenting and communicating the architecture
- Analyzing or evaluating the architecture
- Implementing the system based on the architecture
- Ensuring that the implementation conforms to the architecture

ARCHITECTURE ACTIVITIES

As indicated in the structure of the ABC, architecture activities have comprehensive feedback relationships with each other. We will briefly introduce each activity in the following subsections.

Creating the Business Case for the System.   Creating a business case is broader than simply assessing the market need for a system. It is an important step in creating and constraining any future requirements. How much should the product cost? What is its targeted market? What is its targeted time to market? Will it need to interface with other systems? Are there system limitations that it must work within?

These are all questions that must involve the system's architects. They cannot be decided solely by an architect, but if an architect is not consulted in the creation of the business case, it may be impossible to achieve the business goals.

Understanding the Requirements.   There are a variety of techniques for eliciting requirements from the stakeholders. For example, object-oriented analysis uses scenarios, or "use cases" to embody requirements. Safety-critical systems use more rigorous approaches, such as finite-state-machine models or formal specification languages. In Chapter 4 (Understanding Quality Attributes), we introduce a collection of quality attribute scenarios that support the capture of quality requirements for a system.

One fundamental decision with respect to the system being built is the extent to which it is a variation on other systems that have been constructed. Since it is a rare system these days that is not similar to other systems, requirements elicitation techniques extensively involve understanding these prior systems' characteristics. We discuss the architectural implications of product lines in Chapter 14 (Software Product Lines: Re-using Architectural Assets).

Another technique that helps us understand requirements is the creation of prototypes. Prototypes may help to model desired behavior, design the user interface, or analyze resource utilization. This helps to make the system "real" in the eyes of its stakeholders and can quickly catalyze decisions on the system's design and the design of its user interface.

Regardless of the technique used to elicit the requirements, the desired qualities of the system to be constructed determine the shape of its architecture. Specific tactics have long been used by architects to achieve particular quality attributes. We discuss many of these tactics in Chapter 5 (Achieving Qualities). An architectural design embodies many tradeoffs, and not all of these tradeoffs are apparent when specifying requirements. It is not until the architecture is created that some tradeoffs among requirements become apparent and force a decision on requirement priorities.

Creating or Selecting the Architecture.   In the landmark book *The Mythical Man-Month,* Fred Brooks argues forcefully and eloquently that conceptual integrity is the key to sound system design and that conceptual integrity can only be had by a small number of minds coming together to design the system's architecture. Chapters 5 (Achieving Qualities) and 7 (Designing the Architecture) show how to create an architecture to achieve its behavioral and quality requirements.

Communicating the Architecture.   For the architecture to be effective as the backbone of the project's design, it must be communicated clearly and unambiguously to all of the stakeholders. Developers must understand the work assignments it requires of them, testers must understand the task structure it imposes on them, management must understand the scheduling implications it suggests, and so forth. Toward this end, the architecture's documentation should be informative, unambiguous, and readable by many people with varied backgrounds. We discuss the documentation of architectures in Chapter 9 (Documenting Software Architectures).

Analyzing or Evaluating the Architecture.   In any design process there will be multiple candidate designs considered. Some will be rejected immediately. Others will contend for primacy. Choosing among these competing designs in a rational way is one of the architect's greatest challenges. The chapters in Part Three (Analyzing an Architecture) describe methods for making such choices.

Evaluating an architecture for the qualities that it supports is essential to ensuring that the system constructed from that architecture satisfies its stakeholders' needs. Becoming more widespread are analysis techniques to evaluate the quality attributes that an architecture imparts to a system. Scenario-based techniques provide one of the most general and effective approaches for evaluating an architecture. The most mature methodological approach is found in the Architecture Tradeoff Analysis Method (ATAM) of Chapter 11, while the Cost Benefit Analysis Method (CBAM) of Chapter 12 provides the critical link to the economic implications of architectural decisions.

Implementing Based on the Architecture.   This activity is concerned with keeping the developers faithful to the structures and interaction protocols constrained by the architecture. Having an explicit and well-communicated architecture is the first step toward ensuring architectural conformance. Having an environment or infrastructure that actively assists developers in creating and maintaining the architecture (as opposed to just the code) is better.

Ensuring Conformance to an Architecture.   Finally, when an architecture is created and used, it goes into a maintenance phase. Constant vigilance is required to ensure that the actual architecture and its representation remain faithful to each other during this phase. Although work in this area is comparatively immature, there has been intense activity in recent years. Chapter 10 (Reconstructing Software Architectures) will present the current state of recovering an architecture from an existing system and ensuring that it conforms to the specified architecture.

1.3   What Makes a "Good" Architecture?

If it is true that, given the same technical requirements for a system, two different architects in different organizations will produce different architectures, how can we determine if either one of them is the *right* one?

There is no such thing as an inherently good or bad architecture. Architectures are either more or less fit for some stated purpose. A distributed three-tier client-server architecture may be just the ticket for a large enterprise's financial management system but completely wrong for an avionics application. An architecture carefully crafted to achieve high modifiability does not make sense for a throw-away prototype. One of the messages of this book is that architectures can in fact be evaluated—one of the great benefits of paying attention to them—but only in the context of specific goals.

Nevertheless, there are rules of thumb that should be followed when designing an architecture. Failure to apply any of these does not automatically mean that the architecture will be fatally flawed, but it should at least serve as a warning sign that should be investigated.

We divide our observations into two clusters: process recommendations and product (or structural) recommendations. Our process recommendations are as follows:

- The architecture should be the product of a single architect or a small group of architects with an identified leader.

- The architect (or architecture team) should have the functional requirements for the system and an articulated, prioritized list of quality attributes (such as security or modifiability) that the architecture is expected to satisfy.

- The architecture should be well documented, with at least one static view and one dynamic view (explained in Chapter 2), using an agreed-on notation that all stakeholders can understand with a minimum of effort.

- The architecture should be circulated to the system's stakeholders, who should be actively involved in its review.

- The architecture should be analyzed for applicable quantitative measures (such as maximum throughput) and formally evaluated for quality attributes before it is too late to make changes to it.

- The architecture should lend itself to incremental implementation via the creation of a "skeletal" system in which the communication paths are exercised but which at first has minimal functionality. This skeletal system can then be used to "grow" the system incrementally, easing the integration and testing efforts (see Chapter 7, Section 7.4).

- The architecture should result in a specific (and small) set of resource contention areas, the resolution of which is clearly specified, circulated, and maintained. For example, if network utilization is an area of concern, the architect should produce (and enforce) for each development team guidelines that will result in a minimum of network traffic. If performance is a concern, the architects should produce (and enforce) time budgets for the major threads.

Our structural rules of thumb are as follows:

- The architecture should feature well-defined modules whose functional responsibilities are allocated on the principles of information hiding and separation of concerns. The information-hiding modules should include those that encapsulate idiosyncrasies of the computing infrastructure, thus insulating the bulk of the software from change should the infrastructure change.

- Each module should have a well-defined interface that encapsulates or "hides" changeable aspects (such as implementation strategies and data structure choices) from other software that uses its facilities. These interfaces should allow their respective development teams to work largely independently of each other.

- Quality attributes should be achieved using well-known architectural tactics specific to each attribute, as described in Chapter 5 (Achieving Qualities).

- The architecture should never depend on a particular version of a commercial product or tool. If it depends upon a particular commercial product, it should be structured such that changing to a different product is straightforward and inexpensive.

- Modules that produce data should be separate from modules that consume data. This tends to increase modifiability because changes are often confined to either the production or the consumption side of data. If new data is added, both sides will have to change, but the separation allows for a staged (incremental) upgrade.

- For parallel-processing systems, the architecture should feature well-defined processes or tasks that do not necessarily mirror the module decomposition structure. That is, processes may thread through more than one module; a module may include procedures that are invoked as part of more than one process (the A-7E case study of Chapter 3 is an example of employing this principle).

- Every task or process should be written so that its assignment to a specific processor can be easily changed, perhaps even at runtime.

- The architecture should feature a small number of simple interaction patterns (see Chapter 5). That is, the system should do the same things in the same way throughout. This will aid in understandability, reduce development time, increase reliability, and enhance modifiability. It will also show conceptual integrity in the architecture, which, while not measurable, leads to smooth development.

As you examine the case studies in this book, each of which successfully solves a challenging architectural problem, it is useful to see how many of them followed each of these rules of thumb. This set of rules is neither complete nor absolute but can serve as a guidepost for an architect beginning to make progress on an architectural design problem.

1.4 Summary

In this chapter, we showed that architecture is more than the result of the functional requirements for a system. It is equally the result of the architect's background, the technical environment within which the architect lives, and the sponsoring organization's business goals. The architecture in turn influences the environment that spawned it by adding its presence to the technical environment and by giving the business new marketing possibilities. We introduced the Architecture Business Cycle as the motif for this book, but the reader should be aware that the ABC as described here will be extended in later chapters.

Finally, we posited a set of rules of thumb that generally lead to successful architectures.

Next, we turn our attention to software architecture, per se.

1.5 Discussion Questions

1. How does the nature of your organization affect the architectures that it develops? How do the architectures affect the nature of the organization?

2. What kind of business goals drive (or have driven) the creation of the software architectures of your organization?

3. Who are the stakeholders that exert the most influence over the architecture of systems in your organization? What are their goals? Do the goals ever conflict?

2

What Is Software Architecture?

with Linda Northrop

> *If a project has not achieved a system architecture, including
> its rationale, the project should not proceed to full-scale
> system development. Specifying the architecture as
> a deliverable enables its use throughout the
> development and maintenance process.*
> — Barry Boehm [Boehm 95]

In Chapter 1, we explained that architecture plays a pivotal role in allowing an organization to meet its business goals. Architecture commands a price (the cost of its careful development), but it pays for itself handsomely by enabling the organization to achieve its system goals and expand its software capabilities. Architecture is an asset that holds tangible value to the developing organization beyond the project for which it was created.

In this chapter we will focus on architecture strictly from a software engineering point of view. That is, we will explore the value that a software architecture brings to a development project in addition to the value returned to the enterprise in the ways described in Chapter 1.

2.1 What Software Architecture Is and What It Isn't

Figure 2.1, taken from a system description for an underwater acoustic simulation, purports to describe that system's "top-level architecture" and is precisely

Note: Linda Northrop is a program director at Carnegie Mellon University's Software Engineering Institute.

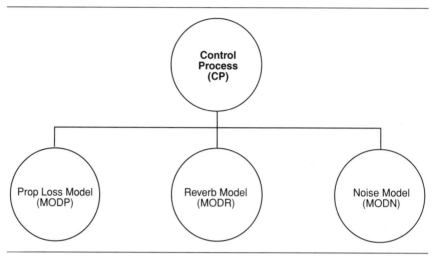

FIGURE 2.1   Typical, but uninformative, presentation of a software architecture

the kind of diagram most often displayed to help explain an architecture. Exactly what can we tell from it?

- The system consists of four elements.
- Three of the elements—Prop Loss Model (MODP), Reverb Model (MODR), and Noise Model (MODN)—might have more in common with each other than with the fourth—Control Process (CP)—because they are positioned next to each other.
- All of the elements apparently have some sort of relationship with each other, since the diagram is fully connected.

Is this an architecture? Assuming (as many definitions do) that architecture is a set of components (of which we have four) and connections among them (also present), this diagram seems to fill the bill. However, even if we accept the most primitive definition, what can we *not* tell from the diagram?

- *What is the nature of the elements?* What is the significance of their separation? Do they run on separate processors? Do they run at separate times? Do the elements consist of processes, programs, or both? Do they represent ways in which the project labor will be divided, or do they convey a sense of runtime separation? Are they objects, tasks, functions, processes, distributed programs, or something else?

- *What are the responsibilities of the elements?* What is it they do? What is their function in the system?

- *What is the significance of the connections?* Do the connections mean that the elements communicate with each other, control each other, send data to each other, use each other, invoke each other, synchronize with each other, share some information-hiding secret with each other, or some combination of these or other relations? What are the mechanisms for the communication? What information flows across the mechanisms, whatever they may be?

- *What is the significance of the layout?* Why is CP on a separate level? Does it call the other three elements, and are the others not allowed to call it? Does it contain the other three in an implementation unit sense? Or is there simply no room to put all four elements on the same row in the diagram?

We *must* raise these questions because unless we know precisely what the elements are and how they cooperate to accomplish the purpose of the system, diagrams such as these are not much help and should be regarded skeptically.

This diagram does not show a software architecture, at least not in any useful way. The most charitable thing we can say about such diagrams is that they represent a start. We now define what *does* constitute a software architecture:

> The software architecture of a program or computing system is the structure or structures of the system, which comprise software elements, the externally visible properties of those elements, and the relationships among them.[1]

"Externally visible" properties are those assumptions other elements can make of an element, such as its provided services, performance characteristics, fault handling, shared resource usage, and so on. Let's look at some of the implications of this definition in more detail.

First, *architecture defines software elements.* The architecture embodies information about how the elements relate to each other. This means that it specifically *omits* certain information about elements that does not pertain to their interaction. Thus, an architecture is foremost an *abstraction* of a system that suppresses details of elements that do not affect how they use, are used by, relate to, or interact with other elements. In nearly all modern systems, elements interact with each other by means of interfaces that partition details about an element into public and private parts. Architecture is concerned with the public side of this division; private details—those having to do solely with internal implementation—are not architectural.

Second, the definition makes clear that *systems can and do comprise more than one structure* and that no one structure can irrefutably claim to be *the* architecture. For example, all nontrivial projects are partitioned into implementation units; these units are given specific responsibilities and are frequently the basis of work assignments for programming teams. This type of element comprises programs and data that software in other implementation units can call or access, and programs and data that are private. In large projects, these elements are almost

---

[1] This is a slight change from the first edition. There the primary building blocks were called "components," a term that has since become closely associated with the component-based software engineering movement, taking on a decidedly runtime flavor. "Element" was chosen here to convey something more general.

certainly subdivided for assignment to subteams. This is one kind of structure often used to describe a system. It is very static in that it focuses on the way the system's functionality is divided up and assigned to implementation teams.

Other structures are much more focused on the way the elements interact with each other at runtime to carry out the system's function. Suppose the system is to be built as a set of parallel processes. The processes that will exist at runtime, the programs in the various implementation units described previously that are strung together sequentially to form each process, and the synchronization relations among the processes form another kind of structure often used to describe a system.

Are any of these structures alone *the* architecture? No, although they all convey architectural information. The architecture consists of these structures as well as many others. This example shows that since architecture can comprise more than one kind of structure, there is more than one kind of element (e.g., implementation unit and processes), more than one kind of interaction among elements (e.g., subdivision and synchronization), and even more than one context (e.g., development time versus runtime). By intention, the definition does not specify what the architectural elements and relationships are. Is a software element an object? A process? A library? A database? A commercial product? It can be any of these things and more.

Third, the definition implies that *every computing system with software has a software architecture* because every system can be shown to comprise elements and the relations among them. In the most trivial case, a system is itself a single element—uninteresting and probably nonuseful but an architecture nevertheless. Even though every system has an architecture, it does not necessarily follow that the architecture is known to anyone. Perhaps all of the people who designed the system are long gone, the documentation has vanished (or was never produced), the source code has been lost (or was never delivered), and all we have is the executing binary code. This reveals the difference between the architecture of a system and the representation of that architecture. Unfortunately, an architecture can exist independently of its description or specification, which raises the importance of *architecture documentation* (described in Chapter 9) and *architecture reconstruction* (discussed in Chapter 10).

Fourth, *the behavior of each element is part of the architecture* insofar as that behavior can be observed or discerned from the point of view of another element. Such behavior is what allows elements to interact with each other, which is clearly part of the architecture. This is another reason that the box-and-line drawings that are passed off as architectures are not architectures at all. They are simply box-and-line drawings—or, to be more charitable, they serve as cues to provide more information that explains what the elements shown actually do. When looking at the names of the boxes (database, graphical user interface, executive, etc.), a reader may well imagine the functionality and behavior of the corresponding elements. This mental image approaches an architecture, but it springs from the observer's mind and relies on information that is not present. We do not mean that the exact behavior and performance of every element must be documented in all circumstances; however, to the extent that an element's behavior influences how another element must be written to interact with it or influences the acceptability of the system as a whole, this behavior is part of the software architecture.

Finally, the definition is indifferent as to whether *the architecture for a system is a good one or a bad one,* meaning that it will allow or prevent the system from meeting its behavioral, performance, and life-cycle requirements. We do not accept trial and error as the best way to choose an architecture for a system—that is, picking an architecture at random, building the system from it, and hoping for the best—so this raises the importance of *architecture evaluation* (Chapters 11 and 12) and *architecture design* (Chapter 7).

2.2   Other Points of View

Software architecture is a growing but still young discipline; hence, it has no single, accepted definition. On the other hand, there is no shortage of definitions. Most of those commonly circulated are consistent in their themes—structure, elements, and connections among them—but they vary widely in the details and are not interchangeable.

The study of software architecture has evolved by observation of the design principles that designers follow and the actions that they take when working on real systems. It is an attempt to abstract the commonalities inherent in system design, and as such it must account for a wide range of activities, concepts, methods, approaches, and results. For that reason, other definitions of architecture are present in the software engineering community, and because you are likely to encounter some of them, you should understand their implications and be able to discuss them. A few of the most often heard definitions follow.

- *Architecture is high-level design.* This is true enough, in the sense that a horse is a mammal, but the two are not interchangeable. Other tasks associated with design are not architectural, such as deciding on important data structures that will be encapsulated. The interface to those data structures is decidedly an architectural concern, but their actual choice is not.

- *Architecture is the overall structure of the system.* This common refrain implies (incorrectly) that systems have but one structure. We know this to be false, and, if someone takes this position, it is usually entertaining to ask which structure they mean. The point has more than pedagogic significance. As we will see later, the different structures provide the critical engineering leverage points to imbue a system with the quality attributes that will render it a success or failure. The multiplicity of structures in an architecture lies at the heart of the concept.

- *Architecture is the structure of the components of a program or system, their interrelationships, and the principles and guidelines governing their design and evolution over time.* This is one of a number of process-centered definitions that include ancillary information such as principles and guidelines. Many people claim that architecture includes a statement of stakeholder needs and a rationale for how those needs are met. We agree that gathering such information is essential and a matter of good professional practice. However, we do not consider them part of the architecture per se any more than an owner's manual for a car is part of the car. Any system has an architecture that can be discovered and analyzed independently of any knowledge of the process by which the architecture was designed or evolved.

- *Architecture is components and connectors.* Connectors imply a runtime mechanism for transferring control and data around a system. Thus, this definition concentrates on the runtime architectural structures. A UNIX pipe is a connector, for instance. This makes the non-runtime architectural structures (such as the static division into responsible units of implementation discussed earlier) second-class citizens. They aren't second class but are every bit as critical to the satisfaction of system goals. When we speak of "relationships" among elements, we intend to capture both runtime and non-runtime relationships.

At the root of all the discussion about software architecture is a focus on reasoning about the *structural* system issues. And although *architecture* is sometimes used to mean a certain architectural pattern, such as client-server, and sometimes refers to a field of study, such as a book about architecture, it is most often used to describe structural aspects of a particular system. That is what we have attempted to capture in our definition.

2.3   Architectural Patterns, Reference Models, and Reference Architectures

Between box-and-line sketches that are the barest of starting points and full-fledged architectures, with all of the appropriate information about a system filled in, lie a host of intermediate stages. Each stage represents the outcome of a set of architectural decisions, the binding of architectural choices. Some of these intermediate stages are very useful in their own right. Before discussing architectural structures, we define three of them.

1. *An architectural pattern is a description of element and relation types together with a set of constraints on how they may be used.* A pattern can be thought of as a set of constraints on an architecture—on the element types and their patterns of interaction—and these constraints define a set or family of architectures that satisfy them. For example, client-server is a common architectural pattern. Client and server are two element types, and their coordination is described in terms of the protocol that the server uses to communicate with each of its clients. Use of the term *client-server* implies only that multiple clients exist; the clients themselves are not identified, and there is no discussion of what functionality, other than implementation of the protocols, has been assigned to any of the clients or to the server. Countless architectures are of the client-server pattern under this (informal) definition, but they are different from each other. An architectural pattern is not an architecture, then, but it still conveys a useful image of the system—it imposes useful constraints on the architecture and, in turn, on the system.

One of the most useful aspects of patterns is that they exhibit known quality attributes. This is why the architect chooses a particular pattern and not one at random. Some patterns represent known solutions to performance problems, others lend themselves well to high-security systems, still others have been used successfully in high-availability systems. Choosing an architectural pattern is often the architect's first major design choice.

The term *architectural style* has also been widely used to describe the same concept.

2. *A reference model is a division of functionality together with data flow between the pieces.* A reference model is a standard decomposition of a known problem into parts that cooperatively solve the problem. Arising from experience, reference models are a characteristic of mature domains. Can you name the standard parts of a compiler or a database management system? Can you explain in broad terms how the parts work together to accomplish their collective purpose? If so, it is because you have been taught a reference model of these applications.

3. *A reference architecture is a reference model mapped onto software elements (that cooperatively implement the functionality defined in the reference model) and the data flows between them.* Whereas a reference model divides the functionality, a reference architecture is the mapping of that functionality onto a system decomposition. The mapping may be, but by no means necessarily is, one to one. A software element may implement part of a function or several functions.

Reference models, architectural patterns, and reference architectures are not architectures; they are useful concepts that capture elements of an archititure. Each is the outcome of early design decisions. The relationship among these design elements is shown in Figure 2.2.

People often make analogies to other uses of the word *architecture*, about which they have some intuition. They commonly associate architecture with physical structure (buildings, streets, hardware) and physical arrangement. A building architect must design a building that provides accessibility, aesthetics, light, maintainability, and so on. A software architect must design a system that provides concurrency, portability, modifiability, usability, security, and the like, and that reflects consideration of the tradeoffs among these needs.

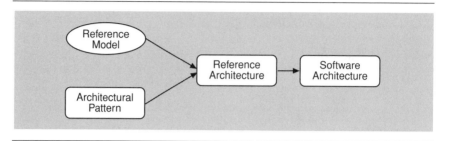

FIGURE 2.2   The relationships of reference models, architectural patterns, reference architectures, and software architectures. (The arrows indicate that subsequent concepts contain more design elements.)

Analogies between buildings and software systems should not be taken too far, as they break down fairly quickly. Rather, they help us understand that the viewer's perspective is important and that structure can have different meanings depending on the motivation for examining it. A precise definition of software architecture is not nearly as important as what investigating the concept allows us to do.

2.4   Why Is Software Architecture Important?

Chapter 1 covered the importance of architecture to an enterprise. In this chapter, we focus on why architecture matters from a technical perspective. In that context, there are fundamentally three reasons for software architecture's importantance.

1. *Communication among stakeholders.* Software architecture represents a common abstraction of a system that most if not all of the system's stakeholders can use as a basis for mutual understanding, negotiation, consensus, and communication.

2. *Early design decisions.* Software architecture manifests the earliest design decisions about a system, and these early bindings carry weight far out of proportion to their individual gravity with respect to the system's remaining development, its deployment, and its maintenance life. It is also the earliest point at which design decisions governing the system to be built can be analyzed.

3. *Transferable abstraction of a system.* Software architecture constitutes a relatively small, intellectually graspable model for how a system is structured and how its elements work together, and this model is transferable across systems. In particular, it can be applied to other systems exhibiting similar quality attribute and functional requirements and can promote large-scale re-use.

We will address each of these points in turn.

ARCHITECTURE IS THE VEHICLE FOR STAKEHOLDER COMMUNICATION

Each stakeholder of a software system—customer, user, project manager, coder, tester, and so on—is concerned with different system characteristics that are affected by the architecture. For example, the user is concerned that the system is reliable and available when needed; the customer is concerned that the architecture can be implemented on schedule and to budget; the manager is worried (as well as about cost and schedule) that the architecture will allow teams to work largely independently, interacting in disciplined and controlled ways. The architect is worried about strategies to achieve all of those goals.

Architecture provides a common language in which different concerns can be expressed, negotiated, and resolved at a level that is intellectually manageable even for large, complex systems (see the sidebar What Happens When I Push This Button?). Without such a language, it is difficult to understand large systems sufficiently to make the early decisions that influence both quality and usefulness. Architectural analysis, as we will see in Part Three, both depends on this level of communication and enhances it.

"What Happens When I Push This Button?"
Architecture as a Vehicle for Stakeholder Communication

The project review droned on and on. The government-sponsored development was behind schedule and over budget and was large enough so that these lapses were attracting Congressional attention. And now the government was making up for past neglect by holding a marathon come-one-come-all review session. The contractor had recently undergone a buyout, which hadn't helped matters. It was the afternoon of the second day, and the agenda called for the software architecture to be presented. The young architect—an apprentice to the chief architect of the system—was bravely explaining how the software architecture for the massive system would enable it to meet its very demanding real-time, distributed, high-reliability requirements. He had a solid presentation and a solid architecture to present. It was sound and sensible. But the audience—about 30 government representatives who had varying roles in the management and oversight of this sticky project—was tired. Some of them were even thinking that perhaps they should have gone into real estate instead of enduring another one of these marathon let's-finally-get-it-right-this-time reviews.

The viewgraph showed, in semiformal box-and-line notation, what the major software elements were in a runtime view of the system. The names were all acronyms, suggesting no semantic meaning without explanation, which the young architect gave. The lines showed data flow, message passing, and process synchronization. The elements were internally redundant, the architect was explaining. "In the event of a failure," he began, using a laser pointer to denote one of the lines, "a restart mechanism triggers along this path when . . ."

"What happens when the mode select button is pushed?" interrupted one of the audience members. He was a government attendee representing the user community for this system.

"Beg your pardon?" asked the architect.

"The mode select button," he said. "What happens when you push it?"

"Um, that triggers an event in the device driver, up here," began the architect, laser-pointing. "It then reads the register and interprets the event code. If it's mode select, well, then, it signals the blackboard, which in turns signals the objects that have subscribed to that event . . ."

"No, I mean what does the system do," interrupted the questioner. "Does it reset the displays? And what happens if this occurs during a system reconfiguration?"

The architect looked a little surprised and flicked off the laser pointer. This was not an architectural question, but since he was an architect and therefore fluent in the requirements, he knew the answer. "If the command line is in setup mode, the displays will reset," he said. "Otherwise an error message will be put on the control console, but the signal will be ignored." He put the laser pointer back on. "Now, the restart mechanism that I was talking about . . ."

"Well, I was just wondering," said the users' delegate, "because I see from your chart that the display console is sending signal traffic to the target location module."

"What *should* happen?" asked another member of the audience, addressing the first questioner. "Do you really want the user to get mode data during its reconfiguring?" And for the next 45 minutes, the architect watched as the audience consumed his time slot by debating what the correct behavior of the system was supposed to be in various esoteric states.

The debate was not architectural, but the architecture (and its graphical rendition) had sparked debate. It is natural to think of architecture as the basis for communication among some of the stakeholders besides architects and developers. Managers, for example, use it to create teams and allocate resources among them. But users? The architecture is invisible to users, after all; why should they latch on to it as a tool for system understanding?

The fact is that they do. In this case, the questioner had sat through two days of viewgraphs all about function, operation, user interface, and testing. But even though he was tired and wanted to go home, it was the first slide on architecture that made him realize he didn't understand something. Attendance at many architecture reviews has convinced me that seeing the system in a new way prods the mind and brings new questions to the surface. For users, architecture often serves as that new way, and the questions that a user poses will be behavioral. In the sidebar Their Solution Just Won't Work in Chapter 11, we describe an architecture evaluation exercise in which the user representatives were much more interested in what the system was going to do than in how it was going to do it, and naturally so. Until that point, their only contact with the vendor had been through its marketers. The architect was the first legitimate expert on the system to whom they had access, and they didn't hesitate to seize the moment.

Of course, careful and thorough requirements specifications can ameliorate this, but for a variety of reasons they are not always created or available.

In their absence, a specification of the architecture often triggers questions and improves clarity. It is probably more prudent to recognize this than to resist it. In Chapter 11, we point out that one of the benefits of an architecture evaluation is the clarification and prioritization of requirements.

Sometimes such an exercise will reveal unreasonable requirements, whose utility can then be revisited. A review of this type that emphasizes synergy between requirements and architecture would have let the young architect in our story off the hook by giving him a place in the overall review session to address that kind of information. And the user representative would not have felt like a fish out of water, asking his question at a clearly inappropriate moment. Of course, he could always go into real estate.

— PCC

ARCHITECTURE MANIFESTS THE EARLIEST SET OF DESIGN DECISIONS

Software architecture represents a system's earliest set of design decisions. These early decisions are the most difficult to get correct and the hardest to change later in the development process, and they have the most far-reaching effects.

The Architecture Defines Constraints on Implementation.   An implementation exhibits an architecture if it conforms to the structural design decisions described by the architecture. This means that the implementation must be divided into the prescribed elements, the elements must interact with each other in the prescribed fashion, and each element must fulfill its responsibility to the others as dictated by the architecture.

Resource allocation decisions also constrain implementations. These decisions may be invisible to implementors working on individual elements. The constraints permit a separation of concerns that allows management decisions to make the best use of personnel and computational capacity. Element builders must be fluent in the specification of their individual elements but not in architectural tradeoffs. Conversely, architects need not be experts in all aspects of algorithm design or the intricacies of the programming language, but they are the ones responsible for the architectural tradeoffs.

The Architecture Dictates Organizational Structure.   Not only does architecture prescribe the structure of the system being developed, but that structure becomes engraved in the structure of the development project (and sometimes, as mentioned in Chapter 1, the structure of the entire organization). The normal method for dividing up the labor in a large system is to assign different groups different portions of the system to construct. This is called the work breakdown structure of a system. Because the system architecture includes the highest-level decomposition of the system, it is typically used as the basis for the work breakdown structure, which in turn dictates units of planning, scheduling, and budget;

interteam communication channels; configuration control and file system organization; integration and test plans and procedures; and even minutiae such as how the project intranet is organized and how many team picnics there are. Teams communicate with each other in terms of the interface specifications to the major elements. The maintenance activity, when launched, will also reflect the software structure, with teams formed to maintain specific structural elements.

A side effect of establishing the work breakdown structure is to freeze some aspects of the software architecture. A group that is responsible for one of the subsystems will resist having its responsibilities distributed across other groups. If these responsibilities have been formalized in a contractual relationship, changing them can become expensive. Tracking progress on a collection of tasks being distributed also becomes much more difficult.

Once the architecture has been agreed on, then, it becomes almost impossible, for managerial and business reasons, to modify it. This is one argument (among many) for carrying out a comprehensive evaluation before freezing the software architecture for a large system.

The Architecture Inhibits or Enables a System's Quality Attributes.   Whether a system will be able to exhibit its desired (or required) quality attributes is substantially determined by its architecture. Chapter 5 will delve into the relationship between architectures and quality in more detail, but for now keep the following in mind:

- If your system requires high performance, you need to manage the time-based behavior of elements and the frequency and volume of inter-element communication.
- If modifiability is important, you need to assign responsibilities to elements such that changes to the system do not have far-reaching consequences.
- If your system must be highly secure, you need to manage and protect inter-element communication and which elements are allowed to access which information. You may also need to introduce specialized elements (such as a trusted kernel) into the architecture.
- If you believe scalability will be needed in your system, you have to carefully localize the use of resources to facilitate the introduction of higher-capacity replacements.
- If your project needs to deliver incremental subsets of the system, you must carefully manage inter-component usage.
- If you want the elements of your system to be re-usable in other systems, you need to restrict inter-element coupling so that when you extract an element it does not come out with too many attachments to its current environment to be useful.

The strategies for these and other quality attributes are supremely architectural. It is important to understand, however, that architecture alone cannot guarantee functionality or quality. Poor downstream design or implementation decisions can always undermine an adequate architectural design. Decisions at all stages of the life cycle—from high-level design to coding and implementation—affect system quality. Therefore, quality is not completely a function of architectural design. To ensure quality, a good architecture is necessary, but not sufficient.

Predicting System Qualities by Studying the Architecture.   Is it possible to tell that the appropriate architectural decisions have been made (i.e., if the system will exhibit its required quality attributes) without waiting until the system is developed and deployed? If the answer were no, choosing an architecture would be a hopeless task—random selection would perform as well as any other method. Fortunately, it *is* possible to make quality predictions about a system based solely on an evaluation of its architecture. Architecture evaluation techniques such as the Architecture Tradeoff Analysis Method of Chapter 11 support top-down insight into the attributes of software product quality that is made possible (and constrained) by software architectures.

The Architecture Makes It Easier to Reason about and Manage Change. The software development community is coming to grips with the fact that roughly 80 percent of a typical software system's cost occurs *after* initial deployment. A corollary of this statistic is that most systems that people work on are in this phase. Many if not most programmers and designers never work on new development—they work under the constraints of the existing body of code. Software systems change over their lifetimes; they do so often and often with difficulty.

Every architecture partitions possible changes into three categories: local, nonlocal, and architectural. A local change can be accomplished by modifying a single element. A nonlocal change requires multiple element modifications but leaves the underlying architectural approach intact. An architectural change affects the fundamental ways in which the elements interact with each other—the pattern of the architecture—and will probably require changes all over the system. Obviously, local changes are the most desirable, and so an effective architecture is one in which the most likely changes are also the easiest to make.

Deciding when changes are essential, determining which change paths have the least risk, assessing the consequences of proposed changes, and arbitrating sequences and priorities for requested changes all require broad insight into relationships, performance, and behaviors of system software elements. These are in the job description for an architect. Reasoning about the architecture can provide the insight necessary to make decisions about proposed changes.

The Architecture Helps in Evolutionary Prototyping.   Once an architecture has been defined, it can be analyzed and prototyped as a skeletal system. This aids the development process in two ways.

1. The system is executable early in the product's life cycle. Its fidelity increases as prototype parts are replaced by complete versions of the software. These prototype parts can be a lower-fidelity version of the final functionality, or they can be surrogates that consume and produce data at the appropriate rates.

2. A special case of having the system executable early is that potential performance problems can be identified early in the product's life cycle.

Each of these benefits reduces the risk in the project. If the architecture is part of a family of related systems, the cost of creating a framework for prototyping can be distributed over the development of many systems.

The Architecture Enables More Accurate Cost and Schedule Estimates.
Cost and schedule estimates are an important management tool to enable the manager to acquire the necessary resources and to understand whether a project is in trouble. Cost estimations based on an understanding of the system pieces are, inherently, more accurate than those based on overall system knowledge. As we have said, the organizational structure of a project is based on its architecture. Each team will be able to make more accurate estimates for its piece than a project manager will and will feel more ownership in making the estimates come true. Second, the initial definition of an architecture means that the requirements for a system have been reviewed and, in some sense, validated. The more knowledge about the scope of a system, the more accurate the estimates.

ARCHITECTURE AS A TRANSFERABLE, RE-USABLE MODEL

The earlier in the life cycle re-use is applied, the greater the benefit that can be achieved. While code re-use is beneficial, re-use at the architectural level provides tremendous leverage for systems with similar requirements. Not only code can be re-used but so can the requirements that led to the architecture in the first place, as well as the experience of building the re-used architecture. When architectural decisions can be re-used across multiple systems, all of the early decision consequences we just described are also transferred.

Software Product Lines Share a Common Architecture.
A software product line or family is a set of software-intensive systems sharing a common, managed set of features that satisfy the specific needs of a particular market segment or mission and that are developed from a common set of core assets in a prescribed way. Chief among these core assets is the architecture that was designed to handle the needs of the entire family. Product line architects choose an architecture (or a family of closely related architectures) that will serve all envisioned members of the product line by making design decisions that apply across the family early and by making other decisions that apply only to individual members late. The architecture defines what is fixed for all members of the product line and what is variable. Software product lines represent a powerful approach to multi-system development that shows order-of-magnitude payoffs in time to market, cost, productivity, and product quality. The power of architecture lies at the heart of the paradigm. Similar to other capital investments, the architecture for a

product line becomes a developing organization's core asset. Software product lines are explained in Chapter 14, and case studies of product lines are given in Chapters 15 and 17.

Systems Can Be Built Using Large, Externally Developed Elements.

Whereas earlier software paradigms focused on *programming* as the prime activity, with progress measured in lines of code, architecture-based development often focuses on *composing* or *assembling elements* that are likely to have been developed separately, even independently, from each other. This composition is possible because the architecture defines the elements that can be incorporated into the system. It constrains possible replacements (or additions) according to how they interact with their environment, how they receive and relinquish control, what data they consume and produce, how they access data, and what protocols they use for communication and resource sharing.

One key aspect of architecture is its organization of element structure, interfaces, and operating concepts. The most significant principle of this organization is *interchangeability*. In 1793, Eli Whitney's mass production of muskets, based on the principle of interchangeable parts, signaled the dawn of the Industrial Age. In the days before reliable physical measurements, this was a daunting notion. Today in software, until abstractions can be reliably delimited, the notion of structural interchangeability is just as daunting and just as significant.

Commercial off-the-shelf components, subsystems, and compatible communications interfaces all depend on the principle of interchangeability. However, there is much about software development through composition that remains unresolved. When the components that are candidates for importation and re-use are distinct subsystems that have been built with conflicting architectural assumptions, unanticipated complications can increase the effort required to integrate their functions. David Garlan and his colleagues coined the term *architectural mismatch* to describe this situation.

Less Is More: It Pays to Restrict the Vocabulary of Design Alternatives.

As useful architectural patterns and design patterns are collected, it becomes clear that, although computer programs can be combined in more or less infinite ways, there is something to be gained by voluntarily restricting ourselves to a relatively small number of choices when it comes to program cooperation and interaction. That is, we wish to minimize the design complexity of the system we are building. Advantages to this approach include enhanced re-use, more regular and simpler designs that are more easily understood and communicated, more capable analysis, shorter selection time, and greater interoperability.

Properties of software design follow from the choice of architectural pattern. Patterns that are more desirable for a particular problem should improve the implementation of the resulting design solution, perhaps by making it easier to arbitrate conflicting design constraints, by increasing insight into poorly understood design contexts, and/or by helping to surface inconsistencies in requirements specifications.

System Architecture versus Software Architecture

Over the past 5 to 10 years, we have had many occasions to give talks on software architecture. Invariably, a question comes from the audience along the lines of "Why are you talking about software architecture? Isn't system architecture just as important?" or "What is the difference between software architecture and system architecture?"

In fact, there is little difference, as we will see. But we mostly talk about *software* architecture because we want to stress the crucial nature of the software decisions that an architect makes concerning overall product quality.

In creating a software architecture, system considerations are seldom absent. For example, if you want an architecture to be high performance, you need to have some idea of the physical characteristics of the hardware platforms that it will run on (CPU speed, amount of memory, disk access speed) and the characteristics of any devices that the system interfaces with (traditional I/O devices, sensors, actuators), and you will also typically be concerned with the characteristics of the network (primarily bandwidth). If you want an architecture that is highly reliable, again you will be concerned with the hardware, in this case with its failure rates and the availability of redundant processing or network devices. On it goes. Considerations of hardware are seldom far from the mind of the architect.

So, when you design a software architecture, you will probably need to think about the entire system—the hardware as well as the software. To do otherwise would be foolhardy. No engineer can be expected to make predictions about the characteristics of a system when only part of that system is specified.

But still we persist in speaking about *software* architecture primarily, and not system architecture. Why is this? Because most of the architect's freedom is in the software choices, not in the hardware choices. It is not that there are no hardware choices to be made, but these may be out of the architect's control (for example, when creating a system that needs to work on arbitrary client machines on the Internet) or specified by others (for reasons of economics, legal issues, or compliance with standards); or they will likely change over time.

For this reason, we feel justified in focusing on the software portion of architecture, for this is where the most fundamental decisions are made, where the greatest freedoms reside, and where there are the greatest opportunities for success (or disaster!).

— RK

An Architecture Permits Template-Based Development.   An architecture embodies design decisions about how elements interact that, while reflected in each element's implementation, can be localized and written just once. Templates can be used to capture in one place the inter-element interaction mechanisms. For instance, a template can encode the declarations for an element's public area where results will be left, or can encode the protocols that the element uses to engage with the system executive. An example of a set of firm architectural decisions enabling template-based development will be discussed in Chapter 8.

An Architecture Can Be the Basis for Training.   The architecture, including a description of how elements interact to carry out the required behavior, can serve as the introduction to the system for new project members. This reinforces our point that one of the important uses of software architecture is to support and encourage communication among the various stakeholders. The architecture is a common reference point.

2.5 Architectural Structures and Views

The neurologist, the orthopedist, the hematologist, and the dermatologist all have a different view of the structure of a human body. Ophthalmologists, cardiologists, and podiatrists concentrate on subsystems. The kinesiologist and psychiatrist are concerned with different aspects of the entire arrangement's behavior. Although these views are pictured differently and have very different properties, all are inherently related: Together they describe the architecture of the human body.

So it is with software. Modern systems are more than complex enough to make it difficult to grasp them all at once. Instead, we restrict our attention at any one moment to one (or a small number) of the software system's structures. To communicate meaningfully about an architecture, we must make clear which structure or structures we are discussing at the moment—which *view* we are taking of the architecture.

We will be using the related terms *structure* and *view* when discussing architecture representation. A view is a representation of a coherent set of architectural elements, as written by and read by system stakeholders. It consists of a representation of a set of elements and the relations among them. A structure is the set of elements itself, as they exist in software or hardware. For example, a module structure is the set of the system's modules and their organization. A module view is the representation of that structure, as documented by and used by some system stakeholders. These terms are often used interchangeably, but we will adhere to these definitions.

Architectural structures can by and large be divided into three groups, depending on the broad nature of the elements they show.

- *Module structures.* Here the elements are modules, which are units of implementation. Modules represent a code-based way of considering the system. They are assigned areas of functional responsibility. There is less emphasis on how the resulting software manifests itself at runtime. Module structures allow us to answer questions such as What is the primary functional responsibility assigned to each module? What other software elements is a module allowed to use? What other software does it actually use?

What modules are related to other modules by generalization or specialization (i.e., inheritance) relationships?

- *Component-and-connector structures.* Here the elements are runtime components (which are the principal units of computation) and connectors (which are the communication vehicles among components). Component-and-connector structures help answer questions such as What are the major executing components and how do they interact? What are the major shared data stores? Which parts of the system are replicated? How does data progress through the system? What parts of the system can run in parallel? How can the system's structure change as it executes?

- *Allocation structures.* Allocation structures show the relationship between the software elements and the elements in one or more external environments in which the software is created and executed. They answer questions such as What processor does each software element execute on? In what files is each element stored during development, testing, and system building? What is the assignment of software elements to development teams?

These three structures correspond to the three broad types of decision that architectural design involves:

- How is the system to be structured as a set of code units (modules)?
- How is the system to be structured as a set of elements that have runtime behavior (components) and interactions (connectors)?
- How is the system to relate to nonsoftware structures in its environment (i.e., CPUs, file systems, networks, development teams, etc.)?

SOFTWARE STRUCTURES

Some of the most common and useful software structures are shown in Figure 2.3. These are described in the following sections.

Module.   Module-based structures include the following.

- *Decomposition.* The units are modules related to each other by the "is a submodule of" relation, showing how larger modules are decomposed into smaller ones recursively until they are small enough to be easily understood. Modules in this structure represent a common starting point for design, as the architect enumerates what the units of software will have to do and assigns each item to a module for subsequent (more detailed) design and eventual implementation. Modules often have associated products (i.e., interface specifications, code, test plans, etc.). The decomposition structure provides a large part of the system's modifiability, by ensuring that likely changes fall within the purview of at most a few small modules. It is often used as the basis for the development project's organization, including the

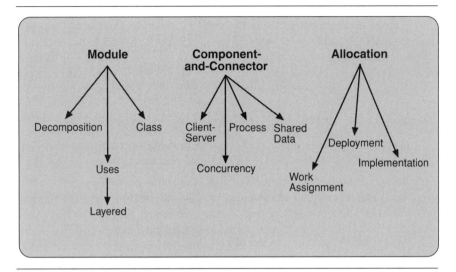

FIGURE 2-3   Common software architecture structures

structure of the documentation, and its integration and test plans. The units in this structure often have organization-specific names. Certain U.S. Department of Defense standards, for instance, define Computer Software Configuration Items (CSCIs) and Computer Software Components (CSCs), which are units of modular decomposition. In Chapter 15, we will see system function groups and system functions as the units of decomposition.

- *Uses.* The units of this important but overlooked structure are also modules, or (in circumstances where a finer grain is warranted) procedures or resources on the interfaces of modules. The units are related by the *uses* relation. One unit uses another if the correctness of the first requires the presence of a correct version (as opposed to a stub) of the second. The uses structure is used to engineer systems that can be easily extended to add functionality or from which useful functional subsets can be easily extracted. The ability to easily subset a working system allows for incremental development, a powerful build discipline that will be discussed further in Chapter 7.

- *Layered.* When the uses relations in this structure are carefully controlled in a particular way, a system of layers emerges, in which a layer is a coherent set of related functionality. In a strictly layered structure, layer n may only use the services of layer $n - 1$. Many variations of this (and a lessening of this structural restriction) occur in practice, however. Layers are often designed as abstractions (virtual machines) that hide implementation specifics below from the layers above, engendering portability. We will see layers in the case studies of Chapters 3, 13, and 15.

- *Class,* or *generalization.* The module units in this structure are called classes. The relation is "inherits-from" or "is-an-instance-of." This view supports reasoning about collections of similar behavior or capability (i.e., the classes that other classes inherit from) and parameterized differences which are captured by subclassing. The class structure allows us to reason about re-use and the incremental addition of functionality.

Component-and-Connector.   These structures include the following.

- *Process,* or *communicating processes.* Like all component-and-connector structures, this one is orthogonal to the module-based structures and deals with the dynamic aspects of a running system. The units here are processes or threads that are connected with each other by communication, synchronization, and/or exclusion operations. The relation in this (and in all component-and-connector structures) is *attachment,* showing how the components and connectors are hooked together. The process structure is important in helping to engineer a system's execution performance and availability.

- *Concurrency.* This component-and-connector structure allows the architect to determine opportunities for parallelism and the locations where resource contention may occur. The units are components and the connectors are "logical threads." A logical thread is a sequence of computation that can be allocated to a separate physical thread later in the design process. The concurrency structure is used early in design to identify the requirements for managing the issues associated with concurrent execution.

- *Shared data,* or *repository.* This structure comprises components and connectors that create, store, and access persistent data. If the system is in fact structured around one or more shared data repositories, this structure is a good one to illuminate. It shows how data is produced and consumed by runtime software elements, and it can be used to ensure good performance and data integrity.

- *Client-server.* If the system is built as a group of cooperating clients and servers, this is a good component-and-connector structure to illuminate. The components are the clients and servers, and the connectors are protocols and messages they share to carry out the system's work. This is useful for separation of concerns (supporting modifiability), for physical distribution, and for load balancing (supporting runtime performance).

Allocation.   Allocation structures include the following.

- *Deployment.* The deployment structure shows how software is assigned to hardware-processing and communication elements. The elements are software (usually a process from a component-and-connector view), hardware entities (processors), and communication pathways. Relations are "allocated-to," showing on which physical units the software elements reside, and "migrates-to," if the allocation is dynamic. This view allows an engineer to reason about performance, data integrity, availability, and security. It is of particular interest in distributed or parallel systems.

- *Implementation.* This structure shows how software elements (usually modules) are mapped to the file structure(s) in the system's development, integration, or configuration control environments. This is critical for the management of development activities and build processes.

- *Work assignment.* This structure assigns responsibility for implementing and integrating the modules to the appropriate development teams. Having a work assignment structure as part of the architecture makes it clear that the decision about who does the work has architectural as well as management implications. The architect will know the expertise required on each team. Also, on large multi-sourced distributed development projects, the work assignment structure is the means for calling out units of functional commonality and assigning them to a single team, rather than having them implemented by everyone who needs them.

Table 2.1 summarizes the software structures. The table lists the meaning of the elements and relations in each structure and tells what each structure might be used for.

TABLE 2.1   Architectural Structures of a System

Software Structure	Relations	Useful for
Decomposition	Is a submodule of; shares secret with	Resource allocation and project structuring and planning; information hiding, encapsulation; configuration control
Uses	Requires the correct presence of	Engineering subsets; engineering extensions
Layered	Requires the correct presence of; uses the services of; provides abstraction to	Incremental development; implementing systems on top of "virtual machines" portability
Class	Is an instance of; shares access methods of	In object-oriented design systems, producing rapid almost-alike implementations from a common template
Client-Server	Communicates with; depends on	Distributed operation; separation of concerns; performance analysis; load balancing
Process	Runs concurrently with; may run concurrently with; excludes; precedes; etc.	Scheduling analysis; performance analysis

continued

TABLE 2.1 Architectural Structures of a System *Continued*

Software Structure	Relations	Useful for
Concurrency	Runs on the same logical thread	Identifying locations where resource contention exists, where threads may fork, join, be created or be killed
Shared Data	Produces data; consumes data	Performance; data integrity; modifiability
Deployment	Allocated to; migrates to	Performance, availability, security analysis
Implementation	Stored in	Configuration control, integration, test activities
Work Assignment	Assigned to	Project management, best use of expertise, management of commonality

Although we often think about a system's structure in terms of its functionality, there are system properties in addition to functionality, such as physical distribution, process communication, and synchronization, that must be considered at an architectural level. Each structure provides a method for reasoning about some of the relevant quality attributes. The uses structure, for instance, must be *engineered* (not merely recorded) to build a system that can be easily extended or contracted. The process structure is *engineered* to eliminate deadlock and reduce bottlenecks. The module decomposition structure is *engineered* to produce modifiable systems, and so forth. Each structure provides the architect with a different view into the system and a different leverage point for design.

RELATING STRUCTURES TO EACH OTHER

Each of these structures provides a different perspective and design handle on a system, and each is valid and useful in its own right. Although the structures give different system perspectives, they are not independent. Elements of one will be related to elements of others, and we need to reason about these relations. For example, a module in a decomposition structure may be manifested as one, as part of one, or as several components in one of the component-and-connector structures, reflecting its runtime alter ego. In general, mappings between structures are many to many.

Individual projects sometimes consider one structure dominant and cast other structures, when possible, in terms of it. Often, but not always, the dominant structure is module decomposition. This is for a good reason: It tends to spawn the project structure. Scenarios, described in Chapter 4, are useful for exercising a given structure as well as its connections to other structures. For example, a software engineer wanting to make a change to the client-server structure of a system would need to consider the process and deployment views because client-server mechanisms typically involve processes and threads, and physical distribution might involve different control mechanisms than would be used if the processes were colocated on a single machine. If control mechanisms need to be changed, the module decomposition or layered view would need to be considered to determine the extent of the changes.

Not all systems warrant consideration of many architectural structures. The larger the system, the more dramatic the differences between these structures tend to be; however, for small systems we can often get by with less. Instead of working with each of several component-and-connector structures, a single one will do. If there is only one process, then the process structure collapses to a single node and need not be carried through the design. If there is to be no distribution (that is, if there is just one processor), then the deployment structure is trivial and need not be considered further.

Structures represent the primary engineering leverage points of an architecture. Individual structures bring with them the power to manipulate one or more quality attributes. They represent a powerful separation-of-concerns approach for creating the architecture (and, later, for analyzing it and explaining it to stakeholders). And, as we will see in Chapter 9, the structures that the architect has chosen as engineering leverage points are also the primary candidates for the basis for architecture documentation.

WHICH STRUCTURES TO CHOOSE?

We have briefly described a number of useful architectural structures, and there are many more. Which ones should an architect work on? Which ones should the architect document? Surely not all of them.

There is no shortage of advice. In 1995, Philippe Kruchten [Kruchten 95] published a very influential paper in which he described the concept of architecture comprising separate structures and advised concentrating on four. To validate that the structures were not in conflict with each other and together did in fact describe a system meeting its requirements, Kruchten advised using key use cases as a check. This so-called "Four Plus One" approach became popular and has now been institutionalized as the conceptual basis of the Rational Unified Process. Kruchten's four views follow:

- *Logical*. The elements are "key abstractions," which are manifested in the object-oriented world as objects or object classes. This is a module view.
- *Process*. This view addresses concurrency and distribution of functionality. It is a component-and-connector view.
- *Development*. This view shows the organization of software modules, libraries, subsystems, and units of development. It is an allocation view, mapping software to the development environment.
- *Physical*. This view maps other elements onto processing and communication nodes and is also an allocation view (which others call the deployment view).

At essentially the same time that Kruchten published his work, Soni, Nord, and Hofmeister [Soni 95] published an influential paper in which they reported the structures put into use across many projects by the software architects in their organization. Their views were conceptual, module interconnection, execution, and code. Once again, these map clearly to the module, component-and-connector, and allocation models.

Other authors followed, and the list of available structures grows ever more rich. Of course, you should not use them all even though most of them will in fact exist in the system you are building. Instead, consider that one of the obligations of the architect is to understand how the various structures lead to quality attributes, and then choose the ones that will best deliver those attributes. This point will be treated at greater length in Chapter 9, on architectural representation.

2.6 Summary

This chapter defined software architecture and also introduced the related concepts of reference model, reference architecture, and architectural pattern. We have explained why architecture is a fundamentally useful concept in software engineering, in terms of the early insights it provides into the system, the communication it enables among stakeholders, and the value it provides as a re-usable asset. All of these themes will be expanded in subsequent chapters.

Our definition of architecture makes clear that systems comprise many structures. We showed several of the most commonly used structures and explained how each serves as an engineering leverage point into the design process.

The next chapter is the first case study of the book. Its purpose is to show the utility of different architectural structures in the design of a complex system.

2.7 For Further Reading

The early work of David Parnas laid much of the conceptual foundation for what became the study of software architecture (see the sidebar Architecture Déjà Vu). A quintessential Parnas reader would include his foundational article on information hiding [Parnas 72] as well as his works on program families [Parnas 76], the structures inherent in software systems [Parnas 74], and introduction of the uses structure to build subsets and supersets of systems [Parnas 79]. All of these papers can be found in the more easily accessible collection of his important papers [Hoffman 00].

Software architectural patterns have been extensively catalogued in *Pattern-Oriented Software Architecture* [Buschmann 96, Schmidt 00].

Early papers on architectural views as used in industrial development projects are [Soni 95] and [Kruchten 95]. The former grew into a book [Hofmeister 00] that presents a comprehensive picture of views as used in development and analysis. The latter grew into the Rational Unified Process, about which there is no shortage of references, both paper and online. A good one is [Kruchten 00].

A discussion of architectural mismatch can be found in Garlan et al. [Garlan 95]. Barry Boehm [Boehm 95] discusses the process issues surrounding software architecture.

The Software Engineering Institute's software architecture Web page [SEI ATA] provides a wide variety of software architecture resources and links, including a broad collection of definitions of the term.

Paulish [Paulish 02] discusses the relationship of cost and schedule to the existence of an architecture.

Architecture Déjà Vu

While architecture is undoubtedly a vital part of system development that is enjoying widespread attention at the moment, it must be pointed out that the field is plowing old ground in several areas. In many ways we are "discovering" fundamental principles that were laid out eloquently and convincingly over a quarter-century ago by Fred Brooks, Edsger Dijkstra, David Parnas, and others.

In programming, the term *architecture* was first used to mean a description of a computer system that applied equally to more than one system. It still carries this meaning today. In 1969, Fred Brooks and Ken Iverson called architecture the "conceptual structure of a computer . . . as seen by the programmer" [Brooks 69]. A few years later, Brooks (crediting G. Blaauw for the term) defined architecture as "the complete and detailed specification of the user interface" [Brooks 75]. A careful distinction was drawn between architecture and implementation. Quoting Blaauw, Brooks writes, "Where architecture tells *what* happens, implementation tells *how* it is made to happen." This distinction survives today, and in the era of object-oriented programming, it thrives.

The term *architecture* is still used today in some communities to refer to the user view of a system, but that is not what we mean by *software* architecture. The structure(s) contained in a software architecture is invisible to the system's end user. However, the conceptual separation between the *what* and the *how* applies. Software architecture is not concerned with how elements do what they do, just as the end user is not concerned with how the system does what it does. The notion of architecture as a common description of a class of systems (i.e., an abstraction, where all the instances are said to exhibit the architecture) remains at the heart of what we call software architecture today.

Also in 1968, Edsger Dijkstra was telling us to be concerned with how software is partitioned and structured as opposed to simply programming to produce a correct result [Dijkstra 68]. He was writing about an operating system and introduced the idea of a layered structure, in which programs were grouped into layers and programs in one layer could communicate only with programs in adjacent layers. Dijkstra pointed out the elegant conceptual integrity exhibited by such an organization, resulting in increased ease of development and maintenance.

David Parnas advanced this line of observation with his fundamental contributions to software engineering in the early 1970s. In his work, more than anyone else's, is to be found many of the fundamental tenets and principles behind software architecture, including the following:

- A design principle for how to break a system into elements to increase maintainability and (as we will see in Chapter 5) re-usability. If architecture has a fundamental principle, it is this one, which Parnas called information hiding [Parnas 72].

- The principle of using an element via its interface only, the conceptual basis of all object-based design [Parnas 72].

- An observation of the various structures to be found in software systems, with an admonition not to confuse them—a lesson often forgotten by today's "architecturists" [Parnas 74].

- Introduction of the uses structure, a principle for controlling the connections between elements in order to increase the extensibility of a system, as well as the ability to field subsets quickly and easily [Parnas 79].

- The principle of detection and handling of errors (now called exceptions) in component-based systems, which is the underlying approach of most modern programming languages [Parnas 72, 76].

- Viewing every program as a member of a family of programs, with principles for taking advantage of the commonalities among the members and ordering the design decisions so that the ones that need to be the easiest to revise are made last. The coarse structuring of the program—part of its architecture—comprises the set of early, family-wide design decisions [Parnas 76].

- Recognition that the structure of a system influences the qualities (such as reliability) of that system [Parnas 76].

Now it is true, and Parnas would agree, that not all of the ideas in his papers were invented by him from whole cloth. About information hiding, for example, he has said that he was writing down what good programmers had been doing for a long time (especially operating systems programmers writing device drivers). However, taken as a body, Parnas's work is a coherent statement of the theme of software architecture: *Structure matters*. His insights form the backbone of software architecture as a study area, and no book on the subject would be complete without acknowledging his fundamental contributions.

Recently a colleague and I had a fine architectural discussion about what exactly constitutes the *interface* to a software element; clearly it is much more than the names of the programs you can call and the parameters they take. My colleague worked out that it is actually the set of assumptions that you can safely make about the element, and that these assumptions vary according to the context of the element's use. I agreed and pulled out Parnas's paper [Parnas 71] in which he said precisely the same thing. My friend looked a little crestfallen for a moment and then said, "Now I know how Scott felt when he reached the South Pole and found Amundsen's flag already planted. He probably said, 'Oh, damn. And now I've got to eat my dogs.'"

Parnas's flag is planted deeply, and often, in our field. In the next chapter, we will present a case study of an architecture created by Parnas to put his ideas into practical use in a demanding real-world application. Even though it ran its course long ago, we know of no other single project that so clearly laid out and faithfully followed architectural principles such as engineering and maintaining separate structures to achieve quality goals; strict information hiding to achieve re-usable elements and a re-usable architecture; and painstaking specification of that architecture, its elements, and their relationships.

While Parnas and others laid the foundations, the field has taken its own turns in the interim. Experience with basic ideas leads to the refinement of those ideas, to embellishments rooted in practicalities, and to entirely new concepts. Thus, while Parnas wrote about *program families* a couple of decades ago, we will see in Chapter 14 that organizational, process, and managerial concerns predominate in the successful development of *product lines*, their conceptual descendant. While Dijkstra wrote about separation of concerns about a quarter-century ago, *objects* (the conceptual descendant) have only fairly recently come into their own as a standard, widely accepted design approach. And while Brooks and Blaauw wrote about architecture even longer ago, we've already seen that architectures cannot be understood except in light of the business issues that spawned them, and we will see ways to analyze architectures without waiting for the system to be built.

Today, architecture as a field of study is large and growing larger, primarily because it has left the realm of deep thinkers and visionaries and made the transition into practice. The early ideas have been refined and applied enough so that it is becoming an accepted state-of-the-practice approach to system building.

— PCC

2.8 Discussion Questions

1. Software architecture is often compared to building architecture. What are the strong points of this comparison? What is the correspondence in buildings to software architecture structures and views? To patterns? What are the weaknesses of the comparison? When does it break down?

2. What is the difference between a reference architecture and an architectural pattern? What can you do with one that you cannot do with the other in terms of organizational planning and architectural analysis?

3. Do the architectures in your organization recognize the different views (structures and relations) inherent in architecture? If so, which ones? If not, why not?

4. Is there a different definition of software architecture that you are familiar with? If so, think about the ways in which this definition supports our acid test of an architecture: Does it abstract information away from the system and yet provide enough information to be a basis for analysis, decision making, and risk reduction?

3

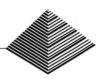

A-7E Avionics System

A Case Study in Utilizing Architectural Structures

*An object-oriented program's runtime structure often bears
little resemblance to its code structure. The code structure
is frozen at compile-time; it consists of classes
in fixed inheritance relationships.
A program's runtime structure consists of rapidly changing
networks of communicating objects. In fact, the two
structures are largely independent. Trying to
[understand] one from the other is like
trying to understand the dynamism
of living ecosystems from the static
taxonomy of plants and animals,
and vice versa.*
— E. Gamma, R. Helms, R. Johnson,
and J. Vlissides [Gamma 95]

In Chapter 2, we stated that software architecture describes elements of a system and the relations among them. We also emphasized that every system has many kinds of elements and that different architectural structures are useful, even necessary, to present a complete picture of the architecture of a system. Each structure concentrates on one aspect of the architecture.

This chapter will present a case study of an architecture designed by engineering and specifying three specific architectural structures: *module decomposition*, *uses*, and *process*. We will see how these structures complement each other to provide a complete picture of how the system works, and we will see how certain qualities of the system are affected by each one. Table 3.1 summarizes the three structures we will discuss.

TABLE 3.1   The A-7E's Architecural Structures

Structure	Elements	Relation among Elements	Has Influence Over
Module Decomposition	Modules (implementation units)	Is a submodule of; shares a secret with	Ease of change
Uses	Procedures	Requires the correct presence of	Ability to field subsets and develop incrementally
Process	Processes; thread of procedures	Synchronizes with; shares CPU with; excludes	Schedulability; achieving performance goals through parallelism

3.1   Relationship to the Architecture Business Cycle

Figure 3.1 shows the ABC as it pertains to the A-7E avionics system described in this chapter. The system was constructed beginning in 1977 for the naval aviators who flew the A-7E aircraft and was paid for by the U.S. Navy. The developing organization was the software engineering group at the U.S. Naval Research Laboratory. The developers were creating the software to test their belief that certain software

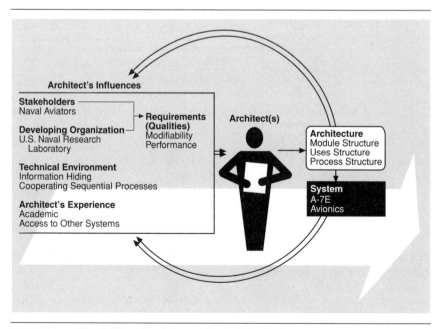

FIGURE 3.1   The ABC as it relates to the A-7E avionics systems

engineering strategies (in this case, information hiding and cooperating sequential processes) were appropriate for high-performance embedded real-time systems.

The architects included one of the authors of this book and one of the leaders in the development of software engineering principles, but the architects had little experience in the avionics domain, although they did have access to other avionics systems and to experts in avionics. There was no compiler available for the target platform.

We will start by explaining the application, what the system does, which qualities were important to achieve, and the software's role in performing the system's task.

3.2 Requirements and Qualities

Figure 3.2 shows the A-7E Corsair II. It is a single-seat, carrier-based attack aircraft used by the U.S. Navy throughout the 1960s, 1970s, and 1980s. An earlier version, the A-7C, was among the very first production aircraft in the world to be equipped with an onboard computer to help the pilot with navigation and "weapon delivery" (the military euphemism for attacking a ground target).

The A-7E's onboard computer is a small, special-purpose IBM machine for which no compiler exists; programming is in assembly language only. The computer has special registers connected to analog-to-digital and digital-to-analog converters that let it receive and send data to almost two dozen devices in the aircraft's avionics suite.

In broad terms, the A-7E software is responsible for reading sensors and updating cockpit displays that help the pilot drop weapons on a target. The A-7E software does not actually fly the aircraft, as more modern avionics systems do.

FIGURE 3.2   An A-7E Corsair II.   Used with permission and under copyright of Squadron/Signal Publications, Inc.

The following are the primary sensors the software reads and manages:

- An air probe that measures barometric pressure and air speed.
- A forward-looking radar that can be aimed in azimuth and elevation and returns the straight-line range to the point on the ground at which it is pointed.
- A Doppler radar that reports ground speed and drift angle (the difference between the direction in which the aircraft's nose is pointed and the direction in which it is moving over the ground).
- An inertial measurement set (IMS) that reports accelerations along each of three orthogonal axes. The software must read these accelerations in a timely manner and integrate them over time to derive velocities, and it must integrate the velocities over time to derive the aircraft's current position in the physical world. It also must manage the alignment and compensate for the drift of the axes to keep them pointed north, east, and vertical, respectively, so that the measurements accurately correspond to the aircraft's frame of reference.
- An interface to the aircraft carrier's inertial measurement system, through which the aircraft can compute its current position while on board a ship.
- Sensors that report which of the A-7E's six underwing bomb racks hold weapons and which of more than 100 kinds of weapons in the aircraft's repertoire they are. The software stores large tables of the parameters for each weapon type, which let it compute how that weapon moves through the atmosphere in a free-fall ballistic trajectory.
- A radar altimeter that measures the distance to the ground.

The cockpit display devices managed by the software include some that are display only and some by which the pilot communicates with the software, as follows:

- A map display that always shows the aircraft's current location by moving a back-lit filmstrip as the aircraft travels. The pilot can choose the map's orientation so that the top corresponds either to the current heading or to true north.
- A heads-up display—a device that projects digital and iconographic information on a clear window between the pilot and the windscreen. Since the pilot's head position is assumed fixed and known, the display can be used to overlay information about the real world, such as the position of the target or a line showing the aircraft's direction of travel.
- A keypad and a trio of small alphanumeric display windows. With the keypad, the pilot can request approximately a hundred kinds of digital information from the computer. A bank of switches on the computer control panel allows the pilot to choose the desired navigation and weapon delivery modes.
- Various lights and dials and an audible signal.

The pilot communicates the location of a ground target (or a navigational waypoint) to the software in a number of ways, including the following:

- Keying in its latitude and longitude via the keypad

- Slewing the map using a joystick until its coordinates are under the center crosshairs and then "designating" it by pushing a special button on the control stick
- Aiming the forward-looking radar to the point and designating it
- Slewing a special symbol on the heads-up display until it overlays the point of interest on the ground and then designating it

The software then provides navigational information (direction, distance, time to go) and directional cues on the heads-up display that take the aircraft to the designated location.

The pilot can choose from over two dozen navigation modes, based on which sensors are most reliable under the conditions of the moment. The software has at least five direct and indirect ways to calculate the aircraft's current altitude, including a trigonometric scheme using the range and elevation angle of the forward-looking radar as components of a triangle (see Figure 3.3). There are more than 20 weapon delivery modes, all demanding in terms of the real-time calculations (repeated 25 times every second) necessary to maintain the A-7E's bombing accuracy.

A-7Es were retired from active duty in the late 1980s, but current-generation fighters feature a heads-up display and weapon delivery and navigation modes that show heavy influence from the Corsair.

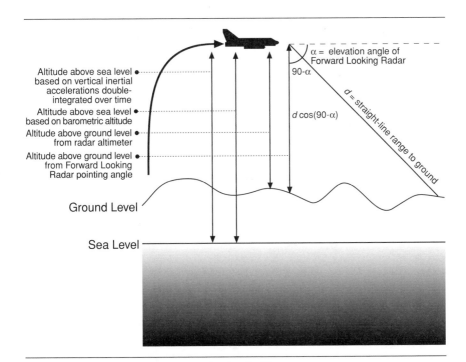

FIGURE 3.3   Calculation of altitude for the A-7E

The architecture we will present in this chapter is not the architecture for the original software but that for a redesign project launched by Navy software engineers using the A-7E as a demonstration project for their ideas (see the sidebar About the A-7 Project). The qualities that the software system was expected to have included real-time performance and modifiability for expected changes. Specifically, the performance requirements were stated in terms of updates per second of the A7-E's displays and weapon delivery calculations. The modifiability requirements dealt with making changes to the weaponry, the platform, the symbology on the display, and the addition of new input through the keypad.

About the A-7 Project

"In the mid-1970s, it was clear to computer scientists at the Naval Research Laboratory (NRL) in Washington, D.C., that much of the computer science technology being developed in academia and laboratories was not being used by the developers of software for Navy systems." So began a typical description of the Navy's Software Cost Reduction (SCR) project, or, as it was more popularly known, the A-7 project. Most descriptions went on to say that NRL's response was to choose a high-fidelity, challenging Navy program (the software for the A-7E aircraft) and then redesign and reimplement it using that under-utilized technology. The point was to create a convincing demonstration of the technology's value in real-world applications.

Between the lines, however, was the fact that those scientists had some very specific computer science technology in mind: primarily, the use of information hiding as the design strategy. This is not surprising, because the impetus behind the A-7 project was the man who first wrote about information hiding as a design technique, David Parnas. Parnas wanted to find out whether his ideas (and others, such as cooperating sequential processes) could be used in a system with inflexible requirements, demanding memory constraints, and tight time budgets. If not, he wanted to find out why not and how to improve his ideas so that they could work. Vague methods demonstrated only on toy problems were clearly not enough. The idea behind the A-7 project was to leave a complete engineering model—documentation, design, code, methodology, principles—that others could emulate, all reported in the open literature.

The project started in 1977 with a couple of people working part-time. It soon chose the demonstration application: The software for the A-7E was a hard real-time system (meaning it absolutely had to meet its timing requirements), it was embedded (having to interface with all sorts of esoteric hardware devices), it was absolutely authentic, and it was very tightly constrained by the computer's tiny memory capacity: only 32,000 16-bit words. If the new techniques succeeded in duplicating *this* program, they would succeed anywhere.

The first product was a requirements specification for the software. It hadn't been intended, but when Parnas asked the Navy if he could obtain the A-7's requirements document, the response was "*What* requirements document?" Realizing that they had to have a standard against which to test and judge when they were done, the software engineers at the NRL reluctantly set about documenting the requirements for the software. The team not only produced a requirements document but, more important, produced a method for producing it. SCR-style requirements documents are now widely used for real-time embedded software systems.

Then the small team concentrated on designing the interfaces to all of the modules. The few people working on the project were pioneering what would today be called object-based design. In designing to accommodate future changes, they were also building what would today be called a domain model. In creating a standard, re-usable design, they were building what would today be called a reference architecture (see Chapter 12). They had to balance their time among inventing new software engineering approaches, learning the avionics domain, writing papers to get the word out and, last but hardly least, producing the software.

The project implementation phase was staged by deploying a tiny subset of the software to demonstrate the ability to generate executable code, and then deploying two successively larger subsets, and finally the entire system. The uses structure, one of the three architectural structures highlighted in the case study, allowed them to define these subsets quickly and easily to meet their needs. By the time the second of the three subsets was under way, it was clear to project management that most of what they had set out to learn had been learned and that slogging through to the complete reimplementation was not going to be practical given the small staff size, small budget, and still infantile expertise in the avionics domain. In 1987, the project demonstrated the successful completion of the second subset and was completed. The subset was carefully chosen to include part of every second-level module and to perform a useful and nontrivial navigation function.

The team concluded that information hiding is not only compatible with real-time embedded systems but in many ways ideal for it. Careful attention to module interfaces and module interface specifications paid off in essentially eliminating integration as a project phase: There were practically no errors of the type usually associated with the integration step. The software was able to meet its timing deadlines but could not compete with years of handcrafted assembly code in terms of memory efficiency. It is hoped that memory efficiency is now and will remain less of a concern than it was in 1977.

The architecture we present in this case study is that of the completed design, the one that led to the subset of 1987. There is no reason to believe that it would not have also led, unchanged, to the full reimplementation of the system. In any case, it is a very good example of paying attention to different architectural structures or views in order to achieve particular goals, and we present it in that light.

Why, after all this time, is the A-7E still interesting? Because it holds two lessons. One is that information hiding is a viable and prudent design discipline—a lesson that has been well heeded by the community. The second is that carefully engineering different structures of an architecture yields payoffs in terms of achievable qualities—a lesson not so well heeded, and so we repeat it in the context of the current interest in software architecture in the hope that, through repetition, the lesson will be better absorbed.

— PCC

3.3   Architecture for the A-7E Avionics System

The architecture for the A-7E avionics system is centered around three architectural structures discussed in Chapter 2:

- Decomposition, a structure of modules
- Uses, a structure of modules
- Process, a structure of components and connectors

We will discuss each in turn.

DECOMPOSITION STRUCTURE

Unless a program is small enough to be produced by a single programmer, we must think how the work will be divided into units that can be implemented separately and how those modules will interact. The unit of the decomposition structure is, of course, the module. A module may be thought of as defining a group of procedures, some public and some private, plus a set of private data structures. The relation among modules in the decomposition structure is "is-a-submodule-of" or "shares-a-secret-with."

Prior to 1977, performance was the overriding goal of embedded (as well as most other) systems. The goal of the A-7E designers was to balance performance with modifiability and demonstrate that it was possible to achieve modifiability without compromising performance.

Information Hiding.   The A-7E module decomposition is based on information hiding. An architectural tactic we will revisit in Chapter 5, information hiding works by encapsulating system details that are likely to change independently in different modules. The interface of a module reveals only those aspects considered unlikely to change; the details hidden by the module interface are the module's secrets.

For instance, if a device such as an aircraft altitude sensor is likely to be replaced over the life of an avionics program, the information-hiding principle makes the details of interacting with that device the secret of one module. The interface to the module provides an abstraction of the sensor, consisting perhaps of a single program that returns the most recent value measured by the sensor, because all replacement sensors probably share this capability. If the sensor is ever replaced, only the internal parts of that module need to change; the rest of the software is unaffected.

Information hiding is enforced by requiring that modules interact only via a defined set of public facilities—their *interfaces.* Each module provides a set of *access procedures,* which may be called by any other module in the system. The access procedures provide the only inter-module means for interacting with information encapsulated in a module.

Of course, this is the philosophy underlying object-based design, with a key difference: Whereas objects are created from the physical objects inherent in the application, or conjured up from intuitive insights about the system, information-hiding modules are derived by cataloging the changes to the software that are perceived to be likely over the system's lifetime.

A module may consist of submodules, or it may be considered a single implementation unit. If it contains submodules, a guide to its substructure is provided. The decomposition into submodules and their design is continued until each module is small enough to be discarded and begun again if the programmer assigned to it leaves the project.

Specific goals of module decomposition are as follows:

- Each module's structure should be simple enough to be understood fully.
- It should be possible to change the implementation of one module without knowledge of the implementation of other modules and without affecting the behavior of other modules.
- The ease of making a change in the design should bear a reasonable relationship to the likelihood of the change being needed; it should be possible to make likely changes without changing any module interfaces; less likely changes may involve interface changes but only for modules that are small and not widely used. Only very unlikely changes should require changes in the interfaces of widely used modules.
- It should be possible to make a major software change as a set of independent changes to individual modules (i.e., except for interface changes, programmers changing the individual modules should not need to communicate). If the module interfaces are not revised, it should be possible to run and test any combination of old and new module versions.

The documentation of the decomposition structure is sometimes called a *module guide*. It defines the responsibilities of each of the modules by stating the design decisions that will be encapsulated by it. Its purpose is to avoid duplication and gaps, to achieve separation of concerns, and, most of all, to help a maintainer find out which modules are affected by a problem report or change request.

The guide states the criteria used to assign a particular responsibility to a module and arranges the modules in such a way that we can find the necessary information without searching through unrelated documentation. It reflects the tree structure of the decomposition structure, dividing the system into a small number of modules and treating each one in the same way until all of them are quite small. Each nonleaf node in the tree represents a module composed of the modules represented by its descendants. The guide does not describe any runtime relationship among the modules: It doesn't talk about how modules interact with each other while the system is executing; rather, it simply describes a design-time relationship among the implementation units that constitute the design phase of a project.

Applying this principle is not always easy. It is an attempt to lower the expected cost of software by anticipating likely changes. Such estimates are necessarily

TABLE 3.2   How the A-7E Module Decomposition Structure Achieves Quality Goals

Goal	How Achieved
Ease of change to: weapons, platform, symbology, input	Information hiding
Understand anticipated changes	Formal evaluation procedure to take advantage of experience of domain experts
Assign work teams so that their interactions were minimized	Modules structured as a hierarchy; each work team assigned to a second-level module and all of its descendants

based on experience, knowledge of the application area, and an understanding of hardware and software technology. Because a designer might not have had all of the relevant experience, formal evaluation procedures were used that were designed to take advantage of the experience of others. Table 3.2 summarizes the role of the module structure in the A-7E architecture.

A-7E Module Decomposition Structure.   To describe the A-7E module decomposition structure, and to give an example of how a module structure is documented, we provide the following excerpts from the A-7E software module guide. The decomposition tree is described beginning with the three highest-level modules. These are motivated by the observation that, in systems like the A-7E, changes tend to come from three areas: the hardware with which the software must interact, the required externally visible behavior of the system, and a decision solely under the jurisdiction of a project's software designer.

Hardware-Hiding Module. The Hardware-Hiding Module includes the procedures that need to be changed if any part of the hardware is replaced by a new unit with a different hardware/software interface but with the same general capabilities. This module implements *virtual hardware,* or a set of abstract devices that are used by the rest of the software. The primary secrets of this module are the hardware/software interfaces. The secondary secrets of this module are the data structures and algorithms used to implement the virtual hardware. One of the submodules of the Hardware-Hiding Module is the Extended Computer Module that hides the details of the processor.

Behavior-Hiding Module. The Behavior-Hiding Module includes procedures that need to be changed if there are changes in requirements affecting the required behavior. Those requirements are the primary secret of this module. These procedures determine the values to be sent to the virtual output devices provided by the Hardware-Hiding Module.

Software Decision Module. The Software Decision Module hides software design decisions that are based on mathematical theorems, physical facts, and programming considerations such as algorithmic efficiency and accuracy. The secrets of this module are not described in the requirements document. This module differs from the other modules in that both the secrets and the interfaces are determined by software designers. Changes in these modules are more likely to be motivated by a desire to improve performance or accuracy than by externally imposed changes.

The module guide goes on to explain how conflicts among these categories (e.g., is a required algorithm part of the behavior or a software decision?) are arbitrated by a complete and unambiguous requirements specification and then provides the second-level decomposition. The following sections describe how the Software Decision Module is decomposed.

Application Data Type Module—The Application Data Type Module supplements the data types provided by the Extended Computer Module with data types that are useful for avionics applications and do not require a computer-dependent implementation. Examples of types include distance (useful for altitude), time intervals, and angles (useful for latitude and longitude). These data types are implemented using the basic numeric data types provided by the Extended Computer; variables of those types are used just as if the types were built into the Extended Computer.

The secrets of the Application Data Type Module are the data representation used in the variables and the procedures used to implement operations on those variables. Units of measurement (such as feet, seconds, or radians) are part of the representation and are hidden. Where necessary, the modules provide conversion operators that deliver or accept real values in specified units.

Data Banker Module—Most data are produced by one module and consumed by another. In most cases, the consumers should receive a value that is as up to date as practical. The time at which a datum should be recalculated is determined both by properties of its consumer (e.g., accuracy requirements) and by properties of its producer (e.g., cost of calculation, rate of change of value). The Data Banker Module acts as a "middleman" and determines when new values for these data are computed.

The Data Banker Module obtains values from producer procedures; consumer procedures obtain data from Data Banker access procedures. The producer and consumers of a particular datum can be written without knowing when a stored value is updated. In most cases, neither the producer nor the consumer need be modified if the updating policy changes.

The Data Banker provides values for all data that report on the internal state of a module or on the state of the aircraft. The Data Banker also signals events involving changes in the values that it supplies. The Data Banker is used as long as consumer and producer are separate modules, even when they are both submodules of a larger module. The Data Banker is not used if consumers require specific members of the sequence of values computed by the producer or if a produced value is solely a function of the values of input parameters given to the producing procedure, such as $\sin(x)$.[1]

---

[1] The Data Banker Module is an example of the use of the blackboard architectural pattern (see Chapter 5, Achieving Qualities).

The choice among updating policies should be based on the consumers' accuracy requirements, how often consumers require the value, the maximum wait that consumers can accept, how rapidly the value changes, and the cost of producing a new value. This information is part of the specification given to the implementor of the Data Banker Module.

Filter Behavior Module—The Filter Behavior Module contains digital models of physical filters. They can be used by other procedures to filter potentially noisy data. The primary secrets of this module are the models used for the estimation of values based on sample values and error estimates. The secondary secrets are the computer algorithms and data structures used to implement those models.

Physical Models Module—The software requires estimates of quantities that cannot be measured directly but can be computed from observables using mathematical models. An example is the time that a ballistic weapon will take to strike the ground. The primary secrets of the Physical Models Module are the models; the secondary secrets are the computer implementations of those models.

Software Utility Module—The Software Utility Module contains those utility routines that would otherwise have to be written by more than one other programmer. The routines include mathematical functions, resource monitors, and procedures that signal when all modules have completed their power-up initialization. The secrets of the module are the data structures and algorithms used to implement the procedures.

System Generation Module—The primary secrets of the System Generation Module are decisions that are postponed until system generation time. These include the values of system-generation parameters and the choice among alternative implementations of a module. The secondary secrets of the System Generation Module are the method used to generate a machine-executable form of the code and the representation of the postponed decisions. The procedures in this module do not run on the onboard computer; they run on the computer used to generate the code for the onboard system.

The module guide describes a third- (and in some cases a fourth-) level decomposition, but that has been omitted here. Figure 3.4 shows the decomposition structure of the A-7E architecture down to the third level. Notice that many of the Device Interface modules have the same names as Function Driver modules. The difference is that the Device Interface modules are programmed with knowledge of how the software interfaces with the devices; the Function Driver modules are programmed with the knowledge of values required to be computed and sent to those devices. This suggests another architectural relationship that we will explore shortly: how the software in these modules cooperates to accomplish work.

But the module decomposition view is not yet complete. Recall from Chapter 2 our definition of architecture as including the behavioral specification for each of the elements. Carefully designed language-independent interfaces are crucial for maintaining portability and achieving interoperability. Here, each module must have an interface specified for it. Chapter 9 discusses documentation for software interfaces.

Hardware-Hiding Module	Behavior-Hiding Module

Extended Computer Module
 Data Module
 Input/Output Module
 Computer State Module
 Parallelism Control Module
 Program Module
 Virtual Memory Module
 Interrupt Handler Module
 Timer Module
Device Interface Module
 Air Data Computer Module
 Angle of Attack Sensor Module
 Audible Signal Device Module
 Computer Fail Device Module
 Doppler Radar Set Module
 Flight Information Displays Module
 Forward Looking Radar Module
 Head-Up Display Module
 Inertial Measurement Set Module
 Input/Output Representation Module
 Master Function Switch Module
 Panel Module
 Projected Map Display Set Module
 Radar Altimeter Module
 Shipboard Inertial Navigation
  System Module
 Slew Control Module
 Switch Bank Module
 TACAN Module
 Visual Indicators Module
 Waypoint Information System Module
 Weapon Characteristics Module
 Weapon Release System Module
 Weight on Gear Module

Function Driving Module
 Air Data Computer Module
 Audible Signal Module
 Computer Fail Signal Module
 Doppler Radar Set Module
 Flight Information Display Module
 Forward Looking Radar Module
 Head-Up Display Module
 Inertial Measurement Set Module
 Panel Module
 Projected Map Display Set Module
 Shipboard Inertial Navigation
  System Module
 Visual Indicator Module
 Weapon Release System Module
 Ground Test Module
Shared Services Module
 Mode Determination Module
 Panel I/O Support Module
 Shared Subroutine Module
 Stage Director Module
 System Value Module

Software Decision Module

Application Data Type Module
 Numeric Data Type Module
 State Transition Event Module
Data Banker Module
 Singular Values Module
 Complex Event Module
Filter Behavior Module
Physical Models Module
 Aircraft Motion Module
 Earth Characteristics Module
 Human Factors Module
 Target Behavior Module
 Weapon Behavior Module
Software Utility Module
 Power-Up Initialization Module
 Numerical Algorithms Module
System Generation Module
 System Generation Parameter
  Module
 Support Software Module

FIGURE 3.4   The module decomposition view of the A-7E software architecture

In the previous chapter, we remarked that architectures serve as the blueprint for the developing project as well as for the software. In the case of the A-7E architecture, this second-level module decomposition structure became enshrined in many ways: Design documentation, online configuration-controlled files, test plans, programming teams, review procedures, and project schedule and milestones all used it as their unit of reference.

USES STRUCTURE

The second major structure of interest in the A-7E architecture is the uses structure. The decomposition structure carries no information about runtime execution of the software; you might make an educated guess as to how two procedures in different modules interact at runtime, but this information is not in fact in the module decomposition. Rather, the uses structure supplies the authoritative picture of how the software interacts.

The Uses Relation.   The concept behind the uses structure is the uses relation. Procedure A is said to *use* procedure B if a correctly functioning procedure B must be present in order for procedure A to meet its requirements. In practice this relation is similar to but not quite the same as the calls relation. Procedure A usually calls procedure B because it uses it. However, here are two cases where uses and calls are different:

1. Procedure A is simply required to call procedure B in its specification, but the future computation performed by A will not depend on what B does. Procedure B must be present in order for procedure A to work, but it need not be correct. A calls, but does not use, B. B might be an error handler, for example.
2. Procedure B performs its function without being called by procedure A, but A uses the results. The results might be an updated data store that B leaves behind. Or B might be an interrupt handler that A assumes exists and functions correctly. A uses, but does not call, B.

The uses relation allows rapid identification of functional subsets. If you know that procedure A needs to be in the subset, you also know that every procedure that A uses must also be there. The transitive closure of this relation defines the subset. It therefore pays to engineer this structure, to impose a discipline on it, so that every subset needn't consist of the entire system. This means specifying an allowed-to-use structure for programmers. After implementation is complete, the actual uses can be cataloged.

The unit of the uses (or allowed-to-use) structure is the access procedure. By dictating what procedures are allowed to use which other procedures (and, by implication, what procedures are *not* allowed to be used by which other procedures), the uses structure is defined.

Although the unit of the uses structure is a procedure, in practice all of the procedures of a module may share usage restrictions. Hence, the name of a module might appear in the uses structure; if so, it is shorthand for all of the access procedures in that module.

The uses (allowed-to-use) structure is conceptually documented with a binary matrix; each row and column lists every procedure in the system. Thus, if element (m,n) is true, then procedure m uses (is allowed to use) procedure n. In practice, this is too cumbersome, and a shorthand was introduced in which rules for whole modules (as opposed to individual procedures within each module) were adopted.

Table 3.3 summarizes the role of the uses structure in the A-7E software architecture.

The A-7E Uses Structure. Recall that the uses structure is first documented in a specification showing the allowed-to-use relation; actual uses are extracted after implementation. The allowed-to-use specification for the A-7E architecture is a seven-page table of which Table 3.4 is a short excerpt. The two-character preface refers to the second-level modules. The names to the right of the period refer to submodule names that we have mostly omitted from this chapter.

TABLE 3.3 How the A-7E Uses Structure Achieves Quality Goals

Goal	How Achieved
Incrementally build and test system functions	Create "is-allowed-to-use" structure for programmers that limits procedures each can use
Design for platform change	Restrict number of procedures that use platform directly
Produce usage guidance of manageable size	Where appropriate, define uses to be a relationship among modules

TABLE 3.4 Excerpt from the A-7E Allowed-to-Use Specification

Using procedures: A procedure in . . .	. . . is allowed to use any procedure in . . .
EC: Extended Computer Module	None
DI: Device Interface Module	EC.DATA, EC.PGM, EC.IO, EC.PAR, AT.NUM, AT.STE, SU
ADC: Air Data Computer	PM.ECM
IMS: Inertial Measurement Set	PM.ACM
FD: Function Driver Module	EC.DATA, EC.PAR, EC.PGM, AT.NUM, AT.STE, SU, DB.SS.MODE, DB.SS.PNL.INPUT, DB.SS.SYSVAL, DB.DI
ADC: Air Data Computer Functions	DB.DI.ADC, DI.ADC, FB
IMS: IMS Functions	DB.DI.IMS, DI.IMS
PNL: Panel Functions	EC.IO, DB.SS.PNL.CONFIG, SS.PNL.FORMAT, DI.ADC, DI.IMS, DI.PMDS, DI.PNL
SS: Shared Services Module	EC.DATA, EC.PGM, EC.PAR, AT.NUM, AT.STE, SU
PNL: Panel I/O Support	DB.SS.MODE, DB.DI.PNL, DB.DI.SWB, SS.PNL.CONFIG, DI.PNL
AT: Application Data Type Module	EC.DATA, EC.PGM
NUM: Numeric Data Types	None additional
STE: State Transition Events	EC.PAR

Notice the pattern that emerges:

- No procedure in the Extended Computer Module is allowed to use a procedure in any other module, but all other modules are allowed to use (portions of) it.
- Procedures in the Application Data Type Module are allowed to use only procedures in the Extended Computer Module and nothing else.
- Procedures in the Device Interface Module (at least the part shown) are allowed to use only Extended Computer, Application Data Type, and Physical Models procedures.
- Function Driver and Shared Services procedures can use Data Banker, Extended Computer, Application Data Type, and Device Interface procedures.
- No procedure can use any procedure in the Function Driver Module.
- Only a Function Driver procedure can use a Shared Services procedure.

What we have is a picture of a system partitioned into *layers*. The Extended Computer Module is the bottommost layer, and the Application Data Type Module is built right on top of it. The two form a virtual machine in which a procedure at a particular level is allowed to use a procedure at the same or any lower level.

At the high end of the layering come the Function Driver and Shared Services modules, which have the freedom to use a wide variety of system facilities to do their jobs. In the middle layers lie the Physical Models, Filter Behavior, and Data Banker modules. The Software Utilities reside in parallel with this structure and are allowed to use anything (except the Function Drivers) necessary to accomplish their individual tasks.

Layered architectures are a well-known architectural pattern and occur in many of the case studies in this book. Layering emerges from the uses structure, but is not a substitute for it as layering does not show what subsets are possible. This is the point of the uses structure—a *particular* Function Driver Module will use a *particular* set of Shared Services, Data Banker, Physical Models, Device Interface, Application Data Type, and Extended Computer operations. The used Shared Services in turn use their own set of lower-level procedures, and so forth. The complete set of procedures derived in this manner constitutes a subset.

The allowed-to-use structure also provides an image of how the procedures of modules interact at runtime to accomplish tasks. Each Function Driver procedure controls the output value associated with one output device, such as the position of a displayed symbol. In general, a Function Driver procedure retrieves data (via Data Banker procedures) from data producers, applies rules for computing the correct value of its assigned output, and sends that value to the device by calling the appropriate Device Interface procedure. Data may come from one of the following:

- Device Interface procedures about the state of the world with which the software interfaces
- Physical Models procedures that compute predictive measures about the outside world (such as where a bomb will strike the earth if released now, given the aircraft's current position and velocity)

- Shared Services procedures about the current mode, the trustworthiness of current sensor readings, or what panel operations the pilot has requested

Once the allowed-to-use structure is designed, implementors know what interfaces they need to be familiar with in order to do their work. After implementation is complete, the actual uses structure can be documented so that subsets can be fielded. The ability to deploy a subset of a system is an important part of the Evolutionary Delivery Life Cycle (see Chapter 7, Designing the Architecture). When budgets are cut (or overrun) and schedules slip, delivering a subset is often the best way to put a positive face on a bad situation. It is probably the case that more subsets would be delivered (instead of nothing at all) if the architectural structure necessary to achieve them—the uses structure—had been carefully designed.

PROCESS STRUCTURE

The third structure of architectural importance to the A-7E is the process structure. Even though the underlying aircraft computer is a uniprocessor, the Extended Computer Module presents a virtual programming interface that features multiprocessing capabilities. This was to plan for if and when the A-7E computer was replaced with an actual multi-processor. Hence, the software was implemented as a set of cooperating sequential processes that synchronize with each other to cooperatively use shared resources. The set was arranged using offline (pre-runtime) scheduling to produce a single executable thread that is then loaded onto the host computer.

A process is a set of programming steps that are repeated in response to a triggering event or to a timing constraint. It has its own thread of control, and it can suspend itself by waiting for an event (usually by invoking one of the event-signaling programs on a module's interface).

Processes are written for two purposes in the A-7E. The first is for the function drivers to compute the output values of the avionics software. They are required to run periodically (e.g., to continuously update a symbol position on the heads-up display) or in response to some triggering event (e.g., when the pilot presses the weapon release button). It is natural to implement these as processes. Conceptually, function driver processes are structured as follows:

- Periodic process: do every 40 milliseconds
  - Call other modules' access procedures to gather the values of all relevant inputs
  - Calculate the resulting output value
  - Call the appropriate Device Interface procedure to send the output value to the outside world
- End periodic process
- Demand process
  - Await triggering event

- Calculate the resulting output outcome
- Call the appropriate Device Interface procedure to trigger the action in the outside world
- End demand process

Processes also occur, although less frequently, as a way to implement certain access procedures. If the value returned by an access procedure is expensive to compute, a programmer might meet the timing requirements by continuously computing the value in the background and simply returning the most recent value immediately when the access procedure is called. For example,

- Process: do every 100 milliseconds
  - Gather inputs to compute value
  - Compute value
  - Store in variable most_recent
- End process
- Procedure get_value(p1)
  - p1 := most_recent.
  - return
- End procedure

The process structure, then, consists of the set of processes in the software. The relation it contains is "synchronizes-with," which is based on events that one process signals and one or more processes await. This relation is used as the primary input to the scheduling activity, which includes deadlock avoidance.

The offline scheduling techniques used in the A-7E software are beyond the scope of this treatment, but they avoid the overhead of a runtime scheduler, and they would not have been possible without the information contained in the process structure. The process structure also allows an optimization trick: merging two otherwise unrelated processes, which makes scheduling easier in many circumstances and avoids the overhead of context switching when one process suspends and another resumes. This technique is invisible to programmers, occurring automatically during system construction. Table 3.5 summarizes the role of the process structure in the A-7E architecture.

TABLE 3.5 How the A-7E Process Structure Achieves Quality Goals

Goal	How Achieved
Map input to output	Each process implemented as cycle that samples, inputs, computes, and presents output
Maintain real-time constraints	Identify process through process structure and then perform offline scheduling
Provide results of time-consuming calculations immediately	Perform calculations in background and return most recent value when queried

The process structure emerged after the other structures had been designed. Function Driver procedures were implemented as processes. Other processes computed time-consuming calculations in the background so that a value would always be available.

Two kinds of information were captured in the process structure. The first documented what procedures were included in the body of each process. This gave a picture of the threads that ran through the system and also told the implementors which procedures must be coded to be re-entrant (i.e., able to carry two or more threads of control simultaneously) by using protected data stores or mutual exclusion. It also gave designers early insight into which procedures were going to be invoked most often, suggesting areas where optimization would pay off.

The second kind of information in the process structure documented which processes (or sequential segments of process threads) could not execute simultaneously. The actual regions of mutual exclusion were not finalized until the processes were completely coded, but the early "excludes" relation among processes let the scheduling team understand some of the quantitative requirements of the offline scheduler and start planning on areas where automation would be most helpful.

Success or Failure?

Bob Glass, in his editorial in the November 1998 issue of *The Journal of Systems and Software* [Glass 98], argues that the A-7E was a failure because the software described in this chapter never flew. I have a great deal of respect for Bob, both personally and professionally, but in this case he is mistaken. He is evaluating a research system by commercial standards.

What do I mean by that? The research world and the commercial world have different cultures and different standards for success. One manifestation of this difference is how the two worlds "sell" to their customers. The commercial world prides itself on delivering, on time and on budget, what is specified. You would justifiably be upset if you went to your local automotive dealer to purchase a car and it wasn't delivered on time, at the cost you contracted for, and performing in the fashion you expected.

The research world "sells" on vision. That is, a research proposal specifies how the world will be different if the funder supports the proposed research. The funder should be upset if, at the end of the research, what is delivered is something that could be purchased at a local commercial establishment. Usually the funder is quite satisfied if the research produces new ideas that have the potential to change the world.

While these characterizations are admittedly idealized, they are by and large accurate. Commercial customers frequently want innovation. Research customers almost always want deliverables. Also, both camps must often promise deliverables that cannot be delivered as a means of securing sales. Still, the heart of this characterization is true.

The goal of the A-7E project described in this chapter was to demonstrate to a skeptical world that "object-oriented techniques" (although the terminology was different then) could be used to construct real-time high-performance software. This is a research objective. The goal was to change the world as it was seen then. From a research perspective, the success of the Software Cost Reduction program (of which the A-7E development was a portion) can be seen in the number of citations it has been given in the research literature (in the hundreds). It can also be seen in the general acceptance of much of what was revolutionary at the time in terms of encapsulation and information hiding.

So the A-7E was a commercial "failure," but it was a research success. To go back to Bob's argument, the question is Did the Navy get what they were paying for? This depends on whether the Navy thought it was paying for a production system or a research effort. Since the effort was housed in the Naval Research Laboratory, it seems clear that the A-7E was a research effort and should be judged by research standards.

— LJB

3.4   Summary

This chapter described the architecture of a highly capable avionics system in terms of three related but quite different structures. A module decomposition structure describes design-time relations among its components, which are implementation units that can be assigned to teams. A uses structure describes runtime usage relations among its components, which are procedures in modules. From it, a picture of a layered architecture emerges. The process structure describes the parallelism of the system and is the basis for assignment for the physical hardware.

It is critical to design each structure correctly because each is the key to a different quality attribute: ease of change, ease of extracting a subset, and increased parallelism and performance. It is also critical to document each structure completely because the information about each is duplicated in no other place.

Even though the structures are orthogonal, they are related, in that modules contain procedures, which use each other and are strung together in processes. Other architectural structures could have been specified for this system. One, a data flow view (a component-and-connector view additional to those introduced in Chapter 2), would have looked something like the one in Figure 3.5. All data comes from the external world via the Device Interface modules and works its way through computation and storage modules to the Function Driver modules, which compute output values to send back to the devices. The A-7E designers never thought data flow views were useful—what quality attribute do they help achieve that the others do not?—but other designers might feel different. The point—and the lesson—about architectural views is that they should enhance

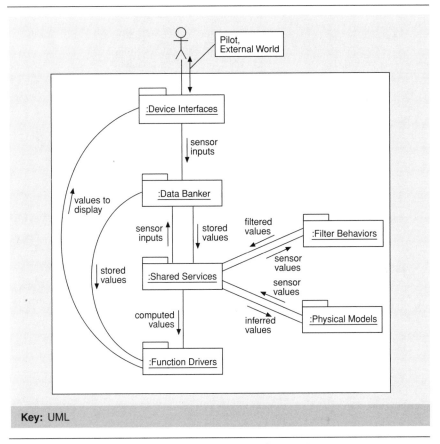

FIGURE 3.5 Coarse-grained data flow view for the A-7E software

understanding of and intellectual control over the system and its attributes. If a view meets these conditions, it is probably one you will want to pay attention to.

We also presented the architecture in terms of the qualities the designers wished to achieve: changeability and understandability. This leads us to the thesis that we explore in the next two chapters: Architectures reflect a set of desired qualities.

3.5 For Further Reading

The A7-E avionics project has been documented in [Parnas 85a]. The data collected about changes to the system was analyzed and described in [Hager 91] and [Hager 89]. Much of the material about the module structure was taken from the

A-7E module guide, which was written by Kathryn Britton and David Parnas [Britton 81].

3.6   Discussion Questions

1. Suppose that a version of the A-7E software were to be developed for installation on a flight trainer version of the aircraft. This aircraft would carry no weapons, but it would teach pilots how to navigate using the onboard avionics. What structures of the architecture would have to change, and how?

2. Chapter 7 will discuss using the architecture as a basis for incremental development: starting small and growing the system but having a working subset at all times. Propose the smallest subset of the A-7E software that still does something (correctly, in accordance with requirements) observable by the pilot. (A good candidate is displaying a value, such as current heading on some cockpit display.) Which modules do you need and which can you do without? Now propose three incremental additions to that subset and specify the development plan (i.e., which modules you need) for those.

3. Suppose that monitors were added to ensure that correct values were being stored in the Data Banker and computed by the Function Drivers. If the monitors detected a disparity between the stored or computed values and what they computed as the correct values, they would signal an error. Show how each of the A-7E's architectural structures would change to accommodate this design. If you add modules, state the information-hiding criteria for placing them in the module hierarchy.

PART TWO

CREATING AN ARCHITECTURE

Part One of this book introduced the Architecture Business Cycle (ABC) and laid the groundwork for the study of software architecture. In particular, it set out the influences at work when an architect begins building a system, and it pointed out that requirements for particular quality attributes such as performance or modifiability often originate from the organization's business goals. How then does an architect create an architecture? That is the focus of Part Two. Because the achievement of quality attributes is critical to the success of a system, we begin by discussing quality and how it is achieved with the contents of the architect's tool box.

Quality is often in the eye of the beholder (to paraphrase Booth Tarkington). What this means for the architect is that customers may dislike a design because their concept of quality differs from the architect's. Quality attribute scenarios are the means by which quality moves from the eye of the beholder to a more objective basis. In Chapter 4, we explore different types of quality that may be appropriate for an architecture. For six important attributes (availability, modifiability, performance, security, testability, and usability), we describe how to generate scenarios that can be used to characterize quality requirements. These scenarios demonstrate what quality means for a particular system, giving both the architect and the customer a basis for judging a design.

Knowing the quality requirements, of course, only provides a goal for the architect. In Chapter 5, we list the tools (tactics and patterns) in the architect's kit that are used to achieve the quality attributes. High availability, for example, depends on having some form of redundancy in either data or code, and this redundancy generates additional considerations for the architect (such as ensuring synchronization among the replicates).

In Chapter 6, we introduce our second case study—a system designed to support the air traffic control functions of the Federal Aviation Administration. This system was designed to achieve ultra-high availability requirements (less than five minutes downtime per year) and illustrates the tactics enumerated in Chapter 5.

Quality attribute scenarios and architectural tactics are some of the tools available for the creation of an architecture. In Chapter 7, we discuss how to apply these tools in designing an architecture and in building a skeletal system, and how the architecture is reflected in the organizational structure.

In Chapter 8, we present our third case study, of flight simulators. These systems were designed to achieve real-time performance and to be readily modified. We show how these goals were achieved.

Once an architecture has been designed, it must be documented. This is a matter of documenting first the relevant views and then the material that extends beyond any particular view. Chapter 9 details how to document an architecture.

Frequently, the architecture for a system is unavailable—because it was never documented, it has been lost, or the as-built system differs from the designed system. Chapter 10 discusses recovering the architecture for an existing system.

4

Understanding Quality Attributes

with Felix Bachmann and Mark Klein

> *"Cheshire-Puss," [Alice] began, rather timidly . . . "Would*
> *you tell me, please, which way I ought to go from here?"*
> *"That depends a good deal on where you want to go to," said the Cat.*
> *"Oh, I don't much care where—" said Alice.*
> *Then it doesn't matter which way you go," said the Cat.*
> *"—so long as I get somewhere," said Alice.*
> *"Oh, you're sure to do that," said the Cat,*
> *"if only you walk long enough."*
> — Lewis Carroll, *Alice's Adventures in Wonderland.*

As we have seen in the Architecture Business Cycle, business considerations determine qualities that must be accommodated in a system's architecture. These qualities are over and above that of functionality, which is the basic statement of the system's capabilities, services, and behavior. Although functionality and other qualities are closely related, as you will see, functionality often takes not only the front seat in the development scheme but the only seat. This is short-sighted, however. Systems are frequently redesigned not because they are functionally deficient—the replacements are often functionally identical—but because they are difficult to maintain, port, or scale, or are too slow, or have been compromised by network hackers. In Chapter 2, we said that architecture was the first stage in software creation in which quality requirements could be addressed. It is the mapping of a system's functionality onto software structures that determines the architecture's support for qualities. In Chapter 5 we discuss how the qualities are supported by architectural design decisions, and in Chapter 7 we discuss how the architect can manage the tradeoffs inherent in any design.

Note: Felix Bachmann and Mark Klein are senior members of the technical staff at the Software Engineering Institute.

Here our focus is on understanding how to express the qualities we want our architecture to provide to the system or systems we are building from it. We begin the discussion of the relationship between quality attributes and software architecture by looking closely at quality attributes. What does it mean to say that a system is modifiable or reliable or secure? This chapter characterizes such attributes and discusses how this characterization can be used to express the quality requirements for a system.

4.1   Functionality and Architecture

Functionality and quality attributes are orthogonal. This statement sounds rather bold at first, but when you think about it you realize that it cannot be otherwise. If functionality and quality attributes were not orthogonal, the choice of function would dictate the level of security or performance or availability or usability. Clearly though, it is possible to independently choose a desired level of each. Now, this is not to say that any level of any quality attribute is achievable with any function. Manipulating complex graphical images or sorting an enormous database might be inherently complex, making lightning-fast performance impossible. But what is possible is that, for any of these functions your choices as an architect will determine the relative level of quality. Some architectural choices will lead to higher performance; some will lead in the other direction. Given this understanding, the purpose of this chapter is, as with a good architecture, to separate concerns. We will examine each important quality attribute in turn and learn how to think about it in a disciplined way.

What is functionality? It is the ability of the system to do the work for which it was intended. A task requires that many or most of the system's elements work in a coordinated manner to complete the job, just as framers, electricians, plumbers, drywall hangers, painters, and finish carpenters all come together to cooperatively build a house. Therefore, if the elements have not been assigned the correct responsibilities or have not been endowed with the correct facilities for coordinating with other elements (so that, for instance, they know when it is time for them to begin their portion of the task), the system will be unable to offer the required functionality.

Functionality may be achieved through the use of any of a number of possible structures. In fact, if functionality were the only requirement, the system could exist as a single monolithic module with no internal structure at all. Instead, it is decomposed into modules to make it understandable and to support a variety of other purposes. In this way, functionality is largely independent of structure. Software architecture constrains its allocation to structure when *other* quality attributes are important. For example, systems are frequently divided so that several people can cooperatively build them (which is, among other things, a time-to-market issue, though seldom stated this way). The interest of functionality is how it interacts with, and constrains, those other qualities.

4.2 Architecture and Quality Attributes

Achieving quality attributes must be considered throughout design, implementation, and deployment. No quality attribute is entirely dependent on design, nor is it entirely dependent on implementation or deployment. Satisfactory results are a matter of getting the big picture (architecture) as well as the details (implementation) correct. For example:

- Usability involves both architectural and nonarchitectural aspects. The nonarchitectural aspects include making the user interface clear and easy to use. Should you provide a radio button or a check box? What screen layout is most intuitive? What typeface is most clear? Although these details matter tremendously to the end user and influence usability, they are not architectural because they belong to the details of design. Whether a system provides the user with the ability to cancel operations, to undo operations, or to re-use data previously entered is architectural, however. These requirements involve the cooperation of multiple elements.
- Modifiability is determined by how functionality is divided (architectural) and by coding techniques within a module (nonarchitectural). Thus, a system is modifiable if changes involve the fewest possible number of distinct elements. This was the basis of the A-7E module decomposition structure in Chapter 3. In spite of having the ideal architecture, however, it is always possible to make a system difficult to modify by writing obscure code.
- Performance involves both architectural and nonarchitectural dependencies. It depends partially on how much communication is necessary among components (architectural), partially on what functionality has been allocated to each component (architectural), partially on how shared resources are allocated (architectural), partially on the choice of algorithms to implement selected functionality (nonarchitectural), and partially on how these algorithms are coded (nonarchitectural).

The message of this section is twofold:

1. Architecture is critical to the realization of many qualities of interest in a system, and these qualities should be designed in and can be evaluated at the architectural level.
2. Architecture, by itself, is unable to achieve qualities. It provides the foundation for achieving quality, but this foundation will be to no avail if attention is not paid to the details.

Within complex systems, quality attributes can *never* be achieved in isolation. The achievement of any one will have an effect, sometimes positive and sometimes negative, on the achievement of others. For example, security and reliability often exist in a state of mutual tension: The most secure system has the fewest points of failure—typically a security kernel. The most reliable system has the most points of failure—typically a set of redundant processes or processors where the failure of any one will not cause the system to fail. Another example of the tension between quality attributes is that almost every quality attribute negatively affects performance. Take portability. The main technique for achieving portable software is to isolate system dependencies, which introduces overhead into the system's execution, typically as process or procedure boundaries, and this hurts performance.

Let's begin our tour of quality attributes. We will examine the following three classes:

1. Qualities of the system. We will focus on availability, modifiability, performance, security, testability, and usability.
2. Business qualities (such as time to market) that are affected by the architecture.
3. Qualities, such as conceptual integrity, that are about the architecture itself although they indirectly affect other qualities, such as modifiability.

4.3 System Quality Attributes

System quality attributes have been of interest to the software community at least since the 1970s. There are a variety of published taxonomies and definitions, and many of them have their own research and practitioner communities. From an architect's perspective, there are three problems with previous discussions of system quality attributes:

- The definitions provided for an attribute are not operational. It is meaningless to say that a system will be modifiable. Every system is modifiable with respect to one set of changes and not modifiable with respect to another. The other attributes are similar.
- A focus of discussion is often on which quality a particular aspect belongs to. Is a system failure an aspect of availability, an aspect of security, or an aspect of usability? All three attribute communities would claim ownership of a system failure.
- Each attribute community has developed its own vocabulary. The performance community has "events" arriving at a system, the security community has "attacks" arriving at a system, the availability community has "failures" of a system, and the usability community has "user input." All of these may actually refer to the same occurrence, but are described using different terms.

A solution to the first two of these problems (nonoperational definitions and overlapping attribute concerns) is to use *quality attribute scenarios* as a means of characterizing quality attributes. A solution to the third problem is to provide a brief discussion of each attribute—concentrating on its underlying concerns—to illustrate the concepts that are fundamental to that attribute community.

QUALITY ATTRIBUTE SCENARIOS

A quality attribute scenario is a quality-attribute-specific requirement. It consists of six parts.

- *Source of stimulus.* This is some entity (a human, a computer system, or any other actuator) that generated the stimulus.
- *Stimulus.* The stimulus is a condition that needs to be considered when it arrives at a system.
- *Environment.* The stimulus occurs within certain conditions. The system may be in an overload condition or may be running when the stimulus occurs, or some other condition may be true.
- *Artifact.* Some artifact is stimulated. This may be the whole system or some pieces of it.
- *Response.* The response is the activity undertaken after the arrival of the stimulus.
- *Response measure.* When the response occurs, it should be measurable in some fashion so that the requirement can be tested.

We distinguish general quality attribute scenarios (general scenarios)—those that are system independent and can, potentially, pertain to any system—from concrete quality attribute scenarios (concrete scenarios)—those that are specific to the particular system under consideration. We present attribute characterizations as a collection of general scenarios; however, to translate the attribute characterization into requirements for a particular system, the relevant general scenarios need to be made system specific.

Figure 4.1 shows the parts of a quality attribute scenario.

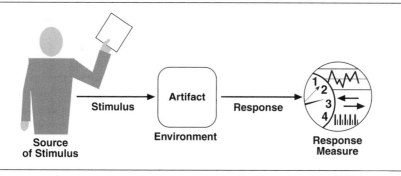

FIGURE 4.1 Quality attribute parts

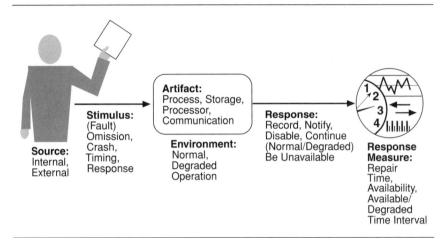

FIGURE 4.2   Availability general scenarios

Availability Scenario.   A general scenario for the quality attribute of availability, for example, is shown in Figure 4.2. Its six parts are shown, indicating the range of values they can take. From this we can derive concrete, system-specific, scenarios. Not every system-specific scenario has all of the six parts. The parts that are necessary are the result of the application of the scenario and the types of testing that will be performed to determine whether the scenario has been achieved.

An example availability scenario, derived from the general scenario of Figure 4.2 by instantiating each of the parts, is "An unanticipated external message is received by a process during normal operation. The process informs the operator of the receipt of the message and continues to operate with no downtime." Figure 4.3 shows the pieces of this derived scenario.

The source of the stimulus is important since differing responses may be required depending on what it is. For example, a request from a trusted source may be treated differently from a request from an untrusted source in a security scenario. The environment may also affect the response, in that an event arriving at a system may be treated differently if the system is already overloaded. The artifact that is stimulated is less important as a requirement. It is almost always the system, and we explicitly call it out for two reasons.

First, many requirements make assumptions about the internals of the system (e.g., "a Web server within the system fails"). Second, when we utilize scenarios within an evaluation or design method, we refine the scenario artifact to be quite explicit about the portion of the system being stimulated. Finally, being explicit about the value of the response is important so that quality attribute requirements are made explicit. Thus, we include the response measure as a portion of the scenario.

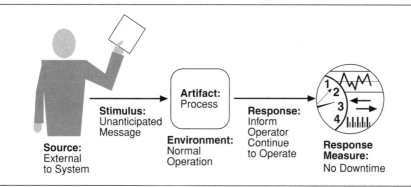

FIGURE 4.3   Sample availability scenario

Modifiability Scenario. A sample modifiability scenario is "A developer wishes to change the user interface to make a screen's background color blue. This change will be made to the code at design time. It will take less than three hours to make and test the change and no side effect changes will occur in the behavior." Figure 4.4 illustrates this sample scenario (omitting a few minor details for brevity).

A collection of concrete scenarios can be used as the quality attribute requirements for a system. Each scenario is concrete enough to be meaningful to the architect, and the details of the response are meaningful enough so that it is possible to test whether the system has achieved the response. When eliciting requirements, we typically organize our discussion of general scenarios by quality attributes; if the same scenario is generated by two different attributes, one can be eliminated.

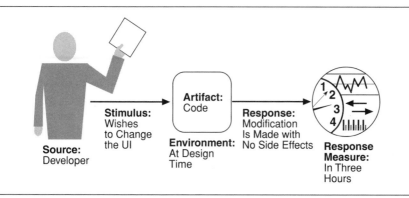

FIGURE 4.4   Sample modifiability scenario

For each attribute we present a table that gives possible system-independent values for each of the six parts of a quality scenario. A general quality scenario is generated by choosing one value for each element; a concrete scenario is generated as part of the requirements elicitation by choosing one or more entries from each column of the table and then making the result readable. For example, the scenario shown in Figure 4.4 is generated from the modifiability scenario given in Table 4.2 (on page 83), but the individual parts were edited slightly to make them read more smoothly as a scenario.

Concrete scenarios play the same role in the specification of quality attribute requirements that use cases play in the specification of functional requirements.

QUALITY ATTRIBUTE SCENARIO GENERATION

Our concern in this chapter is helping the architect generate meaningful quality attribute requirements for a system. In theory this is done in a project's requirements elicitation, but in practice this is seldom rigorously enforced. As we said in Chapter 1, a system's quality attribute requirements are seldom elicited and recorded in a disciplined way. We remedy this situation by generating concrete quality attribute scenarios. To do this, we use the quality-attribute-specific tables to create general scenarios and from these derive system-specific scenarios. Typically, not all of the possible general scenarios are created. The tables serve as a checklist to ensure that all possibilities have been considered rather than as an explicit generation mechanism. We are unconcerned about generating scenarios that do not fit a narrow definition of an attribute—if two attributes allow the generation of the same quality attribute requirement, the redundancy is easily corrected. However, if an important quality attribute requirement is omitted, the consequences may be more serious.

4.4   Quality Attribute Scenarios in Practice

General scenarios provide a framework for generating a large number of generic, system-independent, quality-attribute-specific scenarios. Each is potentially but not necessarily relevant to the system you are concerned with. To make the general scenarios useful for a particular system, you must make them system specific.

Making a general scenario system specific means translating it into concrete terms for the particular system. Thus, a general scenario is "A request arrives for a change in functionality, and the change must be made at a particular time within the development process within a specified period." A system-specific version might be "A request arrives to add support for a new browser to a Web-based system, and the change must be made within two weeks." Furthermore, a single general scenario may have many system-specific versions. The same system that has to support a new browser may also have to support a new media type.

We now discuss the six most common and important system quality attributes, with the twin goals of identifying the concepts used by the attribute community and providing a way to generate general scenarios for that attribute.

AVAILABILITY

Availability is concerned with system failure and its associated consequences. A system failure occurs when the system no longer delivers a service consistent with its specification. Such a failure is observable by the system's users—either humans or other systems. An example of an availability general scenario appeared in Figure 4.3.

Among the areas of concern are how system failure is detected, how frequently system failure may occur, what happens when a failure occurs, how long a system is allowed to be out of operation, when failures may occur safely, how failures can be prevented, and what kinds of notifications are required when a failure occurs.

We need to differentiate between failures and faults. A fault may become a failure if not corrected or masked. That is, a failure is observable by the system's user and a fault is not. When a fault does become observable, it becomes a failure. For example, a fault can be choosing the wrong algorithm for a computation, resulting in a miscalculation that causes the system to fail.

Once a system fails, an important related concept becomes the time it takes to repair it. Since a system failure is observable by users, the time to repair is the time until the failure is no longer observable. This may be a brief delay in the response time or it may be the time it takes someone to fly to a remote location in the mountains of Peru to repair a piece of mining machinery (this example was given by a person who was responsible for repairing the software in a mining machine engine.).

The distinction between faults and failures allows discussion of automatic repair strategies. That is, if code containing a fault is executed but the system is able to recover from the fault without it being observable, there is no failure.

The availability of a system is the probability that it will be operational when it is needed. This is typically defined as

$$\alpha = \frac{\text{mean time to failure}}{\text{mean time to failure} + \text{mean time to repair}}$$

From this come terms like 99.9% availability, or a 0.1% probability that the system will not be operational when needed.

Scheduled downtimes (i.e., out of service) are not usually considered when calculating availability, since the system is "not needed" by definition. This leads to situations where the system is down and users are waiting for it, but the downtime is scheduled and so is not counted against any availability requirements.

Availability General Scenarios. From these considerations we can see the portions of an availability scenario, shown in Figure 4.2.

- *Source of stimulus.* We differentiate between internal and external indications of faults or failure since the desired system response may be different. In our example, the unexpected message arrives from outside the system.

- *Stimulus.* A fault of one of the following classes occurs.
  - *omission.* A component fails to respond to an input.
  - *crash.* The component repeatedly suffers omission faults.
  - *timing.* A component responds but the response is early or late.
  - *response.* A component responds with an incorrect value.

  In Figure 4.3, the stimulus is that an unanticipated message arrives. This is an example of a timing fault. The component that generated the message did so at a different time than expected.

- *Artifact.* This specifies the resource that is required to be highly available, such as a processor, communication channel, process, or storage.

- *Environment.* The state of the system when the fault or failure occurs may also affect the desired system response. For example, if the system has already seen some faults and is operating in other than normal mode, it may be desirable to shut it down totally. However, if this is the first fault observed, some degradation of response time or function may be preferred. In our example, the system is operating normally.

- *Response.* There are a number of possible reactions to a system failure. These include logging the failure, notifying selected users or other systems, switching to a degraded mode with either less capacity or less function, shutting down external systems, or becoming unavailable during repair. In our example, the system should notify the operator of the unexpected message and continue to operate normally.

- *Response measure.* The response measure can specify an availability percentage, or it can specify a time to repair, times during which the system must be available, or the duration for which the system must be available. In Figure 4.3, there is no downtime as a result of the unexpected message.

Table 4.1 presents the possible values for each portion of an availability scenario.

MODIFIABILITY

Modifiability is about the cost of change. It brings up two concerns.

1. *What can change (the artifact)?* A change can occur to any aspect of a system, most commonly the functions that the system computes, the platform the system exists on (the hardware, operating system, middleware, etc.), the environment within which the system operates (the systems with which it must interoperate,

TABLE 4.1 Availability General Scenario Generation

Portion of Scenario	Possible Values
Source	Internal to the system; external to the system
Stimulus	Fault: omission, crash, timing, response
Artifact	System's processors, communication channels, persistent storage, processes
Environment	Normal operation; degraded mode (i.e., fewer features, a fall back solution)
Response	System should detect event and do one or more of the following: record it notify appropriate parties, including the user and other systems disable sources of events that cause fault or failure according to defined rules be unavailable for a prespecified interval, where interval depends on criticality of system continue to operate in normal or degraded mode
Response Measure	Time interval when the system must be available Availability time Time interval in which system can be in degraded mode Repair time

the protocols it uses to communicate with the rest of the world, etc.), the qualities the system exhibits (its performance, its reliability, and even its future modifications), and its capacity (number of users supported, number of simultaneous operations, etc.). Some portions of the system, such as the user interface or the platform, are sufficiently distinguished and subject to change that we consider them separately. The category of platform changes is also called portability. Those changes may be to add, delete, or modify any one of these aspects.

2. *When is the change made and who makes it (the environment)?* Most commonly in the past, a change was made to source code. That is, a developer had to make the change, which was tested and then deployed in a new release. Now, however, the question of when a change is made is intertwined with the question of who makes it. An end user changing the screen saver is clearly making a change to one of the aspects of the system. Equally clear, it is not in the same category as changing the system so that it can be used over the Web rather than on a single machine. Changes can be made to the implementation (by modifying the source code), during compile (using compile-time switches), during build (by choice of libraries), during configuration setup (by a range of techniques, including parameter setting) or during execution (by parameter setting). A change can also be made by a developer, an end user, or a system administrator.

Once a change has been specified, the new implementation must be designed, implemented, tested, and deployed. All of these actions take time and money, both of which can be measured.

Modifiability General Scenarios.   From these considerations we can see the portions of the modifiability general scenarios. Figure 4.4 gives an example: "A developer wishes to change the user interface. This change will be made to the code at design time, it will take less than three hours to make and test the change, and no side-effect changes will occur in the behavior."

- *Source of stimulus.* This portion specifies who makes the changes—the developer, a system administrator, or an end user. Clearly, there must be machinery in place to allow the system administrator or end user to modify a system, but this is a common occurrence. In Figure 4.4, the modification is to be made by the developer.

- *Stimulus.* This portion specifies the changes to be made. A change can be the addition of a function, the modification of an existing function, or the deletion of a function. It can also be made to the qualities of the system—making it more responsive, increasing its availability, and so forth. The capacity of the system may also change. Increasing the number of simultaneous users is a frequent requirement. In our example, the stimulus is a request to make a modification, which can be to the function, quality, or capacity.

    Variation is a concept associated with software product lines (see Chapter 14). When considering variation, a factor is the number of times a given variation must be specified. One that must be made frequently will impose a more stringent requirement on the response measures than one that is made only sporadically.

- *Artifact.* This portion specifies what is to be changed—the functionality of a system, its platform, its user interface, its environment, or another system with which it interoperates. In Figure 4.4, the modification is to the user interface.

- *Environment.* This portion specifies when the change can be made—design time, compile time, build time, initiation time, or runtime. In our example, the modification is to occur at design time.

- *Response.* Whoever makes the change must understand how to make it, and then make it, test it and deploy it. In our example, the modification is made with no side effects.

- *Response measure.* All of the possible responses take time and cost money, and so time and cost are the most desirable measures. Time is not always possible to predict, however, and so less ideal measures are frequently used, such as the extent of the change (number of modules affected). In our example, the time to perform the modification should be less than three hours.

Table 4.2 presents the possible values for each portion of a modifiability scenario.

PERFORMANCE

Performance is about timing. Events (interrupts, messages, requests from users, or the passage of time) occur, and the system must respond to them. There are a

TABLE 4.2   Modifiability General Scenario Generation

Portion of Scenario	Possible Values
Source	End user, developer, system administrator
Stimulus	Wishes to add/delete/modify/vary functionality, quality attribute, capacity
Artifact	System user interface, platform, environment; system that interoperates with target system
Environment	At runtime, compile time, build time, design time
Response	Locates places in architecture to be modified; makes modification without affecting other functionality; tests modification; deploys modification
Response Measure	Cost in terms of number of elements affected, effort, money; extent to which this affects other functions or quality attributes

variety of characterizations of event arrival and the response but basically performance is concerned with how long it takes the system to respond when an event occurs.

One of the things that make performance complicated is the number of event sources and arrival patterns. Events can arrive from user requests, from other systems, or from within the system. A Web-based financial services system gets events from its users (possibly numbering in the tens or hundreds of thousands). An engine control system gets its requests from the passage of time and must control both the firing of the ignition when a cylinder is in the correct position and the mixture of the fuel to maximize power and minimize pollution.

For the Web-based financial system, the response might be the number of transactions that can be processed in a minute. For the engine control system, the response might be the variation in the firing time. In each case, the pattern of events arriving and the pattern of responses can be characterized, and this characterization forms the language with which to construct general performance scenarios.

A performance scenario begins with a request for some service arriving at the system. Satisfying the request requires resources to be consumed. While this is happening the system may be simultaneously servicing other requests.

An arrival pattern for events may be characterized as either periodic or stochastic. For example, a periodic event may arrive every 10 milliseconds. Periodic event arrival is most often seen in real-time systems. Stochastic arrival means that events arrive according to some probabilistic distribution. Events can also arrive sporadically, that is, according to a pattern not capturable by either periodic or stochastic characterizations.

Multiple users or other loading factors can be modeled by varying the arrival pattern for events. In other words, from the point of view of system performance, it does not matter whether one user submits 20 requests in a period of time or whether two users each submit 10. What matters is the arrival pattern at the server and dependencies within the requests.

The response of the system to a stimulus can be characterized by latency (the time between the arrival of the stimulus and the system's response to it), deadlines in processing (in the engine controller, for example, the fuel should ignite when the cylinder is in a particular position, thus introducing a processing deadline), the throughput of the system (e.g., the number of transactions the system can process in a second), the jitter of the response (the variation in latency), the number of events not processed because the system was too busy to respond, and the data that was lost because the system was too busy.

Notice that this formulation does not consider whether the system is networked or standalone. Nor does it (yet) consider the configuration of the system or the consumption of resources. These issues are dependent on architectural solutions, which we will discuss in Chapter 5.

Performance General Scenarios. From these considerations we can see the portions of the performance general scenario, an example of which is shown in Figure 4.5: "Users initiate 1,000 transactions per minute stochastically under normal operations, and these transactions are processed with an average latency of two seconds."

- *Source of stimulus.* The stimuli arrive either from external (possibly multiple) or internal sources. In our example, the source of the stimulus is a collection of users.

- *Stimulus.* The stimuli are the event arrivals. The arrival pattern can be characterized as periodic, stochastic, or sporadic. In our example, the stimulus is the stochastic initiation of 1,000 transactions per minute.

- *Artifact.* The artifact is always the system's services, as it is in our example.

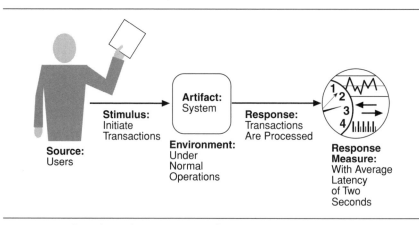

FIGURE 4.5 Sample performance scenario

TABLE 4.3 Performance General Scenario Generation

Portion of Scenario	Possible Values
Source	One of a number of independent sources, possibly from within system
Stimulus	Periodic events arrive; sporadic events arrive; stochastic events arrive
Artifact	System
Environment	Normal mode; overload mode
Response	Processes stimuli; changes level of service
Response Measure	Latency, deadline, throughput, jitter, miss rate, data loss

- *Environment.* The system can be in various operational modes, such as normal, emergency, or overload. In our example, the system is in normal mode.

- *Response.* The system must process the arriving events. This may cause a change in the system environment (e.g., from normal to overload mode). In our example, the transactions are processed.

- *Response measure.* The response measures are the time it takes to process the arriving events (latency or a deadline by which the event must be processed), the variation in this time (jitter), the number of events that can be processed within a particular time interval (throughput), or a characterization of the events that cannot be processed (miss rate, data loss). In our example, the transactions should be processed with an average latency of two seconds.

Table 4.3 gives elements of the general scenarios that characterize performance.

For most of the history of software engineering, performance has been the driving factor in system architecture. As such, it has frequently compromised the achievement of all other qualities. As the price/performance ratio of hardware plummets and the cost of developing software rises, other qualities have emerged as important competitors to performance.

SECURITY

Security is a measure of the system's ability to resist unauthorized usage while still providing its services to legitimate users. An attempt to breach security is called an attack[1] and can take a number of forms. It may be an unauthorized attempt to access data or services or to modify data, or it may be intended to deny services to legitimate users.

---

[1] Some security experts use "threat" interchangeably with "attack."

Attacks, often occasions for wide media coverage, may range from theft of money by electronic transfer to modification of sensitive data, from theft of credit card numbers to destruction of files on computer systems, or to denial-of-service attacks carried out by worms or viruses. Still, the elements of a security general scenario are the same as the elements of our other general scenarios—a stimulus and its source, an environment, the target under attack, the desired response of the system, and the measure of this response.

Security can be characterized as a system providing nonrepudiation, confidentiality, integrity, assurance, availability, and auditing. For each term, we provide a definition and an example.

1. Nonrepudiation is the property that a transaction (access to or modification of data or services) cannot be denied by any of the parties to it. This means you cannot deny that you ordered that item over the Internet if, in fact, you did.
2. Confidentiality is the property that data or services are protected from unauthorized access. This means that a hacker cannot access your income tax returns on a government computer.
3. Integrity is the property that data or services are being delivered as intended. This means that your grade has not been changed since your instructor assigned it.
4. Assurance is the property that the parties to a transaction are who they purport to be. This means that, when a customer sends a credit card number to an Internet merchant, the merchant is who the customer thinks they are.
5. Availability is the property that the system will be available for legitimate use. This means that a denial-of-service attack won't prevent your ordering *this* book.
6. Auditing is the property that the system tracks activities within it at levels sufficient to reconstruct them. This means that, if you transfer money out of one account to another account, in Switzerland, the system will maintain a record of that transfer.

Each of these security categories gives rise to a collection of general scenarios.

Security General Scenarios.   The portions of a security general scenario are given below. Figure 4.6 presents an example. A correctly identified individual tries to modify system data from an external site; system maintains an audit trail and the correct data is restored within one day.

- *Source of stimulus.* The source of the attack may be either a human or another system. It may have been previously identified (either correctly or incorrectly) or may be currently unknown. If the source of the attack is highly motivated (say politically motivated), then defensive measures such as "We know who you are and will prosecute you" are not likely to be effective; in such cases the motivation of the user may be important. If the source has access to vast resources (such as a government), then defensive measures are very difficult. The attack itself is unauthorized access, modification, or denial of service.

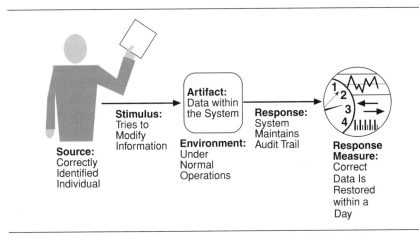

FIGURE 4.6   Sample security scenario

The difficulty with security is allowing access to legitimate users and determining legitimacy. If the only goal were to prevent access to a system, disallowing all access would be an effective defensive measure.

- *Stimulus.* The stimulus is an attack or an attempt to break security. We characterize this as an unauthorized person or system trying to display information, change and/or delete information, access services of the system, or reduce availability of system services. In Figure 4.6, the stimulus is an attempt to modify data.

- *Artifact.* The target of the attack can be either the services of the system or the data within it. In our example, the target is data within the system.

- *Environment.* The attack can come when the system is either online or offline, either connected to or disconnected from a network, either behind a firewall or open to the network.

- *Response.* Using services without authorization or preventing legitimate users from using services is a different goal from seeing sensitive data or modifying it. Thus, the system must authorize legitimate users and grant them access to data and services, at the same time rejecting unauthorized users, denying them access, and reporting unauthorized access. Not only does the system need to provide access to legitimate users, but it needs to support the granting or withdrawing of access. One technique to prevent attacks is to cause fear of punishment by maintaining an audit trail of modifications or attempted accesses. An audit trail is also useful in correcting from a successful attack. In Figure 4.6, an audit trail is maintained.

- *Response measure.* Measures of a system's response include the difficulty of mounting various attacks and the difficulty of recovering from and surviving

TABLE 4.4   Security General Scenario Generation

Portion of Scenario	Possible Values

Source	Individual or system that is
	    correctly identified, identified incorrectly, of unknown identity
	who is
	    internal/external, authorized/not authorized
	with access to
	    limited resources, vast resources

Stimulus	Tries to
	    display data, change/delete data, access system services,
	    reduce availability to system services

Artifact	System services; data within system
Environment	Either online or offline, connected or disconnected, firewalled or open
Response	Authenticates user; hides identity of the user; blocks access to data and/or services; allows access to data and/or services; grants or withdraws permission to access data and/or services; records access/modifications or attempts to access/modify data/services by identity; stores data in an unreadable format; recognizes an unexplainable high demand for services, and informs a user or another system, and restricts availability of services
Response Measure	Time/effort/resources required to circumvent security measures with probability of success; probability of detecting attack; probability of identifying individual responsible for attack or access/modification of data and/or services; percentage of services still available under denial-of-services attack; restore data/services; extent to which data/services damaged and/or legitimate access denied

attacks. In our example, the audit trail allows the accounts from which money was embezzled to be restored to their original state. Of course, the embezzler still has the money, and he must be tracked down and the money regained, but this is outside of the realm of the computer system.

Table 4.4 shows the security general scenario generation table.

TESTABILITY

Software testability refers to the ease with which software can be made to demonstrate its faults through (typically execution-based) testing. At least 40% of the cost of developing well-engineered systems is taken up by testing. If the software architect can reduce this cost, the payoff is large.

In particular, testability refers to the probability, assuming that the software has at least one fault, that it will fail on its *next* test execution. Of course, calculating this probability is not easy and, when we get to response measures, other measures will be used.

For a system to be properly testable, it must be possible to *control* each component's internal state and inputs and then to *observe* its outputs. Frequently this is done through use of a *test harness*, specialized software designed to exercise the software under test. This may be as simple as a playback capability for data recorded across various interfaces or as complicated as a testing chamber for an engine.

Testing is done by various developers, testers, verifiers, or users and is the last step of various parts of the software life cycle. Portions of the code, the design, or the complete system may be tested. The response measures for testability deal with how effective the tests are in discovering faults and how long it takes to perform the tests to some desired level of coverage.

Testability General Scenarios.   Figure 4.7 is an example of a testability scenario concerning the performance of a unit test: A unit tester performs a unit test on a completed system component that provides an interface for controlling its behavior and observing its output; 85% path coverage is achieved within three hours.

- *Source of stimulus.* The testing is performed by unit testers, integration testers, system testers, or the client. A test of the design may be performed by other developers or by an external group. In our example, the testing is performed by a tester.

- *Stimulus.* The stimulus for the testing is that a milestone in the development process is met. This might be the completion of an analysis or design increment, the completion of a coding increment such as a class, the completed integration of a subsystem, or the completion of the whole system. In our example, the testing is triggered by the completion of a unit of code.

- *Artifact.* A design, a piece of code, or the whole system is the artifact being tested. In our example, a unit of code is to be tested.

- *Environment.* The test can happen at design time, at development time, at compile time, or at deployment time. In Figure 4.7, the test occurs during development.

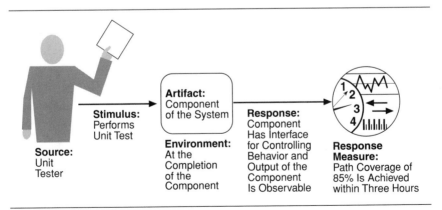

FIGURE 4.7   Sample testability scenario

TABLE 4.5   Testability General Scenario Generation

Portion of Scenario	Possible Values
Source	Unit developer Increment integrator System verifier Client acceptance tester System user
Stimulus	Analysis, architecture, design, class, subsystem integration completed; system delivered
Artifact	Piece of design, piece of code, complete application
Environment	At design time, at development time, at compile time, at deployment time
Response	Provides access to state values; provides computed values; prepares test environment
Response Measure	Percent executable statements executed Probability of failure if fault exists Time to perform tests Length of longest dependency chain in a test Length of time to prepare test environment

- *Response.* Since testability is related to observability and controllability, the desired response is that the system can be controlled to perform the desired tests and that the response to each test can be observed. In our example, the unit can be controlled and its responses captured.

- *Response measure.* Response measures are the percentage of statements that have been executed in some test, the length of the longest test chain (a measure of the difficulty of performing the tests), and estimates of the probability of finding additional faults. In Figure 4.7, the measurement is percentage coverage of executable statements.

Table 4.5 gives the testability general scenario generation table.

USABILITY

Usability is concerned with how easy it is for the user to accomplish a desired task and the kind of user support the system provides. It can be broken down into the following areas:

- *Learning system features.* If the user is unfamiliar with a particular system or a particular aspect of it, what can the system do to make the task of learning easier?

- *Using a system efficiently.* What can the system do to make the user more efficient in its operation?

- *Minimizing the impact of errors.* What can the system do so that a user error has minimal impact?

- *Adapting the system to user needs.* How can the user (or the system itself) adapt to make the user's task easier?

- *Increasing confidence and satisfaction.* What does the system do to give the user confidence that the correct action is being taken?

In the last five years, our understanding of the relation between usability and software architecture has deepened (see the sidebar Usability Mea Culpa). The normal development process detects usability problems through building proto-types and user testing. The later a problem is discovered and the deeper into the architecture its repair must be made, the more the repair is threatened by time and budget pressures. In our scenarios we focus on aspects of usability that have a major impact on the architecture. Consequently, these scenarios must be correct prior to the architectural design so that they will not be discovered during user testing or prototyping.

Usability General Scenarios.   Figure 4.8 gives an example of a usability sce-nario: A user, wanting to minimize the impact of an error, wishes to cancel a sys-tem operation at runtime; cancellation takes place in less than one second. The portions of the usability general scenarios are:

- *Source of stimulus.* The end user is always the source of the stimulus.

- *Stimulus.* The stimulus is that the end user wishes to use a system efficiently, learn to use the system, minimize the impact of errors, adapt the system, or feel comfortable with the system. In our example, the user wishes to cancel an operation, which is an example of minimizing the impact of errors.

- *Artifact.* The artifact is always the system.

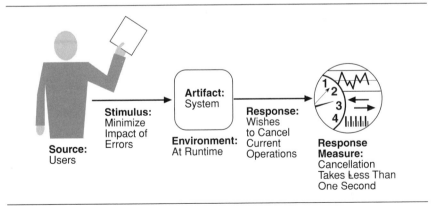

FIGURE 4.8   Sample usability scenario

Usability Mea Culpa (or "*That's* Not Architectural")

About five years ago a number of respected software engineering research-ers publicly made the following bold statement:

> Making a system's user interface clear and easy to use is primarily a mat-ter of getting the details of a user's interaction correct . . . but these details are not architectural.

Sad to say, these researchers were Bass, Clements, and Kazman, and the book was the first edition of *Software Architecture in Practice*. In the interven-ing five years we have learned quite a lot about many quality attributes, and none more so than usability.

While we have always claimed that system quality stems primarily from architectural quality, in the first edition of this book we were, at times, on shaky ground in trying to substantiate this claim. Still, the intervening years have done nothing to lessen the basic truth of the strong relationship between architectural quality and system quality. In fact, all of the evidence points squarely in its favor, and usability has proven to be no exception. Many usability issues *are* architectural. In fact, the usability features that are the most difficult to achieve (and, in particular, the most difficult to add on after the system has been built) turn out to be *precisely* those that are architectural.

If you want to support the ability of a user to cancel an operation in progress, returning to the precise system state in place before the operation was started, you need to plan for this capability in the architecture. Likewise, if you want to support the ability of a user to undo a previous action and if you want to give the user feedback as to an operation's progress. There are many other examples.

The point here is that it is easy to assume that a quality attribute, or signifi-cant portions of a quality attribute, are not architectural. Not everything is architectural it's true, but frequently our assumptions of what is and what is not are based on a superficial analysis of the problem. Probe more deeply, and significant architectural considerations pop up everywhere. And woe to the architect (or architecture writer!) who ignores them.

— RK

- *Environment.* The user actions with which usability is concerned always occur at runtime or at system configuration time. Any action that occurs before then is performed by developers and, although a user may also be the developer, we distinguish between these roles even if performed by the same person. In Figure 4.8, the cancellation occurs at runtime.

- *Response.* The system should either provide the user with the features needed or anticipate the user's needs. In our example, the cancellation occurs as the user wishes and the system is restored to its prior state.

- *Response measure.* The response is measured by task time, number of errors, number of problems solved, user satisfaction, gain of user knowledge, ratio

TABLE 4.6 Usability General Scenario Generation

Portion of Scenario	Possible Values
Source	End user
Stimulus	Wants to learn system features; use system efficiently; minimize impact of errors; adapt system; feel comfortable
Artifact	System
Environment	At runtime or configure time
Response	System provides one or more of the following responses: to support "learn system features" help system is sensitive to context; interface is familiar to user; interface is usable in an unfamiliar context to support "use system efficiently": aggregation of data and/or commands; re-use of already entered data and/or commands; support for efficient navigation within a screen; distinct views with consistent operations; comprehensive searching; multiple simultaneous activities to "minimize impact of errors": undo, cancel, recover from system failure, recognize and correct user error, retrieve forgotten password, verify system resources to "adapt system": customizability; internationalization to "feel comfortable": display system state; work at the user's pace
Response Measure	Task time, number of errors, number of problems solved, user satisfaction, gain of user knowledge, ratio of successful operations to total operations, amount of time/data lost

of successful operations to total operations, or amount of time/data lost when an error occurs. In Figure 4.8, the cancellation should occur in less than one second.

The usability general scenario generation table is given in Table 4.6.

COMMUNICATING CONCEPTS USING GENERAL SCENARIOS

One of the uses of general scenarios is to enable stakeholders to communicate. We have already pointed out that each attribute community has its own vocabulary to describe its basic concepts and that different terms can represent the same occurrence. This may lead to miscommunication. During a discussion of performance, for example, a stakeholder representing users may not realize that the latency of the response to events has anything to do with users. Facilitating this kind of understanding aids discussions of architectural decisions, particularly about tradeoffs.

TABLE 4.7   Quality Attribute Stimuli

Quality Attribute	Stimulus
Availability	Unexpected event, nonoccurrence of expected event
Modifiability	Request to add/delete/change/vary functionality, platform, quality attribute, or capacity
Performance	Periodic, stochastic, or sporadic

Security	Tries to
	    display, modify, change/delete information, access, or reduce
	    availability to system services

Testability	Completion of phase of system development

Usability	Wants to
	    learn system features, use a system efficiently, minimize the impact
	    of errors, adapt the system, feel comfortable

Table 4.7 gives the stimuli possible for each of the attributes and shows a number of different concepts. Some stimuli occur during runtime and others occur before. The problem for the architect is to understand which of these stimuli represent the same occurrence, which are aggregates of other stimuli, and which are independent. Once the relations are clear, the architect can communicate them to the various stakeholders using language that each comprehends. We cannot give the relations among stimuli in a general way because they depend partially on environment. A performance event may be atomic or may be an aggregate of other lower-level occurrences; a failure may be a single performance event or an aggregate. For example, it may occur with an exchange of several messages between a client and a server (culminating in an unexpected message), each of which is an atomic event from a performance perspective.

4.5   Other System Quality Attributes

We have discussed the quality attributes in a general fashion. A number of other attributes can be found in the attribute taxonomies in the research literature and in standard software engineering textbooks, and we have captured many of these in our scenarios. For example, *scalability* is often an important attribute, but in our discussion here scalability is captured by modifying system capacity—the number of users supported, for example. *Portability* is captured as a platform modification.

If some quality attribute—say interoperability—is important to your organization, it is reasonable to create your own general scenario for it. This simply involves filling out the six parts of the scenario generation framework: source, stimulus, environment, artifact, response, and response measure. For interoperability, a stimulus might be a request to interoperate with another system, a response might be a new interface or set of interfaces for the interoperation, and a response measure might be the difficulty in terms of time, the number of interfaces to be modified, and so forth.

4.6 Business Qualities

In addition to the qualities that apply directly to a system, a number of *business* quality goals frequently shape a system's architecture. These goals center on cost, schedule, market, and marketing considerations. Each suffers from the same ambiguity that system qualities have, and they need to be made specific with scenarios in order to make them suitable for influencing the design process and to be made testable. Here, we present them as generalities, however, and leave the generation of scenarios as one of our discussion questions.

- *Time to market.* If there is competitive pressure or a short window of opportunity for a system or product, development time becomes important. This in turn leads to pressure to buy or otherwise re-use existing elements. Time to market is often reduced by using prebuilt elements such as commercial off-the-shelf (COTS) products or elements re-used from previous projects. The ability to insert or deploy a subset of the system depends on the decomposition of the system into elements.

- *Cost and benefit.* The development effort will naturally have a budget that must not be exceeded. Different architectures will yield different development costs. For instance, an architecture that relies on technology (or expertise with a technology) not resident in the developing organization will be more expensive to realize than one that takes advantage of assets already inhouse. An architecture that is highly flexible will typically be more costly to build than one that is rigid (although it will be less costly to maintain and modify).

- *Projected lifetime of the system.* If the system is intended to have a long lifetime, modifiability, scalability, and portability become important. But building in the additional infrastructure (such as a layer to support portability) will usually compromise time to market. On the other hand, a modifiable, extensible product is more likely to survive longer in the marketplace, extending its lifetime.

- *Targeted market.* For general-purpose (mass-market) software, the platforms on which a system runs as well as its feature set will determine the size of the potential market. Thus, portability and functionality are key to market share. Other qualities, such as performance, reliability, and usability also play a role. To attack a large market with a collection of related products, a product line approach should be considered in which a core of the system is common (frequently including provisions for portability) and around which layers of software of increasing specificity are constructed.

Such an approach will be treated in Chapter 14, which discusses software product lines.

- *Rollout schedule.* If a product is to be introduced as base functionality with many features released later, the flexibility and customizability of the architecture are important. Particularly, the system must be constructed with ease of expansion and contraction in mind.

- *Integration with legacy systems.* If the new system has to *integrate* with existing systems, care must be taken to define appropriate integration mechanisms. This property is clearly of marketing importance but has substantial architectural implications. For example, the ability to integrate a legacy system with an HTTP server to make it accessible from the Web has been a marketing goal in many corporations over the past decade. The architectural constraints implied by this integration must be analyzed.

4.7 Architecture Qualities

In addition to qualities of the system and qualities related to the business environment in which the system is being developed, there are also qualities directly related to the architecture itself that are important to achieve. We discuss three, again leaving the generation of specific scenarios to our discussion questions.

Conceptual integrity is the underlying theme or vision that unifies the design of the system at all levels. The architecture should do similar things in similar ways. Fred Brooks writes emphatically that a system's conceptual integrity is of overriding importance, and that systems without it fail:

> I will contend that conceptual integrity is *the* most important consideration in system design. It is better to have a system omit certain anomalous features and improvements, but to reflect one set of design ideas, than to have one that contains many good but independent and uncoordinated ideas. [Brooks 75]

Brooks was writing primarily about the way systems appear to their users, but the point is equally valid for the architectural layout. What Brooks's idea of conceptual integrity does for the user, architectural integrity does for the other stakeholders, particularly developers and maintainers.

In Part Three, you will see a recommendation for architecture evaluation that requires the project being reviewed to make the architect available. If no one is identified with that role, it is a sign that conceptual integrity may be lacking.

Correctness and *completeness* are essential for the architecture to allow for all of the system's requirements and runtime resource constraints to be met. A formal evaluation, as prescribed in Part Three, is once again the architect's best hope for a correct and complete architecture.

Buildability allows the system to be completed by the available team in a timely manner and to be open to certain changes as development progresses. It refers to the ease of constructing a desired system and is achieved architecturally by paying careful attention to the decomposition into modules, judiciously assigning of those modules to development teams, and limiting the dependencies between the modules (and hence the teams). The goal is to maximize the parallelism that can occur in development.

Because buildability is usually measured in terms of cost and time, there is a relationship between it and various cost models. However, buildability is more complex than what is usually covered in cost models. A system is created from certain materials, and these materials are created using a variety of tools. For example, a user interface may be constructed from items in a user interface toolbox (called widgets or controls), and these widgets may be manipulated by a user interface builder. The widgets are the materials and the builder is the tool, so one element of buildability is the match between the materials that are to be used in the system and the tools that are available to manipulate them. Another aspect of buildability is knowledge about the problem to be solved. The rationale behind this aspect is to speed time to market and not force potential suppliers to invest in the understanding and engineering of a new concept. A design that casts a solution in terms of well-understood concepts is thus more buildable than one that introduces new concepts.

4.8 Summary

The qualities presented in this chapter represent those most often the goals of software architects. Since their definitions overlap, we chose to characterize them with general scenarios. We saw that qualities can be divided into those that apply to the system, those that apply to the business environment, and those that apply to the architecture itself.

In the next chapter, we will explore concrete architectural approaches for following the path from qualities to architecture.

4.9 For Further Reading

A discussion of general scenarios and the mapping of scenarios discovered during architectural evaluations to the general scenarios can be found in [Bass 01b]. Further discussion of availability can be found in [Laprie 89] and [Cristian 93]. Security topics can be found in [Ramachandran 02]. The relationship between usability and software architecture is treated in [Gram 96] and [Bass 01a].

[McGregor 01] discusses testability. [Paulish 02] discusses the percentage of development costs associated with testing.

The IEEE maintains standard definitions for quality attributes [ISO 91]. [Witt 94] discusses desirable qualities of architectures (and architects).

4.10   Discussion Questions

1. For the system you are currently working on, what are the most important qualities? What are the system-specific scenarios that capture these qualities and what are the general scenarios they make concrete?

2. Brooks argues that conceptual integrity is the key to successful systems. Do you agree? Can you think of successful systems that have not had this property? If so, what factors made those systems successful anyway? How do you go about measuring a system to see if it meets Brooks's prescription?

3. Generate scenarios for the business and architecture qualities enumerated in Sections 4.4 and 4.5. Have you captured each quality with your scenarios? Which qualities are difficult to capture with scenarios?

5

Achieving Qualities

with Felix Bachmann, Mark Klein, and Bill Wood

> *Every good quality is noxious if unmixed.*
> — Ralph Waldo Emerson

Chapter 4 characterized a number of system quality attributes. That characterization was in terms of a collection of scenarios. Understanding what is meant by a quality attribute enables you to elicit the quality requirements but provides no help in understanding how to achieve them. In this chapter, we begin to provide that help. For each of the six system quality attributes that we elaborated in Chapter 4, we provide architectural guidance for their achievement. The tactics enumerated here do not cover all possible quality attributes, but we will see tactics for integrability in Chapter 8.

We are interested in how the architect achieves particular qualities. The quality requirements specify the responses of the software to realize business goals. Our interest is in the *tactics* used by the architect to create a design using design patterns, architectural patterns, or architectural strategies. For example, a business goal might be to create a product line. A means of achieving that goal is to allow variability in particular classes of functions.

Prior to deciding on a set of patterns to achieve the desired variation, the architect should consider what combination of tactics for modifiability should be applied, as the tactics chosen will guide the architectural decisions. An architectural pattern or strategy implements a collection of tactics. The connection between quality attribute requirements (discussed in Chapter 4) and architectural decisions is the subject of this chapter.

Note: Felix Bachmann, Mark Klein, and Bill Wood are senior members of the technical staff at the Software Engineering Institute.

5.1   Introducing Tactics

What is it that imparts portability to one design, high performance to another, and integrability to a third? The achievement of these qualities relies on fundamental design decisions. We will examine these design decisions, which we call *tactics*. A tactic is a design decision that influences the control of a quality attribute response. We call a collection of tactics an *architectural strategy*, which we will treat in Chapter 12. An architectural pattern packages tactics in a fashion that we will describe in Section 5.8.

A system design consists of a collection of decisions. Some of these decisions help control the quality attribute responses; others ensure achievement of system functionality. In this section, we discuss the quality attribute decisions known as tactics. We represent this relationship in Figure 5.1. The tactics are those that architects have been using for years, and we isolate and describe them. We are not *inventing* tactics here, just capturing what architects do in practice.

Each tactic is a design option for the architect. For example, one of the tactics introduces redundancy to increase the availability of a system. This is one option the architect has to increase availability, but not the only one. Usually achieving high availability through redundancy implies a concomitant need for synchronization (to ensure that the redundant copy can be used if the original fails). We see two immediate ramifications of this example.

1. *Tactics can refine other tactics.* We identified redundancy as a tactic. As such, it can be refined into redundancy of data (in a database system) or redundancy of computation (in an embedded control system). Both types are also tactics. There are further refinements that a designer can employ to make each type of redundancy more concrete. For each quality attribute that we discuss, we organize the tactics as a hierarchy.

2. *Patterns package tactics.* A pattern that supports availability will likely use both a redundancy tactic and a synchronization tactic. It will also likely use more concrete versions of these tactics. At the end of this section, we present an example of a pattern described in terms of its tactics.

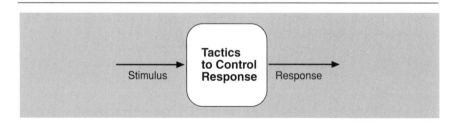

FIGURE 5.1   Tactics are intended to control responses to stimuli.

We organize the tactics for each system quality attribute as a hierarchy, but it is important to understand that each hierarchy is intended only to demonstrate some of the tactics, and that any list of tactics is necessarily incomplete. For each of the six attributes that we elaborated in Chapter 4 (availability, modifiability, performance, security, testability, and usability), we discuss tactical approaches for achieving it. For each, we present an organization of the tactics and a brief discussion. The organization is intended to provide a path for the architect to search for appropriate tactics.

5.2   Availability Tactics

Recall the vocabulary for availability from Chapter 4. A failure occurs when the system no longer delivers a service that is consistent with its specification; this failure is observable by the system's users. A fault (or combination of faults) has the potential to cause a failure. Recall also that recovery or repair is an important aspect of availability. The tactics we discuss in this section will keep faults from becoming failures or at least bound the effects of the fault and make repair possible. We illustrate this in Figure 5.2.

Many of the tactics we discuss are available within standard execution environments such as operating systems, application servers, and database management systems. It is still important to understand the tactics used so that the effects of using a particular one can be considered during design and evaluation. All approaches to maintaining availability involve some type of redundancy, some type of health monitoring to detect a failure, and some type of recovery when a failure is detected. In some cases, the monitoring or recovery is automatic and in others it is manual.

We first consider fault detection. We then consider fault recovery and finally, briefly, fault prevention.

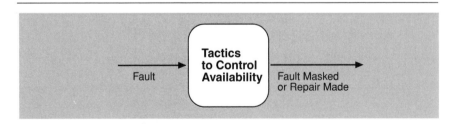

FIGURE 5.2   Goal of availability tactics

FAULT DETECTION

Three widely used tactics for recognizing faults are ping/echo, heartbeat, and exceptions.

- *Ping/echo*. One component issues a ping and expects to receive back an echo, within a predefined time, from the component under scrutiny. This can be used within a group of components mutually responsible for one task. It can also used be used by clients to ensure that a server object and the communication path to the server are operating within the expected performance bounds. "Ping/echo" fault detectors can be organized in a hierarchy, in which a lowest-level detector pings the software processes with which it shares a processor, and the higher-level fault detectors ping lower-level ones. This uses less communications bandwidth than a remote fault detector that pings all processes.

- *Heartbeat (dead man timer)*. In this case one component emits a heartbeat message periodically and another component listens for it. If the heartbeat fails, the originating component is assumed to have failed and a fault correction component is notified. The heartbeat can also carry data. For example, an automated teller machine can periodically send the log of the last transaction to a server. This message not only acts as a heartbeat but also carries data to be processed.

- *Exceptions*. One method for recognizing faults is to encounter an exception, which is raised when one of the fault classes we discussed in Chapter 4 is recognized. The exception handler typically executes in the same process that introduced the exception.

The ping/echo and heartbeat tactics operate among distinct processes, and the exception tactic operates within a single process. The exception handler will usually perform a semantic transformation of the fault into a form that can be processed.

FAULT RECOVERY

Fault recovery consists of preparing for recovery and making the system repair. Some preparation and repair tactics follow.

- *Voting*. Processes running on redundant processors each take equivalent input and compute a simple output value that is sent to a voter. If the voter detects deviant behavior from a single processor, it fails it. The voting algorithm can be "majority rules" or "preferred component" or some other algorithm. This method is used to correct faulty operation of algorithms or failure of a processor and is often used in control systems. If all of the processors utilize the same algorithms, the redundancy detects only a processor fault and not an algorithm fault. Thus, if the consequence of a failure is extreme, such as potential loss of life, the redundant components can be diverse.

One extreme of diversity is that the software for each redundant component is developed by different teams and executes on dissimilar platforms. Less extreme is to develop a single software component on dissimilar platforms. Diversity is expensive to develop and maintain and is used only in exceptional circumstances, such as the control of surfaces on aircraft. It is usually used for control systems in which the outputs to the voter are straightforward and easy to classify as equivalent or deviant, the computations are cyclic, and all redundant components receive equivalent inputs from sensors. Diversity has no downtime when a failure occurs since the voter continues to operate. Variations on this approach include the Simplex approach, which uses the results of a "preferred" component unless they deviate from those of a "trusted" component, to which it defers. Synchronization among the redundant components is automatic since they are all assumed to be computing on the same set of inputs in parallel.

- *Active redundancy (hot restart).* All redundant components respond to events in parallel. Consequently, they are all in the same state. The response from only one component is used (usually the first to respond), and the rest are discarded. When a fault occurs, the downtime of systems using this tactic is usually milliseconds since the backup is current and the only time to recover is the switching time. Active redundancy is often used in a client/server configuration, such as database management systems, where quick responses are necessary even when a fault occurs. In a highly available distributed system, the redundancy may be in the communication paths. For example, it may be desirable to use a LAN with a number of parallel paths and place each redundant component in a separate path. In this case, a single bridge or path failure will not make all of the system's components unavailable.

  Synchronization is performed by ensuring that all messages to any redundant component are sent to all redundant components. If communication has a possibility of being lost (because of noisy or overloaded communication lines), a reliable transmission protocol can be used to recover. A reliable transmission protocol requires all recipients to acknowledge receipt together with some integrity indication such as a checksum. If the sender cannot verify that all recipients have received the message, it will resend the message to those components not acknowledging receipt. The resending of unreceived messages (possibly over different communication paths) continues until the sender marks the recipient as out of service.

- *Passive redundancy (warm restart/dual redundancy/triple redundancy).* One component (the primary) responds to events and informs the other components (the standbys) of state updates they must make. When a fault occurs, the system must first ensure that the backup state is sufficiently fresh before resuming services. This approach is also used in control systems, often when the inputs come over communication channels or from sensors and have to be switched from the primary to the backup on failure. Chapter 6, describing an air traffic control example, shows a system using it. In the air traffic control system, the secondary decides when to take over from the primary, but in other systems this decision can be done in other components. This tactic depends on the standby components taking over reliably. Forcing switchovers periodically—for example, once a day or once a week—increases the availability of the system. Some database systems force a switch with storage of every new data item. The new data item is stored in a shadow page and the old page becomes a backup for recovery. In this case, the downtime can usually be limited to seconds.

Synchronization is the responsibility of the primary component, which may use atomic broadcasts to the secondaries to guarantee synchronization.

- *Spare.* A standby spare computing platform is configured to replace many different failed components. It must be rebooted to the appropriate software configuration and have its state initialized when a failure occurs. Making a checkpoint of the system state to a persistent device periodically and logging all state changes to a persistent device allows for the spare to be set to the appropriate state. This is often used as the standby client workstation, where the user can move when a failure occurs.   The downtime for this tactic is usually minutes.

There are tactics for repair that rely on component reintroduction. When a redundant component fails, it may be reintroduced after it has been corrected. Such tactics are shadow operation, state resynchronization, and rollback.

- *Shadow operation.* A previously failed component may be run in "shadow mode" for a short time to make sure that it mimics the behavior of the working components before restoring it to service.

- *State resynchronization.* The passive and active redundancy tactics require the component being restored to have its state upgraded before its return to service. The updating approach will depend on the downtime that can be sustained, the size of the update, and the number of messages required for the update. A single message containing the state is preferable, if possible. Incremental state upgrades, with periods of service between increments, lead to complicated software.

- *Checkpoint/rollback.* A checkpoint is a recording of a consistent state created either periodically or in response to specific events. Sometimes a system fails in an unusual manner, with a detectably inconsistent state. In this case, the system should be restored using a previous checkpoint of a consistent state and a log of the transactions that occurred since the snapshot was taken.

FAULT PREVENTION

The following are some fault prevention tactics.

- *Removal from service.* This tactic removes a component of the system from operation to undergo some activities to prevent anticipated failures. One

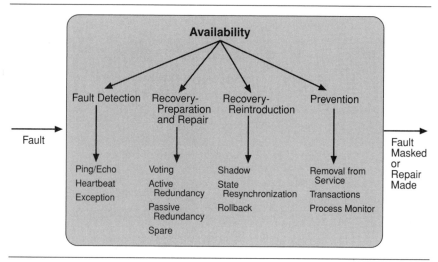

FIGURE 5.3   Summary of availability tactics

example is rebooting a component to prevent memory leaks from causing a failure. If this removal from service is automatic, an architectural strategy can be designed to support it. If it is manual, the system must be designed to support it.

- *Transactions*. A transaction is the bundling of several sequential steps such that the entire bundle can be undone at once. Transactions are used to prevent any data from being affected if one step in a process fails and also to prevent collisions among several simultaneous threads accessing the same data.

- *Process monitor*. Once a fault in a process has been detected, a monitoring process can delete the nonperforming process and create a new instance of it, initialized to some appropriate state as in the spare tactic.

Figure 5.3 summarizes the tactics just discussed.

5.3   Modifiability Tactics

Recall from Chapter 4 that tactics to control modifiability have as their goal controlling the time and cost to implement, test, and deploy changes. Figure 5.4 shows this relationship.

We organize the tactics for modifiability in sets according to their goals. One set has as its goal reducing the number of modules that are directly affected by a

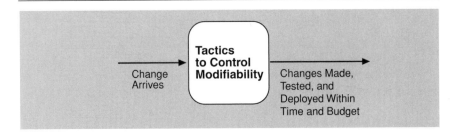

FIGURE 5.4   Goal of modifiability tactics

change. We call this set "localize modifications." A second set has as its goal limiting modifications to the localized modules. We use this set of tactics to "prevent
the ripple effect." Implicit in this distinction is that there are modules directly
affected (those whose responsibilities are adjusted to accomplish the change) and
modules indirectly affected by a change (those whose responsibilities remain
unchanged but whose implementation must be changed to accommodate the
directly affected modules). A third set of tactics has as its goal controlling
deployment time and cost. We call this set "defer binding time."

LOCALIZE MODIFICATIONS

Although there is not necessarily a precise relationship between the number of
modules affected by a set of changes and the cost of implementing those changes,
restricting modifications to a small set of modules will generally reduce the cost.
The goal of tactics in this set is to assign responsibilities to modules during
design such that anticipated changes will be limited in scope. We identify five
such tactics.

- *Maintain semantic coherence.* Semantic coherence refers to the relationships among responsibilities in a module. The goal is to ensure that all of
  these responsibilities work together without excessive reliance on other
  modules. Achievement of this goal comes from choosing responsibilities
  that have semantic coherence. Coupling and cohesion metrics are an attempt
  to measure semantic coherence, but they are missing the context of a change.
  Instead, semantic coherence should be measured against a set of anticipated
  changes. One subtactic is to *abstract common services.* Providing common
  services through specialized modules is usually viewed as supporting re-use.
  This is correct, but abstracting common services also supports modifiability.
  If common services have been abstracted, modifications to them will need to
  be made only once rather than in each module where the services are used.
  Furthermore, modification to the modules using those services will not impact
  other users. This tactic, then, supports not only localizing modifications but

also the prevention of ripple effects. Examples of abstracting common services are the use of application frameworks and the use of other middleware software.

- *Anticipate expected changes.* Considering the set of envisioned changes provides a way to evaluate a particular assignment of responsibilities. The basic question is "For each change, does the proposed decomposition limit the set of modules that need to be modified to accomplish it?" An associated question is "Do fundamentally different changes affect the same modules?" How is this different from semantic coherence? Assigning responsibilities based on semantic coherence assumes that expected changes will be semantically coherent. The tactic of anticipating expected changes does not concern itself with the coherence of a module's responsibilities but rather with minimizing the effects of the changes. In reality this tactic is difficult to use by itself since it is not possible to anticipate all changes. For that reason, it is usually used in conjunction with semantic coherence.

- *Generalize the module.* Making a module more general allows it to compute a broader range of functions based on input. The input can be thought of as defining a language for the module, which can be as simple as making constants input parameters or as complicated as implementing the module as an interpreter and making the input parameters be a program in the interpreter's language. The more general a module, the more likely that requested changes can be made by adjusing the input language rather than by modifying the module.

- *Limit possible options.* Modifications, especially within a product line (see Chapter 14), may be far ranging and hence affect many modules. Restricting the possible options will reduce the effect of these modifications. For example, a variation point in a product line may be allowing for a change of processor. Restricting processor changes to members of the same family limits the possible options.

PREVENT RIPPLE EFFECTS

A ripple effect from a modification is the necessity of making changes to modules not directly affected by it. For instance, if module A is changed to accomplish a particular modification, then module B is changed only because of the change to module A. B has to be modified because it depends, in some sense, on A.

We begin our discussion of the ripple effect by discussing the various types of dependencies that one module can have on another. We identify eight types:

1. Syntax of
   - *data.* For B to compile (or execute) correctly, the type (or format) of the data that is produced by A and consumed by B must be consistent with the type (or format) of data assumed by B.
   - *service.* For B to compile and execute correctly, the signature of services provided by A and invoked by B must be consistent with the assumptions of B.

2. Semantics of
  - *data*. For B to execute correctly, the semantics of the data produced by A and consumed by B must be consistent with the assumptions of B.
  - *service*. For B to execute correctly, the semantics of the services produced by A and used by B must be consistent with the assumptions of B.

3. Sequence of
  - *data*. For B to execute correctly, it must receive the data produced by A in a fixed sequence. For example, a data packet's header must precede its body in order of reception (as opposed to protocols that have the sequence number built into the data).
  - *control*. For B to execute correctly, A must have executed previously · within certain timing constraints. For example, A must have executed no longer than 5ms before B executes.

4. *Identity of an interface of A*. A may have multiple interfaces. For B to compile and execute correctly, the identity (name or handle) of the interface must be consistent with the assumptions of B.

5. *Location of A (runtime)*. For B to execute correctly, the runtime location of A must be consistent with the assumptions of B. For example, B may assume that A is located in a different process on the same processor.

6. *Quality of service/data provided by A*. For B to execute correctly, some property involving the quality of the data or service provided by A must be consistent with B's assumptions. For example, data provided by a particular sensor must have a certain accuracy in order for the algorithms of B to work correctly.

7. *Existence of A*. For B to execute correctly, A must exist. For example, if B is requesting a service from an object A, and A does not exist and cannot be dynamically created, then B will not execute correctly.

8. *Resource behavior of A*. For B to execute correctly, the resource behavior of A must be consistent with B's assumptions. This can be either resource usage of A (A uses the same memory as B) or resource ownership (B reserves a resource that A believes it owns).

With this understanding of dependency types, we can now discuss tactics available to the architect for preventing the ripple effect for certain types.

Notice that none of our tactics necessarily prevent the ripple of semantic changes. We begin with discussion of those that are relevant to the interfaces of a particular module—information hiding and maintaining existing interfaces—and follow with one that breaks a dependency chain—use of an intermediary.

  - *Hide information.* Information hiding is the decomposition of the responsibilities for an entity (a system or some decomposition of a system) into smaller pieces and choosing which information to make private and which to make public. The public responsibilities are available through specified interfaces. The goal is to isolate changes within one module and prevent changes from propagating to others. This is the oldest technique for preventing changes from propagating. It is strongly related to "anticipate expected changes" because it uses those changes as the basis for decomposition.

- *Maintain existing interfaces.* If B depends on the name and signature of an interface of A, maintaining this interface and its syntax allows B to remain unchanged. Of course, this tactic will not necessarily work if B has a semantic dependency on A, since changes to the meaning of data and services are difficult to mask. Also, it is difficult to mask dependencies on quality of data or quality of service, resource usage, or resource ownership. Interface stability can also be achieved by separating the interface from the implementation. This allows the creation of abstract interfaces that mask variations. Variations can be embodied within the existing responsibilities, or they can be embodied by replacing one implementation of a module with another.

  Patterns that implement this tactic include

  - *adding interfaces.* Most programming languages allow multiple interfaces. Newly visible services or data can be made available through new interfaces, allowing existing interfaces to remain unchanged and provide the same signature.
  - *adding adapter.* Add an adapter to A that wraps A and provides the signature of the original A.
  - *providing a stub A.* If the modification calls for the deletion of A, then providing a stub for A will allow B to remain unchanged if B depends only on A's signature.

- *Restrict communication paths.* Restrict the modules with which a given module shares data. That is, reduce the number of modules that consume data produced by the given module and the number of modules that produce data consumed by it. This will reduce the ripple effect since data production/consumption introduces dependencies that cause ripples. Chapter 8 (Flight Simulation) discusses a pattern that uses this tactic.

- *Use an intermediary.* If B has any type of dependency on A other than semantic, it is possible to insert an intermediary between B and A that manages activities associated with the dependency. All of these intermediaries go by different names, but we will discuss each in terms of the dependency types we have enumerated. As before, in the worst case, an intermediary cannot compensate for semantic changes. The intermediaries are

  - *data (syntax).* Repositories (both blackboard and passive) act as intermediaries between the producer and consumer of data. The repositories can convert the syntax produced by A into that assumed by B. Some publish/subscribe patterns (those that have data flowing through a central component) can also convert the syntax into that assumed by B. The MVC and PAC patterns convert data in one formalism (input or output device) into another (that used by the model in MVC or the abstraction in PAC).
  - *service (syntax).* The facade, bridge, mediator, strategy, proxy, and factory patterns all provide intermediaries that convert the syntax of a service

from one form into another. Hence, they can all be used to prevent changes in A from propagating to B.

- *identity of an interface of A*. A broker pattern can be used to mask changes in the identity of an interface. If B depends on the identity of an interface of A and that identity changes, by adding that identity to the broker and having the broker make the connection to the new identity of A, B can remain unchanged.
- *location of A (runtime)*. A name server enables the location of A to be changed without affecting B. A is responsible for registering its current location with the name server, and B retrieves that location from the name server.
- *resource behavior of A or resource controlled by A*. A resource manager is an intermediary that is responsible for resource allocation. Certain resource managers (e.g., those based on Rate Monotonic Analysis in real-time systems) can guarantee the satisfaction of all requests within certain constraints. A, of course, must give up control of the resource to the resource manager.
- *existence of A*. The factory pattern has the ability to create instances as needed, and thus the dependence of B on the existence of A is satisfied by actions of the factory.

DEFER BINDING TIME

The two tactic categories we have discussed thus far are designed to minimize the number of modules that require changing to implement modifications. Our modifiability scenarios include two elements that are not satisfied by reducing the number of modules to be changed—time to deploy and allowing nondevelopers to make changes. Deferring binding time supports both of those scenarios at the cost of requiring additional infrastructure to support the late binding.

Decisions can be bound into the executing system at various times. We discuss those that affect deployment time. The deployment of a system is dictated by some process. When a modification is made by the developer, there is usually a testing and distribution process that determines the time lag between the making of the change and the availability of that change to the end user. Binding at runtime means that the system has been prepared for that binding and all of the testing and distribution steps have been completed. Deferring binding time also supports allowing the end user or system administrator to make settings or provide input that affects behavior.

Many tactics are intended to have impact at loadtime or runtime, such as the following.

- *Runtime registration* supports plug-and-play operation at the cost of additional overhead to manage the registration. Publish/subscribe registration, for example, can be implemented at either runtime or load time.

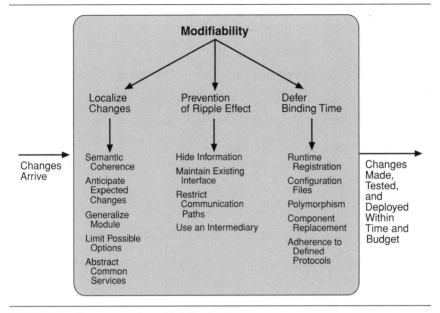

FIGURE 5.5   Summary of modifiability tactics

- *Configuration files* are intended to set parameters at startup.
- *Polymorphism* allows late binding of method calls.
- *Component replacement* allows load time binding.
- *Adherence to defined protocols* allows runtime binding of independent processes.

The tactics for modifiability are summarized in Figure 5.5.

5.4   Performance Tactics

Recall from Chapter 4 that the goal of performance tactics is to generate a response to an event arriving at the system within some time constraint. The event can be single or a stream and is the trigger for a request to perform computation. It can be the arrival of a message, the expiration of a time interval, the detection of a significant change of state in the system's environment, and so forth. The system processes the events and generates a response. Performance tactics control the time within which a response is generated. This is shown in Figure 5.6. Latency is the time between the arrival of an event and the generation of a response to it.

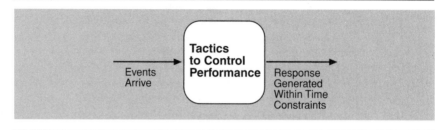

FIGURE 5.6   Goal of performance tactics

After an event arrives, either the system is processing on that event or the processing is blocked for some reason. This leads to the two basic contributors to the response time: resource consumption and blocked time.

1. *Resource consumption.* Resources include CPU, data stores, network communication bandwidth, and memory, but it can also include entities defined by the particular system under design. For example, buffers must be managed and access to critical sections must be made sequential. Events can be of varying types (as just enumerated), and each type goes through a processing sequence. For example, a message is generated by one component, is placed on the network, and arrives at another component. It is then placed in a buffer; transformed in some fashion (*marshalling* is the term the Object Management Group uses for this transformation); processed according to some algorithm; transformed for output; placed in an output buffer; and sent onward to another component, another system, or the user. Each of these phases contributes to the overall latency of the processing of that event.

2. *Blocked time.* A computation can be blocked from using a resource because of contention for it, because the resource is unavailable, or because the computation depends on the result of other computations that are not yet available.

- *Contention for resources.* Figure 5.6 shows events arriving at the system. These events may be in a single stream or in multiple streams. Multiple streams vying for the same resource or different events in the same stream vying for the same resource contribute to latency. In general, the more contention for a resource, the more likelihood of latency being introduced. However, this depends on how the contention is arbitrated and how individual requests are treated by the arbitration mechanism.
- *Availability of resources.* Even in the absence of contention, computation cannot proceed if a resource is unavailable. Unavailability may be caused by the resource being offline or by failure of the component or for some other reason. In any case, the architect must identify places where resource unavailability might cause a significant contribution to overall latency.
- *Dependency on other computation.* A computation may have to wait because it must synchronize with the results of another computation or

because it is waiting for the results of a computation that it initiated. For example, it may be reading information from two different sources, if these two sources are read sequentially, the latency will be higher than if they are read in parallel.

With this background, we turn to our three tactic categories: resource demand, resource management, and resource arbitration.

RESOURCE DEMAND

Event streams are the source of resource demand. Two characteristics of demand are the time between events in a resource stream (how often a request is made in a stream) and how much of a resource is consumed by each request.

One tactic for reducing latency is to reduce the resources required for processing an event stream. Ways to do this include the following.

- *Increase computational efficiency.* One step in the processing of an event or a message is applying some algorithm. Improving the algorithms used in critical areas will decrease latency. Sometimes one resource can be traded for another. For example, intermediate data may be kept in a repository or it may be regenerated depending on time and space resource availability. This tactic is usually applied to the processor but is also effective when applied to other resources such as a disk.

- *Reduce computational overhead.* If there is no request for a resource, processing needs are reduced. In Chapter 17, we will see an example of using Java classes rather than Remote Method Invocation (RMI) because the former reduces communication requirements. The use of intermediaries (so important for modifiability) increases the resources consumed in processing an event stream, and so removing them improves latency. This is a classic modifiability/performance tradeoff.

Another tactic for reducing latency is to reduce the number of events processed. This can be done in one of two fashions.

- *Manage event rate.* If it is possible to reduce the sampling frequency at which environmental variables are monitored, demand can be reduced. Sometimes this is possible if the system was overengineered. Other times an unnecessarily high sampling rate is used to establish harmonic periods between multiple streams. That is, some stream or streams of events are oversampled so that they can be synchronized.

- *Control frequency of sampling.* If there is no control over the arrival of externally generated events, queued requests can be sampled at a lower frequency, possibly resulting in the loss of requests.

Other tactics for reducing or managing demand involve controlling the use of resources.

- *Bound execution times.* Place a limit on how much execution time is used to respond to an event. Sometimes this makes sense and sometimes it does not. For iterative, data-dependent algorithms, limiting the number of iterations is a method for bounding execution times.

- *Bound queue sizes.* This controls the maximum number of queued arrivals and consequently the resources used to process the arrivals.

RESOURCE MANAGEMENT

Even though the demand for resources may not be controllable, the management of these resources affects response times. Some resource management tactics are:

- *Introduce concurrency.* If requests can be processed in parallel, the blocked time can be reduced. Concurrency can be introduced by processing different streams of events on different threads or by creating additional threads to process different sets of activities. Once concurrency has been introduced, appropriately allocating the threads to resources (load balancing) is important in order to maximally exploit the concurrency.

- *Maintain multiple copies of either data or computations.* Clients in a client-server pattern are replicas of the computation. The purpose of replicas is to reduce the contention that would occur if all computations took place on a central server. Caching is a tactic in which data is replicated, either on different speed repositories or on separate repositories, to reduce contention. Since the data being cached is usually a copy of existing data, keeping the copies consistent and synchronized becomes a responsibility that the system must assume.

- *Increase available resources.* Faster processors, additional processors, additional memory, and faster networks all have the potential for reducing latency. Cost is usually a consideration in the choice of resources, but increasing the resources is definitely a tactic to reduce latency. This kind of cost/performance tradeoff is analyzed in Chapter 12.

RESOURCE ARBITRATION

Whenever there is contention for a resource, the resource must be scheduled. Processors are scheduled, buffers are scheduled, and networks are scheduled. The architect's goal is to understand the characteristics of each resource's use and choose the scheduling strategy that is compatible with it.

A scheduling policy conceptually has two parts: a priority assignment and dispatching. All scheduling policies assign priorities. In some cases the assignment is as simple as first-in/first-out. In other cases, it can be tied to the deadline of the request or its semantic importance. Competing criteria for scheduling include optimal resource usage, request importance, minimizing the number of resources used, minimizing latency, maximizing throughput, preventing starvation to ensure fairness, and so forth. The architect needs to be aware of these possibly conflicting criteria and the effect that the chosen tactic has on meeting them.

A high-priority event stream can be dispatched only if the resource to which it is being assigned is available. Sometimes this depends on pre-empting the current user of the resource. Possible preemption options are as follows: can occur anytime; can occur only at specific pre-emption points; and executing processes cannot be pre-empted. Some common scheduling policies are:

1. *First-in/First-out.* FIFO queues treat all requests for resources as equals and satisfy them in turn. One possibility with a FIFO queue is that one request will be stuck behind another one that takes a long time to generate a response. As long as all of the requests are truly equal, this is not a problem, but if some requests are of higher priority than others, it is problematic.

2. *Fixed-priority scheduling.* Fixed-priority scheduling assigns each source of resource requests a particular priority and assigns the resources in that priority order. This strategy insures better service for higher-priority requests but admits the possibility of a low-priority, but important, request taking an arbitrarily long time to be serviced because it is stuck behind a series of higher-priority requests. Three common prioritization strategies are

- *semantic importance.* Each stream is assigned a priority statically according to some domain characteristic of the task that generates it. This type of scheduling is used in mainframe systems where the domain characteristic is the time of task initiation.
- *deadline monotonic.* Deadline monotonic is a static priority assignment that assigns higher priority to streams with shorter deadlines. This scheduling policy is used when streams of different priorities with real-time deadlines are to be scheduled.
- *rate monotonic.* Rate monotonic is a static priority assignment for periodic streams that assigns higher priority to streams with shorter periods. This scheduling policy is a special case of deadline monotonic but is better known and more likely to be supported by the operating system.

3. *Dynamic priority scheduling:*
- *round robin.* Round robin is a scheduling strategy that orders the requests and then, at every assignment possibility, assigns the resource to the next request in that order. A special form of round robin is a cyclic executive where assignment possibilities are at fixed time intervals.
- *earliest deadline first.* Earliest deadline first assigns priorities based on the pending requests with the earliest deadline.

4. *Static scheduling.* A cyclic executive schedule is a scheduling strategy where the pre-emption points and the sequence of assignment to the resource are determined offline.

For Further Reading at the end of this chapter lists books on scheduling theory.

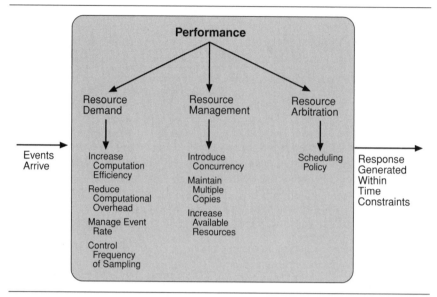

FIGURE 5.7   Summary of performance tactics

The tactics for performance are summarized in Figure 5.7.

5.5   Security Tactics

Tactics for achieving security can be divided into those concerned with resisting attacks, those concerned with detecting attacks, and those concerned with recovering from attacks. All three categories are important. Using a familiar analogy, putting a lock on your door is a form of resisting an attack, having a motion sensor inside of your house is a form of detecting an attack, and having insurance is a form of recovering from an attack. Figure 5.8 shows the goals of the security tactics.

RESISTING ATTACKS

In Chapter 4, we identified nonrepudiation, confidentiality, integrity, and assurance as goals in our security characterization. The following tactics can be used in combination to achieve these goals.

- *Authenticate users.* Authentication is ensuring that a user or remote computer is actually who it purports to be. Passwords, one-time passwords, digital certificates, and biometric identifications provide authentication.

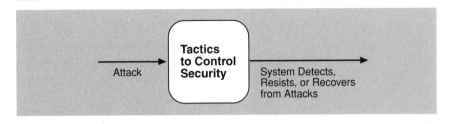

FIGURE 5.8   Goal of security tactics

- *Authorize users.* Authorization is ensuring that an authenticated user has the rights to access and modify either data or services. This is usually managed by providing some access control patterns within a system. Access control can be by user or by user class. Classes of users can be defined by user groups, by user roles, or by lists of individuals.

- *Maintain data confidentiality.* Data should be protected from unauthorized access. Confidentiality is usually achieved by applying some form of encryption to data and to communication links. Encryption provides extra protection to persistently maintained data beyond that available from authorization. Communication links, on the other hand, typically do not have authorization controls. Encryption is the only protection for passing data over publicly accessible communication links. The link can be implemented by a virtual private network (VPN) or by a Secure Sockets Layer (SSL) for a Web-based link. Encryption can be symmetric (both parties use the same key) or asymmetric (public and private keys).

- *Maintain integrity.* Data should be delivered as intended. It can have redundant information encoded in it, such as checksums or hash results, which can be encrypted either along with or independently from the original data.

- *Limit exposure.* Attacks typically depend on exploiting a single weakness to attack all data and services on a host. The architect can design the allocation of services to hosts so that limited services are available on each host.

- *Limit access.* Firewalls restrict access based on message source or destination port. Messages from unknown sources may be a form of an attack. It is not always possible to limit access to known sources. A public Web site, for example, can expect to get requests from unknown sources. One configuration used in this case is the so-called demilitarized zone (DMZ). A DMZ is used when access must be provided to Internet services but not to a private network. It sits between the Internet and a firewall in front of the internal network. The DMZ contains devices expected to receive messages from arbitrary sources such as Web services, e-mail, and domain name services.

DETECTING ATTACKS

The detection of an attack is usually through an *intrusion detection* system. Such systems work by comparing network traffic patterns to a database. In the case of misuse detection, the traffic pattern is compared to historic patterns of known attacks. In the case of anomaly detection, the traffic pattern is compared to a historical baseline of itself. Frequently, the packets must be filtered in order to make comparisons. Filtering can be on the basis of protocol, TCP flags, payload sizes, source or destination address, or port number.

Intrusion detectors must have some sort of sensor to detect attacks, managers to do sensor fusion, databases for storing events for later analysis, tools for offline reporting and analysis, and a control console so that the analyst can modify intrusion detection actions.

RECOVERING FROM ATTACKS

Tactics involved in recovering from an attack can be divided into those concerned with restoring state and those concerned with attacker identification (for either preventive or punitive purposes).

The tactics used in restoring the system or data to a correct state overlap with those used for availability since they are both concerned with recovering a consistent state from an inconsistent state. One difference is that special attention is paid to maintaining redundant copies of system administrative data such as passwords, access control lists, domain name services, and user profile data.

The tactic for identifying an attacker is to *maintain an audit trail*. An audit trail is a copy of each transaction applied to the data in the system together with identifying information. Audit information can be used to trace the actions of an attacker, support nonrepudiation (it provides evidence that a particular request was made), and support system recovery. Audit trails are often attack targets themselves and therefore should be maintained in a trusted fashion.

Figure 5.9 provides a summary of the tactics for security.

5.6 Testability Tactics

The goal of tactics for testability is to allow for easier testing when an increment of software development is completed. Figure 5.10 displays the use of tactics for testability. Architectural techniques for enhancing the software testability have not received as much attention as more mature fields such as modifiability, performance, and availability, but, as we stated in Chapter 4, since testing consumes such a high percentage of system development cost, anything the architect can do to reduce this cost will yield a significant benefit.

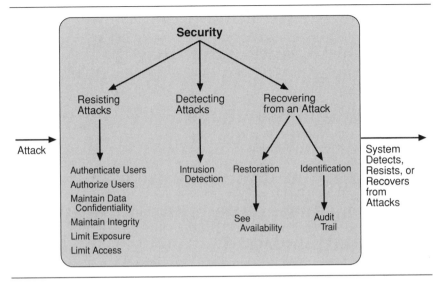

FIGURE 5.9   Summary of tactics for security

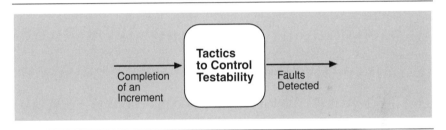

FIGURE 5.10   Goal of testability tactics

Although in Chapter 4 we included design reviews as a testing technique, in this chapter we are concerned only with testing a running system. The goal of a testing regimen is to discover faults. This requires that input be provided to the software being tested and that the output be captured.

Executing the test procedures requires some software to provide input to the software being tested and to capture the output. This is called a test harness. A question we do not consider here is the design and generation of the test harness. In some systems, this takes substantial time and expense.

We discuss two categories of tactics for testing: providing input and capturing output, and internal monitoring.

INPUT/OUTPUT

There are three tactics for managing input and output for testing.

- *Record/playback.* Record/playback refers to both capturing information crossing an interface and using it as input into the test harness. The information crossing an interface during normal operation is saved in some repository and represents output from one component and input to another. Recording this information allows test input for one of the components to be generated and test output for later comparison to be saved.

- *Separate interface from implementation.* Separating the interface from the implementation allows substitution of implementations for various testing purposes. Stubbing implementations allows the remainder of the system to be tested in the absence of the component being stubbed. Substituting a specialized component allows the component being replaced to act as a test harness for the remainder of the system.

- *Specialize access routes/interfaces.* Having specialized testing interfaces allows the capturing or specification of variable values for a component through a test harness as well as independently from its normal execution. For example, metadata might be made available through a specialized interface that a test harness would use to drive its activities. Specialized access routes and interfaces should be kept separate from the access routes and interfaces for required functionality. Having a hierarchy of test interfaces in the architecture means that test cases can be applied at any level in the architecture and that the testing functionality is in place to observe the response.

INTERNAL MONITORING

A component can implement tactics based on internal state to support the testing process.

- *Built-in monitors.* The component can maintain state, performance load, capacity, security, or other information accessible through an interface. This interface can be a permanent interface of the component or it can be introduced temporarily via an instrumentation technique such as aspect-oriented programming or preprocessor macros. A common technique is to record events when monitoring states have been activated. Monitoring states can actually increase the testing effort since tests may have to be repeated with the monitoring turned off. Increased visibility into the activities of the component usually more than outweigh the cost of the additional testing.

Figure 5.11 provides a summary of the tactics used for testability.

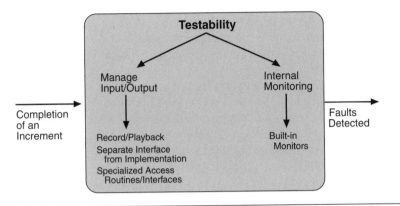

FIGURE 5.11   Summary of testability tactics

5.7   Usability Tactics

Recall from Chapter 4 that usability is concerned with how easy it is for the user to accomplish a desired task and the kind of support the system provides to the user. Two types of tactics support usability, each intended for two categories of "users." The first category, runtime, includes those that support the user during system execution. The second category is based on the iterative nature of user interface design and supports the interface developer at design time. It is strongly related to the modifiability tactics already presented.

Figure 5.12 shows the goal of the runtime tactics.

RUNTIME TACTICS

Once a system is executing, usability is enhanced by giving the user feedback as to what the system is doing and by providing the user with the ability to issue

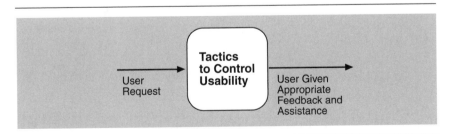

FIGURE 5.12   Goal of runtime usability tactics

usability-based commands such as those we saw in Chapter 4. For example, *cancel, undo, aggregate,* and *show multiple views* support the user in either error correction or more efficient operations.

Researchers in human–computer interaction have used the terms "user intiative," "system initiative," and "mixed initiative" to describe which of the human–computer pair takes the initiative in performing certain actions and how the interaction proceeds. The usability scenarios we enumerated in Chapter 4, Understanding Quality Attributes, combine initiatives from both perspectives. For example, when canceling a command the user issues a cancel—"user initiative"—and the system responds. During the cancel, however, the system may put up a progress indicator—"system initiative." Thus, cancel demonstrates "mixed initiative." We use this distinction between user and system initiative to discuss the tactics that the architect uses to achieve the various scenarios.

When the user takes the initiative, the architect designs a response as if for any other piece of functionality. The architect must enumerate the responsibilities of the system to respond to the user command. To use the cancel example again: When the user issues a cancel command, the system must be listening for it (thus, there is the responsibility to have a constant listener that is not blocked by the actions of whatever is being canceled); the command to cancel must be killed; any resources being used by the canceled command must be freed; and components that are collaborating with the canceled command must be informed so that they can also take appropriate action.

When the system takes the initiative, it must rely on some information—a model—about the user, the task being undertaken by the user, or the system state itself. Each model requires various types of input to accomplish its initiative. The system initiative tactics are those that identify the models the system uses to predict either its own behavior or the user's intention. Encapsulating this information will enable an architect to more easily tailor and modify those models. Tailoring and modification can be either dynamically based on past user behavior or offline during development.

- *Maintain a model of the task.* In this case, the model maintained is that of the task. The task model is used to determine context so the system can have some idea of what the user is attempting and provide various kinds of assistance. For example, knowing that sentences usually start with capital letters would allow an application to correct a lower-case letter in that position.

- *Maintain a model of the user.* In this case, the model maintained is of the user. It determines the user's knowledge of the system, the user's behavior in terms of expected response time, and other aspects specific to a user or a class of users. For example, maintaining a user model allows the system to pace scrolling so that pages do not fly past faster than they can be read.

- *Maintain a model of the system.* In this case, the model maintained is that of the system. It determines the expected system behavior so that appropriate feedback can be given to the user. The system model predicts items such as the time needed to complete current activity.

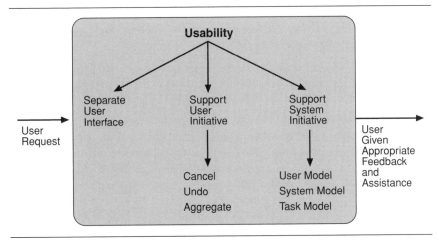

FIGURE 5.13 Summary of runtime usability tactics

DESIGN-TIME TACTICS

User interfaces are typically revised frequently during the testing process. That is, the usability engineer will give the developers revisions to the current user interface design and the developers will implement them. This leads to a tactic that is a refinement of the modifiability tactic of semantic coherence:

- *Separate the user interface from the rest of the application.* Localizing expected changes is the rationale for semantic coherence. Since the user interface is expected to change frequently both during the development and after deployment, maintaining the user interface code separately will localize changes to it. The software architecture patterns developed to implement this tactic and to support the modification of the user interface are:
  - Model-View-Controller
  - Presentation-Abstraction-Control
  - Seeheim
  - Arch/Slinky

Figure 5.13 shows a summary of the runtime tactics to achieve usability.

5.8   Relationship of Tactics to Architectural Patterns

We have presented a collection of tactics that the architect can use to achieve particular attributes. In fact, an architect usually chooses a pattern or a collection of patterns designed to realize one or more tactics. However, each pattern implements multiple tactics, whether desired or not. We illustrate this by discussing the Active Object design pattern, as described by [Schmidt 00]:

> The *Active Object* design pattern decouples method execution from method invocation to enhance concurrency and simplify synchronized access to objects that reside in their own thread of control.

The pattern consists of six elements: a *proxy*, which provides an interface that allows clients to invoke publicly accessible methods on an active object; a *method request*, which defines an interface for executing the methods of an active object; an *activation list*, which maintains a buffer of pending method requests; a *scheduler*, which decides what method requests to execute next; a *servant*, which defines the behavior and state modeled as an active object; and a *future*, which allows the client to obtain the result of the method invocation.

The motivation for this pattern is to enhance concurrency—a performance goal. Thus, its main purpose is to implement the "introduce concurrency" performance tactic. Notice the other tactics this pattern involves, however.

- *Information hiding (modifiability).* Each element chooses the responsibilities it will achieve and hides their achievement behind an interface.
- *Intermediary (modifiability).* The proxy acts as an intermediary that will buffer changes to the method invocation.
- *Binding time (modifiability).* The active object pattern assumes that requests for the object arrive at the object at runtime. The binding of the client to the proxy, however, is left open in terms of binding time.
- *Scheduling policy (performance).* The scheduler implements some scheduling policy.

Any pattern implements several tactics, often concerned with different quality attributes, and any implementation of the pattern also makes choices about tactics. For example, an implementation could maintain a log of requests to the active object for supporting recovery, maintaining an audit trail, or supporting testability.

The analysis process for the architect involves understanding all of the tactics embedded in an implementation, and the design process involves making a judicious choice of what combination of tactics will achieve the system's desired goals.

5.9 Architectural Patterns and Styles

An architectural pattern in software, also known as an architectural style, is analogous to an architectural style in buildings, such as Gothic or Greek Revival or

Queen Anne. It consists of a few key features and rules for combining them so that architectural integrity is preserved. An architectural pattern is determined by:

- A set of element types (such as a data repository or a component that computes a mathematical function).
- A topological layout of the elements indicating their interrelationships.
- A set of semantic constraints (e.g., filters in a pipe-and-filter style are pure data transducers—they incrementally transform their input stream into an output stream, but do not control either upstream or downstream elements).
- A set of interaction mechanisms (e.g., subroutine call, event-subscriber, blackboard) that determine how the elements coordinate through the allowed topology.

Mary Shaw and David Garlan's influential work attempted to catalog a set of architectural patterns that they called architectural *styles* or *idioms*. This has been evolved by the software engineering community into what is now more commonly known as architectural patterns, analogous to design patterns and code patterns.

The motivation of [Shaw 96] for embarking on this project was the observation that high-level abstractions for complex systems exist but we do not study or catalog them, as is common in other engineering disciplines.

These patterns occur not only regularly in system designs but in ways that sometimes prevent us from recognizing them, because in different disciplines the same architectural pattern may be called different things. In response, a number of recurring architectural patterns, their properties, and their benefits have been cataloged. One such catalog is illustrated in Figure 5.14.

In this figure patterns are categorized into related groups in an inheritance hierarchy. For example, an event system is a substyle of independent elements. Event systems themselves have two subpatterns: implicit invocation and explicit invocation.

What is the relationship between architectural patterns and tactics? As shown earlier, we view a tactic as a foundational "building block" of design, from which architectural patterns and strategies are created.

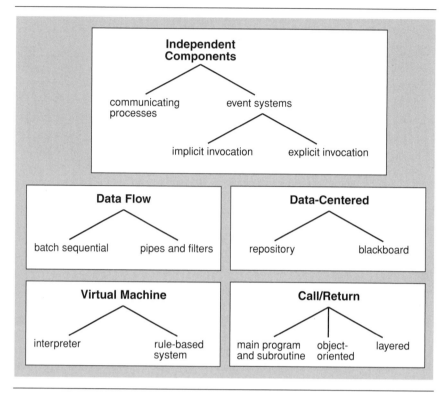

FIGURE 5.14   A small catalog of architectural patterns, organized by is-a relations

5.10   Summary

In this chapter we saw how the architect realizes particular quality attribute requirements. These requirements are the means by which a system achieves business goals. Our interest here was in the *tactics* used by the architect to create a design using architectural patterns and strategies.

We provided a list of well-known tactics for achieving the six quality attributes elaborated in Chapter 4: availability, modifiability, performance, security, testability, and usability. For each we discussed the tactics that are available and widely practiced.

As we discussed, in relating tactics to patterns the architect's task has only just begun when the tactics are chosen. Any design uses multiple tactics, and understanding what attributes are achieved by them, what their side effects are, and the risks of not choosing other tactics is essential to architecture design.

5.11 Discussion Questions

1. As in question 3 from Chapter 4, consider a widely used Web site, such as Amazon or eBay. What tactics would you need to consider when choosing the architectural patterns or architectural strategies for meeting the performance requirements you enumerated in that question?

2. Given the set of tactics you chose in question 1, what tradeoffs with other quality attributes might you expect from using them (such as security, availability, and modifiability)?

3. Usability is not always given due consideration in architecture design, making usability system goals often difficult to achieve because they are treated as an afterthought. Think of a system where you are familiar with the architecture and try to enumerate the usability tactics, if any, it has employed.

5.12 For Further Reading

Further reading about security can be found in [Ramachandran 02]; about the relationship between usability and software architectural patterns, in [Bass 01a]; and about availability techniques for distributed systems, in [Jalote 94]. [McGregor 01] is a source of information about testability.

The two-volume reference on architectural patterns, [Buschmann 96] and [Schmidt 00], discusses the MVC and PAC patterns (vol. 1) and pattern-oriented software architecture (vol. 2).

The Simplex architecture for availability is discussed at *http://www.sei.cmu.edu/ simplex/*.

[Bachmann 02] discusses the use of tactics as a basis for analysis of modifiability and performance; [Chretienne 95] discusses various types of scheduling theory; and [Briand 99] discusses coupling metrics.

The Model-View-Controller pattern is documented in [Gamma 95], the Presentation-Abstraction-Control pattern in [Buschmann 96], the Seeheim pattern in [Pfaff 85], and Arch/Slinky, in [UIMS 92].

6

Air Traffic Control
A Case Study in Designing
for High Availability

> *The FAA has faced this problem [of complexity] throughout its decade-old attempt to replace the nation's increasingly obsolete air traffic control system. The replacement, called Advanced Automation System, combines all the challenges of computing in the 1990s. A program that is more than a million lines in size is distributed across hundreds of computers and embedded into new and sophisticated hardware, all of which must respond around the clock to unpredictable real-time events. Even a small glitch potentially threatens public safety.*
> — W. Wayt Gibbs [Gibbs 94]

Air traffic control (ATC) is among the most demanding of all software applications. It is *hard real time*, meaning that timing deadlines must be met absolutely; it is *safety critical*, meaning that human lives may be lost if the system does not perform correctly; and it is *highly distributed*, requiring dozens of controllers to work cooperatively to guide aircraft through the airways system. In the United States, whose skies are filled with more commercial, private, and military aircraft than any other part of the world, ATC is an area of intense public scrutiny. Aside from the obvious safety issues, building and maintaining a safe, reliable airways system requires enormous expenditures of public money. ATC is a multibillion-dollar undertaking.

This chapter is a case study of one part of a once-planned, next-generation ATC system for the United States. We will see how its architecture—in particular, a set of carefully chosen views (as in Chapter 2) coupled with the right tactics (as in Chapter 5)—held the key to achieving its demanding and wide-ranging requirements. Although this system was never put into operation because of budgetary constraints, it was implemented and demonstrated that the system could meet its quality goals.

In the United States, air traffic is controlled by the Federal Aviation Administration (FAA), a government agency responsible for aviation safety in general.

The FAA is the customer for the system we will describe. As a flight progresses from its departure airport to its arrival airport, it deals with several ATC entities that guide it safely through each portion of the airways (and ground facilities) it is using. *Ground control* coordinates the movement of aircraft on the ground at an airport. Towers control aircraft flying within an airport's *terminal control area*, a cylindrical section of airspace centered at an airport. Finally, *en route centers* divide the skies over the country into 22 large sections of responsibility.

Consider an airline flight from Key West, Florida, to Washington, D.C.'s Dulles Airport. The crew of the flight will communicate with Key West ground control to taxi from the gate to the end of the runway, Key West tower during takeoff and climb-out, and then Miami Center (the en route center whose airspace covers Key West) once it leaves the Key West terminal control area. From there the flight will be handed off to Jacksonville Center, Atlanta Center, and so forth, until it enters the airspace controlled by Washington Center. From Washington Center, it will be handed off to the Dulles tower, which will guide its approach and landing. When it leaves the runway, the flight will communicate with Dulles ground control for its taxi to the gate. This is an oversimplified view of ATC in the United States, but it suffices for our case study. Figure 6.1 shows the hand-off process, and Figure 6.2 shows the 22 en route centers.

The system we will study is called the Initial Sector Suite System (ISSS), which was intended to be an upgraded hardware and software system for the 22 en route centers in the United States. It was part of a much larger government procurement that would have, in stages, installed similar upgraded systems in the towers and ground control facilities, as well as the transoceanic ATC facilities.

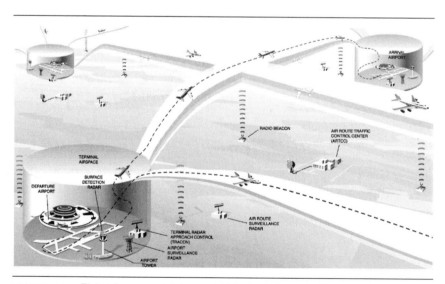

FIGURE 6.1 Flying from point A to point B in the U.S. air traffic control system. Courtesy of Ian Worpole/*Scientific American*, 1994.

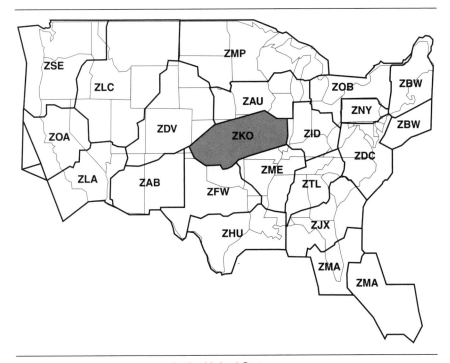

FIGURE 6.2   En route centers in the United States

The fact that ISSS was to be procured as only one of a set of strongly related systems had a profound effect on its architecture. In particular, there was great incentive to adopt common designs and elements where possible because the ISSS developer also intended to bid on the other systems. After all, these different systems (en route center, tower, ground control) share many elements: interfaces to radio systems, interfaces to flight plan databases, interfaces to each other, interpreting radar data, requirements for reliability and performance, and so on. Thus, the ISSS design was influenced broadly by the requirements for all of the upgraded systems, not just the ISSS-specific ones. The complete set of upgraded systems was to be called the Advanced Automation System (AAS).

Ultimately, the AAS program was canceled in favor of a less ambitious, less costly, more staged upgrade plan. Nevertheless, ISSS is still an illuminating case study because, when the program was canceled, the design and most of the code were actually already completed. Furthermore, the architecture of the system (as well as most other aspects) was studied by an independent audit team and found to be well suited to its requirements. Finally, the system that was deployed instead of ISSS borrowed heavily from the ISSS architecture. For these reasons, we will present the ISSS architecture as an actual solution to an extremely difficult problem.

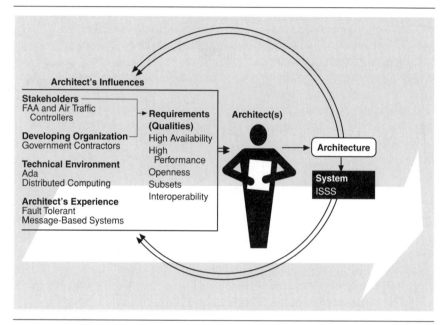

FIGURE 6.3   The ABC applied to the ATC system

6.1   Relationship to the Architecture Business Cycle

Figure 6.3 shows how the air traffic control system relates to the Architecture Business Cycle (ABC). The end users are federal air traffic controllers; the customer is the Federal Aviation Administration; and the developing organization is a large corporation that supplies many other important software-intensive systems to the U.S. government. Factors in the technical environment include the mandated use of Ada as the language of implementation for large government software systems and the emergence of distributed computing as a routine way to build systems and approach fault tolerance.

6.2   Requirements and Qualities

Given that air traffic control is highly visible, with huge amounts of commercial, government, and civilian interest, and given that it involves the potential loss of human life if it fails, its two most important quality requirements are as follows:

   1. Ultrahigh availability, meaning that the system is absolutely prohibited from being inoperative for longer than very short periods. The actual availability requirement for ISSS is targeted at 0.99999, meaning that the system should be unavailable for less than 5 minutes a year. (However, if the system is able to recover from a failure and resume operating within 10 seconds, that failure is not counted as unavailable time.)

2. High performance, meaning that the system has to be able to process large numbers of aircraft—as many as 2,440—without "losing" any of them. Networks have to be able to carry the communication loads, and the software has to be able to perform its computations quickly and predictably.

In addition, the following requirements, although not as critical to the safety of the aircraft and their passengers, are major drivers in the shape of the architecture and the principles behind that shape:

- Openness, meaning that the system has to be able to incorporate commercially developed software components, including ATC functions and basic computing services such as graphics display packages
- The ability to field subsets of the system, to handle the case in which the billion-dollar project falls victim to reductions in budget (and hence functionality)—as indeed happened
- The ability to make modifications to the functionality and handle upgrades in hardware and software (new processors, new I/O devices and drivers, new versions of the Ada compiler)
- The ability to operate with and interface to a bewildering set of external systems, both hardware and software, some decades old, others not yet implemented

Finally, this system is unusual in that is must satisfy a great many stakeholders, particularly the controllers, who are the system's end users. While this does not sound unusual, the difference is that controllers have the ability to reject the system if it is not to their liking, even if it meets all its operational requirements. The implications of this situation were profound for the processes of determining requirements and designing the system, and slowed it down substantially.

The term *sector suite* refers to a suite of controllers (each sitting at a control console like the one in Figure 6.4) that together control all of the aircraft in a particular sector of the en route center's airspace. Our oversimplified view of ATC is now enhanced by the fact that aircraft are handed off not only from center to center but also from sector to sector within each center. Sectors are defined in ways unique to each center. They may be defined to balance the load among the center's controllers; for instance, less-traveled sectors may be larger than densely flown areas.

The ISSS design calls for flexibility in how many control stations are assigned to each sector; anywhere from one to four are allowed, and the number can be changed administratively while the system is in operation. Each sector is required to have at least two controllers assigned to it. The first is the radar controller, who monitors the radar surveillance data, communicates with the aircraft, and is responsible for maintaining safe separations. The controller is responsible for managing the tactical situation in the sector. The second controller is the data

FIGURE 6.4 Controllers at a sector suite. Courtesy of William J. Hughes Technical Center; FAA public domain photo.

controller, who retrieves information (such as flight plans) about each aircraft that is either in the sector or soon will be. The data controller provides the radar controller with the information needed about the aircraft's intentions in order to safely and efficiently guide it through the sector.

ISSS is a large system. Here are some numbers to convey a sense of scale:

- ISSS is designed to support up to 210 consoles per en route center. Each console contains its own workstation-class processor; the CPU is an IBM RS/6000.
- ISSS requirements call for a center to control from 400 to 2,440 aircraft tracks simultaneously.
- There may be 16 to 40 radars to support a single facility.
- A center may have from 60 to 90 control positions (each with one or several consoles devoted to it).
- The code to implement ISSS contains about 1 million lines of Ada.

In summary, the ISSS system must do the following:

- Acquire radar target reports that are stored in an existing ATC system called the Host Computer System.
- Convert the radar reports for display and broadcast them to all of the consoles. Each console chooses the reports that it needs to display; any console is capable of displaying any area.

- Handle conflict alerts (potential aircraft collisions) or other data transmitted by the host computer.
- Interface to the Host for input and retrieval of flight plans.
- Provide extensive monitoring and control information, such as network management, to allow site administrators to reconfigure the installation in real time.
- Provide a recording capability for later playback.
- Provide graphical user interface facilities, such as windowing, on the consoles. Special safety-related provisions are necessary, such as window transparency to keep potentially crucial data from being obscured.
- Provide reduced backup capability in the event of failure of the Host, the primary communications network, or the primary radar sensors.

In the next section, we will explore the architecture that fulfilled these requirements.

6.3   Architectural Solution

Just as an architecture affects behavior, performance, fault tolerance, and maintainability, so it is shaped by stringent requirements in any of these areas. In the case of ISSS, by far the most important driving force is the extraordinarily high requirement for system availability: less than 5 minutes per year of downtime. This requirement, more than any other, motivated architectural decisions for ISSS.

We begin our depiction of the ISSS architecture by describing the physical environment hosting the software. Then we give a number of software architecture views (as described in Chapter 2), highlighting the tactics (as described in Chapter 5) employed by each. During this discussion, we introduce a new view not previously discussed: fault tolerance. After discussing the relationships among views, we conclude the architecture picture for ISSS by introducing a refinement of the "abstract common services" tactic for modifiability and extensibility, namely, code templates.

ISSS PHYSICAL VIEW

ISSS is a distributed system, consisting of a number of elements connected by local area networks. Figure 6.5 shows a physical view of the ISSS system. It does not show any of the support systems or their interfaces to the ISSS equipment. Neither does it show any structure of the software. The major elements of the physical view and the roles its elements play are as follows:

- The Host Computer System is the heart of the en route automation system. At each en route center there are two host computers, one primary and the

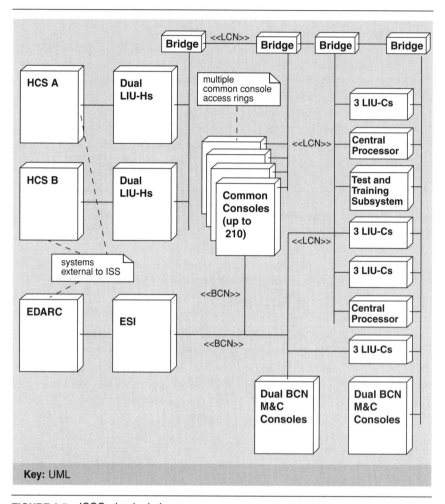

FIGURE 6.5 ISSS physical view

other ready to take over should there be some problem with the primary one. The Host provides processing of both surveillance and flight plan data. Surveillance data is displayed on the en route display consoles used by controllers. Flight data is printed as necessary on flight strip printers, and some flight data elements are displayed on the data tags associated with the radar surveillance information.

- Common consoles are the air traffic controller's workstations. They provide displays of aircraft position information and associated data tags in a plan view format (the radar display), displays of flight plan data in the form of electronic flight strips,[1] and a variety of other information displays. They also allow controllers to modify the flight data and to control the information being displayed and its format. Common consoles are grouped in sector suites of one to four consoles, with each sector suite serving the controller team for one airspace control sector.

- The common consoles are connected to the Host computers by means of the Local Communications Network (LCN), the primary network of ISSS. Each Host is interfaced to the LCN via dual LCN interface units (each called LIU-H), which act as a fault-tolerant redundant pair.

- The LCN is composed of four parallel token ring networks for redundancy and for balancing overall loading. One network supports the broadcast of surveillance data to all processors. One processor is used for point-to-point communications between pairs of processors; one provides a channel for display data to be sent from the common consoles to recording units for layer playback; and one is a spare. Bridges provide connections between the networks of the access rings and those of the backbone. The bridges also provide the ability to substitute the spare ring for a failed ring and to make other alternative routings.

- The Enhanced Direct Access Radar Channel (EDARC) provides a backup display of aircraft position and limited flight data block information to the en route display consoles. EDARC is used in the event of a loss of the display data provided by the host. It provides essentially raw unprocessed radar data and interfaces to an ESI (External System Interface) processor.

- The Backup Communications Network (BCN) is an Ethernet network using TCP/IP protocols. It is used for other system functions besides the EDARC interface and is also used as a backup network in some LCN failure conditions.

- Both the LCN and the BCN have associated *Monitor-and-Control* (M&C) consoles. These give system maintenance personnel an overview of the state of the system and allow them to control its operation. M&C consoles are ordinary consoles that contain special software to support M&C functions and also provide the top-level or global availability management functions.

- The Test and Training subsystem provides the capability to test new hardware and software and to train users without interfering with the ATC mission.

- The central processors are mainframe-class processors that provide the data recording and playback functions for the system in an early version of ISSS.

---

[1] A flight strip is a strip of paper, printed by the system that contains flight plan data about an aircraft currently in or about to arrive in a sector. Before ISSS, these flight strips were annotated by hand in pencil. ISSS was to provide the capability to manipulate strips onscreen.

Each common console is connected to both the LCN and the BCN. Because of the large number of common consoles that may be present at a facility (up to 210), multiple LCN access rings are used to support all of them. This, then, is the physical view for ISSS, highlighting the hardware in which the software resides.

MODULE DECOMPOSITION VIEW

The module elements of the ISSS operational software are called Computer Software Configuration Items (CSCIs), defined in the government software development standard whose use was mandated by the customer. CSCIs correspond largely to work assignments; large teams are devoted to designing, building, and testing them. There is usually some coherent theme associated with each CSCI—some rationale for grouping all of the small software elements (such as packages, processes, etc.) that it contains.

There are five CSCIs in ISSS, as follows:

1. Display Management, responsible for producing and maintaining displays on the common consoles.
2. Common System Services, responsible for providing utilities generally useful in air traffic control software—recall that the developer was planning to build other systems under the larger AAS program.
3. Recording, Analysis, and Playback, responsible for capturing ATC sessions for later analysis.
4. National Airspace System Modification, entailing a modification of the software that resides on the Host (outside the scope of this chapter).
5. The IBM AIX operating system, providing the underlying operating system environment for the operational software.

These CSCIs form units of deliverable documentation and software, they appear in schedule milestones, and each is responsible for a logically related segment of ISSS functionality.

The module decomposition view reflects several modifiability tactics, as discussed in Chapter 5. "Semantic coherence" is the overarching tactic for allocating well-defined and nonoverlapping responsibilities to each CSCI. The Common System Services Module reflects the tactic of "abstract common services." The Recording, Analysis, and Playback CSCI reflects the "record/playback" tactic for testability. The resources of each CSCI are made available through carefully designed software interfaces, reflecting "anticipation of expected changes," "generalizing the module," and "maintaining interface stability."

PROCESS VIEW

The basis of concurrency in ISSS resides in elements called *applications*. An application corresponds roughly to a process, in the sense of Dijkstra's cooperating sequential processes, and is at the core of the approach the ISSS designers adopted for fault tolerance. An application is implemented as an Ada "main" unit (a process schedulable by the operating system) and forms part of a CSCI (which helps us define a mapping between the module decomposition view and this one). Applications communicate by message passing, which is the connector in this component-and-connector view.

ISSS is constructed to operate on a plurality of processors. Processors (as described in the physical view) are logically combined to form a *processor group*, the purpose of which is to host separate copies of one or more applications. This concept is critical to fault tolerance and (therefore) availability. One executing copy is primary, and the others are secondary; hence, the different application copies are referred to as *primary address space* (PAS) or *standby address space* (SAS). The collection of one primary address space and its attendant standby address spaces is called an *operational unit*. A given operational unit resides entirely within the processors of a single processor group, which can consist of up to four processors. Those parts of the ISSS that are not constructed in this fault-tolerant manner (i.e., of coexisting primary and standby versions) simply run independently on different processors. These are called *functional groups* and they are present on each processor as needed, with each copy a separate instance of the program, maintaining its own state.

In summary, an application may be either an operating unit or a functional group. The two differ in whether the application's functionality is backed up by one or more secondary copies, which keep up with the state and data of the primary copy and wait to take over in case the primary copy fails. Operational units have this fault-tolerant design; functional groups do not. An application is implemented as an operational unit if its availability requirements dictate it; otherwise, it is implemented as a functional group.

Applications interact in a client-server fashion. The client of the transaction sends the server a *service request message*, and the server replies with an acknowledgment. (As in all client-server schemes, a particular participant—or application in this case—can be the client in one transaction and the server in another.) Within an operational unit, the PAS sends state change notifications to each of its SASs, which look for time-outs or other signs that they should take over and become primary if the PAS or its processor fails. Figure 6.6 summarizes how the primary and secondary address spaces of an application coordinate with each other to provide backup capability and give their relationship to processor groups.

When a functional group receives a message, it need only respond and update its own state as appropriate. Typically, the PAS of an operational unit receives and responds to messages on behalf of the entire operational unit. It then must update both its own state and the state of its SASs, which involves sending the SASs additional messages.

In the event of a PAS failure, a switchover occurs as follows:

1. A SAS is promoted to the new PAS.
2. The new PAS reconstitutes with the clients of that operational unit (a fixed list for each operational unit) by sending them a message that means,

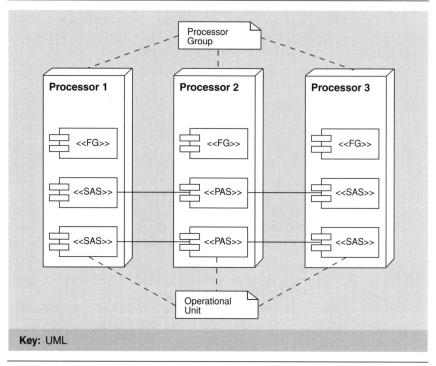

FIGURE 6.6 Functional groups (FG), operational units, processor groups, and primary/standby address spaces

essentially: The operational unit that was serving you has had a failure. Were you waiting for anything from us at the time? It then proceeds to service any requests received in response.

3. A new SAS is started to replace the previous PAS.

4. The newly started SAS announces itself to the new PAS, which starts sending it messages as appropriate to keep it up to date.

If failure is detected within a SAS, a new one is started on some other processor. It coordinates with its PAS and starts receiving state data.

To add a new operational unit, the following step-by-step process is employed:

- Identify the necessary input data and where it resides.
- Identify which operational units require output data from the new operational unit.
- Fit this operational unit's communication patterns into a systemwide acyclic graph in such a way that the graph remains acyclic so that deadlocks will not occur.
- Design the messages to achieve the required data flows.

- Identify internal state data that must be used for checkpointing and the state data that must be included in the update communication from PAS to SAS.
- Partition the state data into messages that fit well on the networks.
- Define the necessary message types.
- Plan for switchover in case of failure: Plan updates to ensure complete state.
- Ensure consistent data in case of switchover.
- Ensure that individual processing steps are completed in less time than a system "heartbeat."
- Plan data-sharing and data-locking protocols with other operational units.

This process is not for novices, but can be navigated straightforwardly by experienced team members. A tactic discussed in a section that follows—code templates—was used to make the process more repeatable and much less error prone.

The process view reflects several availability tactics, including "state resynchronization," "shadowing," "active redundancy," and "removal from service."

CLIENT-SERVER VIEW

Because the applications in the process view interact with each other in client-server fashion, it is reasonable to show a client-server view of ISSS as well, although the behavior it describes largely mirrors that captured by the process view shown earlier. For completeness, Figure 6.7 shows a client-server view of the system.

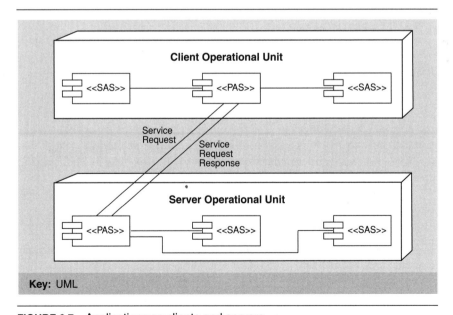

FIGURE 6.7   Applications as clients and servers

The clients and servers were carefully designed to have consistent (as opposed to ad hoc) interfaces. This was facilitated by using simple message-passing protocols for interaction. The result reflects the modifiability tactics of "maintaining interface stability," "component replacement," and "adherence to defined protocols."

CODE VIEW

One view not discussed in Chapter 2 but which sometimes appears in architectures of large systems is the code view. A code view shows how functionality is mapped to code units.

In ISSS, an Ada (main) *program* is created from one or more source files; it typically comprises a number of *subprograms*, some of which are gathered into separately compilable *packages*. The ISSS is composed of several such programs, many of which operate in a client-server manner.

An Ada program may contain one or more *tasks*, which are Ada entities capable of executing concurrently with each other. These are the code-view corollary of the processes described in the process view. Because Ada tasks are managed by the Ada runtime system, ISSS also employs a mapping of Ada tasks onto UNIX (AIX) processes, which means that all individual threads of control (whether separate Ada programs or tasks within a single Ada program) are independent AIX processes operating concurrently.

Applications (i.e., operational units and functional groups) are decomposed into Ada packages, some of which include only type definitions and some of which are re-used across applications. *Packaging* is a design activity intended to embody abstraction and information hiding, and it is carried out by an operational unit's chief designer.

LAYERED VIEW

Underlying the operation of the ATC application programs on the ISSS processors system is a commercial UNIX operating system, AIX. However, UNIX does not provide all the services necessary to support a fault-tolerant distributed system such as ISSS. Therefore, additional system services software was added. Figure 6.8 shows as a set of layers the overall software environment in a typical ISSS processor.[2]

The lowest two rows of elements above AIX represent extensions to AIX that run within the AIX kernel's address space. Because of performance requirements

---

[2] Strictly speaking, Figure 6.8 is an *overlay* between a layered view and a component-and-connector view, because it shows runtime connections between the submodules in the layers. In two cases, AAS Services and Other Device Driver, the connections among these and other submodules within the layered view are not shown, because there are so many that it would clutter the diagram. These services are freely used by most of the layered system. The actual connections would be listed in the supporting documentation for this view.

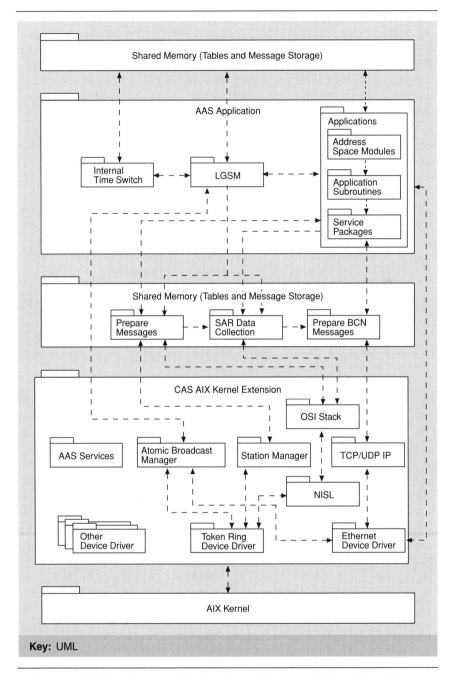

FIGURE 6.8 ISSS software architecture layers. The associations show data and/or control flow, making this an overlay of layers and a component-and-connector view.

and for compatibility with the AIX operating system, these extensions are generally small programs written in the C language. Since they run within the kernels' address space, faults in these programs can potentially damage AIX itself; hence, they must be relatively small, trusted programs reflecting the "limit exposure" tactic, discussed in Chapter 5. Although the tactic is security based—namely, to prevent denial of service—in ISSS it is used to enhance availability, which is a complementary goal. Happily, sometimes tactics serve multiple quality attributes well.

The Atomic Broadcast Manager (ABM) plays a key role in the communication among the Local Availability Manager modules within a sector suite to manage the availability of suite functions. The Station Manager provides datagram services on the LCN and serves as the local representative of the LCN network management services. The Network Interface Sublayer provides a similar function for the point-to-point messages, sharing its network information with the Station Manager.

The next two layers represent operating system extensions that execute outside the AIX kernel's address space and therefore cannot directly damage AIX if they contain faults. These programs are generally written in Ada.

Prepare Messages handles LCN messages for application programs. Prepare BCN Messages performs a similar function for messages to be sent on the BCN. One function of these programs is to determine which of the multiple redundant copies of an application program within a sector suite is the primary and thus is to receive messages. The Local Availability Manager provides the control information needed to make this determination.

The top layer is where the applications reside. The Local Availability Manager and the Internal Time Synchronization programs are application-level system services. The Local Availability Manager is responsible for managing the initiation, termination, and availability of the application programs. It communicates with each address space on its own processor to control its operation and check its status. It also communicates with the Local Availability Manager on the other processors within its sector suite to manage the availability of suite functions, including switching from a primary to a backup copy of an application program when appropriate. The Local Availability Manager communicates with the Global Availability Management application that resides on the M&C consoles to report status and to accept control commands. The Internal Time Synchronization program synchronizes the processor's clock with that of the other ISSS processors, which is crucial to the operation of the availability management functions. (See the fault tolerance view, in Figure 6.9.)

A NEW VIEW: FAULT TOLERANCE

As we said, the views listed in Chapter 2 are not exhaustive. In fact, there is no exhaustive list of views that constitute the complete software architecture for all systems or for any system. A welcome trend in software architecture is the recognition of the importance of architecture in achieving quality attributes, and there-

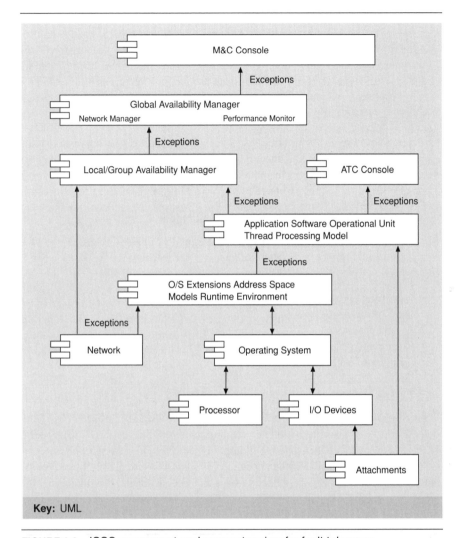

FIGURE 6.9   ISSS component-and-connector view for fault tolerance

fore the importance of explicitly stating the quality attributes that the architecture is to provide. Toward this end, architects often produce views that show how the architecture achieves a particular quality attribute: a security view, for example. For runtime qualities, these views are in the component-and-connector category, showing runtime element interactions. For non-runtime qualities, these views are in the module category, showing how the implementation units are designed to achieve (for example) modifiability.

The high availability requirements for ISSS elevated fault tolerance to an important role in the design of the system. For one thing, a cold system restart in the event of a failure was out of the question. Immediate (or at least rapid) switchover to a component on standby seemed the best approach. As design progressed and this idea became clearer, a new architectural structure emerged: the fault-tolerant hierarchy (Figure 6.9). This structure describes how faults are detected and isolated and how the system recovers. Whereas the PAS/SAS scheme traps and recovers from errors that are confined within a single application, the fault-tolerant hierarchy is designed to trap and recover from errors that are the result of cross-application interaction.

The ISSS fault-tolerant hierarchy provides various levels of fault detection and recovery. Each level asynchronously

- Detects errors in self, peers, and lower levels.
- Handles exceptions from lower levels.
- Diagnoses, recovers, reports, or raises exceptions.

Each level is meant to produce another increment in system availability above that produced by the lower levels. The levels are as follows:

- Physical (network, processor, and I/O devices)
- Operating system
- Runtime environment
- Application
- Local availability
- Group availability
- Global availability
- System monitor and control

Fault detection and isolation are performed at each level in the hierarchy. Fault detection is by built-in tests, event time-outs, network circuit tests, group membership protocol, and, as a last resort, human reaction to alarms and indicators.

Fault recovery is performed at each level in the software hierarchy and can be automatic or manual. For the Local, Group, and Global Availability managers, the recovery methods are table driven. In a PAS, there are four types of recovery from failure. The type of recovery used depends on the current operational status and is determined by the Local Availability Manager using decision tables, as follows:

- In a switchover, the SAS takes over almost immediately from its PAS.
- A warm restart uses checkpoint data (written to nonvolatile memory).
- A cold restart uses default data and loses state history.
- A cutover is used to transition to new (or old) logic or adaptation data.

Redundancy is provided by network hardware (LCN, BCN, and associated bridges), processor hardware (up to four processors per processor group, redundant recording), and software (multiple address spaces per operational unit).

In addition to the availability tactics already seen with the process view, the fault tolerance view adds "ping/echo" and "heartbeat" as ways to detect failures, *exception* to percolate errors to the appropriate place for correction, and *spare* to perform recovery.

RELATING THE VIEWS TO EACH OTHER

During the preceding discussion, the elements in one view made "guest appearances" in other views. Although views form the backbone of understanding a system, deeper insight is often gained by examining the relations the views have to each other and, in particular, from examining mappings from view to view. This imparts a more holistic view of the architecture.

In ISSS, CSCIs are elements in the module decomposition view. They are composed of applications, which in turn are elements in the process view and the client-server view. Applications are implemented as Ada programs and packages, shown in the code view, which in turn map to threads, which are elements in the concurrency view (not shown). The layered view describes the functionality assigned to the modules in the decomposition view in a way that shows what they are allowed to use. Finally, a specialized view focusing on the achievement of a particular runtime quality attribute—the fault tolerance view—uses the elements of the process, layer, and module views.

Chapter 9, which covers how to document a software architecture, will prescribe a special place in the documentation package for capturing view relationships. For ISSS, that mapping would include tables that list the elements from the various views and show how they correspond to each other as described above.

ADAPTATION DATA

ISSS makes extensive use of the modifiability tactic of "configuration files," which it calls adaptation data. Site-specific adaptation data tailors the ISSS system across the 22 en route centers in which it was planned to be deployed, and so-called preset adaptation data tailors the software to changes that arise during development and deployment but which do not represent site-specific differences. Adaptation data represents an elegant and crucial shortcut to modifying the system in the face of site-specific requirements, user- or center-specific preferences, configuration changes, requirements changes, and other aspects of the software that might be expected to vary over time and across deployment sites. In effect, the software has been designed to read its operating parameters and behavioral specifications from input data; it is therefore completely general with respect to the set of behaviors that can be represented in that data (reflecting the "generalize the module" tactic). For example, a requirements change to split the data in one ATC window view into two separate windows—a nontrivial change in many systems—could be accomplished by changing the adaptation data and a few lines of code.

The negative side is that adaptation data presents a complicated mechanism to maintainers. For example, although it is trivial (from an operational point of view) to add new commands or command syntax to the system, the implementation of this flexibility is in fact a complicated interpretive language all its own. Also, complicated interactions may occur between various pieces of adaptation data, which could affect correctness, and there are no automated or semiautomated mechanisms in place to guard against the effects of such inconsistencies. Finally, adaptation data significantly increases the state space within which the operational software must correctly perform, and this has broad implications for system testing.

REFINING THE "ABSTRACT COMMON SERVICES" TACTIC: CODE TEMPLATES FOR APPLICATIONS

Recall that the primary–secondary address space scheme described earlier relies on redundancy to achieve fault tolerance: Copies of the software are stored on different processors. While the primary copy is executing, it sends state information from time to time to all of the secondary copies so that they can take up execution when called on. The implementation plan for these copies called for both to come from true copies of the same *source code*. Even though the primary and secondary copies are never doing the same thing at the same time (the primary is performing its duty and sending state updates to its backups, and the secondaries are waiting to leap into action and accepting state updates), both programs come from identical copies of the same source code. To accomplish this, the contractor developed a standard code template for each application; the template is illustrated in Figure 6.10.

The structure is a continuous loop that services incoming events. If the event is one that causes the application to take a normal (non-fault-tolerant-related) action, it carries out the appropriate action, followed by an update of its backup counterparts' data so that the counterpart can take over if necessary. Most applications process between 50 and 100 normal events. Other events involve the transfer (transmission and reception) of state and data updates. The last set of events involves both the announcement that this unit has become the primary address space and requests from clients for services that the former (now failed) primary address space did not complete.

This template has architectural implications: It makes it simple to add new applications to the system with a minimum of concern for the actual workings of the fault-tolerant mechanisms designed into the approach. Coders and maintainers of applications do not need to know about message-handling mechanisms except abstractly, and they do not need to ensure that their applications are fault tolerant—that has been handled at a higher (architectural) level of design.

Code templates represent a refinement of the "abstract common services" tactic; the part of each application that is common is instantiated in the template. This tactic is related to several other tactics for modifiability. It reflects an "anticipation of expected changes" in the parts it leaves variable and it gives the processes

```
terminate:= false
initialize application/application protocols

ask for current state (image request)
Loop
   Get_event
   Case Event_Type is

   -- "normal" (non-fault-tolerant-related) requests to perform actions;
   -- only happens if this unit is the current primary address space
   when X=> Process X
            Send state data updates to other address spaces
   when Y=>Process Y
            Send state data updates to other address spaces
   ...
   when Terminate_Directive => clean up resources; terminate := true

   when State_Data_Update => apply to state data
   -- will only happen if this unit is a secondary address space, receiving
   -- the update from the primary after it has completed a "normal" action

   -- sending, receiving state data
   when Image_Request =>  send current state data to new address space
   when State_Data_Image => Initialize state data

   when Switch_Directive => notify service packages of change in rank

   -- these are requests that come in after a PAS/SAS switchover; they
   -- report services that they had requested from the old (failed) PAS
   -- which this unit (now the PAS) must complete. A,B, etc. are the names
   -- of the clients.
   when Recon_from_A=>reconstitute A
   when Recon_from_B=>reconstitute B
   ...
   when others=>log error
   end case
exit when terminate
end loop
```

FIGURE 6.10   Code structure template for fault-tolerant ISSS applications

a "semantic coherence," because they all do the same thing when viewed abstractly. The template lets programmers concentrate on the details of their application, leading to "generalizing the module." And by making the interfaces and protocols part of the template, they "maintain interface stability" and achieve "adherence to defined protocols."

Table 6.1 summarizes the approaches and tactics by which the ISSS software architecture met its quality goals.

TABLE 6.1 How the ATC System Achieves Its Quality Goals

Goal	How Achieved	Tactic(s) Used
High Availability	Hardware redundancy (both processor and network); software redundancy (layered fault detection and recovery)	State resynchronization; shadowing; active redundancy; removal from service; limit exposure; ping/echo; heartbeat; exception; spare
High Performance	Distributed multiprocessors; front-end schedulability analysis, and network modeling	Introduce concurrency
Openness	Interface wrapping and layering	Abstract common services; maintain interface stability
Modifiability	Templates and table-driven adaptation data; careful assignment of module responsbilities; strict use of specified interfaces	Abstract common services; semantic coherence; maintain interface stability; anticipate expected changes; generalize the module; component replacement; adherence to defined procotols; configuration files
Ability to Field Subsets	Appropriate separation of concerns	Abstract common services
Interoperability	Client-server division of functionality and message-based communications	Adherence to defined protocols; maintain interface stability

6.4 Summary

Like all of the case studies in this book, ISSS illustrates how architectural solutions can be the key to achieving the needs of an application. Table 6.1 summarized the key approaches used. Because of its projected long life, high cost, large size, important function, and high visibility, ISSS was subject to extraordinary change pressures over and above its demanding operational requirements. Human–computer interfaces, new hardware, new commercial components, operating system and network upgrades, and capacity increases were not just likely but foregone conclusions. The architecture, by using a wide range of fault tolerance mechanisms (and code templates), including hardware and software redundancy and layered fault detection, and by using distributed multiprocess computing with client-server message passing, was able to satisfy its complex, wide-ranging operational requirements.

A footnote to our story is the intensive software audit that was carried out on the ISSS architecture by a blue-ribbon panel of experts when the U.S. government was considering abandoning ISSS in favor of a simpler, less expensive solution. The audit assessed the architecture's ability to deliver the required performance and availability and included modifiability exercises that walked through several change scenarios, including the following:

- Making major modifications to the M&C position's human–computer interface
- Importing third-party-developed air traffic applications into the ISSS system
- Adding new ATC views to the system
- Replacing the RS/6000 processors with a chip of similar capability
- Deleting electronic flight strips from the requirements
- Increasing the system's maximum capacity of flight tracks by 50 percent

In every case, the audit found that the ISSS software architecture had been designed so that the modifications would be straightforward and, in some cases, almost trivial. This is a tribute to its careful design and its explicit consideration of quality attributes and the architectural tactics to achieve them.

6.5 For Further Reading

The saga of the FAA's attempts to upgrade its air traffic control software has been written about extensively; for example, by [Gibbs 94]. The effort to audit the ISSS system for salvageability was reported by [Brown 95]. In these papers, maintainability is treated as a dual quality related not only to the properties of the system but also to the capabilities of the organization slated to perform the maintenance. This important aspect of maintainability—the necessary fit between the maintenance that a system needs and the maintenance that an organization is prepared to provide for it—is not usually discussed.

6.6 Discussion Questions

1. High availability was a main impetus behind the architecture presented in this chapter. How were other quality attributes, such as performance, affected by this requirement? How might the architecture change if this requirement were removed?

2. How many architectural patterns can you recognize in the architecture for ISSS?

3. Construct quality attribute scenarios, as described in Chapter 4, for as many of the requirements given in Section 6.2 as you can. Where necessary information is missing, propose reasonable substitutions.

7

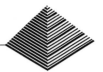

Designing the Architecture

with Felix Bachmann

> *We have observed two traits common to virtually all of the successful*
> *object-oriented systems we have encountered, and noticeably absent*
> *from the ones that we count as failures: the existence of a strong*
> *architectural vision and the application of a well-managed iterative*
> *and incremental development cycle.*
> — Grady Booch [Stikeleather 96]

Up to this point, we have laid the foundations for creating an architecture by presenting a broad set of basic concepts and principles, principally the business aspects of architecture (Chapter 1), architectural views and structures (Chapter 2), quality attributes (Chapter 4), and architectural tactics and patterns for achieving them (Chapter 5). Chapters 3 and 6 presented case studies to cement the concepts presented so far.

We now turn our attention to the design of an architecture and what you can do as it starts to come into being. This chapter will cover four topics:

- Architecture in the life cycle
- Designing the architecture
- Forming the team structure and its relationship to the architecture
- Creating a skeletal system

7.1 Architecture in the Life Cycle

Any organization that embraces architecture as a foundation for its software development processes needs to understand its place in the life cycle. Several life-cycle models exist in the literature, but one that puts architecture squarely in

153

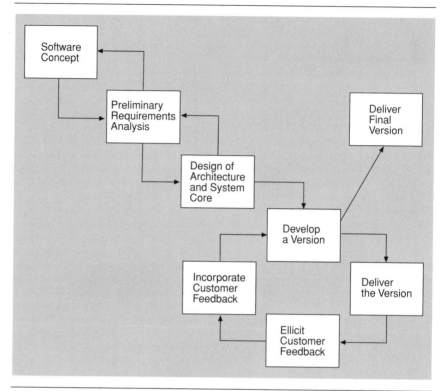

FIGURE 7.1   Evolutionary Delivery Life Cycle

the middle of things is the Evolutionary Delivery Life Cycle model shown in Figure 7.1. The intent of this model is to get user and customer feedback and iterate through several releases before the final release. The model also allows the adding of functionality with each iteration and the delivery of a limited version once a sufficient set of features has been developed. (For more about this life-cycle model, see For Further Reading.)

WHEN CAN I BEGIN DESIGNING?

The life-cycle model shows the design of the architecture as iterating with preliminary requirements analysis. Clearly, you cannot begin the design until you have some idea of the system requirements. On the other hand, it does not take many requirements in order for design to begin.

An architecture is "shaped" by some collection of functional, quality, and business requirements. We call these shaping requirements *architectural drivers* and we see examples of them in our case studies. The architecture of the A-7E discussed in Chapter 3 is shaped by its modifiability and performance requirements.

The architecture for the air traffic control system discussed in Chapter 6 is shaped by its availability requirements. In the flight simulator software presented in Chapter 8, we will see an architecture shaped by performance and modifiability requirements. And so on.

To determine the architectural drivers, identify the highest priority business goals. There should be relatively few of these. Turn these business goals into quality scenarios or use cases. From this list, choose the ones that will have the most impact on the architecture. These are the architectural drivers, and there should be fewer than ten. The Architecture Tradeoff Analysis Method of Chapter 11 uses a *utility tree* to help turn the business drivers into quality scenarios.

Once the architectural drivers are known, the architectural design can begin. The requirements analysis process will then be influenced by the questions generated during architectural design—one of the reverse-direction arrows shown in Figure 7.1.

7.2   Designing the Architecture

In this section we describe a method for designing an architecture to satisfy both quality requirements and functional requirements. We call this method Attribute-Driven Design (ADD). ADD takes as input a set of quality attribute scenarios and employs knowledge about the relation between quality attribute achievement and architecture in order to design the architecture. The ADD method can be viewed as an extension to most other development methods, such as the Rational Unified Process. The Rational Unified Process has several steps that result in the high-level design of an architecture but then proceeds to detailed design and implementation. Incorporating ADD into it involves modifying the steps dealing with the high-level design of the architecture and then following the process as described by Rational.

ATTRIBUTE-DRIVEN DESIGN

ADD is an approach to defining a software architecture that bases the decomposition process on the quality attributes the software has to fulfill. It is a recursive decomposition process where, at each stage, tactics and architectural patterns are chosen to satisfy a set of quality scenarios and then functionality is allocated to instantiate the module types provided by the pattern. ADD is positioned in the life cycle after requirements analysis and, as we have said, can begin when the architectural drivers are known with some confidence.

The output of ADD is the first several levels of a module decomposition view of an architecture and other views as appropriate. Not all details of the views result from an application of ADD; the system is described as a set of containers for functionality and the interactions among them. This is the first articulation of architecture during the design process and is therefore necessarily coarse grained. Nevertheless, it is critical for achieving the desired qualities, and it provides a framework for achieving the functionality. The difference between an architecture resulting from ADD and one ready for implementation rests in the more detailed design decisions that need to be made. These could be, for example, the decision to use specific object-oriented design patterns or a specific piece of middleware that brings with it many architectural constraints. The architecture designed by ADD may have intentionally deferred this decision to be more flexible.

There are a number of different design processes that could be created using the general scenarios of Chapter 4 and the tactics and patterns of Chapter 5. Each process assumes different things about how to "chunk" the design work and about the essence of the design process. We discuss ADD in some detail to illustrate how we are applying the general scenarios and tactics, and hence how we are "chunking" the work, and what we believe is the essence of the design process.

We demonstrate the ADD method by using it to design a product line architecture for a garage door opener within a home information system. The opener is responsible for raising and lowering the door via a switch, remote control, or the home information system. It is also possible to diagnose problems with the opener from within the home information system.

Sample Input.   The input to ADD is a set of requirements. ADD assumes functional requirements (typically expressed as use cases) and constraints as input, as do other design methods. However, in ADD, we differ from those methods in our treatment of *quality requirements*. ADD mandates that quality requirements be expressed as a set of system-specific quality scenarios. The general scenarios discussed in Chapter 4 act as input to the requirements process and provide a checklist to be used in developing the system-specific scenarios. System-specific scenarios should be defined to the detail necessary for the application. In our examples, we omit several portions of a fully fleshed scenario since these portions do not contribute to the design process.

For our garage door example, the quality scenarios include the following:

- The device and controls for opening and closing the door are different for the various products in the product line, as already mentioned. They may include controls from within a home information system. The product architecture for a specific set of controls should be directly derivable from the product line architecture.

- The processor used in different products will differ. The product architecture for each specific processor should be directly derivable from the product line architecture.

- If an obstacle (person or object) is detected by the garage door during descent, it must halt (alternately re-open) within 0.1 second.

- The garage door opener should be accessible for diagnosis and administration from within the home information system using a product-specific diagnosis protocol. It should be possible to directly produce an architecture that reflects this protocol.

Beginning ADD.   We have already introduced architectural drivers. ADD depends on the identification of the drivers and can start as soon as all of them are known. Of course, during the design the determination of which architectural drivers are key may change either as a result of better understanding of the requirements or as a result of changing requirements. Still, the process can begin when the driver requirements are known with some assurance.

In the following section we discuss ADD itself.

ADD Steps.   We begin by briefly presenting the steps performed when designing an architecture using the ADD method. We will then discuss the steps in more detail.

1. *Choose the module to decompose*. The module to start with is usually the whole system. All required inputs for this module should be available (constraints, functional requirements, quality requirements).

2. *Refine the module according to these steps*:
    a. Choose the architectural drivers from the set of concrete quality scenarios and functional requirements. This step determines what is important for this decomposition.
    b. Choose an architectural pattern that satisfies the architectural drivers. Create (or select) the pattern based on the tactics that can be used to achieve the drivers. Identify child modules required to implement the tactics.
    c. Instantiate modules and allocate functionality from the use cases and represent using multiple views.
    d. Define interfaces of the child modules. The decomposition provides modules and constraints on the types of module interactions. Document this information in the interface document for each module.
    e. Verify and refine use cases and quality scenarios and make them constraints for the child modules. This step verifies that nothing important was forgotten and prepares the child modules for further decomposition or implementation.

3. *Repeat the steps above for every module that needs further decomposition.*

1. Choose the Module to Decompose – The following are all modules: system, subsystem, and submodule. The decomposition typically starts with the system, which is then decomposed into subsystems, which are further decomposed into submodules.

In our example, the garage door opener is the system. One constraint at this level is that the opener must interoperate with the home information system.

2.a. Choose the Architectural Drivers – As we said, architectural drivers are the combination of functional and quality requirements that "shape" the architecture or the particular module under consideration. The drivers will be found among the top-priority requirements for the module.

In our example, the four scenarios we have shown are architectural drivers. In the systems on which this example is based, there were dozens of quality scenarios. In examining them, we see a requirement for real-time performance,[1] and modifiability to support product lines. We also see a requirement that online diagnosis be supported. All of these requirements must be addressed in the initial decomposition of the system.

The determination of architectural drivers is not always a top-down process. Sometimes detailed investigation is required to understand the ramifications of particular requirements. For example, to determine if performance is an issue for a particular system configuration, a prototypical implementation of a piece of the system may be required. In our example, determining that the performance requirement is an architectural driver requires examining the mechanics of a garage door and the speed of the potential processors.

We will base our decomposition of a module on the architectural drivers. Other requirements apply to that module, but, by choosing the drivers, we are reducing the problem to satisfying the most important ones. We do not treat all of the requirements as equal; the less important requirements are satisfied within the constraints of the most important. This is a significant difference between ADD and other architecture design methods.

2.b. Choose an Architectural Pattern – As discussed in Chapter 5, for each quality there are identifiable tactics (and patterns that implement these tactics) that can be used in an architecture design to achieve a specific quality. Each tactic is designed to realize one or more quality attributes, but the patterns in which they are embedded have an impact on other quality attributes. In an architecture design, a composition of many such tactics is used to achieve a balance between the required multiple qualities. Achievement of the quality and functional requirements is analyzed during the refinement step.

The goal of step *2b* is to establish an overall architectural pattern consisting of module types. The pattern satisfies the architectural drivers and is constructed by composing selected tactics. Two main factors guide tactic selection. The first is the drivers themselves. The second is the side effects that a pattern implementing a tactic has on other qualities.

For example, a classic tactic to achieve modifiability is the use of an interpreter. Adding an interpreted specification language to a system simplifies the creation of new functions or the modification of existing ones. Macro recording and execution is an example of an interpreter. HTML is an interpreted language

---

[1] A 0.1-second response when an obstacle is detected may not seem like a tight deadline, but we are discussing a mass market where using a processor with limited power translates into substantial cost savings. Also, a garage door has a great deal of inertia and is difficult to stop.

that specifies the look-and-feel of Web pages. An interpreter is an excellent technique for achieving modifiability at runtime, but it has a strong negative influence on performance. The decision to use one depends on the relative importance of modifiability versus performance. A decision may be made to use an interpreter for a portion of the overall pattern and to use other tactics for other portions.

If we examine the available tactics from Chapter 5 in light of our architectural drivers, we see performance and modifiability as the critical quality attributes. The modifiability tactics are "localize changes," "prevent the ripple effect," and "defer binding time." Moreover, since our modifiability scenarios are concerned primarily with changes that will occur during system design, the primary tactic is "localize changes." We choose semantic coherence and information hiding as our tactics and combine them to define virtual machines for the affected areas. The performance tactics are "resource demand" and "resource arbitration." We choose one example of each: "increase computational efficiency" and "choose scheduling policy." This yields the following tactics:

- *Semantic coherence* and *information hiding.* Separate responsibilities dealing with the user interface, communication, and sensors into their own modules. We call these modules *virtual machines* and we expect all three to vary because of the differing products that will be derived from the architecture. Separate the responsibilities associated with diagnosis as well.
- *Increase computational efficiency.* The performance-critical computations should be made as efficient as possible.
- *Schedule wisely.* The performance-critical computations should be scheduled to ensure the achievement of the timing deadline.

Figure 7.2 shows an architectural pattern derived from the combination of these tactics. This is not the only pattern that can be derived, but it is a plausible one.

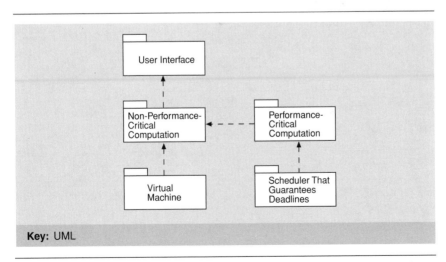

FIGURE 7.2 Architectural pattern that utilizes tactics to achieve garage door drivers

2.c. Instantiate Modules and Allocate Functionality Using Multiple Views – In the preceding section, we discussed how the quality architectural drivers determine the decomposition structure of a module via the use of tactics. As a matter of fact, in that step we defined the module types of the decomposition step. We now show how those module types will be instantiated.

Instantiate modules. In Figure 7.2, we identified a non-performance-critical computation running on top of a virtual machine that manages communication and sensor interactions. The software running on top of the virtual machine is typically an application. In a concrete system we will normally have more than one module. There will be one for each "group" of functionality; these will be instances of the types shown in the pattern. Our criterion for allocating functionality is similar to that used in functionality-based design methods, such as most object-oriented design methods.

For our example, we allocate the responsibility for managing obstacle detection and halting the garage door to the performance-critical section since this functionality has a deadline. The management of the normal raising and lowering of the door has no timing deadline, and so we treat it as non-performance-critical section. The diagnosis capabilities are also non-performance critical. Thus, the non-performance-critical module of Figure 7.2 becomes instantiated as diagnosis and raising/lowering door modules in Figure 7.3. We also identify several responsibilities of the virtual machine: communication and sensor reading and actuator control. This yields two instances of the virtual machine that are also shown in Figure 7.3.

The result of this step is a plausible decomposition of a module. The next steps verify how well the decomposition achieves the required functionality.

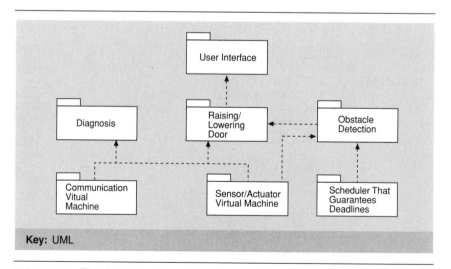

FIGURE 7.3 First-level decomposition of garage door opener

Allocate functionality. Applying use cases that pertain to the parent module helps the architect gain a more detailed understanding of the distribution of functionality. This also may lead to adding or removing child modules to fulfill all the functionality required. At the end, every use case of the parent module must be representable by a sequence of responsibilities within the child modules.

Assigning responsibilities to the children in a decomposition also leads to the discovery of necessary information exchange. This creates a producer/consumer relationship between those modules, which needs to be recorded. At this point in the design, it is not important to define how the information is exchanged. Is the information pushed or pulled? Is it passed as a message or a call parameter? These are all questions that need to be answered later in the design process. At this point only the information itself and the producer and consumer roles are of interest. This is an example of the type of information left unresolved by ADD and resolved during detailed design.

Some tactics introduce specific patterns of interaction between module types. A tactic using an intermediary of type publish-subscribe, for example, will introduce a pattern, "Publish" for one of the modules and a pattern "Subscribe" for the other. These patterns of interaction should be recorded since they translate into responsibilities for the affected modules.

These steps should be sufficient to gain confidence that the system can deliver the desired functionality. To check if the required qualities can be met, we need more than just the responsibilities so far allocated. Dynamic and runtime deployment information is also required to analyze the achievement of qualities such as performance, security, and reliability. Therefore, we examine additional views along with the module decomposition view.

Represent the architecture with views. In Chapter 2, we introduced a number of distinct architectural views. In our experience with ADD, one view from each of the three major groups of views (module decomposition, concurrency, and deployment) have been sufficient to begin with. The method itself does not depend on the particular views chosen, and if there is a need to show other aspects, such as runtime objects, additional views can be introduced. We now briefly discuss how ADD uses these three common views.

- *Module decomposition view.* Our discussion above shows how the module decomposition view provides containers for holding responsibilities as they are discovered. Major data flow relationships among the modules are also identified through this view.

- *Concurrency view.* In the concurrency view dynamic aspects of a system such as parallel activities and synchronization can be modeled. This modeling helps to identify resource contention problems, possible deadlock situations, data consistency issues, and so forth. Modeling the concurrency in a system likely leads to discovery of new responsibilities of the modules, which are recorded in the module view. It can also lead to discovery of new modules, such as a resource manager, in order to solve issues of concurrent access to a scarce resource and the like.

The concurrency view is one of the component-and-connector views. The components are instances of the modules in the module decomposition view, and the connectors are the carriers of *virtual threads*. A "virtual thread" describes an execution path through the system or parts of it. This should not be confused with operating system threads (or processes), which implies other properties like memory/processor allocation. Those properties are not of interest on the level at which we are designing. Nevertheless, after the decisions on an operating system and on the deployment of modules to processing units are made, virtual threads have to be mapped onto operating system threads. This is done during detailed design.

The connectors in a concurrency view are those that deal with threads such as "synchronizes with," "starts," "cancels," and "communicates with." A concurrency view shows instances of the modules in the module decomposition view as a means of understanding the mapping between those two views. It is important to know that a synchronization point is located in a specific module so that this responsibility can be assigned at the right place.

To understand the concurrency in a system, the following use cases are illuminating:

- *Two users doing similar things at the same time.* This helps in recognizing resource contention or data integrity problems. In our garage door example, one user may be closing the door remotely while another is opening the door from a switch.
- *One user performing multiple activities simultaneously.* This helps to uncover data exchange and activity control problems. In our example, a user may be performing diagnostics while simultaneously opening the door.
- *Starting up the system.* This gives a good overview of permanent running activities in the system and how to initialize them. It also helps in deciding on an initialization strategy, such as everything in parallel or everything in sequence or any other model. In our example, does the startup of the garage door opener system depend on the availability of the home information system? Is the garage door opener system always working, waiting for a signal, or is it started and stopped with every door opening and closing?
- *Shutting down the system.* This helps to uncover issues of cleaning up, such as achieving and saving a consistent system state.

In our example, we can see a point of synchronization in the sensor/actuator virtual machine. The performance-critical section must sample the sensor, as must the raising/lowering door section. It is plausible that the performance-critical section will interrupt the sensor/actuator virtual machine when it is performing an action for the raising/lowering door section. We need a synchronization mechanism for the sensor/actuator virtual machine. We see this by examining the virtual thread for the performance-critical section and the virtual thread for the raising/lowering door section, and observing that these two threads both involve the sensor/actuator virtual machine. The crossing of two virtual threads is an indication that some synchronization mechanism should be employed.

Concurrency might also be a point of variation, discussed in Chapter 14 on software product lines. For some products a sequential initialization will work well, while for others everything should be done in parallel. If the decomposition does not support techniques to vary the method of initialization (e.g., by exchanging a component), then the decomposition should be adjusted.

- *Deployment view.* If multiple processors or specialized hardware is used in a system, additional responsibilities may arise from deployment to the hardware. Using a deployment view helps to determine and design a deployment that supports achieving the desired qualities. The deployment view results in the virtual threads of the concurrency view being decomposed into virtual threads within a particular processor and messages that travel between processors to initiate the next entry in the sequence of actions. Thus, it is the basis for analyzing the network traffic and for determining potential congestion.

  The deployment view also helps in deciding if multiple instances of some modules are needed. For example, a reliability requirement may force us to duplicate critical functionality on different processors. A deployment view also supports reasoning about the use of special-purpose hardware.

  The derivation of the deployment view is not arbitrary. As with the module decomposition and concurrency views, the architecture drivers help determine the allocation of components to hardware. Tactics such as replication offer a means to achieve high performance or reliability by deploying replicas on different processors. Other tactics such as a real-time scheduling mechanism actually prohibit deployment on different processors. Functional considerations usually guide the deployment of the parts that are not predetermined by the selected tactics.

The crossing of a virtual thread from one processor to another generates responsibilities for different modules. It indicates a communication requirement between the processors. Some module must be responsible for managing the communication; this responsibility must be recorded in the module decomposition view.

In our example, deployment issues are found in the division of responsibilities between the door opener system and the home information system. Which is responsible for authenticating a remote request, and what is the communication protocol between the two?

2.d. Define Interfaces of the Child Modules – For purposes of ADD, an interface of a module shows the services and properties provided and required. This is different from a signature. It documents what others can use and on what they can depend.

Analyzing and documenting the decomposition in terms of structure (module decomposition view), dynamism (concurrency view), and runtime (deployment view) uncovers the interaction assumptions for the child modules, which should be documented in their interfaces. The module view documents

- producers/consumers of information.
- patterns of interaction that require modules to provide services and to use them.

The concurrency view documents

- interactions among threads that lead to the interface of a module providing or using a service.
- the information that a component is active—for example, has its own thread running.
- the information that a component synchronizes, sequentializes, and perhaps blocks calls.

The deployment view documents

- the hardware requirements, such as special-purpose hardware.
- some timing requirements, such as that the computation speed of a processor has to be at least 10 MIPS.
- communication requirements, such as that information should not be updated more than once every second.

All this information should be available in the modules' interface documentation.

2.e. Verify and Refine Use Cases and Quality Scenarios as Constraints for the Child Modules – The steps enumerated thus far amount to a proposal for a module decomposition. This decomposition must be verified and the child modules must be prepared for their own decomposition.

Functional requirements. Each child module has responsibilities that derive partially from considering decomposition of the functional requirements. Those responsibilities can be translated into use cases for the module. Another way of defining use cases is to split and refine the parent use cases. For example, a use case that initializes the whole system is broken into the initializations of subsystems. This approach has traceability because an analyst can follow the refinement.

In our example, the initial responsibilities for the garage door opener were to open and close the door on request, either locally or remotely; to stop the door within 0.1 second when an obstacle is detected; and to interact with the home information system and support remote diagnostics. The responsibilities are decomposed into the following functional groups corresponding to the modules:

- *User interface.* Recognize user requests and translate them into the form expected by the raising/lowering door module.
- *Raising/lowering door module.* Control actuators to raise or lower the door. Stop the door when it reaches either fully open or fully closed.

- *Obstacle detection.* Recognize when an obstacle is detected and either stop the descent of the door or reverse it.
- *Communication virtual machine.* Manage all communication with the home information system.
- *Sensor/actuator virtual machine.* Manage all interactions with the sensors and actuators.
- *Scheduler.* Guarantee that the obstacle detector will meet its deadlines.
- *Diagnosis.* Manage the interactions with the home information system devoted to diagnosis.

Constraints. Constraints of the parent module can be satisfied in one of the following ways:

- The decomposition satisfies the constraint. For example, the constraint of using a certain operating system can be satisfied by defining the operating system as a child module. The constraint has been satisfied and nothing more needs to be done.
- The constraint is satisfied by a single child module. For example, the constraint of using a special protocol can be satisfied by defining an encapsulation child module for the protocol. The constraint has been designated a child. Whether it is satisfied or not depends on what happens with the decomposition of the child.
- The constraint is satisfied by multiple child modules. For example, using the Web requires two modules (client and server) to implement the necessary protocols. Whether the constraint is satisfied depends on the decomposition and coordination of the children to which the constraint has been assigned.

In our example, one constraint is that the communication with the home information system is maintained. The communication virtual machine will recognize if this communication is unavailable, so the constraint is satisfied by a single child.

Quality scenarios. Quality scenarios also have to be refined and assigned to the child modules.

- A quality scenario may be completely satisfied by the decomposition without any additional impact. It can then be marked as satisfied.
- A quality scenario may be satisfied by the current decomposition with constraints on child modules. For example, using layers might satisfy a specific modifiability scenario, which in turn will constrain the usage pattern of the children.
- The decomposition may be neutral with respect to a quality scenario. For example, a usability scenario pertains to portions of the user interface that are not yet a portion of the decomposition. This scenario should be assigned to one of the child modules.
- A quality scenario may not be satisfiable with the current decomposition. If it is an important one, then the decomposition should be reconsidered. Otherwise,

the rationale for the decomposition not supporting this scenario must be recorded. This is usually the result of a tradeoff with other, perhaps higher-priority scenarios.

In our example, the quality scenarios we identified as architectural drivers are met or refined in the following fashion:

- The devices and controls for opening and closing the door are different for different products in the product line. They may include controls from within a home information system. This scenario is delegated to the user interface module.
- The processor used in different products will differ. The product-specific architecture for each product should be directly derivable from the product line architecture. This scenario is delegated to all of the modules. Each module becomes responsible for not using processor-specific features not supported by standard compilers.
- If an obstacle (person or object) is detected by the garage door during descent, the door must halt (alternately re-open) within 0.1 second. This scenario is delegated to the scheduler and the obstacle detection module.
- The garage door opener should be accessible for diagnosis and administration from within the home information system using a product-specific diagnosis protocol. This scenario is split between the diagnosis and communication modules. The communication module is responsible for the protocol used for communicating with the home information system, and the diagnosis module is responsible for managing the other interactions involving diagnosis.

At the end of this step we have a decomposition of a module into its children, where each child module has a collection of responsibilities; a set of use cases, an interface, quality scenarios, and a collection of constraints. This is sufficient to start the next iteration of decomposition.

Notice from the example how much (or little) progress is made in a single iteration: We have a vocabulary of modules and their responsibilities; we have considered a variety of use cases and quality scenarios and understand some of their ramifications. We have decided the information needs of the modules and their interactions. This information should be captured in the design rationale, as we discuss in Chapter 9, Documenting Software Architectures. We have not decided on most of the details yet. We do not know the language for communication between the user interface module and the raising/lowering modules. We do not know the algorithm for performing obstacle detection. We do not know, in any detail, how the performance-critical section communicates with the non-performance-critical section.

What we have done is defined enough so that if we are designing a large system, we can allocate work teams and give them their charges. If we are designing a small system (such as the garage door opener), we can directly proceed to the next iteration and decide on answers for these questions.

7.3   Forming the Team Structure

Once the first few levels of the architecture's module decomposition structure are fairly stable, those modules can be allocated to development teams. The result is the work assignment view discussed in Chapter 2. This view will either allocate modules to existing development units or define new ones.

As long ago as 1968, the close relationship between an architecture and the organization that produced it was a subject of comment. [Conway 68, 29] makes the point as follows:

> Take any two nodes *x* and *y* of the system. Either they are joined by a branch or they are not. (That is, either they communicate with each other in some way meaningful to the operation of the system or they do not.) If there is a branch, then the two (not necessarily distinct) design groups *X* and *Y* which designed the two nodes must have negotiated and agreed upon an interface specification to permit communication between the two corresponding nodes of the design organization. If, on the other hand, there is no branch between *x* and *y*, then the subsystems do not communicate with each other, there was nothing for the two corresponding design groups to negotiate, and therefore there is no branch between *X* and *Y*.

Conway was describing how to discern organizational structure (at least in terms of communication paths) from system structure, but the relationship between organizational and system structures is bidirectional, and necessarily so.

The impact of an architecture on the development of organizational structure is clear. Once an architecture for the system under construction has been agreed on, teams are allocated to work on the major modules and a work breakdown structure is created that reflects those teams. Each team then creates its own internal work practices (or a system-wide set of practices is adopted). For large systems, the teams may belong to different subcontractors. The work practices may include items such as bulletin boards and Web pages for communication, naming conventions for files, and the configuration control system. All of these may be different from group to group, again especially for large systems. Furthermore, quality assurance and testing procedures are set up for each group, and each group needs to establish liaisons and coordinate with the other groups.

Thus, the teams within an organization work on modules. Within the team there needs to be high-bandwidth communications: Much information in the form of detailed design decisions is being constantly shared. Between teams, low-bandwidth communications are sufficient and in fact crucial. (Fred Brooks's contention is that the overhead of inter-team communication, if not carefully managed, will swamp a project.) This, of course, assumes that the system has been designed with appropriate separation of concerns.

Highly complex systems result when these design criteria are not met. In fact, team structure and controlling team interactions often turn out to be important factors affecting a large project's success. If interactions between the teams need to be complex, either the interactions among the elements they are creating are needlessly complex or the requirements for those elements were not sufficiently "hardened" before development commenced. In this case, there is a need for high-bandwidth connections *between* teams, not just within teams, requiring substantial negotiations and often rework of elements and their interfaces. Like software systems, teams should strive for loose coupling and high cohesion.

Why does the team structure mirror the module decomposition structure? Information hiding, the design principle behind the module decomposition structure of systems, holds that modules should encapsulate, or hide, changeable details by putting up an interface that abstracts away the changeable aspects and presents a common, unified set of services to its users (in this case, the software in other system modules). This implies that each module constitutes its own small domain; we use *domain* here to mean an area of specialized knowledge or expertise. This makes for a natural fit between teams and modules of the decomposition structure, as the following examples show.

- The module is a user interface layer of a system. The application programming interface that it presents to other modules is independent of the particular user interface devices (radio buttons, dials, dialog boxes, etc.) that it uses to present information to the human user, because those might change. The domain here is the repertoire of such devices.
- The module is a process scheduler that hides the number of available processors and the scheduling algorithm. The domain here is process scheduling and the list of appropriate algorithms.
- The module is the Physical Models Module of the A-7E architecture (see Chapter 3). It encapsulates the equations that compute values about the physical environment. The domain is numerical analysis (because the equations must be implemented to maintain sufficient accuracy in a digital computer) and avionics.

Recognizing modules as mini-domains immediately suggests that the most effective use of staff is to assign members to teams according to their expertise. Only the module structure permits this. As the sidebar Organizational and Architecural Structures discusses, organizations sometimes also add specialized groups that are independent of the architectural structures.

The impact of an organization on an architecture is more subtle but just as important as the impact of an architecture on the organization (of the group that builds the system described by the architecture). Suppose you are a member of a group that builds database applications, assigned to work on a team designing an architecture for some application. Your inclination is probably to view the current problem as a database problem, to worry about what database system should be used or whether a home-grown one should be constructed, to assume that data retrievals are constructed as queries, and so on. You therefore press for an architecture that has distinct subsystems for, say, data storage and management, and query formulation and implementation. A person from the telecommunications

Organizational and Architectural Structures

We had just written Section 7.3, about the relationship between organizational structure and architectural structure, when someone who has experience in the telecommunications area proposed a counter-example. The organization he described is committed to responding quickly to customer complaints and requests for changes. In this scheme, every customer-generated change request is assigned to an individual to implement the change. Any particular change may require modifications to a variety of architectural components, and so the individuals on the customer response team make modifications to the whole system and must be outside of any team responsible for any particular group of components. For this reason, an organizational structure aligned only with the architectural structure is not adequate.

At first blush, this counter-example made us nervous, but on further probing we discovered that the organization in question actually made each modification twice: once by the customer service organization to provide quick response to the customer and once by the organizational entity that owned the components affected. Any other possibility would result in rapid degradation of any architecture that is not based strictly on separate components to implement each end-user function.

To explore the argument somewhat: an architecture, as we have emphasized repeatedly, must satisfy many conflicting demands. An architecture that is based on a separate component to implement each end-user function is very good with respect to the modifiability of these functions *as long as the modification is not based on a physical element that affects other functions*. In the maintenance phase, as in the counter-example, this architecture enables modifications to a particular function to be limited to a single component. Of course, such a function-based architecture does not allow re-use of components or sharing of data and is not very efficient with respect to implementation.

The organization under discussion, in fact, had an architecture that attempted to maximize re-use and had organizational units that mirrored component structure. Because modifications would (potentially) involve separate organizational units and the activities of these units had to be coordinated (read this as saying that the reaction time of organizations is slow when multiple units are involved), a separate rapid response unit was established at the cost of making each modification twice.

— LJB

group, on the other hand, views the system in telecommunication terms, and for this person the database is a single (possibly uninteresting) subsystem.

We discussed in Chapter 1 how organizational issues, prior experience, and a desire to employ or develop certain skills will have an effect on the architecture. The scenario above is a concrete example of how that effect might be manifested. As an organization continues to work in a particular domain, it develops particular artifacts to use as a means of obtaining work, and it has organizational groups whose purpose is to maintain these artifacts. We will see this in Chapters 14 and 15, where we discuss software product lines.

7.4   Creating a Skeletal System

Once an architecture is sufficiently designed and teams are in place to begin building to it, a skeletal system can be constructed. The idea at this stage is to provide an underlying capability to implement a system's functionality in an order advantageous to the project.

Classical software engineering practice recommends "stubbing out" sections of code so that portions of the system can be added separately and tested independently. However, which portions should be stubbed? By using the architecture as a guide, a sequence of implementation becomes clear.

First, implement the software that deals with the execution and interaction of architectural components. This may require producing a scheduler in a real-time system, implementing the rule engine (with a prototype set of rules) to control rule firing in a rule-based system, implementing process synchronization mechanisms in a multi-process system, or implementing client-server coordination in a client-server system. Often, the basic interaction mechanism is provided by third-party middleware, in which case the job becomes ones of installation instead of implementation. On top of this communication or interaction infrastructure, you may wish to install the simplest of functions, one that does little more than instigate some rote behavior. At this point, you will have a running system that essentially sits there and hums to itself—but a running system nevertheless. This is the foundation onto which useful functionality can be added.

You can now choose which of the elements providing functionality should be added to the system. The choice may be based on lowering risk by addressing the most problematic areas first, or it may be based on the levels and type of staffing available, or it may be based on getting something useful to market as quickly as possible.

Once the elements providing the next increment of functionality have been chosen, you can employ the uses structure (from Chapter 2) to tell you what additional software should be running correctly in the system (as opposed to just being there in the form of a stub) to support that functionality.

This process continues, growing larger and larger increments of the system, until it is all in place. At no point is the integration and testing task overwhelming; at every increment it is easy to find the source of newly introduced faults. Budgets and schedules are more predictable with smaller increments, which also provide management and marketing with more delivery options.

Even the stubbed-out parts help pave the way for completion. These stubs adhere to the same interfaces that the final version of the system requires, so they can help with understanding and testing the interactions among components even in the absence of high-fidelity functionality. These stub components can exercise this interaction in two ways, either producing hardcoded canned output or reading the output from a file. They can also generate a synthetic load on the system to approximate the amount of time the actual processing will take in the completed working version. This aids in early understanding of system performance requirements, including performance interactions and bottlenecks.

According to Cusumano and Selby, the Evolutionary Delivery Life Cycle is the basis for the strategy that Microsoft uses. In Microsoft's version of this approach, a "complete" skeletal system is created early in a product's life cycle and a "working," but low-fidelity, version is rebuilt at frequent periods—often nightly. This results in a working system for which the features can, at any time, be judged sufficient and the product rolled out. One problem to guard against, however, is that the first development team to complete a portion of the system gets to define the interface to which all subsequent subsystems must conform. This effectively penalizes the complex portions of the system, because they will require more analysis and hence will be less likely to have their interfaces defined first. The effect is to make the complex subsystems even more complex. Our recommendation is first to negotiate the interfaces in the skeletal subsystem and then to use a process that rewards development efficiency.

7.5 Summary

Architecture design must follow requirements analysis, but it does not need to be deferred until requirements analysis is completed. In fact, architecture design can begin once the critical architectural drivers have been determined. When a sufficient portion of the architecture has been designed (again, not necessarily completely designed), a skeletal system can be developed. This skeletal system is the framework on which iterative development (with its associated ability to deliver at any point) is performed.

The quality scenarios and tactics that we presented in Chapters 4 and 5 are critical to architecture design. ADD is a top-down design process based on using quality requirements to define an appropriate architectural pattern and on using functional requirements to instantiate the module types given by that pattern.

Architecture determines some level of organizational structure through determining the necessary communication paths. Existing organizational structure influences architecture as well by providing organizational units with specialized expertise and vested interests.

Where Do Standards Come From?

An interesting discussion flowed around the Usenet a couple of years ago about how the U.S. rail gauge standard became set at the strange-sounding figure of 4 feet, 8-1/2 inches. The discussion has implications for standards in any technology area.

It turns out that the standard was set for two reasons: backward compatibility with legacy systems and the experience of the railroad architects. To be precise, the early creators of the American rail system were trained in Great Britain and had British tools and rolling stock. Of course, this just pushes the question down one level. Why did the British use this strange gauge?

As the story goes, the British built their railroads using this gauge for precisely the same two reasons of legacy compatibility and architects' experience: The trams (which existed before the railroads) used this gauge, and the builders of the new railroad were converted tram builders, initially using tram-building tools.

Of course, trams did not appear without their historical baggage. Early trams were modeled after wagons, and so the early tram builders used the same jigs and tools they had previously used for wagon building. But this still begs the original question: Why did wagons use a wheel spacing of 4 feet, 8-1/2 inches?

They used it because they were constrained by *their* environment, the environment that had been created by the technology of the day. More plainly, any other spacing would have caused their wheels to break because the ruts on the roads in Great Britain at the time were this distance apart.

The roads were another kind of technological legacy, a standard that constrained innovation and determined this important feature of the wagons. This time, however, the legacy came from Rome. The earliest long-distance roads in Great Britain were built by the Romans, in the first four centuries A.D. And, of course, the Romans built these roads the size that they did because this was the size that fit their war chariots. So, the gauge of trains in the United States today is attributable to the design of Roman war chariots built two millennia earlier.

But it doesn't end here.

The spacing of wheels on the Roman war chariot was dictated by the width of the yoke that attached the chariot to the horse. The yoke was made this width to keep the wheel ruts clear of the horse. Thus, the gauge of a modern rail car in the United States, it can be reasonably assumed, was determined by following a set of standards, each of which was dictated by a combination of technical factors, constraints from legacy systems, and the experience of the architects. These factors, combined, mean that the gauge of the U.S. rails was determined by the width of the standard Roman warhorse's derriere.

Although this sounds silly, consider the consequences of ignoring the constraints of existing standards. When Napoleon attacked Russia, his armies made much slower progress than anticipated once they reached eastern Europe because the ruts on the roads there were not to Roman gauge. Because they made slower time than planned, they were caught in the Russian winter. We all know what happened after that.

— RK

7.6 For Further Reading

The Evolutionary Delivery Life Cycle is cited as the "best of breed" of various software development life-cycle models in [McConnell 96]. It is intended to support organizations that have time-to-market pressures with prioritized functionality, as it allows any iteration of a product to be a release. When combined with the construction of a skeletal system and attention to the uses structure, the features in a product release can be implemented so as to maximize market impact.

Christopher Alexander's seminal and innovative work on design patterns for architecture (the house-building kind) served as the basis for the work on software design patterns. [Alexander 77] is essential reading to gain an intuitive understanding of what design patterns are all about. (They are also useful if you plan to build a house one day.)

The most often cited authors on software design patterns are the so-called gang of four [Gamma 95]. [Buschmann 96] documents a set of architectural styles as design patterns, thus bridging these two important conceptual areas.

The Mythical Man-Month [Brooks 95] is required reading for any software engineer, and his revised version discusses the virtues and advantages of architecture-based iterative development, especially as practiced by Microsoft.

[Bosch 00a] provides an architectural design method that differs from ADD by first considering division to achieve functionality and then transforming this division to achieve other qualities.

The Rational Unified Process is described in [Kruchten 00]. [Cusumano 95] provides a detailed description of Microsoft's development practices.

7.7 Discussion Questions

1. Architectures beget the teams that build the modules that compose the architectures. The architectural structure usually reflected in the teams is modular decomposition. What would be the advantages and disadvantages of basing teams around components of some of the other common architectural structures, such as process?

2. ADD provides one method for "chunking" requirements. Architectural drivers are satisfied and other requirements have to be satisfied in the context of the design developed for the drivers. What other chunking methods are there for a decomposition design strategy? Why can't all requirements be satisfied with a single decomposition?

3. What other techniques can you think of for creating an initial version of a software or system architecture. How do these techniques address functional, business, and quality attribute requirements?

4. How does ADD compare to an ad hoc approach to design in terms of the outputs and the time and resources required to run the method? When would ADD be appropriate and when would ad hoc design be appropriate?

8

Flight Simulation
A Case Study in an Architecture
for Integrability

> *The striking conclusion that one draws . . . is that the information*
> *processing capacity of [flight simulation computation] has*
> *been increasing approximately exponentially for nearly*
> *thirty years. There is at this time no clear indication*
> *that the trend is changing.*
> — Laurence Fogarty [Fogarty 67]

Modern flight simulators are among the most sophisticated software systems in existence. They are highly distributed, have rigorous timing requirements, and must be amenable to frequent updates to maintain high fidelity with the ever-changing vehicles and environment they are simulating. The creation and maintenance of these large systems presents a substantial software development challenge in designing for the following:

- Hard real-time performance
- Modifiability, to accommodate changes in requirements and to the simulated aircraft and their environments
- Scalability of function, a form of modifiability, needed to extend these systems so that they can simulate more and more of the real world and further improve the fidelity of the simulation

But, as the title of this chapter makes clear, an overriding concern was designing for *integrability*—a system quality attribute not covered in Chapter 4 but often arising as a driving concern in large systems, especially those developed by distributed teams or separate organizations. Integrability refers to the ease with which separately developed elements, including those developed by third parties, can be made to work together to fulfill the software's requirements. As with other quality attributes, architectural tactics can be brought to bear to achieve integrability (some of which are also aimed at modifiability). These tactics include keeping interfaces small, simple, and stable; adhering to defined protocols; loose

175

coupling or minimal dependencies between elements; using a component framework; and using "versioned" interfaces that allow extensions while permitting existing elements to work under the original constraints.

This chapter will discuss some of the challenges of flight simulation and discuss an architectural pattern created to address them. The pattern is a *Structural Model*, and it emphasizes the following:

- Simplicity and similarity of the system's substructures
- Decoupling of data- and control-passing strategies from computation
- Minimizing module types
- A small number of system-wide coordination strategies
- Transparency of design

These principles result in an architectural pattern that, as we will see, features a high degree of integrability as well as the other quality attributes necessary for flight simulation. The pattern itself is a composite of more primitive patterns.

8.1 Relationship to the Architecture Business Cycle

The segment of the Architecture Business Cycle (ABC) that connects desired qualities to architecture is the focus of this case study. Figure 8.1 shows the ABC for Structural-Model-based flight simulators. The simulators discussed in this chapter are acquired by the U.S. Air Force. Their end users are pilots and crews for the particular aircraft being simulated. Flight simulators are used for pilot training in the operation of the aircraft, for crew training in the operation of the various weapons systems on board, and for mission training for particular missions for the aircraft. Some simulators are intended for standalone use, but more and more are intended to train multiple crews simultaneously for cooperative missions.

The flight simulators are constructed by contractors selected as a result of a competitive bidding process. The simulator systems are large (some as large as 1.5 million lines of code), have long lifetimes (the aircraft being simulated often have lifetimes of 40 years or longer), and have stringent real-time and fidelity requirements (the simulated aircraft must behave exactly like the real aircraft in situations such as normal flight, emergency maneuvers, and equipment failures).

The beginning of the Structural Model pattern dates from 1987 when the Air Force began to investigate the application of object-oriented design techniques. Electronic flight simulators had been in existence since the 1960s, and so this investigation was motivated by problems associated with the existing designs. These included construction problems (the integration phase of development was increasing exponentially with the size and complexity of the systems) and life-cycle problems (the cost of some modifications was exceeding the cost of the original system).

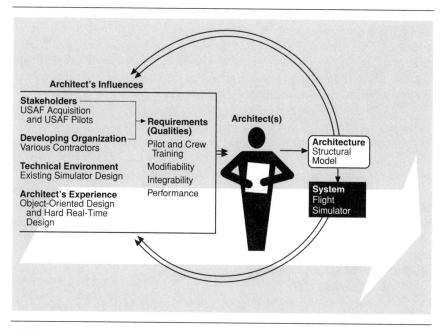

FIGURE 8.1   Initial stages of the ABC for the flight simulator

The Structural Model pattern was able to overcome these problems, as we will see. It has been used in the development of the B-2 Weapons System Trainer, the C-17 Aircrew Training System, and the Special Operations Forces family of trainers, among others.

8.2   Requirements and Qualities

There are three roles involved in a flight training simulator. The first is that of the crew being trained. They sit inside a motion platform surrounded by instruments intended to replicate exactly the aircraft being simulated, and look at visuals that represent what would be seen outside an actual aircraft. We are not going to describe the specifics of either the motion platform or the visual display generator in this chapter. They are driven by special-purpose processors and are outside the scope of the architecture we describe here. The purpose of a flight simulator is to instruct the pilot and crew in how to operate a particular aircraft, how to perform maneuvers such as mid-air refueling, and how to respond to situations such as an attack on the aircraft. The fidelity of the simulation is an important element in the training. For example, the feel of the controls when particular maneuvers are performed must be captured correctly. Otherwise, the pilot and crew are being trained incorrectly and the training may be counter-productive.

The second role associated with a flight simulator is that of the environment. Typically, the environment is a computer model, although with multi-aircraft training exercises it can include individuals other than the pilot and crew. It comprises the atmosphere, threats, weapons, and other aircraft. For example, if the purpose of the training is to practice refueling, the (simulated) refueling aircraft introduces turbulence into the (modeled) atmosphere.

The third role associated with a flight training simulator is that of the simulation instructor. Usually, a training exercise has a specific purpose and specific circumstances. During the exercise, the instructor is responsible for monitoring the performance of the pilot and crew and for initiating training situations. Sometimes these situations are scripted in advance, and other times the instructor introduces them. Typical situations include malfunctions of equipment (e.g., landing gear that does not deploy correctly), attacks on the aircraft from foes, and weather conditions such as turbulence caused by thunderstorms. The instructor has a separate console to monitor the activities of the crew, to inject malfunctions into the aircraft, and to control the environment. Figure 8.2 shows a typical collection of modern flight simulators.

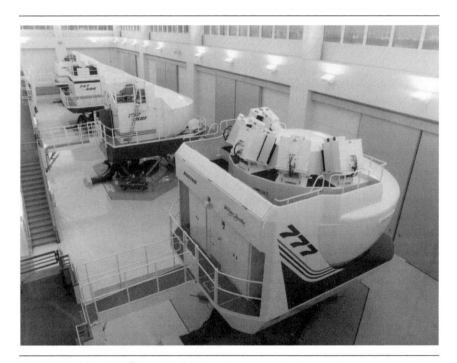

FIGURE 8.2 Modern flight simulators. Courtesy of the Boeing Company.

USE OF MODELS

The models used in the aircraft and the environment are capable of being simulated to almost arbitrary fidelity. As an example of the range of fidelity, consider the modeling of the air pressure affecting the aircraft. A simple model is that the air pressure is affected only by the aircraft altitude. Somewhat more complicated is a model in which the air pressure is affected by altitude and local weather patterns. Modeling local weather patterns takes more computational power but allows consideration of updrafts and downdrafts. An even more complicated model with additional computational requirements is that the air pressure is affected by altitude, local weather patterns, and the behavior of nearby aircraft. One source of turbulence is an aircraft that has recently passed through the airspace of the aircraft being simulated.

A consequence of the capability to simulate the aircraft or the environment to almost arbitrary fidelity is that training simulators in the past always stressed the limits of computational power (and may always do so in the future). Since crew simulator training is an important portion of overall flight training, there are always strong arguments that slightly more fidelity will improve the training and hence the skill set of the crews being trained. Performance, therefore, is one of the important quality requirements for a flight simulator.

STATES OF EXECUTION

A flight simulator can execute in several states.

- *Operate* corresponds to the normal functioning of the simulator as a training tool.
- *Configure* is used when modifications must be made to a current training session. For example, suppose the crew has been training in a single-aircraft exercise and the instructor wishes to switch to mid-air refueling. The simulator is then placed into a configure state.
- *Halt* stops the current simulation.
- *Replay* uses a journal to move through the simulation without crew interaction. Among other functions, it is used to demonstrate to the crew what they have just done, because the crew may get caught up in operating the aircraft and not reflect on their actions. "Record/playback" was identified in Chapter 5 (Achieving Qualities) as an architectural tactic for testing. Here we find it used as a portion of the training process.

The simulators we discuss in this chapter are characterized by the following four properties:

1. *Real-time performance constraints.* Flight simulators must execute at fixed frame rates that are high enough to ensure fidelity. For those not familiar with frame rates, an analogy to motion pictures might be helpful. Each frame is a snapshot in time. When a sufficient number of frames are taken sequentially within a time interval, the user sees or senses continuous motion. Different senses require different frame rates. Common simulator frame rates are 30 Hz or 60 Hz —one-thirtieth or one-sixtieth of a second. Within each frame rate, all computations must run to completion.

All portions of a simulator run at an integral factor of the base rate. If the base rate is 60 Hz, slower portions of the simulation may run at 30, 20, 15, or 12 Hz, and so on. They may not run at a nonintegral factor of the base rate, such as 25 Hz. One reason for this restriction is that the sensory inputs provided by a flight simulator for the crew being trained must be strictly coordinated. It would not do to have the pilot execute a turn but not begin to see or feel the change for even a small period of time (say, one-tenth of a second). Even for delays so small that they are not consciously detectable, a lack of coordination may be a problem. Such delays may result in a phenomenon known as *simulator sickness*, a purely physiological reaction to imperfectly coordinated sensory inputs.

2. *Continuous development and modification.* Simulators exist to train users when the equivalent training on the actual vehicle would be much more expensive or dangerous. To provide a realistic training experience, a flight simulator must be faithful to the actual air vehicle. However, whether civilian or military, air vehicles are continually being modified and updated. The simulator software is therefore almost constantly modified and updated to maintain verisimilitude. Furthermore, the training for which the simulators are used is continually extended to encompass new types of situations, including problems (malfunctions) that might occur with the aircraft and new environmental situations, such as a military helicopter being used in an urban setting.

3. *Large size and high complexity.* Flight simulators typically comprise tens of thousands of lines of code for the simplest training simulation and millions of lines of code for complex, multi-person trainers. Furthermore, the complexity of flight simulators, mapped over a 30-year period, has shown exponential growth.

4. *Developed in geographically distributed areas.* Military flight simulators are typically developed in a distributed fashion for two reasons, one technical and one political. Technically, different portions of the development require different expertise, and so it is common practice for the general contractor to subcontract portions of the work to specialists. Politically, high-technology jobs, such as simulator development, are political plums, so many politicians fight to have a piece of the work in their district. In either case, the integrability of the simulator—already problematic because of the size and complexity of the code—is made more difficult because the paths of communication are long.

In addition, two problems with flight simulators caused the U.S. Air Force to investigate new simulator designs.

1. *Very expensive debugging, testing, and modification.* The complexity of flight simulation software, its real-time nature, and its tendency to be modified regularly all contribute to the costs of testing, integrating, and modifying the software typically exceeding the cost of development. The growth in complexity (and its associated growth in cost) thus caused an emphasis for the architecture on integrability and modifiability.

One of the consequences of the growth in complexity was the increased cost of integration. For example, a large completed Air Force system (1.7 million lines of code) had greatly exceeded its budget for integration. Systems 50% larger were in concept, and they would have been prohibitively expensive. Hence, integrability emerged as a driving architectural concern.

2. *Unclear mapping between software structure and aircraft structure.* Flight simulators have traditionally been built with runtime efficiency as their primary quality goal. This is not surprising given their performance and fidelity requirements and given that simulators were initially built on platforms with extremely limited memory and processing power. Traditional design of flight simulator software was based on following control loops through a cycle. These, in turn, were motivated by the tasks that caused the loop to be activated. For example, suppose the pilot turns the aircraft left. The pilot moves the rudder and aileron controls, which in turn moves the control surfaces, which affects the aerodynamics and causes the aircraft to turn. In the simulator, a model reflects the relationship between the controls, the surfaces, the aerodynamics, and the orientation of the aircraft. In the original flight simulator architecture, this model was contained in a module that might be called Turn. There might be a similar module for level flight, another for takeoff and landing, and so forth. The basic decomposition strategy was based on examining the tasks that the pilot and crew perform, modeling the components that perform the task, and keeping all calculations as local as possible.

This strategy maximizes performance since any task is modeled in a single module (or a small collection of modules) and thus the data movement necessary to perform the calculations is minimized. The problem with this architecture is that the same physical component is represented in multiple models and hence in multiple modules. The extensive interactions among modules cause problems with both modifiability and integration. If the module that controls turning is integrated with the module that controls level flight, and a problem is discovered in the data being provided to the turning module, that same data is probably being accessed by the level flight module. For these reasons, there were many coupling effects to be considered during integration and maintenance.

The architectural pattern, called *Structural Modeling,* that resulted from the reconsideration of the problems of flight simulators will be discussed for the remainder of this chapter. In brief, the pattern includes an object-oriented design to model the subsystems and controller children of the air vehicle. It marries real-time scheduling to this object-oriented design as a means of controlling the execution order of the simulation's subsystems so that fidelity can be guaranteed.

8.3 Architectural Solution

Figure 8.3 shows a reference model for a flight simulator. The three roles we identified earlier (air vehicle, environment, and instructor) are shown interacting with the crew and the various cueing systems. Typically, the instructor is hosted on a different hardware platform from the air vehicle model. The environment model may be hosted either on a separate hardware platform or with the instructor station.

The logical division between the instructor station and the other two portions is clear. The instructor station supports the instructor's control and monitoring of the actions of the crew. The other two portions perform the simulation. The division between the air vehicle and the environment is not as clear. For example, if an aircraft launches a weapon, it is logically a portion of the air vehicle until it leaves the vehicle, at which point it becomes a portion of the environment. Upon firing, the aerodynamics of the weapon are influenced initially by the proximity of the aircraft. Thus, any modeling of the aerodynamics must remain, at least initially, tightly coupled to the air vehicle. If the weapon is always considered a portion of

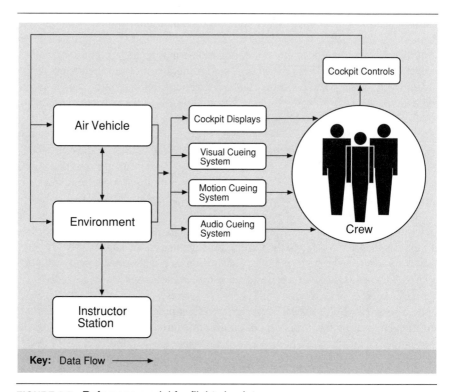

FIGURE 8.3 Reference model for flight simulator

the environment, its modeling involves tight coordination between the air vehicle and the environment. If it is modeled as a portion of the air vehicle and then handed off to the environment when fired, control of the weapon needs to be handed from one to the other.

TREATMENT OF TIME IN A FLIGHT SIMULATOR

Recall from Chapter 5 that resource management is a category of tactics to achieve performance goals. In a real-time simulator, the most important resource to manage is time itself. A flight simulator is supposed to reflect the real world, which it does by creating time-based real-world behaviors. Thus, when the pilot in a simulator activates a particular control, the simulator must provide the same response in the same time as the actual aircraft would. "In the same time" means both within an upper bound of duration after the event and within a lower bound of duration. Reacting too quickly is as bad for the quality of the simulation as reacting too slowly.

There are two fundamentally different ways of managing time in a flight simulator—periodic and event-based—and both of these are used. Periodic time management is used in portions that must maintain real-time performance (such as the air vehicle), and event-based time management is used in portions where real-time performance is not critical (such as the instructor station).

Periodic Time Management. A periodic time-management scheme has a fixed (simulated) time quantum based on the frame rate. That is the basis of scheduling the system processes. This scheme typically uses a non-pre-emptive cyclic scheduling discipline, which proceeds by iterating through the following loop:

- Set initial simulated time.
- Iterate the next two steps until the session is complete.
  - Invoke each of the processes for a fixed (real) quantum. Each process calculates its internal state based on the current simulated time and reports it based on the next period of simulated time. It guarantees to complete its computation within its real-time quantum.
  - Increment simulated time by quantum.

A simulation based on the periodic management of time will be able to keep simulated time and real time in synchronization as long as each process is able to advance its state to the next period within the time quantum allocated to it.

Typically, this is managed by adjusting the responsibilities of the individual processes so that they are small enough to be computed in the allocated quantum. It is the designer's responsibility to provide the number of processors needed to ensure sufficient computational power to enable all processes to receive their quantum of computation.

Event-Based Time Management.   An event-based time-management scheme is similar to the interrupt-based scheduling used in many operating systems. The schedule proceeds by iterating through the following loop:

- Add a simulated event to the event queue.
- While there are events remaining in the event queue,
  - choose the event with the smallest (i.e., soonest) simulated time.
  - set the current simulated time to the time of the chosen event.
  - invoke a process for the chosen event. This process may add events to the event queue.

In this case, simulated time advances by the invoked processes placing events on the event queue and the scheduler choosing the next event to process. In pure event-based simulations, simulated time may progress much faster (as in a war game simulation) or much slower (as in an engineering simulation) than real time.

Mixed-Time Systems.   Returning now to the scheduling of the three portions of the flight simulator, the instructor station is typically scheduled on an event basis—those events that emanate from the instructor's interactions—and the air vehicle model is scheduled on a periodic basis. The environment model can be scheduled using either regime. Thus, the coupling between the air vehicle and the environment may involve matching different time regimes.

Flight simulators must marry periodic time simulation (such as in the air vehicle model) with event-based simulation (such as in the environment model, in some cases) and with other event-based activities that are not predictable (such as an interaction with the instructor station or the pilot setting a switch). Many scheduling policies are possible from the perspective of each process involved in this marriage.

A simple policy for managing events within a periodically scheduled processor is that periodic processing must occur immediately after a synchronization step and complete before any aperiodic processing. Aperiodic processing proceeds within a bounded interval, during which as many messages as possible will be retrieved and processed. Those not processed during a given interval must be deferred to subsequent intervals, with the requirement that all messages be processed in the order received from a single source.

Communication from the portions of the system managed on an event basis to the portions managed using periodic scheduling appears as aperiodic and is scheduled as just discussed. Communication from the portions of the system managed using periodic schedule appears as events to the portions managed on an event basis.

Given this understanding of managing time in a flight simulator, we can now present the architectural pattern that handles this complexity. This pattern is for the air vehicle, and so the time management discussion is from the air vehicle's perspective.

THE STRUCTURAL MODEL ARCHITECTURAL PATTERN

Structural Model is an architectural pattern, as we defined it in Section 2.3. That is, it consists of a collection of element types and a configuration of their coordination at runtime. In this section, we present the Structural Model pattern and discuss the considerations that led to its design. Recall that the air vehicle model itself may be spread over several processors. Thus, the elements of the air vehicle structural model must coordinate internally across processors as well as with the environment model and the instructor portions of the simulation running on (potentially) different processors.

The constituents of the Structural Model architectural pattern are, at the coarsest level, the *executive* and the *application*.

- The *executive* portion handles coordination issues: real-time scheduling of subsystems, synchronization between processors, event management from the instructor–operator station, data sharing, and data integrity.
- The *application* portion handles the computation of the flight simulation: modeling the air vehicle. Its functions are implemented by subsystems and their children.

First we will discuss the air vehicle's executive modules in detail and then return to a discussion of its application modules.

MODULES OF THE AIR VEHICLE MODEL EXECUTIVE

Figure 8.4 shows the air vehicle structural model with the executive pattern given in detail. The modules in the executive are the *Timeline Synchronizer*, the *Periodic Sequencer*, the *Event Handler*, and the *Surrogates* for other portions of the simulator.

Timeline Synchronizer.   The timeline synchronizer is the base scheduling mechanism for the air vehicle model. It also maintains the simulation's internal notion of time. The other three elements of the executive—the periodic sequencer, the event handler, and the surrogates—all must be allocated processor resources. The timeline synchronizer also maintains the current state of the simulation.

The timeline synchronizer passes both data and control to the other three elements and receives data and control from them. It also coordinates time with other portions of the simulator. This can include other processors responsible for a portion of the air vehicle model which have their own timeline synchronizers. Finally, the timeline synchronizer implements a scheduling policy for coordinating both periodic and aperiodic processing. For the sake of continuity, precedence is given to the periodic processing.

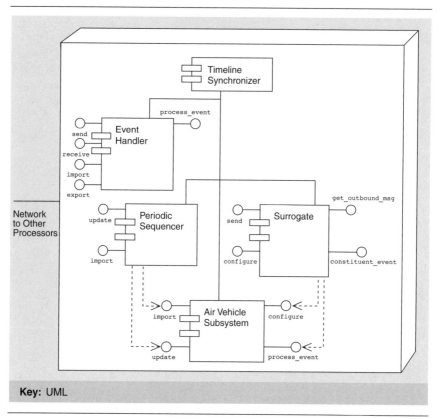

FIGURE 8.4 The Structural Modeling pattern of an air vehicle system processor with focus on the executive

Periodic Sequencer. The periodic sequencer is used to conduct all periodic processing performed by the simulation's subsystems. This involves invoking the subsystems to perform periodic operations according to fixed schedules.

The periodic sequencer provides two operations to the timeline synchronizer. The `import` operation requests that the periodic sequencer invoke subsystems to perform their `import` operation. The `update` operation requests that the periodic sequencer invoke subsystems' `update` operations.

To conduct its processing, the periodic sequencer requires two capabilities. The first is to organize knowledge of a schedule. By *schedule* we mean the patterns of constituent invocations that represent the orders and rates of change propagation through the simulation algorithms realized by the constituents. The enactment of these patterns essentially represents the passage of time within the air vehicle simulation in its various operating states. The second capability is to actually invoke the subsystems through their periodic operations by means of some dispatching mechanism.

Event Handler.   The event handler module is used to orchestrate all aperiodic processing performed by subsystems. This involves invoking their aperiodic operations.

The event handler provides four operations to the timeline synchronizer: `configure` (used to start a new training mission, for example), `constituent_ event` (used when an event is targeted for a particular instance of a module), `get_outbound_msg` (used by the timeline synchronizer to conduct aperiodic processing while in system operating states, such as `operate`, that are predominantly periodic), and `send` (used by subsystem controllers to send events to other subsystem controllers and messages to other systems).

To perform its processing, the event handler requires two capabilities. The first capability is to determine which subsystem controller receives an event, using knowledge of a mapping between event identifiers and subsystem instances. The second capability is to invoke the subsystems and to extract required parameters from events before invocation.

Surrogate.   Surrogates are an application of the "use an intermediary" tactic and are responsible for system-to-system communication between the air vehicle model and the environment model or the instructor station. Surrogates are aware of the physical details of the system with which they communicate and are responsible for representation, communication protocol, and so forth.

For example, the instructor station monitors state data from the air vehicle model and displays it to the instructor. The surrogate gathers the correct data when it gets control of the processor and sends it to the instructor station. In the other direction, the instructor may wish to set a particular state for the crew. This is an event received by the surrogate and passed to the event processor for dispatching to the appropriate subsystems.

This use of surrogates means that both the periodic scheduler and the event handler can be kept ignorant of the details of the instructor station or the platform on which the environment model is operating. All of the system-specific knowledge is embedded in the surrogate. Any change to these platforms will not propagate further than the surrogate in the air vehicle model system.

MODULES OF THE AIR VEHICLE MODEL APPLICATION

Figure 8.5 shows the module types that exist in the application subpart of the air vehicle structural model. There are only two: the *Subsystem Controller* and the *Controller Child.* Subsystem controllers pass data to and from other subsystem controller instances and to their children. Controller children pass data only to and from their parents, not to any other controller children. They also receive control only from their parents and return it only to their parents. These restrictions on data and control passing preclude a controller child from passing data or control even to a sibling. The rationale for this is to assist integration and modifiability by eliminating coupling of a child instance with anything other than its parent.

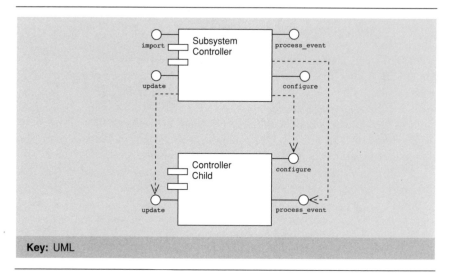

FIGURE 8.5 The application module types

Any effect of modification or integration is mediated by the parent subsystem controller. This is an example of the use of the "restrict communication" tactic.

Subsystem Controller. Subsystem controllers are used to interconnect a set of functionally related children to do the following:

- Achieve the simulation of a subsystem as a whole.
- Mediate control and aperiodic communication between the system and subsystems.

They are also responsible for determining how to use the capabilities of their children to satisfy trainer-specific functionality such as malfunctions and the setting of parameters.

Because the Structural Model pattern restricts communication among controller children, a subsystem controller must provide the capability to make logical connections between its children and those of other subsystems. Inbound connections supply inputs produced outside of the subsystem that the subsystem's children need for their simulation algorithms. Outbound connections satisfy similar needs of other subsystems and of surrogates. These connections appear as sets of names by which a subsystem controller internally refers to data considered to be outside of itself. When such a name is read or written, the appropriate connections are assumed to be made. How the connections are actually made is determined later in the detailed design and is a variation point of the pattern (see Chapter 14, Product Lines, for a discussion of variation points). In addition to making connections between its children and those of other subsystems, the subsystem controller also acts as an intermediary among its own children since restricting communication means that they are not allowed to directly communicate among themselves.

As we mentioned, a flight simulator can be in one of several states. This is translated through the executive to a particular executive state. The executive then reports its current state to the subsystem controller. The two states that are relevant here are *operate* and *stabilize*. The operate state instructs the subsystem controller to perform its normal computations relevant to advancing the state of the simulation. The stabilize state tells the subsystem controller to terminate its current computation in a controlled fashion (to prevent the motion platform from harming the crew through uncontrolled motion) as follows:

- Retrieve and locally store the values of inbound connections under the direct control of an executive. Such a capability addresses issues of data consistency and time coherence.
- Stabilize the simulation algorithms of its children under the control of executive instances and report whether it considers the subsystem as a whole to be currently stable.

Subsystem controllers *must* be able to do the following:

- Initialize themselves and each of their children to a set of initial conditions in response to an event.
- Route requests for malfunctions and the setting of simulation parameters to their children based on knowledge of child capabilities.

Finally, subsystem controllers may support the reconfiguration of mission parameters such as armaments, cargo loads, and the starting location of a training mission. Subsystem controllers realize these capabilities through periodic and aperiodic operations made available to the periodic sequencer and event handler, respectively.

Subsystem controllers must support the two periodic operations—update and import—and may support two others (which are aperiodic)—process_event and configure.

Update – The update operation causes the subsystem controller to perform periodic processing appropriate to the current system operating state, which is provided as an input parameter. In the *operate* state, the update operation causes the subsystem controller to retrieve inputs needed by its children by means of inbound connections, to execute operations of its children in some logical order so that changes can be propagated through them, and to retrieve their outputs for use in satisfying another's inputs or the subsystem's outbound connections. More than just a sequencer, this algorithm provides a logical "glue" that cements the children into some coherent, aggregate simulation. This glue may include computations as well as data transformations and conversions.

In the *stabilize* state, the update operation is used to request that the subsystem controller perform one iteration of its stabilization algorithm, and to determine whether locally defined stability criteria are satisfied. The update operation provides one output parameter, indicating whether the subsystem controller considers the subsystem to be currently stable. This assumes that such a determination can be made locally, which may not be valid in all circumstances.

Subsystem controllers *may* provide the capability to do the following tasks.

Import – The import operation is used to request that the subsystem controller complete certain of its inbound connections by reading their values and to locally store their values for use in a subsequent `update` operation.

There are two aperiodic operations provided by subsystem controllers: `process_event` and `configure`.

Process_event – The `process_event` operation is used in operating states that are predominantly periodic, such as operate, to ask the subsystem controller to respond to an event. The event is provided by an input parameter to the operation. Several events from the instructor–operator station fall into this category, such as `process_malfunction`, `set_parameter`, and `hold_parameter`.

Configure – The `configure` operation is used in system operating states, like *initialize*, in which the processing is predominantly aperiodic. This operation is used to establish a named set of conditions such as some training device configuration or training mission. The information the subsystem controller needs to establish the condition may be provided as an input parameter on the operation, as a location in a memory on secondary storage, or in a database where the information has been stored for retrieval. To complete the operation, the subsystem controller invokes operations of its children that cause the children to establish the conditions.

Controller Children.   Air vehicle model controller children may be simulations of real aircraft components, such as a hydraulic pump, an electrical relay, or a fuel tank. They can support simulator-specific models such as forces and moments, weights and balances, and the equations of motion. They can localize the details of cockpit equipment, such as gauges, switches, and displays. No matter what specific functionality they simulate, controller children are all considered to be of the same module type.

In general, controller children support the simulation of an individual part, or object, within some functional assembly. Each child provides a simulation algorithm that determines its own state based on the following:

- Its former state
- Inputs that represent its connections with logically adjacent children
- Some elapsed time interval

A child makes this determination as often as it is requested to do so by its subsystem controller, which provides the required inputs and receives the child's outputs. This capability is called *updating*.

A child can support the capability of producing abnormal outputs, reflecting a malfunction condition. In addition to potentially modeling changes in normal operating conditions, such as wear and tear, which can result in malfunctions over time, children can be told to start and stop malfunctioning by their subsystem controller.

A controller child can also support the setting of a simulation parameter to a particular value. Simulation parameters are external names for performance parameters and decision criteria used in the controller child's simulation algorithm. Each child can initialize itself to some known condition. Like other child capabilities, parameter setting and initialization must be requested by the subsystem controller.

The updating, malfunctioning, parameter setting, and initializing capabilities differ in the incidence of their use by the subsystem controller. The child is requested to update on a periodic basis, effecting the passage of time within the simulation. Requests for the other capabilities are made only sporadically.

Controller children support these capabilities through a set of periodic and aperiodic operations made available to the subsystem controller. `update` is the single periodic operation and is used to control the periodic execution of the simulation algorithm. The child receives external inputs and returns its outputs through parameters on the operation. Two aperiodic operations are provided by the children: `process_event` and `configure`.

All logical interactions among children are mediated by the subsystem controller, which is encoded with knowledge of how to use the child operations to achieve the simulation requirements allocated to the subsystem as a whole. This includes the following:

- Periodically propagating state changes through the children using their `update` operations
- Making logical connections among children using the input and output parameters on these operations
- Making logical connections among children and the rest of the simulation using the subsystem's inbound and outbound connections

Controller child malfunctions are assumed to be associated with abnormal operating conditions of the real-world components being modeled. Therefore, the presence and identities of these malfunctions are decided by the child's designer and made known to the subsystem controller's designer for use in realizing subsystem malfunction requests. Subsystem malfunctions need not correspond directly to those supported by the children, and certain of them can be realized as some aggregation of more primitive failures supported by children. It is the subsystem controller's responsibility to map between low-level failures and subsystem-level malfunctions.

Likewise, the presence and identities of simulation parameters are decided by the controller child's designer based on the characteristics of the child's simulation algorithm. They are made known to the subsystem controller's designer for use in realizing subsystem requests or for other purposes for which they are intended or are suitable to support.

SKELETAL SYSTEM

What we have thus far described is the basis for a skeletal system, as defined in Chapter 7. We have a structural framework for a flight simulator, but none of the details—the actual simulator functionality—have been filled in. This is a general simulation framework that can be used for helicopter and even nuclear reactor simulation. The process of making a working simulation consists of fleshing out this skeleton with subsystems and controller children appropriate to the task at hand. This fleshing out is dictated by the functional partitioning process, which we will discuss next.

It is rather striking that an entire flight simulator, which can easily comprise millions of lines of code, can be completely described by only six module types: controller children, subsystem controllers, timeline synchronizer, periodic sequencer, event handler, and surrogate. This makes the architecture (comparatively) simple to build, understand, integrate, grow, and otherwise modify.

Equally important, with a standard set of fundamental patterns one can create specification forms, code templates, and exemplars that describe those patterns. This allows for consistent analysis. When the patterns are mandated, an architect can insist that a designer use *only* the provided building blocks. While this may sound draconian, a small number of fundamental building blocks can, in fact, free a designer to concentrate on the functionality—the reason that the system is being built in the first place.

ALLOCATING FUNCTIONALITY TO CONTROLLER CHILDREN

Now that we have described the architectural pattern with which the air vehicle model is built, we still need to discuss how operational functionality is allocated to instances of the modules in that pattern. We do this by defining instances of the subsystem controllers, to detail the specifics of the aircraft to be simulated. The actual partitioning depends on the systems on the aircraft, the complexity of the aircraft, and the types of training for which the simulator is designed.

In this section, we sketch a sample partitioning. We begin with a desire to partition the functionality to controller children based on the underlying physical aircraft. To accomplish this we use an object-oriented decomposition approach, which has a number of virtues, as follows:

- It maintains a close correspondence between the aircraft partitions and the simulator, and this provides us with a set of conceptual models that map closely to the real world. Our understanding of how the parts interact in the aircraft helps us understand how the parts interact in the simulator. It also makes it easier for users and reviewers to understand the simulator because they are familiar with the aircraft (the problem domain) and can easily transfer this familiarity to it (i. e., the solution domain).

- Experience with past flight simulators has taught us that a change in the aircraft is easily identifiable with aircraft partitions. Thus, the locus of change in the simulator corresponds to analogous aircraft partitions, which tends to keep the simulator changes localized and well defined. It also makes it easier to understand how changes in the aircraft affect the simulator, therefore making it easier to assess the cost and time required for changes to be implemented.

- The number and size of the simulator interfaces are reduced. This derives from a strong semantic cohesion within partitions, placing the largest interfaces within partitions instead of across them.

- Localization of malfunctions is also achieved as they are associated with specific pieces of aircraft equipment. It is easier to analyze the effects of malfunctions when dealing with this physical mapping, and the resulting implementations exhibit good locality. Malfunction effects are readily propagated in a natural fashion by the data that the malfunctioning partition produces. Higher-order effects are handled the same as first-order effects. For example, a leak in a hydraulic connection is a first-order effect and is directly modeled by a controller child. The manifestation of this leak as the inability to manipulate a flight control is a higher-order effect but it happens naturally as a result of the propagation of simulation data from child to subsystem controller and from one subsystem to another.

In breaking down the air vehicle modeling problem into more manageable units, the airframe becomes the focus of attention. Groups exist for the airframe, the forces on it, the things outside it, and the things inside it but ancillary to its operation. This typically results in the following specific groups:

- *Kinetics.* Elements that deal with forces exerted on the airframe
- *Aircraft systems.* Parts concerned with common systems that provide the aircraft with various kinds of power or that distribute energy within the airframe
- *Avionics.* Things that provide some sort of ancillary support to the aircraft but that are not directly involved in the kinetics of the air vehicle model, the vehicle's control, or operation of the basic flight systems (e.g., radios)
- *Environment.* Things associated with the environment in which the air vehicle model operates

GROUP DECOMPOSITION

The coarsest decomposition of the air vehicle model is the group. Groups decompose into systems, which in turn decompose into subsystems. Subsystems provide the instances of the subsystem controllers. Groups and systems are not directly reflected in the architecture— there is no group controller—and exist to organize the functionality assigned to the various instances of subsystem control-lers. This decomposition is managed via a process using *n-square charts*.

***n*-Square Charts.**   One method of presenting information about the interfaces in a system is *n*-square charts. We will make use of this presentation method to illustrate how the partitions we selected relate to each other. Because some of the factors we consider in making partitioning decisions are based on the partition interfaces, *n*-square charts are useful in evaluating those decisions. They are a good method for capturing the input and output of a module and can illustrate the abstractions used in various parts of the design.

An example of an *n*-square chart is shown in Figure 8.6. The boxes on the main diagonal represent the system partitions. Their inputs are found in the col-umn in which the partition lies; their outputs are shown in the corresponding row. The full set of inputs to a partition is thus the union of all the cell contents of the partition's column. Conversely, the full set of outputs is the union of all the cell contents in the row in which the partition resides. The flow of data from one par-tition to another is to the right, then down, to the left, and then up.

Figure 8.7 shows an *n*-square chart depicting the interfaces between the groups identified above. Interfaces external to the air vehicle model have been omitted for simplicity. These interfaces terminate in interface subsystems. The data elements shown on this chart are aggregate collections of data to simplify the presentation. The interfaces are not named here; nor are they typed. As we investigate partitions, looking at more limited sets of elements, the information presented becomes more detailed. Systems engineers can use this approach to the point where all of the primitive data objects in the interfaces are shown. During detailed design, the interface types and names will be determined.

Not all of the air vehicle models will correspond to aircraft structure. The aerodynamics models are expressions of the underlying physics of the vehicle's interaction with the environment. There are few direct analogs to aircraft parts. Partitioning this area means relying on the mathematical models and physical

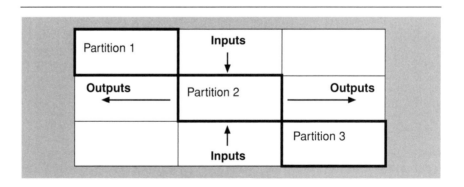

FIGURE 8.6 The *n*-square chart

Kinetics Group	Loads	Vehicle State Vector	Vehicle Position
Power	**Aircraft Systems Group**	Power	
Inertial State	Loads	**Avionics Group**	Ownship Emissions
Atmosphere, Terrain, and Weather Data		Environment Emitter Data	**Environment Group**

FIGURE 8.7   Air vehicle model domain *n*-square for groups

entities that describe the vehicle's dynamics. Partitioning correctly based on mathematical models that affect the total aircraft is more difficult than partitioning based on the aircraft's physical structure.

DECOMPOSING GROUPS INTO SYSTEMS

The next step is to refine groups into systems. A system and a group can be units of integration: The functionality of a system is a relatively self-contained solution to a set of simulation problems. These units are a convenient focus for testing and validation. Group partitions exist as collections of code modules implemented by one engineer or a small group of engineers. We can identify systems within the groups we have defined. We will look briefly at the kinetics group systems as an example.

Systems in the Kinetics Group.   These systems consist of elements concerned with the kinetics of the vehicle. Included in this group are elements directly involved in controlling the vehicle's motion and modeling the interaction of the vehicle and its control surfaces with the environment. The systems identified in this group are:

- Airframe
- Propulsion
- Landing gear
- Flight controls

All of the subsystems in the propulsion system shown in Figure 8.8 deal with the model of the aircraft's engines. Multiple engines are handled by creating

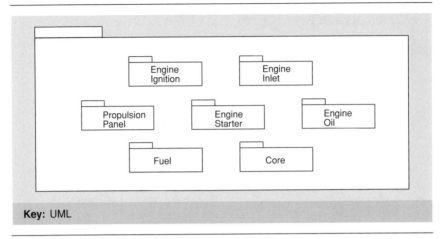

Key: UML

FIGURE 8.8   A propulsion subsystem

multiple sets of state variables and duplicate instances of objects, where appropriate. This system's principal purpose is to calculate engine thrust, moments caused by rotation of engine parts, and the forces and moments caused by mass distribution of fuel.

The aircraft's fuel system is grouped here because its primary interface is to the engines. It calculates the forces acting on the airframe from the movement of the fuel within the tanks as well as the gravitational effect of the fuel mass.

At this point we have identified the division of functionality, its allocation to subsystems and subsystem controllers, and the connections among subsystems. To complete the architecture, we need to do the following:

- Identify the controller children instances for the propulsion subsystem.
- Similarly decompose the other groups, their systems, and their subsystems.

To summarize, we decomposed the air vehicle into four groups: kinetics, aircraft systems, avionics, and environment. We then decomposed the kinetics group into four systems: airframe, propulsion, landing gear, and flight controls. Finally, we presented a decomposition of the propulsion system into a collection of subsystems.

8.4 Summary

In this chapter, we described an architecture for flight simulators that was designed to achieve the quality attributes of performance, integrability, and modifiability. And projects were able to achieve these results with cost savings. For

TABLE 8.1   How the Structural Modeling Pattern Achieves Its Goals

Goal	How Achieved	Tactics Used
Performance	Periodic scheduling strategy using time budgets	Static scheduling
Integrability	Separation of computation from coordination Indirect data and control connections	Restrict communication Use intermediary
Modifiability	Few module types Physically based decomposition	Restrict communication Semantic coherence Interface stability

example, onsite installation teams were 50% of the size previously required because they could locate and correct faults more easily. The design achieves those qualities by restricting the number of module type configurations in the Structural Model architectural pattern, by restricting communication among the module types, and by decomposing the functionality according to anticipated changes in the underlying aircraft.

The improvements in these simulators have principally accrued from a better understanding of, and adherence to, a well-analyzed and well-documented software architecture. Chastek and Brownsword describe some of the results achieved through the use of this pattern [Chastek 96, 28]:

> In a previous data-driven simulator of comparable size (the B-52), 2000–3000 test descriptions (test problems) were identified during factory acceptance testing. With their structural modeling project, 600–700 test descriptions were reported. They found the problems easier to correct; many resulted from misunderstandings with the documentation. . . . Staff typically could isolate a reported problem off-line rather than going to a site. . . . Since the use of structural modeling, defect rates for one project are half that found on previous data-driven simulators.

At the start of this chapter we identified three quality goals of the Structural Model pattern: performance, integrability, and modifiability for operational requirements. Here, we recap how the pattern achieves these goals. Table 8.1 summarizes this information.

PERFORMANCE

A key quality goal of the Structural Model pattern is real-time performance. This is achieved primarily through operation of the executive and use of a periodic scheduling strategy. Each subsystem invoked by the executive has a time budget, and the hardware for the simulator is sized so that it can accommodate the sum of all time budgets. Sometimes this involves a single processor; other times, multiple processors. Given this scheduling strategy, the achievement of real-time performance comes from requiring the sum of the times allocated to the subsystems involved in the control loops to be within one period of the simulator. Thus, real-time performance is guaranteed by a combination of architectural patterns (the executive module configurations) and the functional decomposition (how the instances are invoked).

INTEGRABILITY

In the Structural Model pattern, both the data connections and the control connections between two subsystems are deliberately minimized. First, within a subsystem the controller children can pass neither control nor data directly to any sibling. All data and control transfers occur only through mediation by the subsystem controller. Thus, integrating another controller child into a subsystem requires that the data in the subsystem controller be internally consistent and that the data transferred between the subsystem controller and the controller children be correct. This is a much simpler process than if a new child communicated with other children because all of them would be involved in the integration. That is, achieving integration has been reduced to a problem that is linear, rather than exponential, in the number of children.

When integrating two subsystems, none of their children interact directly and so the problem is again reduced to ensuring that the two subsystems pass data consistently. It is possible that the addition of a new subsystem will affect several other subsystems, but because the number of subsystems is substantially less than the number of controller children, this problem is limited in complexity.

In the Structural Model, therefore, integrability is simplified by deliberately restricting the number of possible connections. The cost of this restriction is that the subsystem controllers often act purely as data conduits for the various controller children, and this adds complexity and performance overhead. In practice, however, the benefits far outweigh the cost. These benefits include the creation of a skeletal system that allows incremental development and easier integration. Every project that has used structural modeling has reported easy, smooth integration.

MODIFIABILITY

Modifiability is simplified when there are few base module configurations for the designer and maintainer to understand and when functionality is localized so that there are fewer subsystem controllers or controller children involved in a particular modification. Using n-square charts helps to reduce connections.

Furthermore, for subsystems that are physically based, the decomposition follows the physical structure, as do modifications. Those subsystems that are not physically based, such as the equations of motion, are less likely to be changed. Users of structural modeling reported that side effects encountered during modifications were rare.

8.5 For Further Reading

For an historical introduction to the computation and engineering involved in creating flight simulators, see [Fogarty 67], [Marsman 85], and [Perry 66].

The Structural Modeling pattern has evolved since 1987. Some of the early writings on this pattern can be found in [Lee 88], [Rissman 90], and [Abowd 93]. A report on results of using the pattern can be found in [Chastek 96].

The reader interested in more details about the functional decomposition used in example flight simulators is referred to [ASCYW 94].

8.6 Discussion Questions

1. The strong relationship between the structure of the system being simulated and the structure of the simulating software is one of the things that makes the Structural Modeling pattern so flexible with respect to mirroring the modeled system in the event of change, extension, or contraction. Suppose the application domain were something other than simulation. Would the Structural Modeling pattern still be a reasonable approach? Why or why not? Under what circumstances would it or would it not be?

2. The data and control flow constraints on subsystem controllers and controller children are very stringent. As a designer and implementor, do you think you would welcome these constraints or find them too restrictive?

3. How does the use of a skeletal system restrict the designer? How is this beneficial and how is it detrimental?

9

Documenting Software Architectures

with Felix Bachmann, David Garlan, James Ivers,
Reed Little, Robert Nord, and Judith Stafford

*Books are the bees which carry the quickening
pollen from one to another mind.*
— James Russell Lowell

As we have seen over and over, the software architecture for a system plays a central role in system development and in the organization that produces it. The architecture serves as the blueprint for both the system and the project developing it. It defines the work assignments that must be carried out by design and implementation teams and it is the primary carrier of system qualities such as performance, modifiability, and security—none of which can be achieved without a unifying architectural vision. Architecture is an artifact for early analysis to make sure that the design approach will yield an acceptable system. Moreover, architecture holds the key to post-deployment system understanding, maintenance, and mining efforts. In short, architecture is the conceptual glue that holds every phase of the project together for all of its many stakeholders.

Documenting the architecture is the crowning step to crafting it. Even a perfect architecture is useless if no one understands it or (perhaps worse) if key stakeholders misunderstand it. If you go to the trouble of creating a strong architecture, you *must* describe it in suffcent detail, without ambiguity, and organized in such a way that others can quickly find needed information. Otherwise, your effort will have been wasted because the architecture will be unusable.

This chapter will help you decide what information about an architecture is important to capture, and it will discuss guidelines for capturing it. It will also discuss notations that are available, including UML.

Note: Felix, James, Reed, and Robert are members of the SEI technical staff; David is an associate professor at Carnegie Mellon University's School of Computer Science; and Judith is an assistant professor at Tufts University's Department of Computer Science.

9.1 Uses of Architectural Documentation

The architecture for a system depends on the requirements levied on it, so too does the documentation for an architecture depend on the requirements levied on it—that is, how we expect it will be used. Documentation is decidedly *not* a case of "one size fits all." It should be sufficiently abstract to be quickly understood by new employees but sufficiently detailed to serve as a blueprint for analysis. The architectural documentation for, say, security analysis may well be different from the architectural documentation we would hand to an implementor. And both of these will be different from what we put in a new hire's familiarization reading list.

Architecture documentation is both prescriptive and descriptive. That is, for some audiences it prescribes what should be true by placing constraints on decisions to be made. For other audiences it describes what is true by recounting decisions already made about a system's design.

All of this tells us that different stakeholders for the documentation have different needs—different kinds of information, different levels of information, and different treatments of information. We should not expect to produce one architectural document and have every consumer read it in the same way. Rather, we should produce documentation that helps a stakeholder quickly find the information that stakeholder is interested in, with a minimum of information that is irrelevant (to that stakeholder) standing in the way.

This might mean producing different documents for different stakeholders. More likely, it means producing a single documentation suite with a roadmap that will help different stakeholders navigate through it.

One of the most fundamental rules for technical documentation in general, and software architecture documentation in particular, is to write from the point of view of the reader. Documentation that was easy to write but is not easy to read will not be used, and "easy to read" is in the eye of the beholder—or in this case, the stakeholder.

Understanding who the stakeholders are and how they will want to use the documentation will help us organize it and make it accessible to and usable for them. Back in Chapter 2, we said that a primary purpose of architecture was to serve as a communication vehicle among stakeholders. Documentation facilitates that communication. Some examples of architectural stakeholders and the information they might expect to find in the documentation are given in Table 9.1.

In addition, each stakeholders come in two varieties: seasoned and new. A new stakeholder will want information similar in content to what his seasoned counterpart wants, but in smaller and more introductory doses. Architecture documentation is a key means for educating people who need an overview: new developers, funding sponsors, visitors to the project, and so forth.

Perhaps one of the most avid consumers of architectural documentation is none other than the architect at some time in the project's future—either the same person or a replacement but in either case someone guaranteed to have an enor-

Documentation as an Introduction to Software Architecture

I had just finished my presentation on the Attribute Driven Design (ADD) method (see Chapter 7). The customer, a group within a business unit of a large manufacturing company, had seen most of our wares: ATAM (Chapter 11), reconstruction (Chapter 10), and our overall product line pitch (Chapter 14). I sat back, satisfied, and waited expectantly.

The customer had a problem however. They wanted to do architecture-based development, but they had a small development group and it would take several years to internalize all that we had shown them. In the meantime, they had products to make and contracts to meet. They just did not have the resources to do all of what they had seen. We needed something to let them get started on the architecture path without having to understand everything involved.

The discussion turned to documentation and the book we were writing on documenting software architecture. The customer was interested in documentation as a means of maintaining corporate knowledge about their products. We ended this meeting agreeing to do an exercise in architectural reconstruction and to document the results according to the principles described in this chapter.

I had always thought of documentation as the tail end of the design and development process. It is necessary for all of the reasons that architecture is necessary (communication, analysis, and education), but it is a derivative, not a driver.

The customer had a different perspective. They viewed documenting the software architecture as an ideal training vehicle for their developers. They had to do documentation in any case, so giving them a template for what to document was squarely in the corporate culture. In the process of filling in the templates, they would have to document different views (part of the engagement was for us to define the views useful to them), they would need to argue about how the artifact they were designing satisfied different quality goals, and, in general, they could learn about architectural concepts in the process of documentation.

This use of documentation as a training vehicle was a new one to me, but it has a great deal of power. For someone enmeshed in the details of the bits, thinking about architecture and architectural issues is a big jump. Understanding the mindset involved in software architecture through documentation seems to be a very good educational tool without a great deal of overhead for the consumer.

— LJB

mous stake in it. New architects are interested in learning how their predecessors tackled the difficult issues of the system and why particular decisions were made.

Even if the future architect is the same person, that architect will use the documentation as a repository of thought, as a storehouse of detailed design decisions too numerous and intertwined to be reproducible from memory alone.

TABLE 9.1   Stakeholders and the Communication Needs Served by Architecture

Stakeholder	Use
Architect and requirements engineers who represent customer(s)	To negotiate and make tradeoffs among competing requirements
Architect and designers of constituent parts	To resolve resource contention and establish performance and other kinds of runtime resource consumption budgets
Implementors	To provide inviolable constraints (plus exploitable freedoms) on downstream development activities
Testers and integrators	To specify the correct black-box behavior of the pieces that must fit together
Maintainers	To reveal areas a prospective change will affect
Designers of other systems with which this one must interoperate	To define the set of operations provided and required, and the protocols for their operation
Quality attribute specialists	To provide the model that drives analytical tools such as rate-monotonic real-time schedulability analysis, simulations and simulation generators, theorem provers, verifiers, etc. These tools require information about resource consumption, scheduling policies, dependencies, and so forth. Architecture documentation must contain the information necessary to evaluate a variety of quality attributes such as security, performance, usability, availability, and modifiability. Analyses for each attributes have their own information needs.
Managers	To create development teams corresponding to work assignments identified, to plan and allocate project resources, and to track progress by the various teams
Product line managers	To determine whether a potential new member of a product family is in or out of scope, and if out by how much
Quality assurance team	To provide a basis for conformance checking, for assurance that implementations have been faithful to the architectural prescriptions

Source: Adapted from [Clements 03]

9.2   Views

Perhaps the most important concept associated with software architecture documentation is the *view*. Recall from Chapter 2 that we defined a software architecture for a system as "the structure or structures of the system, which comprise elements, the externally visible properties of those elements, and the relationships among them." And we said that a view is a representation of a coherent set of architectural elements, as written by and read by system stakeholders. A structure is the set of elements itself, as they exist in software or hardware.

Also in Chapter 2 we discussed a software architecture as a complex entity that cannot be described in a simple one-dimensional fashion. The analogy with building architecture, if not taken too far, proves illuminating. There is no single rendition of a building architecture but many: the room layouts, the elevation drawings, the electrical diagrams, the plumbing diagrams, the ventilation diagrams, the traffic patterns, the sunlight and passive solar views, the security system plans, and many others. Which of these views *is* the architecture? None of them. Which views *convey* the architecture? All of them.

The concept of a view, which you can think of as capturing a structure, provides us with the basic principle of documenting software architecture:

> Documenting an architecture is a matter of documenting the relevant views and then adding documentation that applies to more than one view.

This principle is useful because it breaks the problem of architecture documentation into more tractable parts, which provide the structure for the remainder of this chapter:

- Choosing the relevant views
- Documenting a view
- Documenting information that applies to more than one view

9.3   Choosing the Relevant Views

Recall that we introduced a set of structures and views in Chapter 2. What are the relevant views? This is where knowing your stakeholders and the uses they plan to make of the documentation will help you construct the documentation package they need. The many purposes that architecture can serve—as a mission statement for implementors, as the starting point for system understanding and asset recovery, as the blueprint for project planning, and so forth—are each represented by a stakeholder wanting and expecting to use the documentation to serve that purpose. Similarly, the quality attributes of most concern to you and the other stakeholders in the system's development will affect the choice of what views to document. For instance, a *layered view* will tell you about your system's portability. A *deployment view* will let you reason about your system's performance and reliability. And so it goes. These quality attributes are "spoken for" in the documentation by analysts (perhaps even the architect) who need to examine the architecture to make sure the quality attributes are provided.

In short, different views support different goals and uses. This is fundamentally why we do not advocate a particular view or a collection of views. The views you should document depend on the uses you expect to make of the documentation. Different views will highlight different system elements and/or relationships.

Table 9.2 shows a representative population of stakeholders and the kind of views they tend to find useful. You should use it to help you think about who your stakeholders are and what views might serve them well. Which views are available from which to choose? Chapter 2 listed a set of views, some of which are

TABLE 9.2   Stakeholders and the Architecture Documentation They Might Find Most Useful

Stakeholder	Module Views				C&C Views	Allocation Views	
	Decomposition	Uses	Class	Layer	Various	Deployment	Implementation
Project Manager	s	s		s		d	
Member of Development Team	d	d	d	d	d	s	s
Testers and Integrators		d	d		s	s	s
Maintainers	d	d	d	d	d	s	s
Product Line Application Builder		d	s	o	s	s	s
Customer					s	o	
End User					s	s	
Analyst	d	d	s	d	s	d	
Infrastructure Support	s	s		s		s	d
New Stakeholder	x	x	x	x	x	x	x
Current and Future Architect	d	d	d	d	d	d	s

Key: d = detailed information, s = some details, o = overview information, x = anything
Source: Adapted from [Clements 03].

reflected in Table 9.2. Chapter 2 divided views into these three groups: module, component-and-connector (C&C), and allocation. This three-way categorization reflects the fact that architects need to think about their software in at least three ways at once:

1. How it is structured as a set of implementation units
2. How it is structured as a set of elements that have runtime behavior and interactions
3. How it relates to non-software structures in its environment

Other views are available. A view simply represents a set of system elements and relationships among them, so whatever elements and relationships you deem useful to a segment of the stakeholder community constitute a valid view. Here is a simple three-step procedure for choosing the views for your project.

1. *Produce a candidate view list.* Begin by building a stakeholder/view table, like Table 9.2, for your project. Your stakeholder list is likely to be different from the one in the table, but be as comprehensive as you can. For the columns, enumerate the views that apply to your system. Some views (such as decomposition

or uses) apply to every system, while others (the layered view, most component-and-connector views such as client-server or shared data) only apply to systems designed that way. Once you have the rows and columns defined, fill in each cell to describe how much information the stakeholder requires from the view: none, overview only, moderate detail, or high detail.

2. *Combine views.* The candidate view list from step 1 is likely to yield an impractically large number of views. To reduce the list to a manageable size, first look for views in the table that require only overview depth or that serve very few stakeholders. See if the stakeholders could be equally well served by another view having a stronger constituency. Next, look for views that are good candidates to be combined—that is, a view that gives information from two or more views at once. For small and medium projects, the implementation view is often easily overlaid with the module decomposition view. The module decomposition view also pairs well with uses or layered views. Finally, the deployment view usually combines well with whatever component-and-connector view shows the components that are allocated to hardware elements—the process view, for example.

3. *Prioritize.* After step 2 you should have an appropriate set of views to serve your stakeholder community. At this point you need to decide what to do first. How you decide depends on the details specific to your project, but remember that you don't have to complete one view before starting another. People can make progress with overview-level information, so a breadth-first approach is often the best. Also, some stakeholders' interests supersede others. A project manager or the management of a company with which yours is partnering demands attention and information early and often.

9.4 Documenting a View

There is no industry-standard template for documenting a view, but the seven-part standard organization that we suggest in this section has worked well in practice. First of all, whatever sections you choose to include, make sure to *have* a standard organization. Allocating specific information to specific sections will help the documentation writer attack the task and recognize completion, and it will help the documentation reader quickly find information of interest at the moment and skip everything else.

1. *Primary presentation* shows the elements and the relationships among them that populate the view. The primary presentation should contain the information you wish to convey about the system (in the vocabulary of that view) first. It should certainly include the primary elements and relations of the view, but under some circumstances it might not include all of them. For example, you may wish to show the elements and relations that come into play during normal operation, but relegate error handling or exceptional processing to the supporting documentation.

The primary presentation is usually graphical. In fact, most graphical notations make their contributions in the form of the primary presentation and little else. If the primary presentation is graphical, it must be accompanied by a key that explains, or that points to an explanation of, the notation or symbology used.

Sometimes the primary presentation can be tabular; tables are often a superb way to convey a large amount of information compactly. An example of a textual primary presentation is the A-7E module decomposition view illustrated in Chapter 3. A textual presentation still carries the obligation to present a terse summary of the most important information in the view. In Section 9.6 we will discuss using UML for the primary presentation.

2. *Element catalog* details at least those elements and relations depicted in the primary presentation, and perhaps others. Producing the primary presentation is often what architects concentrate on, but without backup information that explains the picture, it is of little value.[1] For instance, if a diagram shows elements A, B, and C, there had better be documentation that explains in sufficient detail what A, B, and C are, and their purposes or the roles they play, rendered in the vocabulary of the view. For example, a module decomposition view has elements that are modules, relations that are a form of "is part of," and properties that define the responsibilities of each module. A process view has elements that are processes, relations that define synchronization or other process-related interaction, and properties that include timing parameters.

In addition, if there are elements or relations relevant to the view that were omitted from the primary presentation, the catalog is where those are introduced and explained.

The behavior and interfaces of elements are two other aspects of an element catalog; these will be discussed shortly.

3. *Context diagram* shows how the system depicted in the view relates to its environment in the vocabulary of the view. For example, in a component-and-connector view you show which component and connectors interact with external components and connectors, via which interfaces and protocols.

4. *Variability guide* shows how to exercise any variation points that are a part of the architecture shown in this view. In some architectures, decisions are left unbound until a later stage of the development process, and yet the architecture must still be documented. An example of variability is found in software product lines where the product line architecture is suitable for multiple particular systems (discussed in Chapter 14). A variability guide should include documentation about each point of variation in the architecture, including

- the options among which a choice is to be made. In a module view, the options are the various versions or parameterizations of modules. In a component-and-connector view, they might include constraints on replication, scheduling, or choice of protocol. In an allocation view, they

---

[1] To emphasize that it is but a sketch of the complete picture, we call a primary presentation by itself an architectural *cartoon*.

might include the conditions under which a software element would be allocated to a particular processor.
- the binding time of the option. Some choices are made at design time, some at build time, and others at runtime.

5. *Architecture background* explains why the design reflected in the view came to be. The goal of this section is to explain to someone why the design is as it is and to provide a convincing argument that it is sound. An architecture background includes
- rationale, explaining why the decisions reflected in the view were made and why alternatives were rejected.
- analysis results, which justify the design or explain what would have to change in the face of a modification.
- assumptions reflected in the design.

6. *Glossary of terms* used in the views, with a brief description of each.

7. *Other information.* The precise contents of this section will vary according to the standard practices of your organization. They might include management information such as authorship, configuration control data, and change histories. Or the architect might record references to specific sections of a requirements document to establish traceability. Strictly speaking, information such as this is not architectural. Nevertheless, it is convenient to record it alongside the architecture, and this section is provided for that purpose. In any case, the first part of this section must detail its specific contents.

Figure 9.1 summarizes the parts of the documentation just described.

DOCUMENTING BEHAVIOR

Views present structural information about the system. However, structural information is not sufficient to allow reasoning about some system properties. Reasoning about deadlock, for example, depends on understanding the sequence of interactions among the elements, and structural information alone does not present this sequencing information. Behavior descriptions add information that reveals the ordering of interactions among the elements, opportunities for concurrency, and time dependencies of interactions (at a specific time or after a period of time).

Behavior can be documented either about an element or about an ensemble of elements working in concert. Exactly what to model will depend on the type of system being designed. For example, if it is a real-time embedded system, you will need to say a lot about timing properties and the time of events. In a banking system, the sequence of events (e.g., atomic transactions and rollback procedures) is more important than the actual time of events being considered. Different modeling techniques and notations are used depending on the type of analysis to be performed. In UML, sequence diagrams and statecharts are examples of behavioral descriptions. These notations are widely used.

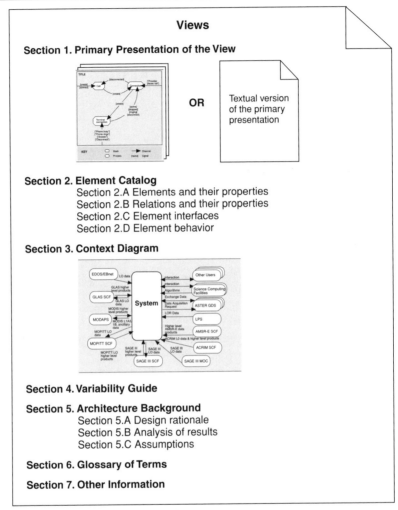

Source: Adapted from [Clements 03].

FIGURE 9.1   The seven parts of a documented view

Statecharts are a formalism developed in the 1980s for describing reactive systems. They add a number of useful extensions to traditional state diagrams such as nesting of state and "and" states, which provide the expressive power to model abstraction and concurrency. Statecharts allow reasoning about the totality of the system. All of the states are assumed to be represented and the analysis techniques are general with respect to the system. That is, it is possible to answer a question such as Will the response time to this stimulus always be less than 0.5 seconds?

A sequence diagram documents a sequence of stimuli exchanges. It presents a collaboration in terms of component instances and their interactions and shows the interaction arranged in time sequence. The vertical dimension represents time and the horizontal dimension represents different components. Sequence diagrams allow reasoning based on a particular usage scenario. They show how the system reacts to a particular stimulus and represent a choice of paths through the system. They make it possible to answer a question such as What parallel activities occur when the system is responding to these specific stimuli under these specific conditions?

DOCUMENTING INTERFACES

An *interface* is a boundary across which two independent entities meet and interact or communicate with each other. Our definition of software architecture in Chapter 2 made it clear that elements' interfaces—carriers of the properties externally visible to other elements—are architectural. Since you cannot perform analyses or system building without them, documenting interfaces is an important part of documenting architecture.

Documenting an interface consists of naming and identifying it and documenting its syntactic and semantic information. The first two parts constitute an interface's "signature." When an interface's resources are invokable programs, the signature names the programs and defines their parameters. Parameters are defined by their order, data type, and (sometimes) whether or not their value is changed by the program. A signature is the information that you would find about the program, for instance, in an element's C or C++ header file or in a Java interface.

Signatures are useful (for example, they can enable automatic build checking), but are only part of the story. Signature matching will guarantee that a system will compile and/or link successfully. However, it guarantees nothing about whether the system will operate successfully, which is after all the ultimate goal. That information is bound up in the semantics to the interface, or what happens when resources are brought into play.

An interface is documented with an interface specification, which is a statement of element properties the architect chooses to make known. The architect should expose only what is needed to interact with the interface. Put another way, the architect chooses what information is permissible and appropriate for people to assume about the element, and what is unlikely to change. Documenting an interface is a matter of striking a balance between disclosing too little information and disclosing too much. Too little information will prevent developers from successfully interacting with the element. Too much will make future changes to the system more difficult and widespread and make the interface too complicated for people to understand. A rule of thumb is to focus on how elements interact with their operational environments, not on how they are implemented. Restrict the documentation to phenomena that are externally visible.

Elements that occur as modules often correspond directly to one or more elements in a component-and-connector view. The module and component-and-connector elements are likely to have similar, if not identical, interfaces and documenting them in both places would produce needless duplication. To avoid that, the interface specification in the component-and-connector view can point to the interface specification in the module view, and only contain the information specific to its view. Similarly, a module may appear in more than one module view—such as the module decomposition or uses view. Again, choose one view to hold the interface specification and refer to it in the others.

A Template for Documenting Interfaces.   Here is a suggested standard organization for interface documentation. You may wish to modify it to remove items not relevant to your situation, or add items unique to it. More important than which standard organization you use is the practice of using one. Use what you need to present an accurate picture of the element's externally visible interactions for the interfaces in your project.

1. *Interface identity.* When an element has multiple interfaces, identify the individual interfaces to distinguish them. This usually means naming them. You may also need to provide a version number.

2. *Resources provided.* The heart of an interface document is the resources that the element provides. Define them by giving their syntax, their semantics (what happens when they are used), and any restrictions on their usage. Several notations exist for documenting an interface's syntax. One is the OMG's Interface Definition Language (IDL), used in the CORBA community. It provides language constructs to describe data types, operations, attributes, and exceptions. The only language support for semantic information is a comment mechanism. Most programming languages have built-in ways to specify the signature of an element. C header (.h) files and Ada package specifications are two examples. Finally, using the <<interface>> stereotype in UML (as shown in Figure 9.4) provides the means for conveying syntactic information about an interface. At a minimum, the interface is named; the architect can also specify signature information.

- *Resource syntax.* This is the resource's signature. The signature includes any information another program will need to write a syntactically correct program that uses the resource. The signature includes the resource name, names and logical data types of arguments (if any), and so forth.
- *Resource semantics.* This describes the result of invoking the resource. It might include
  - assignment of values to data that the actor invoking the resource can access. It might be as simple as setting the value of a return argument or as far-reaching as updating a central database.

- events that will be signaled or messages that will be sent as a result of using the resource.
- how other resources will behave in the future as the result of using this resource. For example, if you ask a resource to destroy an object, trying to access that object in the future through other resources will produce quite a different outcome (an error).
- humanly observable results. These are prevalent in embedded systems; for example, calling a program that turns on a display in a cockpit has a very observable effect: The display comes on.

In addition, the statement of semantics should make it clear whether the resource execution will be atomic or may be suspended or interrupted. The most widespread notation for conveying semantic information is natural language. Boolean algebra is often used to write down preconditions and postconditions, which provide a relatively simple and effective method for expressing semantics. Traces are also used to convey semantic information by writing down sequences of activities or interactions that describe the element's response to a specific use.

- *Resource usage restrictions.* Under what circumstances may this resource be used? Perhaps data must be initialized before it can be read, or a particular method cannot be invoked unless another is invoked first. Perhaps there is a limit on the number of actors that can interact via this resource at any instant. Perhaps only one actor can have ownership and be able to modify the element whereas others have only read access. Perhaps only certain resources or interfaces are accessible to certain actors to support a multilevel security scheme. If the resource requires that other resources be present, or makes other assumptions about its environment, these should be documented.

3. *Data type definitions.* If any interface resources employ a data type other than one provided by the underlying programming language, the architect needs to communicate the definition of that data type. If it is defined by another element, then a reference to the definition in that element's documentation is sufficient. In any case, programmers writing elements using such a resource need to know (a) how to declare variables and constants of the data type; (b) how to write literal values in the data type; (c) what operations and comparisons may be performed on members of the data type; and (d) how to convert values of the data type into other data types, where appropriate.

4. *Exception definitions.* These describe exceptions that can be raised by the resources on the interface. Since the same exception might be raised by more than one resource, it is often convenient to simply list each resource's exceptions but define them in a dictionary collected separately. This section is that dictionary. Common exception-handling behavior can also be defined here.

5. *Variability provided by the interface.* Does the interface allow the element to be configured in some way? These *configuration parameters* and how they affect the semantics of the interface must be documented. Examples of variability include the capacities of visible data structures and the performance characteristics of underlying algorithms. Name and provide a range of values for each configuration parameter and specify the time when its actual value is bound.

6. *Quality attribute characteristics of the interface.* The architect needs to document what quality attribute characteristics (such as performance or reliability) the interface makes known to the element's users. This information may be in the form of constraints on implementations of elements that will realize the interface. Which qualities you choose to concentrate on and make promises about will depend on context.

7. *Element requirements.* What the element requires may be specific, named resources provided by other elements. The documentation obligation is the same as for resources provided: syntax, semantics, and any usage restrictions. Often it is convenient to document information like this as a set of assumptions that the element's designer has made about the system. In this form, they can be reviewed by experts who can confirm or repudiate the assumptions before design has progressed too far.

8. *Rationale and design issues.* As with rationale for the architecture (or architectural views) at large, the architect should record the reasons for an element's interface design. The rationale should explain the motivation behind the design, constraints and compromises, what alternative designs were considered and rejected (and why), and any insight the architect has about how to change the interface in the future.

9. *Usage guide.* Item 2 and item 7 document an element's semantic information on a per resource basis. This sometimes falls short of what is needed. In some cases semantics need to be reasoned about in terms of how a broad number of individual interactions interrelate. Essentially, a *protocol* is involved that is documented by considering a sequence of interactions. Protocols can represent the complete behavior of the interaction or patterns of usage that the element designer expects to come up repeatedly. If interacting with the element via its interface is complex, the interface documentation should include a static behavioral model such as a statechart, or examples of carrying out specific interactions in the form of sequence diagrams. This is similar to the view-level behaviors presented in the previous section, but focused on a single element.

Figure 9.2 summarizes this template which is an expansion of section 2.C from Figure 9.1.

```
          Section 2C. Element Interface Specification

Section 2.C.1.  Interface identity
Section 2.C.2.  Resources provided
                   Section 2.C.a. Resource syntax
                   Section 2.C.b. Resource semantics
                   Section 2.C.c. Resource usage restrictions
Section 2.C.3.  Locally defined data types
Section 2.C.4.  Exception definitions
Section 2.C.5.  Variability provided
Section 2.C.6.  Quality attribute characteristics
Section 2.C.7.  Element requirements
Section 2.C.8.  Rationale and design issues
Section 2.C.9.  Usage guide
```

Source: Adapted from [Clements 03].

FIGURE 9.2   The nine parts of interface documentation

9.5   Documentation across Views

We now turn to the complement of view documentation, which is capturing the information that applies to more than one view or to the documentation package as a whole. Cross-view documentation consists of just three major aspects, which we can summarize as how-what-why:

1. *How* the documentation is laid out and organized so that a stakeholder of the architecture can find the information he or she needs efficiently and reliably. This part consists of a view catalog and a view template.

2. *What* the architecture is. Here, the information that remains to be captured beyond the views themselves is a short system overview to ground any reader as to the purpose of the system; the way the views are related to each other; a list of elements and where they appear; and a glossary that applies to the entire architecture.

3. *Why* the architecture is the way it is: the context for the system, external constraints that have been imposed to shape the architecture in certain ways, and the rationale for coarse-grained large-scale decisions.

Figure 9.3 summarizes these points.

Documentation across Views

How the document is organized:
    1.1 View catalog
    1.2 View template

What the architecture is:
    2.1 System overview
    2.2 Mapping between views
    2.3 List of elements and where they appear
    2.4 Project glossary

Why the architecture is the way it is:
    3.1 Rationale

Source: Adapted from [Clements 03].

FIGURE 9.3   Summary of cross-view documentation

HOW THE DOCUMENTATION IS ORGANIZED TO SERVE A STAKEHOLDER

Every suite of architectural documentation needs an introductory piece to explain its organization to a novice stakeholder and to help that stakeholder access the information he or she she is most interested in. There are two kinds of "how" information:

- A view catalog
- A view template

View Catalog.   A view catalog is the reader's introduction to the views that the architect has chosen to include in the suite of documentation.

When using the documentation suite as a basis for communication, it is necessary for a new reader to determine where particular information can be found. A catalog contains this information. When using the documentation suite as a basis for analysis, it is necessary to know which views contain the information necessary for a particular analysis. In a performance analysis, for example, resource consumption is an important piece of information, A catalog enables the analyst to determine which views contain properties relevant to resource consumption.

There is one entry in the view catalog for each view given in the documentation suite. Each entry should give the following:

1. The name of the view and what style it instantiates
2. A description of the view's element types, relation types, and properties
3. A description of what the view is for

4. Management information about the view document, such as the latest version, the location of the view document, and the owner of the view document

The view catalog is intended to describe the documentation suite, not the system being documented. Specifics of the system belong in the individual views, not in the view catalog. For instance, the actual elements contained in a view are listed in the view's element catalog.

View Template.   A view template is the standard organization for a view. Figure 9.1 and the material surrounding it provide a basis for a view template by defining the standard parts of a view document and the contents and rules for each. The purpose of a view template is that of any standard organization: It helps a reader navigate quickly to a section of interest, and it helps a writer organize the information and establish criteria for knowing how much work is left to do.

WHAT THE ARCHITECTURE IS

This section provides information about the system whose architecure is being documented, the relation of the views to each other, and an index of architectural elements.

System Overview.   This is a short prose description of what the system's function is, who its users are, and any important background or constraints. The intent is to provide readers with a consistent mental model of the system and its purpose. Sometimes the project at large will have a system overview, in which case this section of the architectural documentation simply points to that.

Mapping between Views.   Since all of the views of an architecture describe the same system, it stands to reason that any two views will have much in common. Helping a reader of the documentation understand the relationships among views will give him a powerful insight into how the architecture works as a unified conceptual whole. Being clear about the relationship by providing mappings between views is the key to increased understanding and decreased confusion.

For instance, each module may map to multiple runtime elements, such as when classes map to objects. Complications arise when the mappings are not one to one, or when runtime elements of the system do not exist as code elements at all, such as when they are imported at runtime or incorporated at build or load time. These are relatively simple one- (or none-) to-many mappings. In general, though, *parts* of elements in one view can map to *parts* of elements in another view.

It is not necessary to provide mappings between every pair of views. Choose the ones that provide the most insight.

Element List.   The element list is simply an index of all of the elements that appear in any of the views, along with a pointer to where each one is defined. This will help stakeholders look up items of interest quickly.

Project Glossary.   The glossary lists and defines terms unique to the system that have special meaning. A list of acronyms, and the meaning of each, will also be appreciated by stakeholders. If an appropriate glossary already exists, a pointer to it will suffice here.

WHY THE ARCHITECTURE IS THE WAY IT IS: RATIONALE

Similar in purpose to the rationale for a view or the rationale for an interface design, cross-view rationale explains how the overall architecture is in fact a solution to its requirements. One might use the rationale to explain

- the implications of system-wide design choices on meeting the requirements or satisfying constraints.
- the effect on the architecture when adding a foreseen new requirement or changing an existing one.
- the constraints on the developer in implementing a solution.
- decision alternatives that were rejected.

In general, the rationale explains why a decision was made and what the implications are in changing it.

9.6   Unified Modeling Language

We have concentrated on the kind of information that should be included in architecture documentation. Architecture in some sense expresses what is essential about a software system, and that essence is independent of languages and notations to capture it. Nevertheless, today the Unified Modeling Language (UML) has emerged as the de facto standard notation for documenting a software architecture. However, it must be said that UML makes its main contribution in a view's primary presentation, and its secondary contribution in the behavior of an element or group of elements. It is up to the architect to augment the UML pictures with the necessary supporting documentation (the element catalog, the rationale, and so forth) that a responsible job requires. UML provides no direct support for components, connectors, layers, interface semantics, or many other aspects of a system that are supremely architectural.

Still, in most cases we can use the constructs that UML does offer to achieve satisfactory effects, at least in crafting the primary presentations of architectural views. We begin by discussing module views.

MODULE VIEWS

Recall that a module is a code or implementation unit and a module view is an enumeration of modules together with their interfaces and their relations.

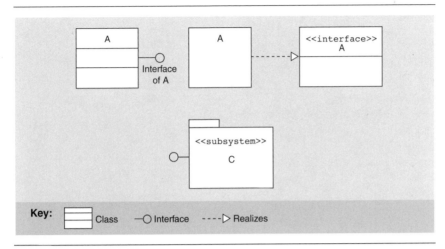

FIGURE 9.4   Interfaces in UML

Interfaces.   Figure 9.4 shows how module interfaces can be represented in UML. UML uses a "lollipop" to denote an interface, which can be appended to classes and subsystems, among other things.

UML also allows a class symbol (box) to be stereotyped as an interface; the open-headed dashed arrow shows that an element realizes an interface. The bottom of the class symbol can be annotated with the interface's signature information: method names, arguments, argument types, and so forth. The lollipop notation is normally used to show dependencies from elements to the interface, while the box notation allows a more detailed description of the interface's syntax, such as the operations it provides.

Modules.   UML provides a variety of constructs to represent different kinds of modules. Figure 9.5 shows some examples. UML has a class construct, which is the object-oriented specialization of a module. Packages can be used in cases where grouping of functionality is important, such as to represent layers and classes. The subsystem construct can be used if a specification of interface and behavior is required.

Figure 9.6 shows how the relations native to module views are denoted using UML. Module decomposition relies on the "is-part-of" relation. The module uses view relies on the dependency relation, and the module class view relies on the generalization, or "is-a" relation (also called "inheritance").

Aggregation.   In UML, the subsystem construct can be used to represent modules that contain other modules; the class box is normally used for the leaves of the decomposition. Subsystems are used both as packages and as classifiers. As packages, they can be decomposed and hence are suitable for module aggregation. As

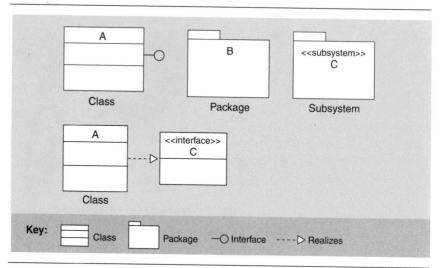

FIGURE 9.5 Examples of module notations in UML

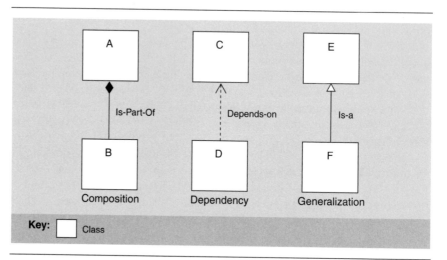

FIGURE 9.6 Examples of relation notations in UML. Module B is part of module A, module D depends on module C, and module F is a type of module E.

classifiers, they encapsulate their contents and can provide an explicit interface. Aggregation is depicted in one of three ways in UML:

- Modules may be nested (see Figure 9.7 *left*).
- A succession of two diagrams (possibly linked) can be shown, where the second is a depiction of the contents of a module shown in the first.

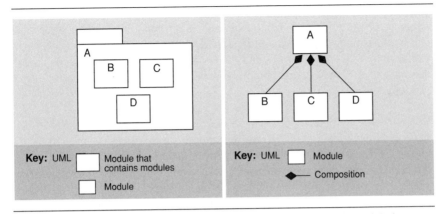

FIGURE 9.7   Decomposition in UML with nesting. The aggregate module is shown as a package (*left*); decomposition in UML with arcs (*right*).

- An arc denoting composition is drawn between the parent and the children (see Figure 9.7 *right*).

In UML, composition is a form of aggregation with implied strong ownership—that is, parts live and die with the whole. If module A is composed of modules B and C, then B or C cannot exist without A, and if A is destroyed at runtime, so are B and C. Thus, UML's composition relation has implications beyond the structuring of the implementation units; the relation also endows the elements with a runtime property. As an architect, you should make sure you are comfortable with this property before using UML's composition relation.

Generalization.   Expressing generalization is at the heart of UML in which modules are shown as classes (although they may also be shown as subsystems). Figure 9.8 shows the basic notation available in UML.

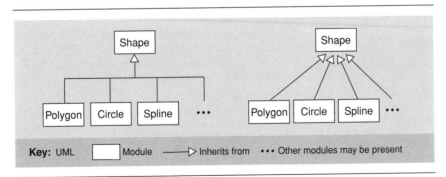

FIGURE 9.8   Documenting generalization in UML with two line styles

The two diagrams in Figure 9.8 are semantically identical. UML allows an ellipsis (. . .) in place of a submodule, indicating that a module can have more children than shown and that additional ones are likely. Module Shape is the parent of modules Polygon, Circle, and Spline, each of which is a subclass, child, or descendant of Shape. Shape is more general, while its children are specialized versions.

Dependency.   The basic notation for dependency was shown in Figure 9.6. The most architecturally significant manifestation of dependency is found in layers. Sadly, UML has no built-in primitive corresponding to a layer. However, it can represent simple layers using *packages,* as shown in Figure 9.9. These are general-purpose mechanisms for organizing elements into groups. UML has predefined packages for systems and subsystems. We can introduce an additional package for layers by defining it as a package stereotype. A layer can be shown as a UML package with the constraints that it groups modules together and that the dependency between packages is "allowed to use." We can designate a layer using the package notation with the stereotype name <<layer>> preceding the layer name, or introduce a new visual form, such as a shaded rectangle.

COMPONENT-AND-CONNECTOR VIEWS

There is no single preferred strategy to document component-and-connector (C&C) views in UML, but a number of alternatives. Each alternative has its advantages and disadvantages. One natural candidate for representing component-and-connector types begins with the UML class concept.

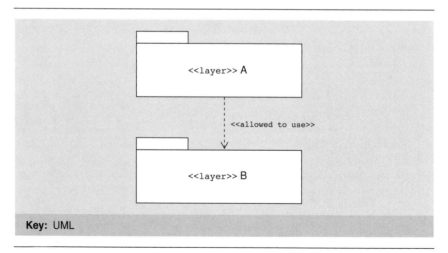

FIGURE 9.9   A simple representation of layers in UML

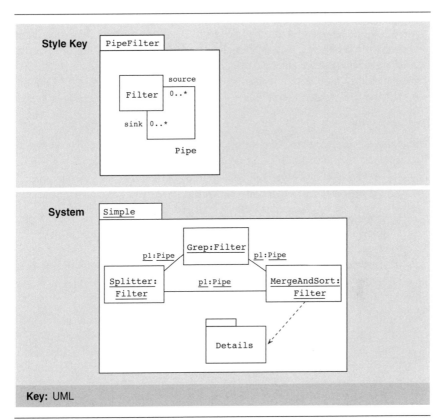

FIGURE 9.10   Types as classes, and instances as objects, exemplified with
a simple pipe and filter

Figure 9.10 illustrates the general idea using a simple pipe-and-filter system.
Here, the filter architectural type is represented as the UML class `Filter`.
Instances of filters, such as `Splitter`, are represented as corresponding objects
in an object instance diagram. To provide a namespace boundary, we enclose the
descriptions in packages. The representation of `MergeAndSort`, denoted `Details`,
would be shown as another package elsewhere.

We now take a closer look at this strategy.

Components.   The type/instance relationship in architectural descriptions is a
close match to the class/object relationship in a UML model. UML classes, like
component types in architectural descriptions, are first-class entities and are rich
structures for capturing software abstractions. The full set of UML descriptive
mechanisms is available to describe the structure, properties, and behavior of a
class, making this a good choice for depicting detail and using UML-based analysis tools. Properties of architectural components can be represented as class

attributes or with associations; behavior can be described using UML behavioral models; and generalization can be used to relate a set of component types. The semantics of an instance or type can also be elaborated by attaching one of the standard stereotypes; for example, the «process» stereotype can be attached to a component to indicate that it runs as a separate process. Note that the relationship between MergeAndSort and its substructure is indicated using a dependency relation.

Interfaces.   Interfaces to components, sometimes called ports, can be shown in five ways, as shown in Figure 9.11, described in increasing order of expressiveness. However, as expressiveness rises so does complexity, so you should pick the first strategy that will serve your purposes.

- *Option 1: No explicit representation.* Leaving out interfaces leads to the simplest diagrams but suffers from the obvious problem that there is no way to characterize the names or the properties of the interfaces in the primary presentation. Still, this choice might be reasonable if the components have only one interface, if the interfaces can be inferred from the system topology, or if the diagram is refined elsewhere.

- *Option 2: Interfaces as annotations.* Representing interfaces as annotations provides a home for information about them, although annotations have no semantic value in UML so cannot be used as a basis for analysis. Again, if the detailed properties of an interface are not of concern, this approach might be reasonable.

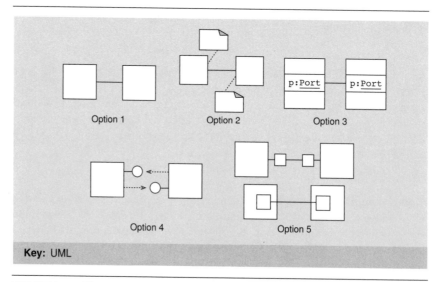

FIGURE 9.11   Five ways to represent interfaces to components (ports)

- *Option 3: Interfaces as class/object attributes.* Treating interfaces as attributes of a class/object makes them part of the formal structural model, but they can have only a simple representation in a class diagram—essentially, a name and a type. This restriction limits the expressiveness of this option.

- *Option 4: Interfaces as UML interfaces.* The UML lollipop notation provides a compact description of an interface in a class diagram depicting a component type. In an instance diagram, a UML association role, corresponding to an interface instance and qualified by the interface type name, provides a compact way to show that a component instance is interacting through a particular interface instance. This approach provides visually distinct depictions of components and interfaces, in which interfaces can clearly be seen as subservient.

  However, this strategy provides no means to depict the services required from a component's environment, often a key part of an interface. Furthermore, it is meaningful for a component type to have several instances of the same interface type, but it is not meaningful to say that a class realizes several versions of one UML interface. For example, there is no easy way to define a `Splitter` filter type that has two output ports of the same "type" using this technique. Finally, unlike classes, UML interfaces do not have attributes or substructure.

- *Option 5: Interfaces as classes.* Describing interfaces as classes contained by a component type overcomes the lack of expressiveness of the previous alternatives: We can now represent interface substructure and indicate that a component type has several interfaces of the same type. A component instance is modeled as an object containing a set of interface objects. However, by representing interfaces as classes, we not only clutter the diagram but also lose clear visual discrimination between interfaces and components. We could use a notational variation in which the interfaces are contained classes, as shown in the lower part of option 5 in Figure 9.11. Indicating points of interaction is counterintuitive, however, as containment usually indicates that a class owns other classes whose instances may or may not be accessible through instances of the parent class.

Connectors.   There are three reasonable options for representing connectors. Again, the choice is between expressiveness and semantic match on the one hand and complexity on the other.

- *Option 1: Connector types as associations and connector instances as links.* In an architectural box-and-line diagram of a system, the lines between components are connectors. One tempting way to represent connectors in UML is as associations between classes or links between objects. This approach is visually simple, provides a clear distinction between components and connectors, and uses the most familiar relationship in UML class diagrams: association. Moreover, associations can be labeled, and a direction associated with the connector can be indicated with an arrow. Unfortunately, connectors and associations have different meanings. A system in an architectural description is built up by choosing components with behavior exposed through their interfaces and connecting them with connectors that coordinate their behaviors. A system's behavior is defined as the collective behavior of a set of components whose interaction is defined and limited by the connections between them.

In contrast, although an association, or link, in UML represents a potential for interaction between the elements it relates, the association mechanism is primarily a way of describing a conceptual relationship between two elements. In addition, an association is a relationship between UML elements, so it cannot stand on its own in a UML model. Consequently, a connector type cannot be represented in isolation. Instead, you must resort to naming conventions or to stereotypes whose meanings are captured by description in UML's object constraint language. Further, the approach does not allow you to specify a connector's interfaces.

- *Option 2: Connector types as association classes.* One solution to the lack of expressiveness is to qualify the association with a class that represents the connector type. In this way, the connector type or connector attributes can be captured as attributes of a class or object. Unfortunately, this technique still does not provide any way of explicitly representing connector interfaces.

- *Option 3: Connector types as classes and connector instances as objects.* One way to give connectors first-class status in UML is to represent connector types as classes and connector instances as objects. Using classes and objects, we have the same four options for representing roles as we had for interfaces: not at all, as annotations, as interfaces realized by a class, or as child classes contained by a connector class. Given a scheme for representing interfaces, an attachment between a component's interface and a connector's interface may be represented as an association or a dependency.

Systems.   In addition to representing individual components and connectors and their types, we also need to encapsulate graphs of components and connectors: systems. Three options are available.

- *Option 1: Systems as UML subsystems.* The primary UML mechanism for grouping related elements is the package. In fact, UML defines a standard package stereotype, called «`subsystem`», to group UML models that represent a logical part of a system. The choice of subsystems is appropriate for any mapping of components and connectors, and it works particularly well for grouping classes. One of the problems with using subsystems, as defined in UML 1.4, is that, although they are both a classifier and a package, the meaning is not entirely clear. Some have argued that we should be able to treat a subsystem as an atomic class-like entity at certain stages in the development process and later be able to refine it in terms of a more detailed substructure. Having the ability to do this would make the subsystem construct more appropriate for modeling architectural components.

- *Option 2: Systems as contained objects.* Object containment can be used to represent systems. Components are represented as instances of contained classes, and connectors are modeled using one of the options outlined earlier. Objects provide a strong encapsulation boundary and carry with them the notion that each instance of the class has the associated "substructure." However, this approach has problems, the most serious being that associations, used to model connectors, between contained classes are not scoped by the class. That is, it is not possible to say that a pair of classes interacts via a particular connector, modeled as an association, only in the context of a particular system. So, for example, indicating that two contained classes interact via an association is valid for instances of classes used anywhere else in the model.

- *Option 3: Systems as collaborations.* A set of communicating objects connected by links is described in UML using a collaboration. If we represent components as objects, we can use collaborations to represent systems. A collaboration defines a set of participants and relationships that are meaningful for a given purpose, which in this case is to describe the runtime structure of the system. The participants define classifier roles that objects play, or conform to, when interacting. Similarly, the relationships define association roles that links must conform to.

    Collaboration diagrams can be used to present collaborations at either the specification or the instance level. A specification-level collaboration diagram shows the roles, defined within the collaboration, arranged in a pattern to describe the system substructure. An instance-level collaboration diagram shows the objects and links conforming to the roles at the specification level and interacting to achieve the purpose. Therefore, a collaboration presented at the instance level is best used to represent the runtime structure of the system.

    Figure 9.12 illustrates this approach. The `Filter` architectural type is represented as previously. Instances of filters and pipes are represented as corresponding classifier roles—for example, `/Splitter` indicates the `Splitter` role—and association roles. The objects and links conforming to those roles are shown in the collaboration diagram at the instance level, indicated by underscored names.

    Although this is a natural way to describe runtime structures, it leaves no way to explicitly represent system-level properties. There is also a semantic mismatch; a collaboration describes a representative interaction between objects and provides a partial description, whereas an architectural configuration is meant to capture a complete description.

ALLOCATION VIEWS

In UML, a deployment diagram is a graph of nodes connected by communication associations. Figure 9.13 provides an example. Nodes may contain component instances, which indicates that the component lives or runs on the node. Components

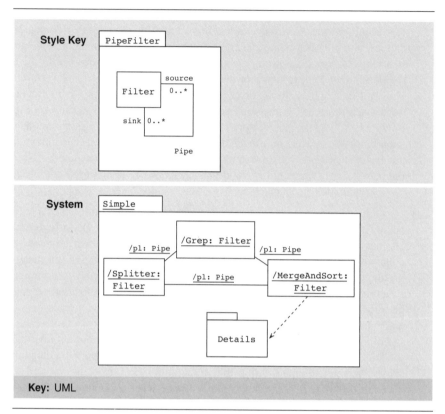

FIGURE 9.12   Systems as collaborations

may contain objects, which indicates that the object is part of the component. Components are connected to other components by dashed-arrow dependencies (possibly through interfaces). This indicates that one component uses the services of another; a stereotype may be used to indicate the precise dependency if needed. The deployment type diagram may also be used to show which components may run on which nodes, by using dashed arrows with the stereotype «supports».

A node is a runtime physical object that represents a processing resource, generally having at least a memory and often processing capability as well. Nodes include computing devices but also human or mechanical processing resources. Nodes may represent types of instances. Runtime computational instances, both objects and components, may reside on node instances.

Nodes may be connected by associations to other nodes. An association indicates a communication path between them. The association may have a stereotype to indicate the nature of the communication path (for example, the kind of channel or network).

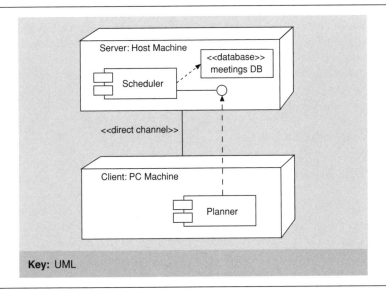

FIGURE 9.13   A deployment view in UML

The nesting of symbols within the node symbol signifies a composition association between a node class and constituent classes or a composition link between a node object and constituent objects.

9.7 Summary

An architecture is worthless if nobody can understand what it is or how to use it. Documenting an architecture is the crowning step in creating it, freeing the architect from having to answer hundreds of questions about it and serving to capture it for current and future stakeholders.

You must understand the stakeholders of the architecture and how they expect to use the documentation. Treat the task of documenting an architecture as documenting the set of relevant views and then supplementing that with cross-view information. Use the stakeholders to help choose the relevant views.

Box-and-line diagrams, whether rendered in an informal notation or in something like UML, tell only a small part of the story. Augment them with supporting documentation that explains the elements and relationships shown in the primary presentation. Interfaces and behavior are important parts of the architecture picture.

This chapter presented a prescriptive organization for documenting software architectures. You may ask why we have not strictly adhered to it in the architectural case studies in this book. A fundamental principle of technical documentation of any kind, and software architecture documentation in particular, is to write so that the material is of the most use to the anticipated readers. Here, the reader wants an overview of the system, its motivations, and how it meets its quality goals—the reader isn't going to analyze it or build to it. Thus, the descriptions that we provide are less formal and less detailed than what we would recommend for construction or analysis. In that spirit, we use primary presentations (cartoons) to convey general information; however, in lieu of a formal element catalog to fill in the detail, we give a narrative description.

9.8 For Further Reading

Much of the material in this chapter was adapted from [Clements 03]. For a more comprehensive treatment of architectural documentation, the interested reader should look there. The reader is also referred to [IEEE 00] for a communitywide standard for architectural documentation that is both consistent with this chapter and gives slightly different terminology.

Finally, there are many good references for the UML. However, the first, and the standard [Rumbaugh 99], still serves as a useful and comprehensive introduction. The Object Management Group is currently generating a version of UML intended to better enable the representation of the software architecture of a system. You can follow the progress of this effort at *http://www.omg.org/uml/*.

9.9 Discussion Questions

1. What views from this chapter are pertinent to a system you are currently working on? What views have you documented? Why is there a difference?

2. You are a new hire to a project. Lay out a sequence of documentation you would like to have to acquaint you with your new position.

3. What documentation would you need to do performance analysis?

10

Reconstructing
Software Architectures

with Jeromy Carrière, Liam O'Brien, and Chris Verhoef

> *One veil hangs over past, present, and future, and it is the province*
> *of the historian to find out, not what was, but what is.*
> — Henry David Thoreau

10.1 Introduction

Throughout this book we have treated architecture as something largely under your control and shown how to make architectural decisions (and, as we will see in Part Three, how to analyze those decisions) to achieve the goals and requirements in place for a system under development. But there is another side to the picture. Suppose we have a system that already exists, but we do not know its architecture. Perhaps the architecture was never recorded by the original developers. Perhaps it was recorded but the documentation has been lost. Or perhaps it was recorded but the documentation is no longer synchronized with the system after a series of changes. How do we maintain such a system? How do we manage its evolution to maintain the quality attributes that its architecture (whatever it may be) has provided for us?

This chapter is about a way to answer these questions using *architecture reconstruction*, in which the "as-built" architecture of an implemented system is obtained from an existing system. This is done through a detailed analysis of the system using tool support. The tools extract information about the system and aid in building and aggregating successive levels of abstraction. If the tools are successful, the end result is an architectural representation that aids in reasoning about the system. In some cases, it may not be possible to generate a useful representation.

Note: Jeromy Carrière is an associate at Microsoft; Liam O'Brien is a member of the SEI team; Chris Verhoef is employed by Free University in Amsterdam.

231

This is sometimes the case with legacy systems that have no coherent architectural design to recover (although that in itself is useful to know).

Architecture reconstruction is an interpretive, interactive, and iterative process involving many activities; it is not automatic. It requires the skills and attention of both the reverse engineering expert and the architect (or someone who has substantial knowledge of the architecture), largely because architectural constructs are not represented explicitly in the source code. There is no programming language construct for "layer" or "connector" or other architectural elements that we can easily pick out of a source code file. Architectural patterns, if used, are seldom labeled. Instead, architectural constructs are realized by many diverse mechanisms in an implementation, usually a collection of functions, classes, files, objects, and so forth. When a system is initially developed, its high-level design/architectural elements are mapped to implementation elements. Therefore, when we reconstruct those elements, we need to apply the inverses of the mappings. Coming up with those requires architectural insight. Familiarity with compiler construction techniques and utilities such as grep, sed, awk, perl, python, and lex/yacc is also important.

The results of architectural reconstruction can be used in several ways. If no documentation exists or if it is out of date, the recovered architectural representation can be used as a basis for redocumenting the architecture, as discussed in Chapter 9. This approach can also be used to recover the as-built architecture, to check conformance against an "as-designed" architecture. This assures us that our maintainers (or our developers, for that matter) have followed the architectural edicts set forth for them and are not eroding the architecture, breaking down abstractions, bridging layers, compromising information hiding, and so forth. The reconstruction can also be used as the basis for analyzing the architecture (see Chapters 11 and 12) or as a starting point for re-engineering the system to a new desired architecture. Finally, the representation can be used to identify elements for re-use or to establish an architecture-based software product line (see Chapter 14).

Architecture reconstruction has been used in a variety of projects ranging from MRI scanners to public telephone switches and from helicopter guidance systems to classified NASA systems. It has been used

- to redocument architectures for physics simulation systems.
- to understand architectural dependencies in embedded control software for mining machinery.
- to evaluate the conformance of a satellite ground system's implementation to its reference architecture .
- to understand different systems in the automotive industry.

THE WORKBENCH APPROACH

Architecture reconstruction requires tool support, but no single tool or tool set is always adequate to carry it out. For one thing, tools tend to be language-specific and we may encounter any number of languages in the artifacts we examine. A mature MRI scanner, for example, can contain software written in 15 languages. For another thing, data extraction tools are imperfect; they often return incomplete results or false positives, and so we use a selection of tools to augment and check on each other. Finally, the goals of reconstruction vary, as discussed above. What you wish to do with the recovered documentation will determine what information you need to extract, which in turn will suggest different tools.

Taken together, these have led to a particular design philosophy for a tool set to support architecture reconstruction known as the *workbench*. A *workbench* should be open (easy to integrate new tools as required) and provide a lightweight integration framework whereby tools added to the tool set do not affect the existing tools or data unnecessarily.

An example of a workbench, which we will use to illustrate several of the points in this chapter, is Dali, developed at the SEI. For Further Reading at the end of the chapter describes others.

RECONSTRUCTION ACTIVITIES

Software architecture reconstruction comprises the following activities, carried out iteratively:

1. *Information extraction.* The purpose of this activity is to extract information from various sources.
2. *Database construction.* Database construction involves converting this information into a standard form such as the Rigi Standard Form (a tuple-based data format in the form of `relationship <entity1> <entity2>`) and an SQL-based database format from which the database is created.
3. *View fusion.* View fusion combines information in the database to produce a coherent view of the architecture.
4. *Reconstruction.* The reconstruction activity is where the main work of building abstractions and various representations of the data to generate an architecture representation takes place.

As you might expect, the activities are highly iterative. Figure 10.1 depicts the architecture reconstruction activities and how information flows among them.

The reconstruction process needs to have several people involved. These include the person doing the reconstruction (reconstructor) and one or more individuals who are familiar with the system being reconstructed (architects and software engineers).

The reconstructor extracts the information from the system and either manually or with the use of tools abstracts the architecture from it. The architecture is obtained by the reconstructor through a set of hypotheses about the system. These hypotheses reflect the inverse mappings from the source artifacts to the design (ideally the opposite of the design mappings). They are tested by generating the inverse mappings and applying them to the extracted information and validating the result. To most effectively generate these hypotheses and validate them, people familiar

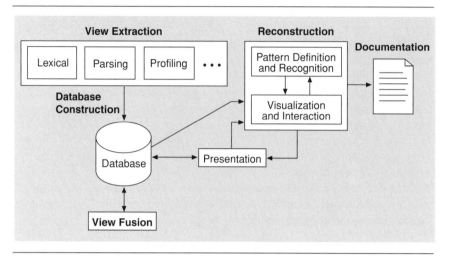

FIGURE 10.1   Architecture reconstruction activities. (The arrows show how information flows among the activities.)

with the system must be involved, including the system architect or engineers who have worked on it (who initially developed it or who currently maintain it).

In the following sections, the various activities of architecture reconstruction are outlined in more detail along with some guidelines for each. Most of these guidelines are not specific to the use of a particular workbench and would be applicable even if the architecture reconstruction was carried out manually.

10.2   Information Extraction

Information extraction involves analyzing a system's existing design and implementation artifacts to construct a model of it. The result is a set of information placed in a database, which is used in the view fusion activity to construct a view of the system.

Information extraction is a blend of the ideal—what information do you want to discover about the architecture that will most help you meet the goals of your reconstruction effort—and the practical—what information can your available tools actually extract and present. From the source artifacts (e.g., code, header files, build files) and other artifacts (e.g., execution traces), you can identify and capture the elements of interest within the system (e.g., files, functions, variables) and their relationships to obtain several base system views. Table 10.1 shows a typical list of the elements and several relationships among them that might be extracted.

Each of the relationships between the elements gives different information about the system. The `calls` relationship between functions helps us build a call

TABLE 10.1   Typical Extracted Elements and Relations

Source Element	Relation	Target Element	Description
File	"includes"	File	C preprocessor #include of one file by another
File	"contains"	Function	Definition of a function in a file
File	"defines_var"	Variable	Definition of a variable in a file
Directory	"contains"	Directory	Directory contains a subdirectory
Directory	"contains"	File	Directory contains a file
Function	"calls"	Function	Static function call
Function	"access_read"	Variable	Read access on a variable
Function	"access_write"	Variable	Write access on a variable

graph. The `includes` relationship between the files gives us a set of dependencies between system files. The `access_read` and `access_write` relationships between functions and variables show us how data is used. Certain functions may write a set of data and others may read it. This information is used to determine how data is passed between various parts of the system. We can determine whether or not a global data store is used or whether most information is passed through function calls.

If the system being analyzed is large, capturing how source files are stored within the directory structure may be important to the reconstruction process. Certain elements or subsystems may be stored in particular directories, and capturing relations such as `dir_contains_file` and `dir_contains_dir` is useful when trying to identify elements later.

The set of elements and relations extracted will depend on the type of system being analyzed and the extraction support tools available. If the system to be reconstructed is object oriented, classes and methods are added to the list of elements to be extracted, and relationships such as `class is_subclass_of_ class` and `class_contains_method` are extracted and used.

Information obtained can be categorized as either static or dynamic. Static information is obtained by observing only the system artifacts, while dynamic information is obtained by observing how the system runs. The goal is to fuse both to create more accurate system views. (View fusion is discussed in Section 10.4.) If the architecture of the system changes at runtime (e.g., a configuration file is read in by the system at startup and certain elements are loaded as a result), that runtime configuration should be captured and used when carrying out the reconstruction.

To extract information, a variety of tools are used, including these:

- Parsers (e.g., Imagix, SNiFF+, CIA, rigiparse)
- Abstract syntax tree (AST) analyzers (e.g., Gen++, Refine)
- Lexical analyzers (e.g., LSME)

- Profilers (e.g., gprof)
- Code instrumentation tools
- Ad hoc (e.g., grep, perl)

Parsers analyze the code and generate internal representations from it (for the purpose of generating machine code). Typically, however, it is possible to save this internal representation to obtain a view. AST analyzers do a similar job, but they build an explicit tree representation of the parsed information. We can build analysis tools that traverse the AST and output selected pieces of architecturally relevant information in an appropriate format.

Lexical analyzers examine source artifacts purely as strings of lexical elements or tokens. The user of a lexical analyzer can specify a set of code patterns to be matched and output. Similarly, a collection of ad hoc tools such as grep and perl can carry out pattern matching and searching within the code to output some required information. All of these tools—code-generating parsers, AST-based analyzers, lexical analyzers, and ad hoc pattern matchers—are used to output static information.

Profiling and code coverage analysis tools can be used to output information about the code as it is being executed, and usually do not involve adding new code to the system. On the other hand, code instrumentation, which has wide applicability in the field of testing, involves adding code to the system to output specific information while the system is executing. These tools generate dynamic system views.

Tools to analyze design models, build files, makefiles, and executables can also be used to extract further information as required. For instance, build files and makefiles include information on module or file dependencies that exist within the system and may not be reflected in the source code.

Much architecture-related information may be extracted statically from source code, compile-time artifacts, and design artifacts. Some architecturally relevant information, however, may not exist in the source artifacts because of late binding. Examples of late binding include the following:

- Polymorphism
- Function pointers
- Runtime parameterization

The precise topology of a system may not be determined until runtime. For example, multi-process and multi-processor systems, using middleware such as J2EE, Jini, or .NET, frequently establish their topology dynamically, depending on the availability of system resources. The topology of such systems does not live in its source artifacts and hence cannot be reverse engineered using static extraction tools.

For this reason, it may be necessary to use tools that can generate dynamic information about the system (e.g., profiling tools). Of course, this requires that such tools be available on the platform on which the system executes. Also, it may be difficult to collect the results from code instrumentation. Embedded systems often have no way to output such information.

GUIDELINES

The following are some practical considerations in applying this step of the method.

- *Use the "least effort" extraction.* Consider what information you need to extract from a source corpus. Is this information lexical in nature? Does it require the comprehension of complex syntactic structures? Does it require some semantic analysis? In each case, a different tool could be applied successfully. In general, lexical approaches are the cheapest to use, and they should be considered if your reconstruction goals are simple.

- *Validate the information you have extracted.* Before starting to fuse or manipulate the various views obtained, make sure that the correct view information has been captured. It is important that the tools being used to analyze the source artifacts do their job correctly. First perform detailed manual examination and verification of a subset of the elements and relations against the underlying source code, to establish that the correct information is being captured. The precise amount of information that needs to be verified manually is up to you. Assuming that this is a statistical sampling, you can decide on a desired confidence level and choose the sampling strategy to achieve it.

- *Extract dynamic information where required*, such as where there is a lot of runtime or late binding and the architecture is dynamically configurable.

10.3   Database Construction

The extracted information is converted into a standard format for storage in a database during database construction. It is necessary to choose a database model. When doing so, consider the following:

- It should be a well-known model, to make replacing one database implementation with another relatively simple.
- It should allow for efficient queries, which is important given that source models can be quite large.
- It should support remote access of the database from one or more geographically distributed user interfaces.
- It supports view fusion by combining information from various tables.
- It supports query languages that can express architectural patterns.
- Checkpointing should be supported by implementations, which means that intermediate results can be saved. This is important in an interactive process in that it gives the user the freedom to explore with the comfort that changes can always be undone.

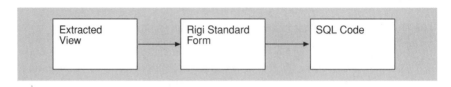

FIGURE 10.2   Conversion of the extracted information to SQL format

The Dali workbench, for example, uses a relational database model. It converts the extracted views (which may be in many different formats depending on the tools used to extract them) into the Rigi Standard Form. This format is then read in by a perl script and output in a format that includes the necessary SQL code to build the relational tables and populate them with the extracted information. Figure 10.2 gives an outline of this process.

An example of the generated SQL code to build and populate the relational tables is shown in Figure 10.3.

When the data is entered into the database, two additional tables are generated: *elements* and *relationships*. These list the extracted elements and relationships, respectively.

Here, the workbench approach makes it possible to adopt new tools and techniques, other than those currently available, to carry out the conversion from whatever format(s) an extraction tool uses. For example, if a tool is required to handle a new language, it can be built and its output can be converted into the workbench format.

In the current version of the Dali workbench, the POSTGRES relational database provides functionality through the use of SQL and perl for generating and manipulating the architectural views (examples are shown in Section 10.5). Changes can easily be made to the SQL scripts to make them compatible with other SQL implementations.

```
create table calls( caller text, callee text );
create table access( func text, variable text );
create table defines_var( file text, variable text );
...
insert into calls values( 'main', 'control' );
insert into calls values( 'main', 'clock' );
...
insert into accesses values( 'main', 'stat 1' );
```

FIGURE 10.3   Example of SQL code generated in Dali

GUIDELINES

When constructiong the database, consider the following.

- Build database tables from the extracted relations to make processing of the data views easier during view fusion. For example, build a table that stores the results of a particular query so that the query need not be run again. If the results are required, you can access them easily through the table.

- As with any database construction, carefully consider the database design before you get started. What will the primary (and possibly secondary) key be? Will any database joins be particularly expensive, spanning multiple tables? In reconstruction the tables are usually quite simple—on the order of `dir_contains_dir` or `function_calls_function`—and the primary key is a function of the entire row.

- Use simple lexical tools like perl and awk to change the format of data that was extracted using any tools into a format that can be used by the workbench.

10.4   View Fusion

View fusion involves defining and manipulating extracted information (now stored in a database) to reconcile, augment, and establish connections between the elements. Different forms of extraction should provide complementary information. Fusion is illustrated using the examples given in the following sections.

IMPROVING A VIEW

Consider the two excerpts shown in Figure 10.4, which are from the sets of methods (each shown preceded by its respective class) extracted from a system implemented in C++. These tables include static and dynamic information about an object-oriented segment of code. We can see from the dynamic information that, for example, `List::getnth` is called. However, this method is not included in the static analysis because the static extractor tool missed it. Also, the calls to the constructor and destructor methods of `InputValue` and `List` are not included in the static information and need to be added to the class/method table that reconciles both sources of information.

In addition, the static extraction in this example shows that the `PrimitiveOp` class has a method called `Compute`. The dynamic extraction results show no such class, but they do show classes, such as `ArithmeticOp`, `AttachOp`, and `StringOp`, each of which has a `Compute` method and is in fact a subclass of `PrimitiveOp`. `PrimitiveOp` is purely a superclass and so never actually called in an executing program. But it is the call to `PrimitiveOp` that a static

Static Extraction	Dynamic Extraction
InputValue::GetValue InputValue::SetValue List::[ ] List::length List::attachr List::detachr PrimitiveOp::Compute	InputValue::GetValue InputValue::SetValue InputValue::~InputValue InputValue::InputValue List::[ ] List::length List::getnth List::List ArithmeticOp::Compute AttachOp::Compute . . . StringOp::Compute

FIGURE 10.4   Static and dynamic data information about the class_contains_method relation

extractor sees when scanning the source code, since the polymorphic call to one of PrimitiveOp's subclasses occurs at runtime.

To get an accurate view of the architecture, we need to reconcile the PrimitiveOp static and dynamic information. To do this, we perform a fusion using SQL queries over the extracted calls, actually_calls, and has_subclass relations. In this way, we can see that the calls to PrimitiveOp::Compute (obtained from the static information) and to its various subclasses (obtained from the dynamic information) are really the same thing.

The lists in Figure 10.5 show the items added to the fused view (in addition to the methods that the static and dynamic information agreed upon) and those removed from it (even though included in either the static or the dynamic information).

Added to Fused View	Not Added
InputValue::ValueValue InputValue::~InputValue List::List List::length List::~List List::getnth	ArithmeticOp::Compute AttachOp::Compute . . . StringOp::Compute

FIGURE 10.5   Items added to and omitted from the overall view

DISAMBIGUATING FUNCTION CALLS

In a multi-process application, name clashes are likely to occur. For example, several processes might have a procedure called `main`. It is important that clashes be identified and disambiguated within the extracted views. Once again, by fusing information that can be easily extracted, we can remove this potential ambiguity. In this case, we need to fuse the static `calls` table with a "file/function containment" table (to determine which functions are defined in which source files) and a "build dependency" table (to determine which files are compiled to produce which executables). The fusion of these information sources allows potentially ambiguous procedure or method names to be made unique and hence unambiguously referred to in the architecture reconstruction process. Without view fusion, this ambiguity would persist into the architecture reconstruction.

GUIDELINES

The following are some practical considerations in applying this step of the method.

- Fuse tables when no single extracted table provides the needed information.

- Fuse tables when there is ambiguity within one of them, and it is not possible to disambiguate using a single table.

- Consider different extraction techniques to extract different information; for example, you can use dynamic and static extraction. Or you might want to use different instances of the same technique, such as different parsers for the same language, if you feel that a single instance might provide erroneous or incomplete information.

10.5 Reconstruction

At this point, the view information has been extracted, stored, and refined or augmented to improve its quality. The reconstruction operates on views to reveal broad, coarse-grained insights into the architecture. Reconstruction consists of two primary activities: *visualization and interaction* and *pattern definition and recognition*. Each is discussed next.

Visualization and interaction provides a mechanism by which the user may interactively visualize, explore, and manipulate views. In Dali, views are presented to the user as a hierarchically decomposed graph of elements and relations, using the Rigi tool. An example of an architectural view is shown in Figure 10. 6.

Pattern definition and recognition provides facilities for architectural reconstruction: the definition and recognition of the code manifestation of architectural patterns. Dali's reconstruction facilities, for example, allow a user to construct

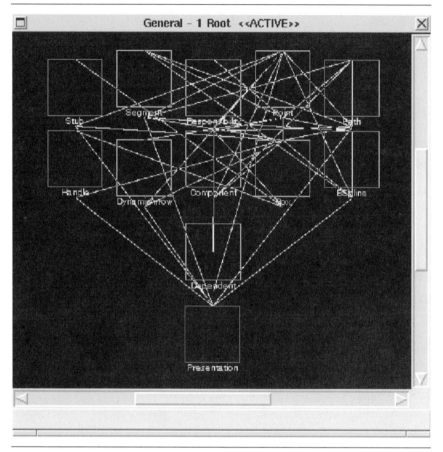

FIGURE 10.6 An architectural view represented in Dali

more abstract views of a software system from more detailed views by identifying aggregations of elements. Patterns are defined in Dali, using a combination of SQL and perl, which we call *code segments*. An SQL query is used to identify elements from the Dali repository that will contribute to a new aggregation, and perl expressions are used to transform names and perform other manipulations of the query results. Code segments are retained, and users can selectively apply and re-use them.

Based on the architectural patterns that the architect expects to find in the system, the reconstructor can build various queries. These queries result in new aggregations that show various abstractions or clusterings of the lower-level elements (which may be source artifacts or abstractions). By interpreting these views and actively analyzing them, it is possible to refine the queries and aggregations to produce several hypothesized architectural views that can be interpreted, further refined, or rejected. There are no universal completion criteria for this process; it

Element	Relationship	Element
f	defines_var	a
f	defines_var	b
g	calls	f
f	calls	h

FIGURE 10.7   Subset of elements and relationships

is complete when the architectural representation is sufficient to support analysis and documentation.

Suppose that our database contains the subset of elements and relations shown in Figure 10.7. In this example variables a and b are defined in function f; that is, they are local to f. We can graphically represent this information as shown in Figure 10.8.

An architectural reconstruction is not interested in the local variables because they lend very little insight into the architecture of the system. Therefore, we can aggregate instances of local variables into the functions in which they occur. An example of the SQL and perl code to accomplish this is shown in Figure 10.9.

The first code portion updates the visual representation by adding a "+" after each function name. The function is now aggregated together with the local variables defined inside it. The SQL query selects functions from the elements table, and the perl expression is executed for each line of the query result. The $fields array is automatically populated with the fields resulting from the query; in this case, only one field is selected (tName) from the table, so

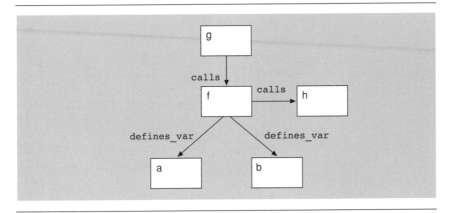

FIGURE 10.8   Graphical representation of elements and relationships

```
#Local Variable aggregation
SELECT tName
     FROM Elements
     WHERE tType='Function';
print ''$fields[0]+ $fields[0] Function\n'';

SELECT dl.func, dl.local_variable
     FROM defines_var dl;
print ''$fields[0] $fields[1] Function\n'';
```

FIGURE 10.9 SQL and perl to aggregate local variables to the function in which they are defined

$fields[0] will store its value for each tuple selected. The expression generates lines of the form:

```
<function>+   <function>   Function
```

this specifies that the element <function> should be aggregated into <function>+, which will have the type Function.

The second code portion hides the local variables from the visualization. The SQL query identifies the local variables for each function defined by selecting each tuple in the defines_var table. Thus in the perl expression, $fields[0] corresponds to the func field and $fields[1] corresponds to the local_variable field. So the output is of the form:

```
<function>+   <variable>   Function
```

That is, each local variable for a function is to be added to that function's <function>+ aggregate. The order of execution of these two code segments is not important, as the final results of applying both of these queries is sorted.

The result of applying the code segments is represented graphically in Figure 10.10.

The primary mechanism for manipulating the extracted information is inverse mappings. Examples include the following:

- Identify types
- Aggregate local variables into functions
- Aggregate members into classes
- Compose architecture-level elements

An example of a query that identifies an architectural element is shown in Figure 10.11. This query identifies the Logical_Interaction architectural element, and says that if the class name is Presentation, Bspline, or Color, or if the class is a subclass of Presentation, it belongs in the Logical_Interaction element.

Code segments are written in this way for abstracting from the lower-level information to generate architecture-level views. The reconstructor builds these segments to test hypotheses about the system. If a particular segment does not

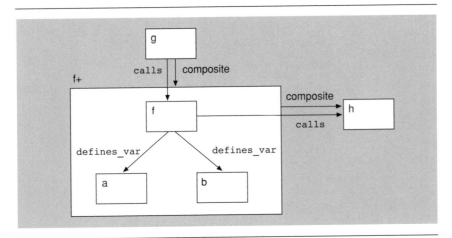

FIGURE 10.10   Result of applying the code segment in Figure 10.9

```
SELECT tSubclass
     FROM has_subclass
     WHERE tSuperclass='Presentation';
print ''Logical_Interaction $fields[0]'';

SELECT tName
     FROM element
     WHERE tName='Presentation'
     OR tName='BSpline'
     OR tName='Color';
print ''Logical_Interaction $fields[0]'';
```

FIGURE 10.11   Query to identify the `Logical_Interaction` element

yield useful results, it can be discarded. The reconstructor iterates through this process until useful architectural views have been obtained.

GUIDELINES

The following are some practical considerations in applying this step of the method.

- Be prepared to work with the architect closely and to iterate several times on the architectural abstractions that you create. This is particularly so in cases where the system has no explicit, documented architecture. (See the sidebar Playing "Spot the Architecture.") In such cases, you can create architectural abstractions as hypotheses and test these hypotheses by creating the views and showing them to the architect and other stakeholders. Based on the false negatives and false positives found, the reconstructor may decide to create

```
SELECT tName
      FROM element
      WHERE tName='vanish-xforms.cc'
      OR tName='PrimativeOp'
      OR tName='Mapping'
      OR tName='MappingEditor'

      OR tName='InputValue'
      OR tName='Point'
      OR tName='VEC'
      OR tName='MAT'
      OR ((tName ~ 'Dbg$' OR tName ~ 'Event$')
         AND tType='Class');
print ''Dialogue $fields[0]'';
```

FIGURE 10.12   Example of a bad code segment that relies on the explicit listing of elements of interest

new abstractions, resulting in new Dali code segments to apply (or perhaps even new extractions that need to be done).

- When developing code segments, try to build ones that are succinct and that do not list every source element. The code segment shown in Figure 10.11 is an example of a good segment; an example of a bad one in this regard, is shown in Figure 10.12. In the latter, the source elements comprising the architectural element of interest are simply listed; this makes the segment difficult to use, understand, and re-use.

- Code segments can be based on naming conventions, if the naming conventions are used consistently throughout the system. An example is one where all functions, data, and files that belong to the *Interface* element begin with i_.

- Code segments can be based on the directory structure where files and functions are located. Element aggregations can be based on these directories.

- Architecture reconstruction is the effort of redetermining architectural decisions, given only the result of these decisions in the actual artifacts (i.e., the code that implements them). As reconstruction proceeds, information must be added to re-introduce the architectural decisions which introduces bias from the reconstructor and thus reinforces the need for a person knowledgeable in the architecture to be involved.

Playing "Spot the Architecture"

Beginning the process of recovering a "lost" architecture can be daunting. The architecture recovery team begins with a blank slate, from which they need to reconstruct an architecture that is, hopefully, both representative of what is actually there and useful for reasoning about the system, maintaining it, evolving it, and so forth.

But you would not embark on an architectural reconstruction project unless the architectural documentation was either lost completely or at least muddied by time and many revisions by many hands. So, how to begin?

In our first few architectural reconstruction efforts this was not our starting point. We had created Dali and needed some examples to test it on, so we chose a couple of systems that we had architected and built ourselves. We had created these systems with explicit architectures in mind, and so recovering them was not too difficult. Still, the process was not without surprises. We discovered architectural violations even in the relatively small systems we had designed and coded. This encouraged us, for if even our own small and conscientiously architected systems had problems, how bad would large, long-lived commercial systems be? We were emboldened by our successes and eager to tackle such a system.

Our chance came in the form of a large, complex physics simulation. This system had been in development for about six years. It was written in two languages, had no formal architectural documentation, and had not been created with a formal architecture design effort. However, the chief architect felt that there was in fact an architecture in there and that we could recover it with a bit of digging. The system had about 300,000 lines of code, but was probably the most complex system that I had ever seen, and that remains true to this day.

In advance of the architect working with us we were able to get a copy of the code base, from which we extracted many useful low-level relations (such as `function_calls_function` and `function_defines_global_variable`). We loaded the database with these tables.

We then sat down with the architect. He sketched out his view of what the architecture was, and we turned that view into a set of SQL queries, ran these over the database, and visualized the result. It was a mess, with thousands of unclassified elements and thousands of relations going everywhere. Viewing this, the architect thought some more and then proposed a different organization. We again turned this into a set of SQL queries, reorganized the database along these lines and visualized the result. The result was once again a mess.

We continued this for the rest of the day and did more the next day. At the end of that time we finally arrived at an architecture that the architect was reasonably happy with, but it always remained somewhat messy.

What is the moral of this story? First, your initial guesses as to the structure of the architecture may be wrong. You may be required to iterate a number of times before you get something that approaches a rational looking structure. Second, if a product was not created with an architecture in mind, chances are that no amount of post-facto organization will create one for you. You can play "spot the architecture" all you like, but there may in fact be no coherent architecture to spot.

— RK

10.6   Example

To illustrate the process of reconstruction, we will walk through a typical set of code segments created in Dali to reconstruct the architecture for UCMEdit, a system for creating and editing Buhr-style use case maps. We will show how the reconstructor moved from the raw data of a set of extracted views to a simple, elegant picture of the software architecture.

INFORMATION EXTRACTION

Table 10.2 shows the elements and relations initially extracted from the UCMEdit source code. Variable accesses are *not* included; that is, there are no `function_reads_variable` or `function_assigns_variable` relations. However, since these relations might be important for determining architectural coupling, a second extraction is engineered to capture them. Additionally, `file depends_on file` relations are extracted by processing the output from running the GNU `make` utility on the application's makefile.

Once the views of interest are extracted, functions thought to be "uninteresting" are filtered out, among them built-in functions, such as `return`, and standard C library functions, such as `scanf` and `printf`.

DATABASE CONSTRUCTION

Next, an SQL database is populated with the extracted relations. As mentioned in Section 10.3, two additional database tables are constructed to catalog the elements

TABLE 10.2   Elements and Relations Extracted from UCMEdit

Relation	Source Element		Target Element	
	Element Type	Element Name	Element Type	Element Name
`calls`	Function	`tCaller`	Function	`tCallee`
`contains`	File	`tContainer`	Function	`tContainee`
`defines`	File	`tFile`	Class	`tClass`
`has_subclass`	Class	`tSuperclass`	Class	`tSubclass`
`has_friend`	Class	`tClass`	Class	`tFriend`
`defines_fn`	Class	`tDefined_by`	Function	`tDefines`
`has_member`	Class	`tClass`	Member variable	`tMember`
`defines_var`	Function	`tDefiner`	Local variable	`tVariable`
`has_instance`	Class	`tClass`	Variable	`tVariable`
`defines_global`	File	`tDefiner`	Global variable	`tVariable`

Example   **249**

and relationships—one identifies all defined elements; the other lists all identified relation types. The elements table has a field (called `type`) that stores the element's type (file, function, etc.).

VIEW FUSION AND RECONSTRUCTION

Figure 10.13 shows the raw extracted model of those elements and relations, containing 830 nodes and 2,507 relations. At this point, the first order of business is to begin applying code segments to search for order within the chaos.

A reliable first step is to aggregate a function and all of the local variables that it defines into a new composite element. After the code segment shown in Figure 10.9 is applied, the models for UCMEdit *still* appear as an inscrutable web of nodes and arcs, but it is simpler than the extracted views of Figure 10.13 prior to the application of the function aggregation code segments. The UCMEdit model now shows 710 nodes and 2,321 relations.

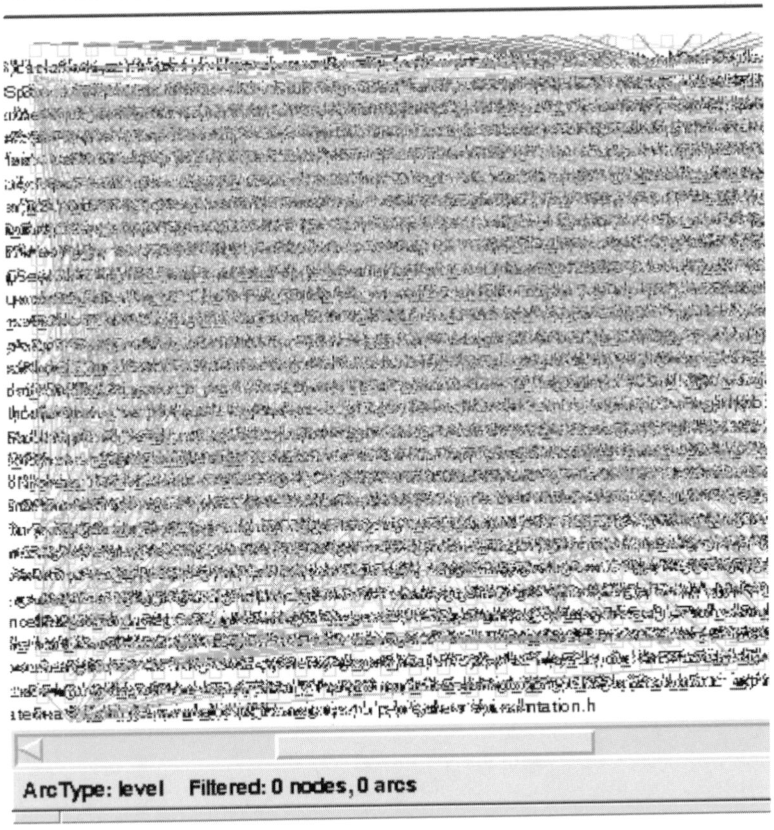

ArcType: level   Filtered: 0 nodes, 0 arcs

FIGURE 10.13   A raw set of extracted elements and relations: white noise

We know that UCMEdit is an object-oriented system, and the next low-level code segment applied takes advantage of that knowledge. Similar in nature to that for collapsing functions, this code segment collapses together classes and their member variables and functions, representing them as a single class node. The resulting model was shown in Figure 10.5; it contains 233 nodes and 518 arcs—a significant visual simplification, although still not tractable.

But there are still many elements remaining that are unrelated to any extracted class. Hence, we have exposed either a deficiency in the extractors applied or ways in which these systems deviate from pure object-oriented design. In fact, both of these cases obtain.

Closer examination reveals that false positives are generated by the extraction code segments in the form of apparent calls to global functions that are actually calls to member functions. Moreover, several functions are indeed global, belonging to no class defined in the system. Of course, some global functions, in the form of system calls or windowing system primitives, are necessary. How these "leftover" cases are separated from the rest of the architecture is discussed next.

The model for UCMEdit is now a collection of files, classes, leftover functions, and global variables. Local variables have been aggregated into the functions in which they are defined, and member functions and member variables have been aggregated into their associated classes. At this point we can compose global variables and functions into the files in which they are defined, in much the same manner as functions and classes were composed. The resulting models, shown in Figure 10.14, contain three separate groups of elements: files, classes, and the remaining leftover functions. Again, a significant visual improvement but still not tractable.

Until now, each code segment applied has been application independent but specific to the extraction techniques and to the domain of C++ software. The next code segment sets to be applied use expert knowledge of the UCMEdit architecture. Here the reconstruction process diverges from a rote analysis, where we apply off-the-shelf code segments, into opportunistic pattern recognition and definition, leveraging the kinds of information that a designer or experienced system programmer should know about a specific system's architecture.

The first application-specific knowledge that we apply to our sample system is as follows:

- It is an interactive, graphical application.
- It attempts to encapsulate access to the underlying windowing and graphics subsystem within a layer.
- The functions comprising the graphics libraries used (Xlib, XForms, and Mesa) have characteristic naming conventions.

These observations lead us to expect architectural patterns—the existence of subsystems, perhaps, or certain patterns of interaction. These expectations are in effect hypotheses, and to test them we check for the existence of the patterns. If the result simplifies the picture and matches our expectations, then our hypothesis is

Example   **251**

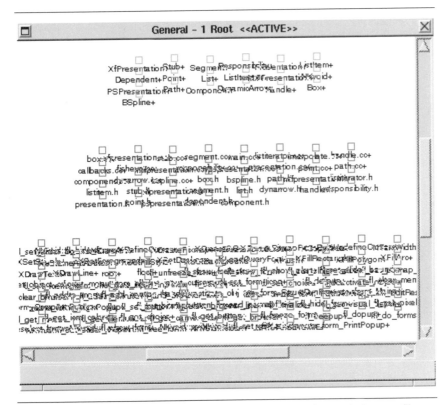

FIGURE 10.14 The UCMEdit model showing (from top to bottom) classes, files, and "leftover" functions (arcs are hidden)

confirmed. We have likely discovered what the architect had in mind. Even if not, we have discovered a reasonable and useful handle with which to understand the system.

In the code segments shown in Figure 10.15, which are intended to identify the graphics subsystem, those external functions provide rendering and interaction functionality to the application. Consider the first code segment: It constructs a new table from the `elements` table by filtering out all functions that are members of classes (those that appear as the `tDefines` field in a tuple of the `defines_fn` relation). Then it selects from this new table all functions called by functions defined by subclasses of the `Presentation` class. Note that this code segment references subclasses of `Presentation`. In doing so, it implicitly identifies the layer that the original designers created to encapsulate accesses to the graphics subsystem. This information will be leveraged further. The second, third, and fourth code segments in this sequence identify functions defined by the Mesa, XForms, and Xlib libraries, respectively, by specifying code segments over the function names.

```
# 1: Identify calls from graphics access layer.
    DROP TABLE tmp;
    SELECT * INTO TABLE tmp
            FROM elements;
    DELETE FROM tmp
            WHERE tmp.tName=defines_fn.tDefines;
    SELECT t1.tName
            FROM tmp t1, calls c1, defines_fn d1,
                    has_subclass s1, has_subclass s2
            WHERE t1.tName=c1.tCallee AND c1.tCaller=d1.tDefines
    AND d1.tDefined_by=s1.tSubclass
    AND s1.tSuperclass='Presentation';

print "Graphics $fields[0]+ null\n";

# 2: Identify calls to Mesa functions.
SELECT tName
            FROM elements
            WHERE tType='Function' AND tName LIKE 'gl%';

print "Graphics $fields[0]+ null\n";

# 3: Identify calls to XForms functions.
SELECT tName
            FROM elements
            WHERE tType='Function' AND tName LIKE 'fl_%';

print "Graphics $fields[0]+ null\n";

# 4: Identify calls to Xlib functions.
DROP TABLE tmp;
    SELECT * INTO TABLE tmp
            FROM elements;
    DELETE FROM tmp
            WHERE tmp.tName=defines_fn.tDefines;
    SELECT c1.tName
            FROM tmp c1
            WHERE tType='Function'
            AND tName LIKE 'X%';

print "Graphics $fields[0]+ null\n";
```

FIGURE 10.15 Code segments for the UCMEdit graphics subsystem

Code segments 2, 3, and 4 collectively identify an architectural element, Graphics, which does not exist in the extracted information but does exist in the as-designed architecture. This is an example of relating the as-implemented and as-designed architectures through a cumulative series of code segment applications. The results, in UCMEdit model, are shown in Figure 10.16.

Note that the names of the elements to be aggregated into the Graphics element include the '+' that was appended by the code segments in the figure. This technique thus refers to previously constructed composite elements without the code segments explicitly querying the database for them.

Examining Figure 10.16, we see that there are only two leftover functions remaining: fabs and [ ]; the latter is obviously an extraction error while the former is a math library function that should have been filtered out along with

Example 253

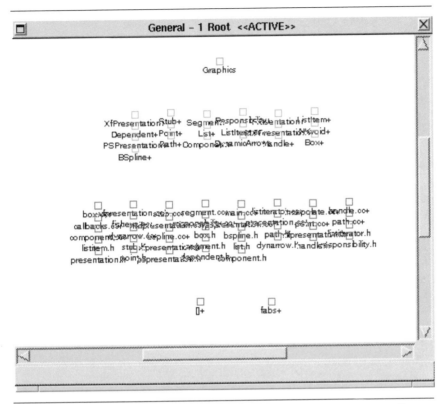

FIGURE 10.16 UCMEdit model showing the graphics subsystem, classes, files, and remaining functions (arcs are hidden)

standard C library and built-in functions. Regardless, neither is of interest and so they can be pruned from the model.

Of course, the determination of which functions are "interesting" or "uninteresting" depends on the goals of the reconstruction. A reconstructor interested in a different aspect of the system, such as how its subsystems depend on platform-specific or operating-system-specific libraries, would not have pruned these functions from the concrete model, but would more likely have aggregated them into a layer to analyze how they are used by the rest of the application. We are interested in constructing an architectural representation of the application-specific part of the system, so we remove these functions.

A second common application-based code segment takes advantage of knowledge about the relationship between classes and files in the example applications. First, a source (.cc) file will contain functions for at most one class; second, a header (.h) file will contain a definition for at most one class. This makes it possible to define a unique containment relationship: A class can include the

```
SELECT DISTINCT tDefined_by
     FROM defines_fn;

print "$fields[0]+ $fields[0]+ Class $fields[0]++\n";

SELECT DISTINCT d1.tDefined_by, c1.tContainer
     FROM defines_fn d1, contains c1
          WHERE c1.tContainee=d1.tDefines;

print "$fields[0]+ $fields[1]+ Class\n";

SELECT d1.tClass, d1.tFile
     FROM defines d1;

print "$fields[0]+ $fields[1] Class\n";
```

FIGURE 10.17   Code segments for class/file containment

header file in which it is defined and the source file that contains its functions. The code segment that generates these aggregations is shown in Figure 10.17.

We see one additional feature of these specifications in this example: The last field in the perl expression associated with the first code segment ($fields[0]++) specifies a renaming of the element being aggregated. In this code segment, we are aggregating classes (named with trailing '+'s because of the class-collapsing code segments of Section 10.4) into new composite elements. The names of the new composites are <class>+; the original class composites are renamed <class>++. The results are shown in Figure 10.18.

UCMEdit was constructed as a prototype intended to demonstrate the advantages of computer-based editing of use case maps. Since over-arching architectural design of the application was not considered at the start of development, identification of architectural elements from the concrete model must be guided by an understanding of the application's structure as it stands at the completion of development. Our understanding of the application will be imposed on the model via direct manipulation, as follows.

First, we know (and can tell by observation of the model) that `callbacks.cc` is central to the structure of the application, containing all of the system's event handlers and the bulk of the user interface implementation. Second, we can observe the obvious relationships between the two remaining files and the classes to which they are connected—`interpolate.cc` is associated exclusively with `BSpline`, and `fisheye.cc` is used only by `Box` and `Component`. Third, we may now reapply our knowledge of the structure of the system's graphics encapsulation, or *presentation,* layer; it is embodied in the `Presentation` class and its subclasses. Fourth, we can make the observation that the `List`, `ListItem`, and `ListIterator` classes are functionally related to one another and are used by almost all of the other classes.

We realize the above observations by

- identifying the `callbacks.cc` file with an architectural element, `Interaction`.

Example   **255**

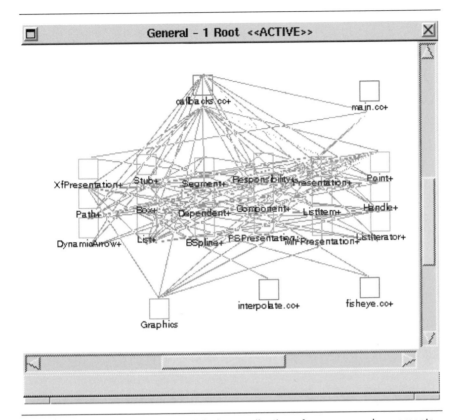

FIGURE 10.18   The UCMEdit model after application of common code segments

- aggregating `interpolate.cc` into the `BSpline` element.
- aggregating the `Presentation` class and its subclasses into a
  `Presentation` element.
- aggregating the `List`, `ListItem`, and `ListIterator` classes into a
  `List` element and hiding it, treating it as a "utility layer."

The results of these changes to the model are shown in Figure 10.19.

At this point, we need to carefully consider how we may further simplify this model. Automatic clustering based on graph-theoretic properties, such as interconnection strength, does not provide any insight. Another option is to attempt to build layers based on the organization generated by the graph layout algorithm, as shown in Figure 10.19, but this approach results in little functional consistency within the layers. In other words, these two hypotheses did not seem to be confirmed by the system, and so we did not pursue them. Considering the domain of use case maps, however, will suggest another hypothesis.

After looking at concepts from use case maps, we identified two broad categories of elements: those related to components and those related to paths,

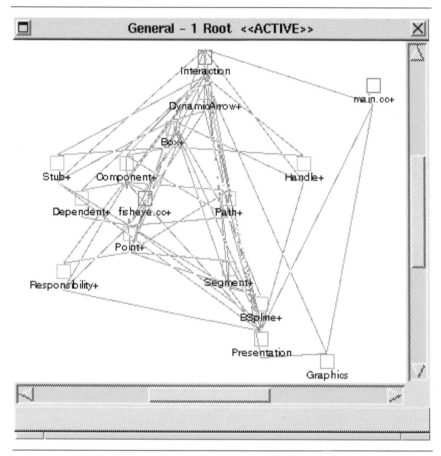

FIGURE 10.19 UCMEdit model after application-specific direct manipulation

these being the two primary constructs comprising a use case map. DynamicArrow, Path, Point, Responsibility, Segment, Stub, and BSpline are related to paths; Box, Component, Dependent, Handle, and fisheye.cc are related to components. Figure 10.20 shows the effect of clustering these elements into two architectural elements: Path and Component.

In probing the connections among elements, we find that there are still a large number of interrelationships. While this is not necessarily harmful in itself, it suggests that UCMEdit's architecture lacks functional consistency within the elements and their connections.

Unfortunately, there are no significant improvements we can make to the UCMEdit model. The system was not well designed in that the mapping from functionality to software structure is complex. This makes the abstraction of function-ally coherent high-level elements within UCMEdit's architecture impossible.

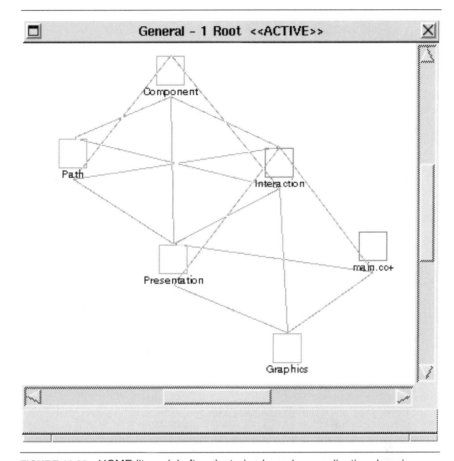

FIGURE 10.20   UCMEdit model after clustering based on application domain

However, we can take advantage of what we have learned to suggest improvements and to document what we know. The latter is especially important since we have discovered that UCMEdit lacks the conceptual integrity that often brings about intuitive understanding.

10.7   Summary

Because architectures are intangible, they often become lost or eroded over a system's lifetime. That is why we need techniques to recover or extract an architecture from a legacy system. This chapter provided an overview of a standard architecture reconstruction and showed an extended example of its application.

The mapping between architectures and source-code-level system artifacts is complex, and this makes architecture reconstruction a complex process that works best when it engages available human knowledge about the system under consideration. Tools are invaluable, especially when arrayed in a lightweight workbench ensemble, but human knowledge and insight are even more invaluable to guide the reconstruction process.

10.8 For Further Reading

There are several reconstruction workbenches in existence. The Software Engineering Institute (SEI) has developed Dali [Kazman 99a]. Other examples include Sneed's reengineering workbench [Sneed 98], the software renovation factories of Verhoef and associates [Brand 97], and the rearchitecting tool suite by Philips Research [Krikhaar 99].

The Rigi Standard Form is discussed in [Müller 93]. The Rigi tool is described in [Wong 94].

[Bowman 99] outlines a method similar to Dali for extracting architectural documentation from the code of an implemented system. In one example, they reconstructed the architecture of the Linux system, analyzing source code using a cfx program (c-code fact extractor) to obtain symbol information from the code and generating a set of relations between the symbols. Then they manually created a tree-structured decomposition of the Linux system into subsystems and assigned the source files to them. Next, they used the grok fact manipulator tool to determine relations between the identified subsystems, and the lsedit visualization tool to visualize the extracted system structure. Refinement of the resultant structure was carried out by moving source files between subsystems.

Harris and associates outline a framework for architecture reconstruction using a combined bottom-up and top-down approach [Harris 95]. The framework consists of three parts: the architecture representation, the source code recognition engine and supporting library of recognition queries, and a "bird's-eye" program overview capability. The bottom-up analysis uses the bird's-eye view to display the system's file structure and source elements and to reorganize information into more meaningful clusters. The top-down analysis uses particular architectural patterns to define elements that should be found in the software. Recognition queries are then run to determine if the expected elements exist.

[Guo 99] outlines the semi-automatic architecture recovery method called ARM, for systems that are designed and developed using patterns. It consists of four main steps: (1) develop a concrete pattern recognition plan, (2) extract a source model, (3) detect and evaluate pattern instances, and (4) reconstruct and analyze the architecture. Case studies have been presented showing the use of the ARM method to reconstruct systems and check their conformance against their documented architectures.

10.9 Discussion Questions

1. Suppose you believed that the architecture for a system was layered. What information would you want to extract from the source code to confirm or refute this hypothesis?

2. Suppose you believed that the architecture for a system followed a shared repository style. What information would you want to extract from the source code to confirm or refute this hypothesis?

3. For each use of reconstruction mentioned in Section 10.1, specify the architectural views you would want to reconstruct.

4. Chapter 6 described a code template used to provide a consistent approach to high availability across the ISSS air traffic control system. Suppose you wanted to confirm that developers and maintainers had remained faithful to this template over the lifetime of the system. Describe the reconstruction process you would undertake.

PART THREE

ANALYZING ARCHITECTURES

Our tour of the ABC has gotten us to the stage where an architect has designed and documented an architecture. This leads us to discuss how to evaluate or to analyze the architecture to make sure it is the one that will do the job. That is the focus of Part Three, which we begin by answering some basic questions about architectural evaluations—why, when, cost, benefits, techniques, planned or unplanned, preconditions, and results.

WHY

One of the most important truths about the architecture of a system is that knowing it will tell you important properties of the system itself—even if the system does not yet exist. Architects make design decisions because of the downstream effects they will have on the system(s) they are building, and these effects are known and predictable. If they were not, the process of crafting an architecture would be no better than throwing dice: We would pick an architecture at random, build a system from it, see if the system had the desired properties, and go back to the drawing board if not. While architecture is not yet a cookbook science, we know we can do much better than random guessing.

Architects by and large know the effects their design decisions will have. As we saw in Chapter 5, architectural tactics and patterns in particular bring known properties to the systems in which they are used. Hence, design choices—that is to say, architectures—are analyzable. Given an architecture, we can deduce things about the system, even if it has not been built yet.

Why evaluate an architecture? Because so much is riding on it, and because you can. An effective technique to assess a candidate architecture—*before* it becomes the project's accepted blueprint—is of great economic value. With the advent of repeatable, structured methods (such as the ATAM, presented in Chapter 11), architecture evaluation has come to provide relatively a low-cost risk mitigation capability. Making sure the architecture is the right one simply makes good sense. *An architecture evaluation should be a standard part of every architecture-based development methodology.*

WHEN

It is almost always cost-effective to evaluate software quality as early as possible in the life cycle. If problems are found early, they are easier to correct—a change to a requirement, specification, or design is all that is necessary. Software quality cannot be appended late in a project, but must be inherent from the beginning, built in by design. It is in the project's best interest for prospective candidate designs to be evaluated (and rejected, if necessary) during the design phase, before long-term institutionalization.

However, architecture evaluation can be carried out at many points during a system's life cycle. If the architecture is still embryonic, you can evaluate those decisions that have already been made or are being considered. You can choose among architectural alternatives. If the architecture is finished, or nearly so, you can validate it before the project commits to lengthy and expensive development. It also makes sense to evaluate the architecture of a legacy system that is undergoing modification, porting, integration with other systems, or other significant upgrades. Finally, architecture evaluation makes an excellent discovery vehicle: Development projects often need to understand how an inherited system meets (or whether it meets) its quality attribute requirements.

Furthermore, when *acquiring* a large software system that will have a long lifetime, it is important that the acquiring organization develop an understanding of the underlying architecture of the candidate. This makes an assessment of their suitability possible with respect to qualities of importance.

Evaluation can also be used to choose between two competing architectures by evaluating both and seeing which one fares better against the criteria for "goodness."

COST

The cost of an evaluation is the staff time required of the participants. AT&T, having performed approximately 300 full-scale architecture reviews on projects requiring a minimum of 700 staff-days, reported that, based on estimates from individual project managers, the average cost was 70 staff-days. ATAM-based reviews require approximately 36 staff-days.[1] If your organization adopts a standing unit for carrying out evaluations, then costs for supporting it must be included, as well as time to train the members.

BENEFITS

We enumerate six benefits that flow from holding architectural inspections.

1. *Financial.* At AT&T, each project manager reports perceived savings from an architecture evaluation. On average, over an eight-year period, projects receiving a full architecture evaluation have reported a 10% reduction in project costs. Given the cost estimate of 70 staff-days, this illustrates that on projects of 700 staff-days or longer the review pays for itself.

Other organizations have not publicized such strongly quantified data, but several consultants have reported that more than 80% of their work was repeat business. Their customers recognized sufficient value to be willing to pay for additional evaluations.

There are many anecdotes about estimated cost savings for customers' evaluations. A large company avoided a multi-million-dollar purchase when the architecture of the global information system they were procuring was found to be incapable of providing the desired system attributes. Early architectural analysis of an electronic funds transfer system showed a $50 billion transfer capability per night, which was only half of the desired capacity. An evaluation of a retail merchandise system revealed early that there would be peak order performance problems that no amount of hardware could fix, and a major business failure was prevented. And so on.

There are also anecdotes of architecture evaluations that did not occur but should have. In one, a rewrite of a customer accounting system was estimated to take two years but after seven years the system had been reimplemented three

---

[1] These figures are for the evaluation team. The ATAM also requires participation from project stakeholders and decision makers, which adds to the total.

times. Performance goals were never met despite the fact that the latest version used sixty times the CPU power of the original prototype version. In another case, involving a large engineering relational database system, performance problems were largely attributable to design decisions that made integration testing impossible. The project was canceled after $20 million had been spent.

2. *Forced preparation for the review.* Indicating to the reviewees the focus of the architecture evaluation and requiring a representation of the architecture before the evaluation is done means that reviewees must document the system's architecture. Many systems do not have an architecture that is understandable to all developers. The existing description is either too brief or (more commonly) too long, perhaps thousands of pages. Furthermore, there are often misunderstandings among developers about some of the assumptions for their elements. The process of preparing for the evaluation will reveal many of these problems.

3. *Captured rationale.* Architecture evaluation focuses on a few specific areas with specific questions to be answered. Answering these questions usually involves explaining the design choices and their rationales. A documented design rationale is important later in the life cycle so that the implications of modifications can be assessed. Capturing a rationale after the fact is one of the more difficult tasks in software development. Capturing it as presented in the architecture evaluation makes invaluable information available for later use.

4. *Early detection of problems with the existing architecture.* The earlier in the life cycle that problems are detected, the cheaper it is to fix them. The problems that can be found by an architectural evaluation include unreasonable (or expensive) requirements, performance problems, and problems associated with potential downstream modifications. An architecture evaluation that exercises system modification scenarios can, for example, reveal portability and extensibility problems. In this way an architecture evaluation provides early insight into product capabilities and limitations.

5. *Validation of requirements.* Discussion and examination of how well an architecture meets requirements opens up the requirements for discussion. What results is a much clearer understanding of the requirements and, usually, their prioritization. Requirements creation, when isolated from early design, usually results in conflicting system properties. High performance, security, fault tolerance, and low cost are all easy to demand but difficult to achieve, and often impossible to achieve simultaneously. Architecture evaluations uncover the conflicts and tradeoffs, and provide a forum for their *negotiated* resolution.

6. *Improved architectures.* Organizations that practice architecture evaluation as a standard part of their development process report an improvement in the quality of the architectures that are evaluated. As development organizations learn to anticipate the questions that will be asked, the issues that will be raised, and the documentation that will be required for evaluations, they naturally pre-position themselves to maximize their performance on the evaluation. Architecture evaluations result in better architectures not only after the fact but before the fact as well. Over time, an organization develops a culture that promotes good architectural design.

In sum, architecture evaluations tend to increase quality, control cost, and decrease budget risk. Architecture is the framework for all technical decisions and as such has a tremendous impact on product cost and quality. An architecture evaluation does not guarantee high quality or low cost, but it can point out areas of risk. Other factors, such as testing or quality of documentation and coding, contribute to the eventual cost and quality of the system.

TECHNIQUES

The ATAM and CBAM methods discussed in the next two chapters are examples of *questioning techniques*. Both use scenarios as the vehicle for asking probing questions about how the architecture under review responds to various situations. Other questioning techniques include checklists or questionnaires. These are effective when an evaluation unit encounters the same kind of system again and again, and the same kind of probing is appropriate each time. All questioning techniques essentially rely on thought experiments to find out how well the architecture is suited to its task.

Complementing questioning techniques are *measuring techniques*, which rely on quantitative measures of some sort. One example of this technique is architectural metrics. Measuring an architecture's coupling, the cohesiveness of its modules, or the depth of its inheritance hierarchy suggests something about the modifiability of the resulting system. Likewise, building simulations or proto-types and then measuring them for qualities of interest (here, runtime qualities such as performance or availability) are measuring techniques.

While the answers that measuring techniques give are in some sense more concrete than those questioning techniques provide, they have the drawback that they can be applied only in the presence of a working artifact. That is, measuring techniques have to have something that exists that can be measured. Questioning techniques, on the other hand, work just fine on hypothetical architectures, and can be applied much earlier in the life cycle.

PLANNED OR UNPLANNED

Evaluations can be planned or unplanned. A planned evaluation is considered a normal part of the project's development cycle. It is scheduled well in advance, built into the project's work plans and budget, and follow-up is expected. An unplanned evaluation is unexpected and usually the result of a project in serious trouble and taking extreme measures to try to salvage previous effort.

The planned evaluation is ideally considered an asset to the project, at worst a distraction from it. It can be perceived not as a challenge to the technical authority of the project's members but as a validation of the project's initial direction. Planned evaluations are pro-active and team-building.

An unplanned evaluation is more of an ordeal for project members, consuming extra project resources and time in the schedule from a project already struggling with both. It is initiated only when management perceives that a project has a substantial possibility of failure and needs to make a mid-course correction. Unplanned evaluations are reactive, and tend to be tension filled. An evaluation's team leader must take care not to let the activities devolve into finger pointing.

Needless to say, planned evaluations are preferable.

PRECONDITIONS

A successful evaluation will have the following properties:

1. *Clearly articulated goals and requirements for the architecture.* An architecture is only suitable, or not, in the presence of specific quality attributes. One that delivers breathtaking performance may be totally wrong for an application that needs modifiability. Analyzing an architecture without knowing the exact criteria for "goodness" is like beginning a trip without a destination in mind. Sometimes (but in our experience, almost never), the criteria are established in a requirements specification. More likely, they are elicited as a precursor to or as part of the actual evaluation. Goals define the purpose of the evaluation and should be made an explicit portion of the evaluation contract, discussed subsequently.

2. *Controlled scope.* In order to focus the evaluation, a small number of explicit goals should be enumerated. The number should be kept to a minimum— around three to five—an inability to define a small number of high-priority goals is an indication that the expectations for the evaluation (and perhaps the system) may be unrealistic.

3. *Cost-effectiveness.* Evaluation sponsors should make sure that the benefits of the evaluation are likely to exceed the cost. The types of evaluation we describe are suitable for medium- and large-scale projects but may not be cost-effective for small projects.

4. *Key personnel availability.* It is imperative to secure the time of the architect or at least someone who can speak authoritatively about the system's architecture and design. This person (or these people) primarily should be able to communicate the facts of the architecture quickly and clearly as well as the motivation behind the architectural decisions. For very large systems, the designers for each major component need to be involved to ensure that the architect's notion of the system design is in fact reflected and manifested in its more detailed levels. These designers will also be able to speak to the behavioral and quality attributes of the components. For the ATAM, the architecture's stakeholders need to be identified and represented at the evaluation. It is essential to identify the customer(s) for the evaluation report and to elicit their values and expectations.

5. *Competent evaluation team.* Ideally, software architecture evaluation teams are separate entities within a corporation, and must be perceived as impartial, objective, and respected. The team must be seen as being composed of people appropriate to carry out the evaluation, so that the project personnel will not regard the evaluation as a waste of time and so that its conclusions will carry weight. It must include people fluent in architecture and architectural issues and be led by someone with solid experience in designing and evaluating projects at the architectural level.

6. *Managed expectations.* Critical to the evaluation's success is a clear, mutual understanding of the expectations of the organization sponsoring it. The evaluation should be clear about what its goals are, what it will produce, what areas it will (and will not) investigate, how much time and resources it will take from the project, and to whom the results will be delivered.

RESULTS

The evaluation should produce a report in which all of the issues of concern, along with supporting data, are described. The report should be circulated in draft form to all evaluation participants in order to catch and correct any misconceptions and biases and to correlate elements before it is finalized. Ideally, the issues should be ranked by their potential impact on the project if left unaddressed.

Information about the evaluation process itself should also be collected. The aggregated output from multiple evaluations leads to courses, training, and improvements to system development and the architecture evaluation processes. Costs and benefits of the evaluation should be collected. Estimates of the benefits are best collected from the manager of the development. The information about the evaluation should be retained by the reviewing organization and used both to improve future evaluations and to provide cost/benefit summaries to the managers of the reviewing organization.

This part has three chapters. The ATAM (discussed in Chapter 11) is a structured method for evaluating architectures. It results in a list of risks that the architecture will not meet its business goals. The CBAM (discussed in Chapter 12) is a method of determining which risks to attack first. In a large system, the number of risks found can be very high. Deciding which to attack first is a matter of balancing the costs of modifying the architecture to reduce the risk against the benefits of removing that risk. The CBAM provides a structure for dealing with this organizational and economic question. Chapter 13 is another case study, which describes systems that support the World Wide Web and how their evolution is an example of several cycles of the ABC.

FOR FURTHER READING

The material in this introduction was derived from [Abowd 96] "Recommended Best Industrial Practice for Architecture Evaluation," which grew out of a series of workshops organized by the authors and others at the Software Engineering Institute. These workshops were attended by representatives of eight industrial and consulting organizations.

Architectural evaluations based on checklists or questionnaires are a form of *active design review* as described in [Parnas 85b]. An active design evaluation is one in which the participants take an active part by using the documentation to answer specific questions prepared in advance. This is as opposed to an opportunistic or unstructured evaluation in which the participants are merely asked to report any anomalies they might discover.

[Cusumano 95] treats the use of metrics to uncover places of likely change. Some of AT&T's rich experience with performing architectural evaluations is documented in [AT&T 93].

11

The ATAM
A Comprehensive Method for Architecture Evaluation

with Mark Klein

> *We evaluate the services that anyone renders to us according*
> *to the value he puts on them, not according*
> *to the value they have for us.*
> — Friedrich Nietzsche

In this chapter, we will introduce the Architecture Tradeoff Analysis Method (ATAM), a thorough and comprehensive way to evaluate a software architecture. The ATAM is so named because it reveals how well an architecture satisfies particular quality goals, and (because it recognizes that architectural decisions tend to affect more than one quality attribute) it provides insight into how quality goals interact—that is, how they trade off.

Evaluating an architecture for a large system is a complicated undertaking. First, a large system will have a comparably large architecture that will be difficult to understand in a limited amount of time. Second, according to Nietzsche and the Architecture Business Cycle (ABC), a computer system is intended to support business goals and the evaluation will need to make connections between those goals and the technical decisions. Finally, a large system usually has multiple stakeholders and acquiring their different perspectives in a limited amount of time requires careful management of an evaluation process. As you can see from this set of difficulties, managing the limited time for an architecture evaluation is a central problem.

Note: Mark Klein is a senior member of the technical staff at the Software Engineering Institute.

The ATAM is designed to elicit the business goals for the system as well as for the architecture. It is also designed to use those goals and stakeholder participation to focus the attention of the evaluators on the portion of the architecture that is central to the achievement of the goals.

This chapter will introduce the steps of the ATAM and discuss them in light of their intended purpose. It will also presents an ATAM case study (based on one of our applications of the method).

11.1   Participants in the ATAM

The ATAM requires the participation and mutual cooperation of three groups:

1. *The evaluation team.* This group is external to the project whose architecture is being evaluated. It usually consists of three to five people. Each member of the team is assigned a number of specific roles to play during the evaluation. (See Table 11.1 for a description of these roles, along with a set of desirable characteristics for each.) The evaluation team may be a standing unit in which architecture evaluations are regularly performed, or its members may be chosen from a pool of architecturally savvy individuals for the occasion. They may work for the same organization as the development team whose architecture is on the table, or they may be outside consultants. In any case, they need to be recognized as competent, unbiased outsiders with no hidden agendas or axes to grind.

2. *Project decision makers.* These people are empowered to speak for the development project or have the authority to mandate changes to it. They usually include the project manager, and, if there is an identifiable customer who is footing the bill for the development, he or she will be present (or represented) as well. The architect is always included—a cardinal rule of architecture evaluation is that the architect must willingly participate. Finally, the person commissioning the evaluation is usually empowered to speak for the development project; even if not, he or she should be included in the group.

3. *Architecture stakeholders.* Stakeholders have a vested interest in the architecture performing as advertised. They are the ones whose ability to do their jobs hinges on the architecture promoting modifiability, security, high reliability, or the like. Stakeholders include developers, testers, integrators, maintainers, performance engineers, users, builders of systems interacting with the one under consideration, and others. Their job during an evaluation is to articulate the specific quality attribute goals that the architecture should meet in order for the system to be considered a success. A rule of thumb—and that is all it is—is that you should expect to enlist the services of twelve to fifteen stakeholders for the evaluation.

TABLE 11.1   ATAM Evaluation Team Roles

Role	Responsibilities	Desirable characteristics
Team Leader	Sets up the evaluation; coordinates with client, making sure client's needs are met; establishes evaluation contract; forms evaluation team; sees that final report is produced and delivered (although the writing may be delegated)	Well-organized, with managerial skills; good at interacting with client; able to meet deadlines
Evaluation Leader	Runs evaluation; facilitates elicitation of scenarios; administers scenario selection/prioritization process; facilitates evaluation of scenarios against architecture; facilitates onsite analysis	Comfortable in front of audience; excellent facilitation skills; good understanding of architectural issues; practiced in architecture evaluations; able to tell when protracted discussion is leading to a valuable discovery or when it is pointless and should be re-directed
Scenario Scribe	Writes scenarios on flipchart or whiteboard during scenario elicitation; captures agreed-on wording of each scenario, halting discussion until exact wording is captured	Good handwriting; stickler about not moving on before an idea (scenario) is captured; can absorb and distill the essence of technical discussions
Proceedings Scribe	Captures proceedings in electronic form on laptop or workstation, raw scenarios, issue(s) that motivate each scenario (often lost in the wording of the scenario itself), and resolution of each scenario when applied to architecture(s); also generates a printed list of adopted scenarios for handout to all participants	Good, fast typist; well organized for rapid recall of information; good understanding of architectural issues; able to assimilate technical issues quickly; unafraid to interrupt the flow of discussion (at opportune times) to test understanding of an issue so that appropriate information is captured
Timekeeper	Helps evaluation leader stay on schedule; helps control amount of time devoted to each scenario during the evaluation phase	Willing to interrupt discussion to call time
Process Observer	Keeps notes on how evaluation process could be improved or deviated from; usually keeps silent but may make discreet process-based suggestions to the evaluation leader during the evaluation; after evaluation, reports on how the process went and lessons learned for future improvement; also responsible for reporting experience to architecture evaluation team at large	Thoughtful observer; knowledgeable in the evaluation process; should have previous experience in the architecture evaluation method
Process Enforcer	Helps evaluation leader remember and carry out the steps of the evaluation method	Fluent in the steps of the method, and willing and able to provide discreet guidance to the evaluation leader

(Continued)

TABLE 11.1 *Continued*

Role	Responsibilities	Desirable characteristics
Questioner	Raise issues of architectural interest that stakeholders may not have thought of	Good architectural insights; good insights into needs of stakeholders; experience with systems in similar domains; unafraid to bring up contentious issues and pursue them; familiar with attributes of concern

Source: Adapted from [Clements 02a].

11.2 Outputs of the ATAM

An ATAM-based evaluation will produce at least the following outputs:

- *A concise presentation of the architecture.* Architecture documentation is often thought to consist of the object model, a list of interfaces and their signatures, or some other voluminous list. But one of the requirements of the ATAM is that the architecture be presented in one hour, which leads to an architectural presentation that is both concise and, usually, understandable.

- *Articulation of the business goals.* Frequently, the business goals presented in the ATAM are being seen by some of the development team for the first time.

- *Quality requirements in terms of a collection of scenarios.* Business goals lead to quality requirements. Some of the important quality requirements are captured in the form of scenarios.

- *Mapping of architectural decisions to quality requirements.* Architectural decisions can be interpreted in terms of the qualities that they support or hinder. For each quality scenario examined during an ATAM, those architectural decisions that help to achieve it are determined.

- *A set of identified sensitivity and tradeoff points.* These are architectural decisions that have a marked effect on one or more quality attributes. Adopting a backup database, for example, is clearly an architectural decision as it affects reliability (positively), and so it is a sensitivity point with respect to reliability. However, keeping the backup current consumes system resources and so affects performance negatively. Hence, it is a tradeoff point between reliability and performance. Whether this decision is a risk or a nonrisk depends on whether its performance cost is excessive in the context of the quality attribute requirements of the architecture.

- *A set of risks and nonrisks.* A risk is defined in the ATAM as an architectural decision that may lead to undesirable consequences in light of stated quality attribute requirements. Similarly, a nonrisk is an architectural decision that, upon analysis, is deemed safe. The identified risks can form the basis for an architectural risk mitigation plan.

- *A set of risk themes.* When the analysis is complete, the evaluation team will examine the full set of discovered risks to look for over-arching themes that identify systemic weaknesses in the architecture or even in the architecture process and team. If left untreated, these risk themes will threaten the project's business goals.

The outputs are used to build a final written report that recaps the method, summarizes the proceedings, captures the scenarios and their analysis, and catalogs the findings.

There are secondary outputs as well. Very often, representations of the architecture will have been created expressly for the evaluation and may be superior to whatever existed before. This additional documentation survives the evaluation and can become part of the project's legacy. Also, the scenarios created by the participants are expressions of the business goals and requirements for the architecture and can be used to guide the architecture's evolution. Finally, the analysis contained in the final report can serve as a statement of rationale for certain architectural decisions made (or not made). The secondary outputs are tangible and enumerable.

There are intangible results of an ATAM-based evaluation. These include a palpable sense of community on the part of the stakeholders, open communication channels between the architect and the stakeholders, and a better overall understanding on the part of all participants of the architecture and its strengths and weaknesses. While these results are hard to measure, they are no less important than the others and often are the longest-lasting.

11.3 Phases of the ATAM

Activities in an ATAM-based evaluation are spread out over four phases.

In phase 0, "Partnership and Preparation," the evaluation team leadership and the key project decision makers informally meet to work out the details of the exercise. The project representatives brief the evaluators about the project so that the team can be supplemented by people who possess the appropriate expertise. Together, the two groups agree on logistics, such as the time and place of meetings, who brings the flipcharts, and who supplies the donuts and coffee. They also agree on a preliminary list of stakeholders (by name, not just role), and they negotiate on when the final report is to be delivered and to whom. They handle formalities such as a statement of work or nondisclosure agreements. They work out delivery to the evaluation team of whatever architectural documentation exists and may be useful. Finally, the evaluation team leader explains what information the manager and architect will be expected to show during phase 1, and helps them construct their presentations if necessary.

TABLE 11.2   ATAM Phases and Their Characteristics

Phase	Activity	Participants	Typical Duration
0	Partnership and preparation	Evaluation team leadership and key project decision makers	Proceeds informally as required, perhaps over a few weeks
1	Evaluation	Evaluation team and project decision makers	1 day followed by a hiatus of 2 to 3 weeks
2	Evaluation (continued)	Evaluation team, project decision makers, and stakeholders	2 days
3	Follow-up	Evaluation team and evaluation client	1 week

Source: Adapted from [Clements 02a].

Phase 1 and phase 2 are the evaluation phases, where everyone gets down to the business of analysis. By now the evaluation team will have studied the architecture documentation and will have a good idea of what the system is about, the overall architectural approaches taken, and the quality attributes that are of paramount importance. During phase 1, the evaluation team meets with the project decision makers (usually for about a day) to begin information gathering and analysis. For phase 2, the architecture's stakeholders join the proceedings and analysis continues, typically for two days. The exact steps of phase 1 and phase 2 are detailed in the next section.

Phase 3 is follow-up in which the evaluation team produces and delivers a written final report. The essence of this phase, however, is team self-examination and improvement. During a post-mortem meeting, the team discusses what went well and what didn't. They study the surveys handed out to participants during phase 1 and phase 2, and the process observer makes his or her report. Team members look for improvements in how they carry out their functions so that the next evaluation can be smoother or more effective. The team catalogs how much effort was spent during the evaluation, on the part of each of the three participating groups. After an appropriate number of months, the team leader contacts the evaluation client to gauge the long-term effects of the exercise so that costs and benefits can be compared.

Table 11.2 shows the four phases of the ATAM, who participates in each one, and an approximate timetable.

STEPS OF THE EVALUATION PHASES

The ATAM analysis phases (phase 1 and phase 2) consist of nine steps. Steps 1 through 6 are carried out in phase 1. In phase 2, with all stakeholders present, those steps are summarized and steps 7 through 9 are carried out.

The analysis steps are nominally carried out in sequential order according to a set agenda, but sometimes there must be dynamic modifications to the schedule to accommodate personnel availability or architectural information. Every evaluation is unique, and there may be times when the team returns briefly to an earlier step, jumps forward to a later step, or iterates among steps, as the need dictates.

Step 1—Present the ATAM.   The first step calls for the evaluation leader to present the ATAM to the assembled project representatives. This time is used to explain the process that everyone will be following, to answer questions, and to set the context and expectations for the remainder of the activities. Using a standard presentation, the leader will describe the ATAM steps in brief and the outputs of the evaluation.

Step 2—Present Business Drivers.   Everyone involved in the evaluation— the project representatives as well as the evaluation team members—needs to understand the context for the system and the primary business drivers motivating its development. In this step, a project decision maker (ideally the project manager or the system's customer) presents a system overview from a business perspective. The presentation should describe the following:

- The system's most important functions
- Any relevant technical, managerial, economic, or political constraints
- The business goals and context as they relate to the project
- The major stakeholders
- The architectural drivers (that is, the major quality attribute goals that shape the architecture)

Step 3—Present Architecture.   Here, the lead architect (or architecture team) makes a presentation describing the architecture at an appropriate level of detail. The "appropriate level" depends on several factors: how much of the architecture has been designed and documented; how much time is available; and the nature of the behavioral and quality requirements.

In this presentation the architect covers technical constraints such as operating system, hardware, or middleware prescribed for use, and other systems with which the system must interact. Most important, the architect describes the architectural approaches (or patterns, if the architect is fluent in that vocabulary) used to meet the requirements.

To make the most of limited time, the architect's presentation should have a high signal-to-noise ratio. That is, it should convey the essence of the architecture and not stray into ancillary areas or delve too deeply into the details of just a few aspects. Thus, it is extremely helpful to brief the architect beforehand about the information the evaluation team requires. A template such as the one in Figure 11.1 can help the architect prepare the presentation. Depending on the architect, a dress rehearsal can be included as part of the phase 1 activities.

Architecture Presentation (~20 slides; 60 minutes)

Driving architectural requirements, the measurable quantities you associate with these requirements, and any existing standards/models/approaches for meeting these (2–3 slides)

Important Architectural Information (4–8 slides)

- Context diagram—the system within the context in which it will exist. Humans or other systems with which the system will interact.
- Module or layer view—the modules (which may be subsystems or layers) that describe the system's decomposition of functionality, along with the objects, procedures, functions that populate these, and the relations among them (e.g., procedure call, method invocation, callback, containment).
- Component-and-connector view—processes, threads along with the synchronization, data flow, and events that connect them.
- Deployment view—CPUs, storage, external devices/sensors along with the networks and communication devices that connect them. Also shown are the processes that execute on the various processors.

Architectural approaches, patterns, or tactics employed, including what quality attributes they address and a description of how the approaches address those attributes (3–6 slides)

- Use of commercial off-the-shelf (COTS) products and how they are chosen/integrated (1–2 slides)
- Trace of 1 to 3 of the most important use case scenarios. If possible, include the runtime resources consumed for each scenario (1–3 slides)
- Trace of 1 to 3 of the most important change scenarios. If possible, describe the change impact (estimated size/difficulty of the change) in terms of the changed modules or interfaces (1–3 slides)
- Architectural issues/risks with respect to meeting the driving architectural requirements (2–3 slides)
- Glossary (1 slide)

FIGURE 11.1   Example of a template for the architecture presentation. *Source:* Adapted from [Clements 02a].

As may be seen in the presentation template, we expect architectural views, as described in Chapter 2, to be the primary vehicle for the architect to convey the architecture. Context diagrams, component-and-connector views, module decomposition or layered views, and the deployment view are useful in almost every evaluation, and the architect should be prepared to show them. Other views can be presented if they contain information relevant to the architecture at hand, especially information relevant to achieving important quality attribute goals. As a rule of thumb, the architect should present the views that he or she found most important during the creation of the architecture.

During the presentation, the evaluation team asks for clarification based on their phase 0 examination of the architecture documentation and their knowledge of the business drivers from the previous step. They also listen for and write down any architectural tactics or patterns they see employed.

Step 4—Identify Architectural Approaches.   The ATAM focuses on analyzing an architecture by understanding its architectural approaches. As we saw in Chapter 5, architectural patterns are useful for (among other reasons) the known ways in which each one affects particular quality attributes. A layered pattern tends to bring portability to a system, possibly at the expense of performance. A data repository pattern is usually scalable in the number of producers and consumers of data. And so forth.

By now, the evaluation team will have a good idea of what patterns and approaches the architect used in designing the system. They will have studied the architecture documentation, and they will have heard the architect's presentation in step 3. During that step, the architect is asked to explicitly name the patterns and approaches used, but the team should also be adept at spotting ones not mentioned.

In this short step, the evaluation team simply catalogs the patterns and approaches that are evident. The list is publicly captured by the scribe for all to see and will serve as the basis for later analysis.

Step 5—Generate Quality Attribute Utility Tree.   An architecture is either suitable or unsuitable with respect to its ability to deliver particular quality attributes to the system(s) built from it. The highest-performance architecture may be totally wrong for a system in which performance is not nearly as important as, say, security. The important quality attribute goals for the architecture under consideration were named in step 2, when the business drivers were presented, but not to any degree of specificity that would permit analysis. Broad goals such as "modifiability" or "high throughput" or "ability to be ported to a number of machines" establish important context and direction, and provide a backdrop against which subsequent information is presented. However, they are not specific enough to let us tell if the architecture suffices. Modifiable in what way? Throughput that is how high? Ported to what machines?

In this step, the quality attribute goals are articulated in detail via a mechanism known as the utility tree. Here, the evaluation team works with the project decision makers to identify, prioritize, and refine the system's most important quality attribute goals, which are expressed as scenarios. The utility tree serves to make the requirements concrete, forcing the architect and customer representatives to define precisely the relevant quality requirements that they were working to provide.

A utility tree begins with *utility* as the root node. Utility is an expression of the overall "goodness" of the system. Quality attributes form the second level because these are the components of utility. Quality attributes named in the business drivers presentation in step 2 make up the initial or seed set of this second level. Typically, performance, modifiability, security, usability, and availability are the children of utility, but participants are free to name their own. Sometimes different stakeholder groups use different names for the same ideas (for example, some stakeholders prefer to speak of "maintainability"). Sometimes they introduce quality attribute names that are meaningful in their own culture but not widely used elsewhere, such as "flextensibility." Any names the stakeholders introduce are fine as long as they are able to explain what they mean through refinement at the next levels. (See the sidebar What's in a Name?)

Under each of these quality attributes are specific quality attribute refinements. For example, performance might be decomposed into "data latency" and "transaction throughput." This is a step toward refining the attribute goals into quality attribute scenarios that are concrete enough for prioritization and analysis. Data latency might be further refined into "Lower storage latency on customer database to 20 ms." and "Deliver 20 frame/second video in real time" because both kinds of data latency are relevant to the system.

Scenarios (as described in Chapter 4) are the mechanism by which broad (and ambiguous) statements of desired qualities are made specific and testable. They form the leaves of the utility tree, grouped by the quality attributes they express. Their six-part form, as shown in Chapter 4, is simplified for purposes of evaluation. ATAM scenarios consist of three parts: stimulus (what condition arrives at a system, who generated it, and what system artifact it stimulates), environment (what is going on at the time), and response (system's reaction to the stimulus expressed in a measurable way).

Now we have something tangible against which to evaluate the architecture. In fact, the analysis steps of the ATAM consist of choosing one scenario at a time and seeing how well the architecture responds to, or achieves, it. More on that in the next step.

Some scenarios might express more than one quality attribute and so might appear in more than one place in the tree. That is not necessarily a problem, but the evaluation leader should guard against scenarios that try to cover too much diverse territory because they will be difficult to analyze. Try to split such scenarios into constituents that each attach smaller concerns.

Not only does the team need to understand the precise goals levied on the architecture, but it also needs to understand their relative importance. A utility tree can easily contain fifty scenarios at its leaves, and there will not be time during the evaluation meeting to analyze them all. Hence, utility tree generation also includes a prioritization step. By consensus, the decision makers assign a priority to each scenario. This prioritization may be on a 0 to 10 scale or use relative rankings such as high, medium, and low. (We prefer the high/medium/low approach because it works well with diverse groups and takes less time than assigning precise numbers.)

After that, scenarios are prioritized a second time, using a different criterion. The architect is asked to rank each scenario by how difficult he or she believes it

What's in a Name?

The architecture evaluation methods in this book use scenarios as a way to capture quality attributes because quality attributes by themselves are too vague for analysis. And yet the ATAM's utility tree uses quality attribute names as an organizing vehicle. Is that a contradiction? In fact, it is not because we do not care what qualities the stakeholders choose. As long as it stimulates their thinking, they are free to choose any quality attribute names they like. For instance, in the utility tree shown in Table 11.5 later in this chapter, you might argue that "configurability" and "modularity" are special kinds of "modifiability" and therefore should appear as a refinement of it. I would probably agree with you. But at that particular evaluation the stakeholders felt they were different enough to warrant their own categories in the utility tree, and so we accommodated them. What really matters is the scenarios at the leaves, not the structure of the branches.

We almost never see the same quality attribute names from evaluation to evaluation. One organization's "maintainability" is another organization's "changeability." Sometimes "portability" is a kind of modifiability, but many times the stakeholders stand it on its own. Reliability and availability are often interchanged, and we have also seen some esoteric quality attribute names that had well-known meaning within the organizations we were visiting: "deployability" and "sellability," for example. What did those mean? We did not know precisely, but it is a happy property of the ATAM that we never need to spend valuable time haggling over definitions. The scenarios provided the operational meaning. What mattered was that the terms meant something to the stakeholders who brought them up, who were then able to use them to conjure up scenarios articulating the concerns for which they stood.

In one ATAM exercise we ran, the developing organization had a very real concern about attracting talented personnel to its headquarters in a small, quiet city in the American Midwest. This business driver actually led to an architectural concern—that the architecture employ sufficiently interesting and state-of-the-art software technology so as to make people want to come work with it.

You will not find "Iowa-bility" in any list of IEEE, ISO, or ANSI standard quality attribute names, but it found its way into one of our ATAM utility trees, where it served as a means to stimulate thinking about scenarios to express the concern.

— PCC

will be for the architecture to satisfy. Again, a simple high/medium/low scheme works well here.

Now each scenario has an associated ordered pair: (H,H), (H,M), (H,L), and so forth. The scenarios that are the most important and the most difficult will be the ones where precious analysis time will be spent and the remainder will be kept as part of the record. A scenario that is considered either unimportant (L,*) or very easy to achieve (*,L) is not likely to receive much attention.

The output of utility tree generation is a prioritized list of scenarios that serves as a plan for the remainder of the ATAM evaluation. It tells the ATAM team where to spend its (relatively limited) time and, in particular, where to probe for architectural approaches and risks. The utility tree guides the evaluators toward the architectural approaches for satisfying the high-priority scenarios at its leaves.

At this point in the evaluation, all of the information necessary for analysis is on the table: the important qualities expected of the architecture that came from step 2's business drivers and step 5's utility tree, and the architecture in place as captured in step 3's architecture presentation and step 4's catalog of approaches used. An example of a utility tree, shown in tabular form (omitting the root utility node) is given in Table 11.5.

Step 6—Analyze Architectural Approaches. Here the evaluation team examines the highest-ranked scenarios one at a time; the architect is asked to explain how the architecture supports each one. Team members—especially the questioners—probe for the architectural approaches that the architect used to carry out the scenario. Along the way, the team documents the relevant architectural decisions and identifies and catalogs their risks, nonrisks, sensitivity points, and tradeoffs. For well-known approaches, the team asks how the architect overcame known weaknesses in the approach or how the architect gained assurance that the approach sufficed. The goal is for the evaluation team to be convinced that the instantiation of the approach is appropriate for meeting the attribute-specific requirements for which it is intended.

For example, the number of simultaneous database clients will affect the number of transactions that a database can process per second. Thus, the assignment of clients to the server is a sensitivity point with respect to the response as measured in transactions per second. Some assignments will result in unacceptable values of this response—these are risks. When it turns out that an architectural decision is a sensitivity point for more than one attribute, it is designated as a tradeoff point.

The scenario walkthrough leads to a discussion of possible risks, nonrisks, sensitivity points, or tradeoff points. These, in turn, may catalyze a deeper analysis, depending on how the architect responds. For example, if the architect cannot characterize the number of clients and cannot say how load balancing will be achieved by allocating processes to hardware, there is little point in a sophisticated queuing or rate-monotonic performance analysis. If such questions can be answered, the evaluation team can perform at least a rudimentary, or back-of-the-envelope, analysis to determine if these architectural decisions are problematic vis-à-vis the quality attribute requirements they are meant to address. The analysis is not meant to be comprehensive. The key is to elicit sufficient architectural information to establish some link between the architectural decisions that have been made and the quality attribute requirements that need to be satisfied.

Figure 11.2 shows a form for capturing the analysis of an architectural approach for a scenario. As shown, based on the results of this step the evaluation

Scenario #: A12		Scenario: Detect and recover from HW failure of main switch.			
Attribute(s)	Availability				
Environment	Normal operations				
Stimulus	One of the CPUs fails				
Response	0.999999 availability of switch				
Architectural decisions		Sensitivity	Tradeoff	Risk	Nonrisk
Backup CPU(s)		S2		R8	
No backup data channel		S3	T3	R9	
Watchdog		S4			N12
Heartbeat		S5			N13
Failover routing		S6			N14
Reasoning	Ensures no common mode failure by using different hardware and operating system (see Risk 8) Worst-case rollover is accomplished in 4 seconds as computing state takes that long at worst Guaranteed to detect failure within 2 seconds based on rates of heartbeat and watchdog Watchdog is simple and has proved reliable Availability requirement might be at risk due to lack of backup data channel ... (see Risk 9)				
Architecture diagram					

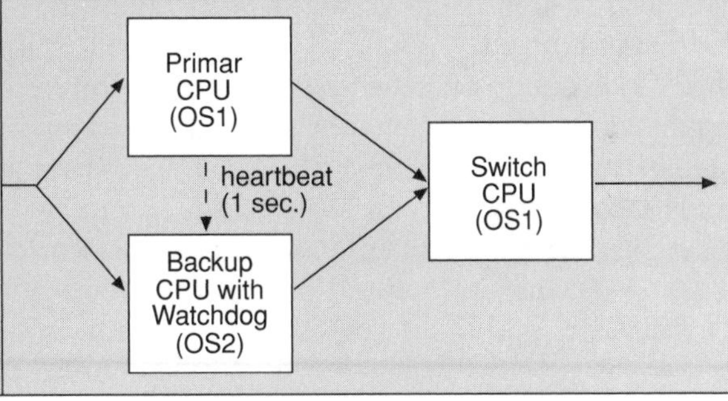

FIGURE 11.2 Example of architectural approach analysis *Source:* Adapted from [Clements 02a].

team can identify and record a set of sensitivity points and tradeoff points, risks and nonrisks. All sensitivity points and tradeoff points are candidate risks. By the end of the ATAM exercise, all of them should be categorized as either one or the other. The risks, nonrisks, sensitivity points, and tradeoff points are gathered in separate lists. The numbers R8, T3, S4, N12, and so forth, in Figure 11.2 are simply pointers into these lists.

At the end of this step, the evaluation team should have a clear picture of the most important aspects of the entire architecture, the rationale for key design decisions, and a list of risks, nonrisks, sensitivity points, and tradeoff points.

Hiatus and Start of Phase 2.   At this point, phase 1 is concluded. The evaluation team retreats to summarize what it has learned and interacts informally (usually by phone) with the architect during a hiatus of a week or two. More scenarios might be analyzed during this period, if desired, or questions of clarification can be resolved.

When the project's decision makers are ready to resume and the stakeholders are assembled, phase 2 commences. This phase is enacted by an expanded list of participants with additional stakeholders attending. First, step 1 is repeated so that the stakeholders understand the method and the role they are to play. Then the evaluation leader recaps the results of steps 2 through 6, and shares the current list of risks, nonrisks, sensitivity points, and tradeoff points. Now the stakeholders are up to speed with the evaluation results so far, and the remaining three steps can be carried out.

Step 7—Brainstorm and Prioritize Scenarios.   While utility tree generation is used primarily to understand how the architect perceived and handled quality attribute architectural drivers, the purpose of scenario brainstorming is to take the pulse of the larger stakeholder community. Scenario brainstorming works well in larger groups, creating an atmosphere in which the ideas and thoughts of one person stimulate others' ideas. The process fosters communication and creativity, and serves to express the collective mind of the participants. The prioritized list of brainstormed scenarios is compared with those from the utility tree exercise. If they agree, it indicates good alignment between what the architect had in mind and what the stakeholders actually wanted. If additional driving scenarios are discovered, this may itself be a risk showing that there was some disagreement in goals between the stakeholders and the architect.

In this step, the evaluation team asks the stakeholders to brainstorm scenarios that are operationally meaningful with respect to the stakeholders' individual roles. A maintainer will likely propose a modifiability scenario, for example, while a user will probably come up with a scenario that expresses useful functionality or ease of operation.

Utility tree scenarios that have not been analyzed are fair game. Stakeholders are free to put them into the brainstorm pool, which gives them the opportunity to revisit scenarios from step 5 and step 6 that they might feel received too little attention.

Once the scenarios have been collected, they must be prioritized, for the same reasons that the scenarios in the utility tree needed to be prioritized: The evaluation team needs to know where to devote its limited analytical time. First, stakeholders are asked to merge scenarios they feel represent the same behavior or quality concern. Then they vote for those they feel are most important. Each stakeholder is allocated a number of votes equal to 30% of the number of scenarios,[1] rounded up. So, if there were twenty scenarios collected, each stakeholder would be given six votes. These votes can be allocated in any way that the stakeholder sees fit: all six votes for one scenario, one vote for each of the six, or anything in between.

Each stakeholder casts his or her votes publicly; our experience tells us it is more fun that way and builds unity among the participants. Once the votes are tallied, the evaluation leader orders the scenarios by vote total and looks for a sharp drop-off in the number of votes. Scenarios "above the line" are adopted and carried forth to subsequent steps. So for example, a team might consider only the top five scenarios.

Step 8—Analyze Architectural Approaches.   After the scenarios have been collected and prioritized, the evaluation team guides the architect in the process of carrying out the highest ranked scenarios from step 7. The architect explains how relevant architectural decisions contribute to realizing each one. Ideally this activity will be dominated by the architect's explanation of scenarios in terms of previously discussed architectural approaches.

In this step the evaluation team performs the same activities as in step 6, mapping the highest-ranked, newly generated scenarios onto the architectural artifacts uncovered thus far.

Step 9—Present Results.   Finally, the collected information from the ATAM needs to be summarized and presented once again to stakeholders. This presentation typically takes the form of a verbal report accompanied by slides, but it might be accompanied by a more comprehensive written report delivered subsequent to the ATAM evaluation. In this presentation the evaluation leader recapitulates the steps of the ATAM and all the information collected in the steps of the method, including the business context, driving requirements, constraints, and architecture. Then the following outputs are presented:

- The architectural approaches documented
- The set of scenarios and their prioritization from the brainstorming
- The utility tree
- The risks discovered
- The nonrisks documented
- The sensitivity points and tradeoff points found

These outputs are all uncovered, publicly captured, and cataloged during the evaluation. In step 9, however, the evaluation team adds value by grouping risks into risk themes, based on some common underlying concern or systemic deficiency. For example, a group of risks about inadequate or out-of-date documentation might be grouped into a risk theme stating that documentation is given insufficient consideration. A group of risks about the system's inability to function in the face of various hardware and/or software failures might lead to a risk theme about insufficient attention to backup capability or providing high availability.

---

[1] This is a common facilitated brainstorming technique.

For each risk theme, the evaluation team identifies which of the business drivers listed in step 2 are affected. Identifying risk themes and then relating them to specific drivers brings the evaluation full circle by relating the final results to

---

Their Solution Just Won't Work

The steps of the ATAM might suggest that the stakeholders' role is merely to help craft the statement of goals for the architecture and then help articulate the scenarios. However, their presence at the presentation and evaluation of the architecture has been vital on more than one occasion. Only the stakeholders have the depth of knowledge necessary to tell when the architecture—or its presenter—is glossing over an important issue. For example, in the evaluation of a financial management system, the ATAM-ites were not expert in the application area of financial management systems. Hence, several exchanges took place during the evaluation, such as the following:

ATAM-ITE: Okay, let's move to the next scenario. Does your system provide that capability?

VENDOR (smiling kindly): Oh, yes, it sure does. All the user has to do is enter the account number, bring up the accounts receivable table, and transfer the results to the sponsor alert file.

ATAM-ITE (nodding, checking "non-risk" for that scenario, and thinking that this evaluation was going to be easier than he thought): Okay, great. Now the next scenario. . . .

SYSTEM USER 1 (indignantly): Wait a minute! You mean there's no way to automatically transfer that data? You're telling me I have to type it all in to *each* alert file?

VENDOR (looking a little nervous): Um, well . . .

SYSTEM USER 1 (sensing vulnerability): Do you know how many sponsors a major university like this has?

VENDOR (tugging at his collar): A lot?

SYSTEM USER 1 (now it's her turn to smile kindly): Yes. A lot.

SYSTEM USER 2: And what if I don't know the account number to enter? That was the whole reason to initiate this transaction in the first place, right? Because otherwise, you'd just open a payout update voucher.

SYSTEM USER 1 (to the ATAM-ITES): Their solution just won't work.

ATAM-ITE (trying to remember what a sponsor alert file was, wondering if he had ever heard of a payout update voucher, and discreetly erasing his previous check mark): OK, well, this sure sounds like we might have a risk here. Now what would you have to change . . . ?

The point is that expert stakeholders are required to sniff out a problem that outsiders might not catch.

— PCC

the initial presentation, thus providing a satisfying closure to the exercise. As important, it elevates the risks that were uncovered to the attention of management. What might otherwise have seemed to a manager like an esoteric technical issue is now identified unambiguously as a threat to something the manager is on record as caring about.

Table 11.3 summarizes the nine steps of the ATAM and shows how each step contributes to the outputs the ATAM delivers after an evaluation. A "**" means that the step is a primary contributor to the output; a "*" means that it is a secondary contributor.

TABLE 11.3 Steps and ATAM Outputs, Correlated

Steps	ATAM Outputs					
	Prioritized Statement of Quality Attribute Requirements	Catalog of Architectural Approaches Used	Approach- and Quality Attribute-Specific Analysis Questions	Mapping of Architectural Approaches to Quality Attributes	Risks and Non-risks	Sensitivity and Tradeoff Points
1. Present ATAM						
2. Present business drivers	*a				*b	
3. Present architecture		**			*c	*d
4. Identify architectural approaches		**	**		*e	*f
5. Generate quality attribute utility tree	**					
6. Analyze architectural approaches		*g	**	**	**	**
7. Brainstorm and prioritize scenarios	**					
8. Analyze architectural approaches		*	**	**	**	**
9. Present results						

a. The business drivers include the first, coarse description of the quality attributes.
b. The business drivers presentation might disclose an already identified or long-standing risk that should be captured.
c. The architect may identify a risk in his or her presentation.
d. The architect may identify a sensitivity of tradeoff point in his or her presentation.
e. Many architectural approaches have standard associated risks.
f. Many architectural approaches have associated standard sensitivities and quality attribute tradeoffs.
g. The analysis steps might reveal one or more architectural approaches not identified in step 4, which will then produce new approach-specific questions.

Source: Adapted from [Clements 02a].

USING THE LIMITED TIME OF AN EVALUATION EFFECTIVELY

In the introduction, we identified limited time as one of the main problems in conducting an architectural evaluation. Now we can see how the ATAM solves that problem. The business goals are used as motivation for the collection of scenarios that represent the utility tree. Other scenarios are prioritized, essentially, as a bottom-up check on the top-down scenario generation of the utility tree. Only the high-priority and difficult scenarios are analyzed. The evaluators are guided to these important but problematic areas of the architecture by the steps of the method. These are the areas that will yield the most important results.

11.4   The Nightingale System: A Case Study in Applying the ATAM

This section will describe the ATAM in practice using a case study based on an actual evaluation. Identifying information has been changed to protect the client's confidentiality.

PHASE 0: PARTNERSHIP AND PREPARATION

The client or organization for the evaluation, which had approached us after reading about the ATAM on our Web site, was a major producer of health care systems software, aimed at the hospital, clinic, and HMO markets. The system under consideration was called Nightingale. We learned that it was a large system expected to comprise several million lines of code and that it was well into implementation. Nightingale already had its first customer, a hospital chain with forty-some hospitals throughout the southwestern United States.

Why, we wanted to know, was our client interested in an architecture evaluation when the system was already well on its way to being fielded and sold? There were two reasons. First, if the architecture was fundamentally flawed in any way, it was much better to discover it sooner rather than later; second, the organization had strong ambitions to sell the system to many other customers, but recognized that it would have to tailor it specifically to the needs, applications, and regulatory environments of each one. Hence, while the architecture might be adequate for the first, kickoff customer, the client wanted to make sure that it was sufficiently robust and modifiable to serve as the basis for an entire product family of health care management systems.

The system would serve as the information backbone for the health care institutions in which it was installed. It would provide data about patients' treatment history as well as track their insurance and other payments. And it would provide a data-warehousing capability to help spot trends (such as predictors for relapses of certain diseases). The system would produce a large number of on-

TABLE 11.4   Evaluation Team Role Assignments

Member	Role
1	Team leader, evaluation leader, questioner
2	Evaluation leader, questioner
3	Timekeeper, questioner
4	Scenario scribe, questioner, data gatherer
5	Questioner, process enforcer
6	Proceedings scribe, process observer

demand and periodic reports, each tailored to the institution's specific needs. For those patients making payments on their own, it would manage the work flow associated with initiating and servicing what amounts to a loan throughout its entire life. Further, since the system would either run (or at least be accessible) at all of the health care institution's facilities, it had to be able to respond to a specific office's configuration needs. Different offices might run different hardware configurations, for instance, or require different reports. A user might travel from one site to another, and the system would have to recognize that user and his or her specific information needs, no matter the location.

Negotiations to sign a statement of work took about a month—par for the course when legalities between two large organizations are involved—and when it was complete we formed an evaluation team of six people,[2] assigning roles as shown in Table 11.4.

For this exercise, we assigned two evaluation leaders who would take turns facilitating the proceedings. We have found this scheme markedly helpful in reducing fatigue and stress, and it makes for better results. We chose our questioners based on their familiarity with performance and modifiability. We also chose people with experience in integrating COTS products, since our client told us early on that Nightingale employed a few dozen commercial software packages. Happily, one of our questioners also had experience working in the health care industry.

We held a one-day kickoff meeting attended by the evaluation team, the project manager, the lead architect, and the project manager for Nightingale's first customer. The last three constituted the decision makers for Nightingale. At the meeting, we heard more about Nightingale's capabilities and requirements, received a catalog of available architectural documentation (from which we chose those we wanted to examine), and compiled a list of stakeholders to attend phase 2. We agreed on a schedule for the phase 1 and phase 2 meetings and for the delivery of the final report. Finally, we went over the presentations that the

---

[2] Six is a large team. As we mentioned earlier, teams are usually three to five people and four is average. In this case, two of the team members were new to the ATAM process and were added to give them experience.

project manager and the architect, respectively, would be requested to make for steps 2 and 3 of phase 1, and made sure they were clear on the information we would want to see.

Later, before phase 1, our team met for two hours. The team leader went over the role assignments once again and made sure everyone knew his or her duties. Also, we walked through the architecture documentation we had received, making note of the patterns and tactics it indicated. This pre-meeting helped the team arrive at the evaluation somewhat knowledgeable about the architecture (thus increasing everyone's confidence), and it laid the groundwork for step 4, in which patterns and approaches would be cataloged.

In the Nightingale evaluation, the meeting also raised a red flag about the documentation, which was incomplete and unclear. Whole sections had not yet been written, and by and large the architecture was presented as a set of inadequately defined box-and-line diagrams. We felt that, were we to begin phase 1 at this point, we would not be on a firm conceptual footing. So we telephoned the architect and asked him to verbally fill in some of the blanks. Then, though we knew there were still gaps in our knowledge, at least we felt comfortable enough to begin the evaluation. We made a note that inadequate documentation was a risk that we needed to catalog.

PHASE 1: EVALUATION

As called for in phase 1, the evaluation team met with the project's decision makers. In addition to those who had attended the kickoff meeting (the project manager, the lead architect, and the project manager for Nightingale's kickoff customer), two lead designers participated.

Step 1: Present ATAM. The evaluation leader used our organization's standard viewgraph package that explains the method. The hour-long presentation lays out the method's steps and phases, describes the conceptual foundations underlying the ATAM (such as scenarios, architectural approaches, sensitivity points, and the like), and lists the outputs that will be produced by the end of the exercise.

The decision makers were already largely familiar with ATAM, having heard it described during the phase 0 discussions, so this step proceeded without a hitch.

Step 2: Present Business Drivers. At the evaluation, the project manager for the client organization presented the business objectives for the Nightingale system from the development organization, as well as from organizations they hoped would be customers for the system. For the development organization, Nightingale addressed business requirements that included

- support for their kickoff customer's diverse uses (e.g., treatment tracking, payment histories, trend spotting, etc.).

- creation of a new version of the system (e.g., to manage doctors' offices) that the development organization could market to customers other than the kickoff customer.

The second business driver alerted us to the fact that this architecture was intended for an entire software product line (see Chapter 14), not just one system.

For the kickoff customer, Nightingale was to replace the multiple existing legacy systems, which were

- old (one was more than 25 years old).
- based on aging languages and technology (e.g., COBOL and IBM assembler).
- difficult to maintain.
- unresponsive to the current and projected business needs of the health care sites.

The kickoff customer's business requirements included

- the ability to deal with diverse cultural and regional differences.
- the ability to deal with multiple languages (especially English and Spanish) and currencies (especially the U.S. dollar and Mexican peso).
- a new system at least as fast as any legacy system being replaced.
- a new single system combining distinct legacy financial management systems.

The business constraints for the system included

- a commitment to employees of no lost jobs via retraining of existing employees.
- the adoption of a "buy rather than build" approach to software.
- recognition that the customer's marketplace (i.e., number of competitors) had shrunk.

The technical constraints for the system included

- use of off-the-shelf software components whenever possible.
- a two-year time frame to implement the system with the replacement of physical hardware occurring every 26 weeks.

The following quality attributes were identified as high priority:

- *Performance.* Health care systems require quick response times to be considered useful. The 5-second transaction response time of the legacy system was too slow, as were the legacy response times for online queries and reports. System throughput was also a performance concern.
- *Usability.* There was a high turnover of users of the system, so retraining was an important customer issue. The new system had to be easy to learn and use.
- *Maintainability.* The system had to be maintainable, configurable, and extensible to support new markets (e.g., managing doctors' offices), new customer requirements, changes in state laws and regulations, and the needs of the different regions and cultures.

The manager identified the following quality attributes as important, but of somewhat lower priority:

- *Security.* The system had to provide the normal commercial level of security (e.g., confidentiality and data integrity) required by financial systems.
- *Availability.* The system had to be highly available during normal business hours.
- *Scalability.* The system had to scale up to meet the needs of the largest hospital customers and down to meets the needs of the smallest walk-in clinics.
- *Modularity.* The developing organization was entertaining the possibility of selling not just new versions of Nightingale but individual components of it. Providing this capability required qualities closely related to maintainability and scalability.
- *Testability and supportability.* The system had to be understandable by the customer's technical staff since employee training and retention was an issue.

Step 3: Present Architecture.   During the evaluation team's interactions with the architect, before as well as during the evaluation exercise, several views of the architecture and the architectural approaches emerged. Key insights included the following:

- Nightingale consisted of two major subsystems: OnLine Transaction Manager (OLTM) and Decision Support and Report Generation Manager (DSRGM). OLTM carries interactive performance requirements, whereas DSRGM is more of a batch processing system whose tasks are initiated periodically.
- Nightingale was built to be highly configurable.
- The OnLine Transaction Manager subsystem was strongly layered.
- Nightingale was a repository-based system; a large commercial database lay at its heart.
- Nightingale relied heavily on COTS software, including the central database, a rules engine, a work flow engine, CORBA, a Web engine, a software distribution tool, and many others.
- Nightingale was heavily object oriented, relying on object frameworks to achieve much of its configurability.

Figure 11.3 shows a layered view of OLTM rendered in the informal notation used by the architect. Figure 11.4 depicts how OLTM works at runtime by showing the major communication and data flow paths among the parts of the system deployed on various hardware processors. We present these figures basically as we were given them to give you a better understanding of the reality of an ATAM evaluation. Note that they do not cleanly map; that is, in Figure 11.3 there is a transaction manager and CORBA, but these do not occur in Figure 11.4. This type of omission is typical of many of our ATAM evaluations, and one of the activities that occurs during step 3 is that the evaluators ask questions about the inconsistencies in the diagrams in an attempt to come to some level of understanding

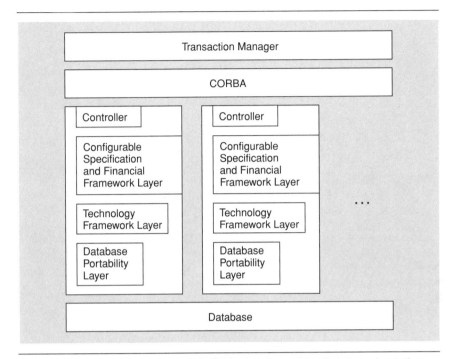

FIGURE 11.3   Layered view of the OLTM in the the architect's informal notation

of the architecture. Figure 11.5 shows a similar runtime view of OLTM in which a transaction can be traced throughout the system, again with similar inconsistencies and, in this case, without a description of the meaning of the arrows. We determined that these arrows also represented data flow.

All of these views of the Nightingale are equally legitimate and carry important information. Each shows an aspect relevant to different concerns, and all were used to carry out the analysis steps of the ATAM exercise.

Step 4—Catalog Architectural Approaches.   After the architecture presentation, the evaluation team listed the architectural approaches they had heard, plus those they had learned about during their pre-evaluation review of the documentation. The main ones included

- layering, especially in OLTM.
- object orientation.
- use of configuration files to achieve modifiability without recoding or recompiling.
- client-server transaction processing.
- a data-centric architectural pattern, with a large commercial database at its heart.

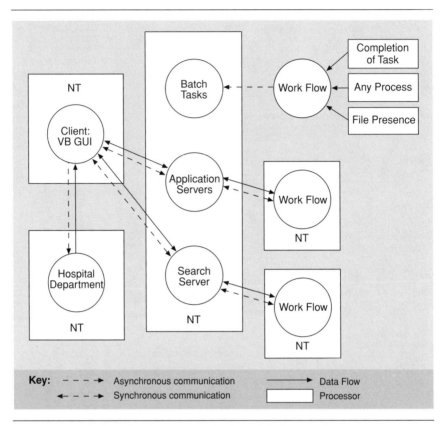

FIGURE 11.4 A view showing communication, data flow, and processors of the OLTM

These and other approaches gave the evaluation team a conceptual footing from which to begin asking probing questions when scenario analysis began.

Step 5—Generate Quality Attribute Utility Tree. Table 11.5 shows the utility tree generated during the Nightingale ATAM exercise. Notice that all of the quality attributes identified during step 2 appear and that each is refined into one or more specific meanings.

A few of the quality attribute refinements have no scenarios associated with them. That often happens and it is not a problem. People are sometimes able to think of a reasonable-sounding refinement for a quality attribute, but, when pressed to instantiate it in the context of their own system, discover that it does not really apply.

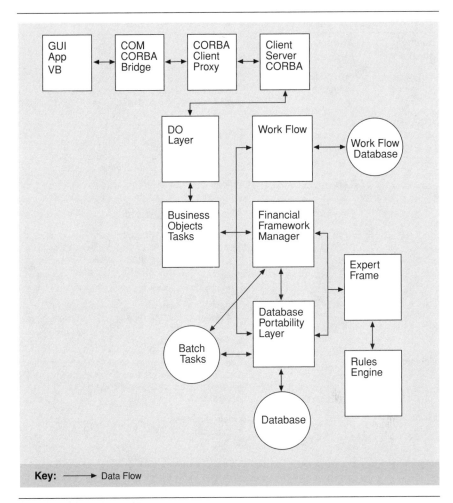

FIGURE 11.5   Data flow architectural view of the OLTM

To capture the utility tree for all to see, the proceedings scribe used a flip-chart page for each quality attribute and taped it to the wall. Then, as that quality attribute was refined and instantiated with scenarios, she captured the information on that flipchart or on continuation flipcharts taped underneath.[3]

---

[3] We have also experimented with capturing the utility tree online in a table like Table 11.5 and projecting it directly from the computer. This makes the tree easier to build and modify but the participants can see only one screen's worth at any time. Seeing the whole utility tree helps stimulate thinking and identify gaps. Collaborative-work software systems would seem to be ideal here, but it is hard to beat flipcharts and masking tape for simplicity, reliability, and economy.

TABLE 11. 5   Tabular Form of the Utility Tree for the Nightingale ATAM Exercise

Quality Attribute	Attribute Refinement	Scenarios
Performance	Transaction response time	A user updates a patient's account in response to a change-of-address notification while the system is under peak load, and the transaction completes in less than 0.75 second. (H,M)
		A user updates a patient's account in response to a change-of-address notification while the system is under twice the current peak load, and the transaction completes in less than 4 seconds. (L,M)
	Throughput	At peak load, the system is able to complete 150 normalized transactions per second. (M,M)
	Generating reports	No scenarios suggested.
Usability	Proficiency training	A new hire with two or more years experience in the business becomes proficient in Nightingale's core functions in less than 1 week. (M,L)
		A user in a particular context asks for help, and the system provides help for that context. (H,L)
	Normal operations	A hospital payment officer initiates a payment plan for a patient while interacting with that patient and completes the process without the system introducing delays. (M,M)
Configurability		A hospital increases the fee for a particular service. The configuration team makes the change in 1 working day; no source code needs to change. (H,L)
Maintainability		A maintainer encounters search- and response-time deficiencies, fixes the bug, and distributes the bug fix. (H,M)
		A reporting requirement requires a change to the report-generating metadata. (M,L)
		The database vendor releases a new version that must be installed in a minimum amount of time. (H,M)
Extensibility	Adding new product	A product that tracks blood bank donors is created. (M,M)
Security	Confidentiality	A physical therapist is allowed to see the part of a patient's record dealing with orthopedic treatment, but not other parts nor any financial information. (H,M)
	Integrity	The system resists unauthorized intrusion. (H,M)
Availability		The database vendor releases new software, which is hot-swapped into place. (H,L)
		The system supports 24/7 Web-based account access by patients. (L,L)

TABLE 11. 5   *Continued*

Quality Attribute	Attribute Refinement	Scenarios
Scalability	Growing the system	The kickoff customer purchases a health care company three times its size, requiring a partitioning of the database. (L,H)
		The kickoff customer divests a business unit. (L,M)
		The kickoff customer consolidates two business units. (L,M)
		The developing organization wants to sell components of Nightingale. (M,L)
Modularity	Functional subsets	Build a system that can function autonomously with core functionality. (M,L)
	Flexibility to replace COTS products	Replace the commercial database with one by another vendor. (H,M)
		Replace the operating system. (H,M)
		Replace the database portability layer. (H,M)
		Replace the transaction manager. (H,M)
		Replace the work flow engine. (H,M)
		Replace the commercial accounting package. (H,M)
		Replace Solaris on the Sun platforms that host the database. (H,M)
		Replace the rules engine. (H,M)
Interoperability		Build a system that interfaces with the epidemiological database at the National Centers for Disease Control. (M,M)
Testability		
Supportability		

The scenarios in Table 11.5 are annotated with the priority rankings assigned by the decision makers present. The first of each ordered pair indicates the importance of the capability; the second indicates the architect's estimation of the difficulty in achieving it.

Notice that some of the scenarios are well formed according to our earlier discussion, others have no stimulus, and still others have no responses. At this stage, the imprecision in scenario specification is permissible as long as the stakeholders understand the meaning. If the scenarios are selected for analysis, then the stimulus and response must be made explicit.

Step 6—Analyze Architectural Approaches. The utility tree exercise produced no scenarios ranked (H,H), which indicates high-importance, high-difficulty scenarios that merit high analytical priority. So we looked for (H,M) scenarios, a cluster of which appeared under "Modularity," hypothesizing the replacement of various COTS products in the system. Although extensive use of COTS was a purposeful strategy to reduce development risk, it was also worrisome to the project's management because it was felt that the system (and the customers to whom it was sold) would be at the mercy of a large number of COTS vendors. Therefore, achieving architectural flexibility to swap out COTS products was of keen interest.

We walked through each of the scenarios with the architect. Each consumed, on average, about a half hour.[4] Since these were scenarios about changes, we asked about the range and impact of the changes. We learned the following.

- Replacing the commercial database with a database supplied by another vendor would be difficult. A dialect of SQL (a superset of ANSI-standard SQL) specific to the current database vendor was used throughout Nightingale, as were several vendor-specific tools and components. The architect considered replacing the database as highly unlikely and so was not concerned that shifting to another system would be very expensive. This was news to the project manager, however, who was not so sure that the scenario was out of the question. We recorded our first analysis-based architectural risk: "Because Nightingale uses vendor-specific tools, components, and an SQL dialect not supported by or compatible with databases supplied by other vendors, replacing the database would be extremely difficult and expensive, requiring several staff-years of effort." The architectural decision to wed the architecture to the database was also recorded as a sensitivity point, negatively affecting modifiability.

- Replacing one operating system with another would be a reasonably straightforward change. On the server side, the operating system was insulated by a layer, which would confine the necessary changes to a small portion. However, OLTM relies on NT authentication facilities directly, and a replacement operating system would have to provide something similar for the change to be straightforward. On the DSRGM side, all operating system dependencies had already been eliminated in the source code; DSRGM was developed on a Windows NT platform but deployed on UNIX, providing compelling evidence that it was already independent of the operating system. Here we recorded our first nonrisk: "Because operating system dependencies have been localized or eliminated from OLTM and DSRGM, replacing the operating system with another one would require only a small modification." Encapsulating operating system dependencies was recorded as a sensitivity point, positively affecting modifiability.

- Changing the rules engine raised several issues of concern. This scenario was not a farfetched one, because we learned that there were associated performance

---

[4] In evaluation after evaluation, the first scenario analyzed invariably takes the most time, perhaps as much as three times the average.

and maintainability concerns associated with using the rules engine. The likely scenario would be to remove, not replace, the rules engine and then implement the rules directly in C++. Since forward chaining among the rules had been disallowed (specifically—and wisely—to keep this option open), the rules were effectively procedural and could be compiled. Such a change would have several serious effects:

- It would likely improve performance (although this question had not yet been answered authoritatively).
- It would obviate the need for personnel trained in the rules language and knowledgeable about the rules engine.
- It would deprive the development team of a useful rules development and simulation environment.
- It would lead to the possibility that the rules could become "buried" in the rest of the C++ code and make it easier for them to become entangled in functional code not strictly related to rules, and hence harder to recognize and maintain.
- It would remove the possibility that the rules could reference some object that in fact did not exist, a possibility that exists today and represents an error that could conceivably survive past testing and into a production system. Writing the rules in C++ would eliminate this error at compile time.

To facilitate this change, a rule-to-C++ code generator would need to be written, a development effort of significant scope and unknown difficulty. For this scenario, we recorded as a risk the major effort needed to remove the rules engine. We also recorded using a rules engine (as opposed to C++ code) as a tradeoff point in the architecture. This made development easier and changes to the rule base easier; however, these benefits came at the cost of decreased performance, specially trained developers, and more difficult testing.

And so forth. We continued this scenario, investigating replacement of the commercial Web-hosting engine, the commercial accounting package, the work flow engine, and the Solaris operating system on the Sun platforms.

At this point, the phase 1 meeting ended. We had recorded six sensitivity points, one tradeoff point, four risks, and five nonrisks.

PHASE 2: EVALUATION (CONTINUED)

The phase 2 meeting commenced after a hiatus of two weeks. During the break, the evaluation team wrote up those parts of the final report that could be completed: the business drivers, the presented architecture, the list of approaches, the utility tree, and the phase 1 analysis. We also interacted via telephone with the architect to check our understanding of some technical points, and with the project manager to make sure that a good stakeholder representation would be present for phase 2.

For phase 2, we had nine stakeholders present in addition to the project decision makers present during phase 1. They included developers, maintainers, representatives from the kickoff customer, and two end users.

The first activities of phase 2 were to repeat step 1 (describing the ATAM) for the new participants, and then recap the results of phase 1 to bring everyone up to speed. After that, steps 7, 8, and 9 were carried out.

Step 7—Brainstorm and Prioritize Scenarios. The stakeholders were a productive group, contributing a total of 72 scenarios during this step. More than a dozen of those scenarios were found at the leaves of step 5's utility tree but were not analyzed during phase 1. This was not only proper but encouraged. In this way, the stakeholders were expressing the view that some scenarios deserved more attention than they had received during phase 1.

Table 11.6 contains a selection of some of the more interesting scenarios that emerged during step 7. Notice that many of them are not particularly well structured, and some are downright cryptic. This reflects the spontaneous nature of a brainstorming exercise in which everyone is actively engaged. Rather than spend several minutes structuring and wordsmithing each scenario as it arises, we like to concentrate on capturing thoughts while they are fresh in people's minds. If a scenario's meaning needs to be polished before voting occurs or before it is analyzed, then we are happy to spend the necessary time doing so (with the help of the person who proposed it).

TABLE 11.6   Brainstormed Scenarios

Number	Scenario
1	Previously public data is made private, and access is adjusted accordingly.
2	Data in the information hub is replicated to a branch clinic, and performance is degraded.
3	A rule in the rule engine fires, and data access is too slow.
4	A user posts a patient's payment at a busy time, and response is slow (in a testing environment).
5	A user in one business unit needs to perform actions on behalf of other business units.
6	Decide to support German.
7	Add an epidemiologist role and supporting functionality.
8	Sell Nightingale to a five-person doctor's office and have it support their business.
9	A user requests a new field for asynchronous queries.
10	In response to a complaint, a hospital discovers it has been incorrectly charging for bedpans for six months.
11	A hospital needs to centralize the record maintenance process across multiple affiliates; associated business process is re-engineered.
12	A manager wants a report on historical payment delinquency rates for people who were treated for cuts and lacerations.

TABLE 11.6 *Continued*

Number	Scenario
13	"What-if" scenario: A proposed law change is applied to an account.
14	A defect corrupts data and is not detected until the next reporting cycle.
15	Nightingale is installed in a hospital, and the hospital's existing database must be converted.
16	An error in the replication process causes a transaction database to be out of sync with the backup database.
17	An error in the system causes all payments to accounts in Arizona to be unpostable.
18	A transaction log audit trail fails for three days (how to recover?).
19	An affiliate redefines a business day and month.
20	Receive payment post information from an insurance company's database system, given its metadata definition.
21	Introduce a new work flow process for patient check-in and check-out.
22	Batch processes are initiated based on time and events.
23	Main communication to branch clinics from the information hub goes down.
24	A branch clinic database server fails to boot.
25	A report needs to be generated using information from two hospitals that use different configurations.
26	A remittance center submits the same batch of payments twice, and activity occurs after the second submission.
27	A rehabilitation therapist is assigned to another hospital, but needs read-only access to the treatment histories of his or her former patients.
28	Distribute a set of changes to a set of health care sites consistently (forms and configurations).
29	A fire in the data center forces the information hub to be moved to a new location.
30	One hospital sells a large number of accounts payable to another business unit.
31	Change the rules for generating a warning about conflicting medications.
32	A user in a hospital's finance office wants to change output from paper to online viewing.
33	The phone company changes an area code.
34	A malicious account administrator has slowly transferred small amounts into various accounts of his friends. How to discover and determine extent?

After merging a few almost-alike scenarios, the stakeholders voted. We assigned 22 votes to each stakeholder (72 scenarios times 30%, rounded up to the nearest even integer), which they cast in two passes. We tallied the votes and spent a half-hour with the group placing the dozen or so highest-priority scenarios in the utility tree created during step 5. For this exercise, all of the high-priority step 7 scenarios were straightforwardly placed as new leaves of existing branches in the utility tree. This suggested that the architect was thinking along the same lines as the stakeholders in terms of important quality attributes.

After reconciling the new scenarios with the utility tree, we began analyzing the scenarios that received the most votes.

Step 8—Analyze Architectural Approaches.   During step 8, we analyzed seven additional scenarios, a number slightly above average for an ATAM exercise. In deference to space limitations, the Scenario 15 sidebar summarizes the analysis for just one of them.

Step 9—Present Results.   Step 9 is a one- to two-hour presentation summarizing the results and findings of the exercise. It begins with a boilerplate set of slides that contains a method recap and blank template slides that can be filled in with the business drivers summary, the architecture summary, the list of approaches, the utility tree, the scenario analysis, and the list of analysis outputs.

The evaluation team meets during the evenings of phase 2 to compile all the results gathered so far. The phase 2 agenda also contains a block of time before step 9 when the team can caucus and complete the package.

In addition to the risks, nonrisks, sensitivity points, and tradeoff points, the team presents risk themes that seem to systematically underlie the problematic areas of the architecture, if any. This is the only part of the results that the participants will not have already seen (and, for that matter, helped to identify). For each one, we also state why it matters in terms that will be meaningful to the client: We identify the stated business drivers that each risk theme jeopardizes.

Scenario 15: Nightingale is installed in a hospital and the hospital's existing database must be converted.

Not surprisingly, the architect had given this scenario a lot of thought, since carrying it out successfully was essential to the success of Nightingale. There was a documented procedure in place, which the architect drew for us on the whiteboard.

It often happens that a scenario leads to a deeper understanding of the architecture than was present before. Here, the architect had the information, but (reasonably) did not include it in the step 3 presentation, considering it ancillary.

Walking through the migration process convinced the evaluation team that a well-thought-out procedure was in place, with known strengths and reasonable limitations. It did not surprise us that the architect did not mention the process during his presentation of step 3. What did surprise us was that we saw nothing about it in the documentation package we received and reviewed prior to phase 1. When pressed about this, the architect admitted that the procedure was not yet documented, which we recorded as a risk. Offsetting this risk, however, was a nonrisk that we recorded: "The architecture supports a straightforward and effective data conversion and migration facility to support Nightingale installation."

For Nightingale, we identified three risk themes:

1. *Over-reliance on specific COTS products.* Here we cited the difficulties in swapping out the database, in removing the rules engine, and in relying on an old and possibly no-longer-supported version of the database portability layer. This risk theme threatened the business driver of a system that is maintainable.

2. *Error recovery processes were not fully defined. The customer's knowledge of available tools was incomplete.* Several scenarios dealt with discovering errors in the database and backing them out. While the architecture supported those procedures well enough, it was clear that the architects and designers were thinking about some of them for the first time. The representatives of the kickoff customer reported that they had no procedures in place (either of their own or inherited from the developing organization) for making such error corrections. This risk theme threatened the business driver of usability and support for the customer's enterprise.

3. *Documentation issues.* The state of documentation on the Nightingale project was inadequate. The team began to realize this as far back as the pre-phase 1 meeting, and several scenarios analyzed during phase 2 reinforced this opinion. While a large volume of detailed documentation (such as that produced via UML and the Rose model) existed, there was almost no introductory or over-view documentation of the architecture, which is critical for training, adding people to the project, maintenance, and guiding development and testing. The extensive rule base that governed the behavior of Nightingale was undocumented, as was the data conversion and migration procedure. Lacking such documentation, the system would be unmaintainable by the kickoff customer, who was on the verge of inheriting it, thus jeopardizing one of the key business drivers for Nightingale—support for the customer's enterprise.

PHASE 3: FOLLOW-UP

The tangible output of the ATAM is a final report that contains a list of risks, non-risks, sensitivity points, and tradeoff points. It also contains a catalog of architectural approaches used, the utility tree and brainstormed scenarios, and the record of analysis of each selected scenario. Finally, the final report contains the set of risk themes identified by the evaluation team and an indication of which business drivers are jeopardized by each one.

Like the presentation of results, we use a boilerplate template that has many of the standard sections (such as a description of the ATAM) completed and templates for other sections ready to be filled in. We also write some of the final report—for instance, the utility tree and step 6 analysis—during the hiatus between phases 1 and 2. Preparation pays off; whereas it used to take about two weeks to produce a final report for an ATAM client, we can now produce a high-quality comprehensive report in about two days.

11.5 Summary

The ATAM is a robust method for evaluating software architectures. It works by having project decision makers and stakeholders articulate a precise list of quality attribute requirements (in the form of scenarios) and by illuminating the architectural decisions relevant to carrying out each high-priority scenario. The decisions can then be cast as risks or nonrisks to find any trouble spots in the architecture.

In addition to understanding what the ATAM is, it is also important to understand what it is not.

- The ATAM is not an evaluation of requirements. That is, an ATAM-based evaluation will not tell anyone whether all of the requirements for a system will be met. It will discern whether gross requirements are satisfiable given the current design.
- The ATAM is not a code evaluation. Because it is designed for use early in the life cycle, it makes no assumptions about the existence of code and has no provision for code inspection.
- The ATAM does not include actual system testing. Again because the ATAM is designed for use early in the life cycle, it makes no assumptions of the existence of a system and has no provisions for any type of actual testing.
- The ATAM is not a precise instrument, but identifies possible areas of risk within the architecture. These risks are embodied in the sensitivity points and the tradeoffs. The ATAM relies on the knowledge of the architect, and so it is possible that some risks will remain undetected. In addition, risks that are detected are not quantified. That is, there is no attempt to say that a particular sensitivity point will have a particular dollar value if not corrected. This final point will be addressed in Chapter 12 when we discuss the Cost Benefit Analysis Method (CBAM).

We have participated in a large number of evaluations using the ATAM and taught and observed others performing them. In virtually every case, the reaction among the technical people being evaluated is amazement that so many risks can be found in such a short time. The reaction among management is that now they can understand why a particular technical issue threatens the achievement of their business goals. The ATAM has proven itself as a useful tool.

11.6 For Further Reading

As this book was going to press, an initial draft of a training course on the ATAM was being tested. Details can be found on SEI's architecture tradeoff analysis Web site *http://www.sei.cmu.edu/ata/ata-init.html*. For a more comprehensive treatment of the ATAM, including a case study of applying it to a NASA satellite data system, see [Clements 02a].

[Chung 00] is an interesting treatment of quality attribute requirements and their relationship to design decisions. It refers to [Boehm76], which presents a tree of software quality characteristics very similar to the utility trees used in the ATAM.

To understand the historical roots of the ATAM, and to see a second (simpler) architecture evaluation method, you can read about the software architecture analysis method (SAAM) in [Kazman 94].

11.7   Discussion Questions

1. Think of an important software system in your organization. Could you present the business drivers or discuss the architecture using the template given in this chapter? If not, what information is missing? Could you sketch a utility tree for the system?

2. If you were going to evaluate the architecture for this system, who would you want to participate? What would be the stakeholder roles and who could you get to represent those roles?

12

The CBAM

A Quantitative Approach to Architecture Design Decision Making

with Jai Asundi and Mark Klein

> *A billion here, a billion there, pretty soon it adds up to real money.*
> — U.S. Senator Everett Dirksen (1896–1969)

As we saw in Chapter 11, the Architecture Tradeoff Analysis Method (ATAM) provides software architects a means of evaluating the technical tradeoffs faced while designing or maintaining a software system. In the ATAM, we are primarily investigating how well the architecture—real or proposed—has been designed with respect to the quality attributes that its stakeholders have deemed important. We are also analyzing architectural tradeoffs—the places where a decision might have consequences for several quality attributes simultaneously.

However, the ATAM is missing an important consideration: The biggest tradeoffs in large, complex systems usually have to do with economics. How should an organization invest its resources in a manner that will maximize its gains and minimize its risk? In the past, this question primarily focused on costs, and even then these were primarily the costs of building the system in the first place and not the long-term costs through cycles of maintenance and upgrade. As important, or perhaps more important than costs, are the *benefits* that an architectural decision may bring to an organization.

Given that the resources for building and maintaining a system are finite, there must be a rational process that helps us choose among architectural options, during both an initial design phase and subsequent upgrade periods. These options will have different costs, will consume differing amounts of resources, will implement different features (each of which brings some benefit to the organization), and will have some inherent risk or uncertainty. To capture these

---

Note: Jai Asundi teaches at the University of Texas, Dallas; Mark Klein is on the technical staff at the Software Engineering Institute.

aspects we need *economic* models of software that take into account costs, bene-fits, risks, and schedule implications.

To address this need for economic decision making, we have developed a method of economic modeling of software systems, centered on an analysis of their architectures. Called the Cost Benefit Analysis Method (CBAM), it builds on the ATAM to model the costs and the benefits of architectural design decisions and is a means of optimizing such decisions. The CBAM provides an assessment of the technical and economic issues and architectural decisions.

12.1 Decision-Making Context

The software architect or decision maker wishes to maximize the difference between the benefit derived from the system and the cost of implementing the design. The CBAM begins where the ATAM concludes and, in fact, depends upon the artifacts that the ATAM produces as output. Figure 12.1 depicts the con-text for the CBAM.

Because architectural strategies have technical and economic implications, the business goals of a software system should influence the strategies used by software architects or designers. The direct economic implication is the cost of implementing the system. The technical implications are the characteristics of the system—namely, the quality attributes. In turn the quality attributes have eco-nomic implications because of the benefits that can be derived.

Recall that when an ATAM has been applied to a software system, we have as a result a set of artifacts documented on completion. They are:

- A description of the business goals that are crucial to the success of the system
- A set of architectural views that document the existing or proposed architecture

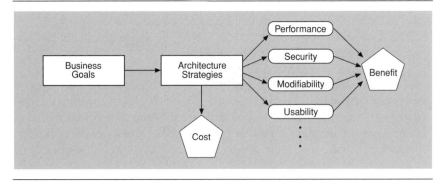

FIGURE 12.1 Context for the CBAM

- A utility tree that represents a decomposition of the stakeholders' goals for the architecture, starting with high-level statements of quality attributes and ending with specific scenarios
- A set of risks that have been identified
- A set of sensitivity points (architectural decisions that affect some quality attribute measure of concern)
- A set of tradeoff points (architectural decisions that affect more than one quality attribute measure, some positively and some negatively)

The ATAM identifies the set of key architectural decisions relevant to the quality attribute scenarios elicited from the stakeholders. These decisions result in some specific quality attribute responses—namely, particular levels of availability, performance, security, usability, modifiability, and so forth. But each architectural decision also has associated costs. For example, using redundant hardware to achieve a desired level of availability has a cost; checkpointing to a disk file has a different cost. Furthermore, both of these architectural decisions will result in (presumably different) measurable levels of availability that will have some value to the organization developing the system. Perhaps the organization believes that its stakeholders will pay more for a highly available system (a telephone switch or medical monitoring software, for example) or that it will be sued if the system fails (for example, the software that controls anti-lock brakes in an automobile).

The ATAM uncovers the architectural decisions made in the system and links them to business goals and quality attribute response measures. The CBAM builds on this base by eliciting the costs and benefits associated with these decisions. Given this information, the stakeholders can then decide whether to use redundant hardware, checkpointing, or some other tactic to achieve the system's desired availability. Or they can choose to invest their finite resources in some other quality attribute—perhaps believing that higher performance will have a better benefit-to-cost ratio. A system always has a limited budget for creation or upgrade, so every architectural choice is, in some sense, competing with every other one for inclusion.

The CBAM does not make decisions for the stakeholders, just as a financial advisor does not tell you how to invest your money. It simply aids in the elicitation and documentation of the costs, benefits, and uncertainty of a "portfolio" of architectural investments and gives the stakeholders a framework within which they can apply a rational decision-making process that suits their needs and their risk aversion.

To briefly summarize, the idea behind the CBAM is that architectural strategies (a collection of architectural tactics) affect the quality attributes of the system and these in turn provide system stakeholders with some benefit. We refer to this benefit as *utility*. Each architectural strategy provides a specific level of utility to the stakeholders. Each also has cost and takes time to implement. Given this information, the CBAM can aid the stakeholders in choosing architectural strategies based on their *return on investment* (ROI)—the ratio of benefit to cost.

12.2   The Basis for the CBAM

We now describe the key ideas that form the basis for the CBAM. The practical realization of these ideas as a series of steps will be described in Section 12.3. Our goal here is to develop the theory underpinning a measure of ROI for various architectural strategies in light of scenarios chosen by the stakeholders.

We begin by considering a collection of scenarios generated either as a portion of an ATAM or especially for the CBAM evaluation. We examine how they differ in the values of their projected responses and then assign utility to those values. The utility is based on the importance of each scenario being considered with respect to its anticipated response value. We next consider the architectural strategies that lead to the various projected responses. Each strategy has a cost, and each impacts multiple quality attributes. That is, an architectural strategy could be implemented to achieve some projected response, but while achieving that response it also affects some other quality attributes. The utility of these "side effects" must be taken into account when considering a strategy's overall utility. It is this overall utility that we combine with the project cost of an architectural strategy to calculate a final ROI measure.

UTILITY

Utility is determined by considering the issues described in the following sections.

Variations of Scenarios.   The CBAM uses scenarios as a way to concretely express and represent specific quality attributes, just as in the ATAM. Also as in the ATAM, we structure scenarios into three parts: stimulus (an interaction with the system), environment (the system's state at the time), and response (the measurable quality attribute that results). However, there is a difference between the methods: The CBAM actually uses a *set* of scenarios (generated by varying the values of the responses) rather than individual scenarios as in the ATAM. This leads to the concept of a utility-response curve.

Utility-Response Curves.   Every stimulus-response value pair in a scenario provides some utility to the stakeholders, and the utility of different possible values for the response can be compared. For example, a very high availability in response to failure might be valued by the stakeholders only slightly more than moderate availability. But low latency might be valued substantially more than moderate latency. We can portray each relationship between a set of utility measures and a corresponding set of response measures as a graph—a utility-response curve. Some examples of utility-response curves are shown in Figure 12.2. In each, points labeled a, b, or c represent different response values. The utility-response curve thus shows utility as a function of the response value.

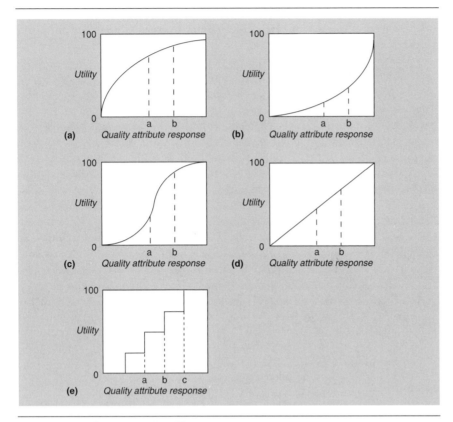

FIGURE 12.2   Some sample utility-response curves

The utility-response curve depicts how the utility derived from a particular response varies as the response varies. As seen in Figure 12.2, the utility could vary nonlinearly, linearly, or even as a step-function. For example, graph (c) portrays a steep rise in utility over a narrow change in a quality attribute response level, such as the performance example stated above. The availability example might be better characterized by graph (a), where a modest change in the response level results in only a very small change in utility to the user.

Eliciting the utility characteristics from the stakeholders can be a long and tedious process. To make it practical we have chosen to elicit only rough approximations of these curves from the stakeholders, using five values of the quality attribute response for the scenario. We now explain the four of these values that can be derived without consideration of any architectural strategy. The fifth value depends on the architectural strategy used, and we discuss this later.

To build the utility-response curve, we first determine the quality attribute levels for the best-case and worst-case situations. The best-case quality attribute level is that above which the stakeholders foresee no further utility. For example, a system response to the user of 0.1 second is perceived as instantaneous, so improving it further so that it responds in 0.03 second has no utility. Similarly, the worst-case quality attribute level is a minimum threshold above which a system *must* perform; otherwise it is of no use to the stakeholders. These levels— best-case and worst-case—are assigned utility values of 100 and 0, respectively.

We must then determine the *current* and *desired* utility levels for the scenario. The respective utility values (between 0 and 100) for the current and desired cases are elicited from the stakeholders, using the best-case and worst-case values as reference points (e.g., we are currently half as good as we would like to be, but if we reach the desired quality attribute level, we will have 90% of the maximum utility; hence, the current utility level is set to 50 and the desired utility level is set to 90). In this manner the curves are generated for all of the scenarios.

Priorities of Scenarios. Different scenarios within a given system have different levels of importance to the stakeholders and hence different utilities. To characterize the relative importance of each scenario, a weight is assigned through a two-step voting exercise. In the first step the stakeholders vote on the scenarios to establish an ordering among them. This voting is based on each scenario's "expected" response value. The stakeholders then assign a weight of 1 to the highest-rated scenario and a fractional amount to the other scenarios based on their relative importance.

If, at some future date, additional scenarios need to be added, they can be assigned a weight. The stakeholders, through consensus, can make sure that the scenarios weights accord with their intuition.

Architectural Strategies. It is the job of the architect, or architects, to determine the architectural strategies for moving from the *current* quality attribute response level to the *desired* or even *best-case* level. A portion of the CBAM is devoted to this task. For each strategy, we can derive

- the expected value of the response in each scenario. The utility of the expected value is calculated using interpolation from the four values already elicited from the stakeholders.
- the effect of the architectural strategy on other attributes of interest.
- a cost estimate for implementing the architectural strategy.

Side effects – Each architectural strategy will impact not only the quality attribute from the scenario being considered currently but will typically also affect other quality attributes (this is why there are architectural tradeoffs!). It is important to determine the utility of these additional *side effect* attribute responses that arise as a result of applying the architectural strategy. In the worst case, we must create a new version of the scenario for the side effect attribute and determine its utility-response curve. However, in practice, if the quality attribute is important to the stakeholders, then it has occurred in one of the other scenarios and the utility-response curve has already been constructed for that response. In this case, the only thing left to determine is the expected utility associated with that quality attribute for the given architectural strategy. Notice that it is possible that the expected utility for a particular attribute may be negative if the architectural strategy is designed to emphasize an attribute in conflict with the one whose utility we are currently calculating.

Once this additional information has been elicited we can calculate the benefit of applying an architectural strategy by summing its benefits to all relevant quality attributes.

Determining benefit and normalization – We calculate the overall utility of an architectural strategy across scenarios from the utility-response curves by summing the utility associated with each one (weighted by the importance of the scenario). For each architectural strategy, i, we calculate a benefit, B_i as follows:

$$B_i = \sum_j (b_{i,j} \times W_j)$$

where $b_{i,j}$ is the benefit accrued to strategy i due to its effect on scenario j and W_j is the weight of scenario j. Referring to Figure 12.2, each $b_{i,j}$ is calculated as the change in utility brought about by the architectural strategy with respect to this scenario: $b_{i,j} = U_{expected} - U_{current}$; that is, the utility of the expected value of the architectural strategy minus the utility of the current system relative to this scenario. The effect of multiplying the weight, W_j, is to normalize this utility value by the relative importance of the various scenarios, as already described.

CALCULATING ROI

The ROI value for each architectural strategy is the ratio of the total benefit, B_i, to the Cost, C_i, of implementing it. The cost is calculated using a model appropriate for the system and the environment being developed.

$$R_i = \frac{B_i}{C_i}$$

Using this ROI score, the architectural strategies can be rank-ordered; this rank ordering can then be used to determine the optimal order for implementation of the various strategies.

Consider curves (a) and (b) in Figure 12.2. Curve (a) "flattens out" as the quality attribute response improves. In this case, it is likely that a point is reached past which ROI decreases as the quality attribute response improves. In other words, spending more money will not yield a significant increase in utility. On the other hand, consider curve (b), for which a small improvement in quality attribute response can yield a very significant increase in utility. There an architectural strategy whose ROI is too low might rank significantly higher with a modest improvement in its quality attribute response.

The Importance of Cost Modeling

Random visitor: You're supposed to know something about availability, aren't you?

Len Bass: I know something, but I'm not a real expert.

RV: Well, maybe you can help me. I have a problem with how much availability to put into my system. My boss tells me, whenever I have a problem, to look at the Big Stock Broker Company's Web site to get ideas.

LB: Well, they have millions of customers and certainly have rigid availability requirements.

RV: That's exactly my problem. The system I'm building will have a couple hundred users who are probably happy with five days a week, ten hours a day availability. How do I convince my boss he's going way overboard?

So far we have presented many techniques for achieving particular qualities, but we have not presented any method for keeping management expectations under control. Our assumption has been that there is a business case for the system under construction. This business case begets particular requirements, and the architect's job is to satisfy them to the extent possible. What is the architect to do when this assumption is false and the requirements are overkill for the business goals of the system?

After giving the matter some thought, the best I could come up with is that the main weapon the architect has to combat overengineered requirements is the argument of cost. It is the same reason I do not drive a fancy luxury car—I do not want to pay the price.

Maintaining high availability requires a high level of redundancy with a rollover capability. Developing this capability takes time and personnel. Personnel cost money, as do purchasing highly available software and adapting it for particular needs.

In software engineering, cost is estimated using cost models. A cost model makes certain assumptions about the character of the system being constructed, environmental parameters, and personnel expertise, and then produces an estimate based on historical data.

Cost models (especially early in the life cycle) are imperfect for a wide variety of reasons, but they are the only tools available to constrain requirements. As such, they are invaluable to the architect.

— LJB

12.3 Implementing the CBAM

Turning the foundations for the CBAM into a set of practical steps involves taking the bases we discussed in the previous section and performing them in a fashion that minimizes the work that is needed. Part of being "practical" involves limiting the size of the decision space.

STEPS

A process flow diagram for the CBAM is given in Figure 12.3. The first four steps are annotated with the relative number of scenarios they consider. That number steadily decreases, ensuring that the method concentrates the stakeholders' time on the scenarios believed to be of the greatest potential in terms of ROI.

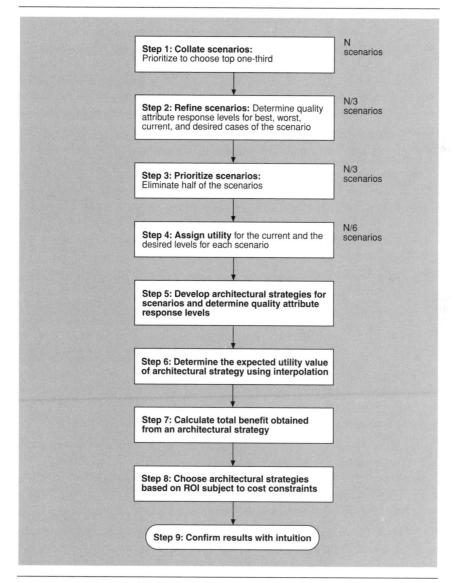

FIGURE 12.3   Process flow diagram for the CBAM

- *Step 1: Collate scenarios.* Collate the scenarios elicited during the ATAM exercise, and give the stakeholders the chance to contribute new ones. Prioritize these scenarios based on satisfying the business goals of the system and choose the top one-third for further study.

- *Step 2: Refine scenarios.* Refine the scenarios output from step 1, focusing on their stimulus-response measures. Elicit the worst-case, current, desired, and best-case quality attribute response level for each scenario.

- *Step 3: Prioritize scenarios.* Allocate 100 votes to each stakeholder and have them distribute the votes among the scenarios, where their voting is based on the *desired* response value for each scenario. Total the votes and choose the top 50% of the scenarios for further analysis. Assign a weight of 1.0 to the highest-rated scenario; assign the other scenarios a weight relative to the highest rated. This becomes the weighting used in the calculation of a strategy's overall benefit. Make a list of the quality attributes that concern the stakeholders.

- *Step 4: Assign utility.* Determine the utility for each quality attribute response level (worst-case, current, desired, best-case) for the scenarios from step 3.

- *Step 5: Develop architectural strategies for scenarios and determine their expected quality attribute response levels.* Develop (or capture already developed) architectural strategies that address the chosen scenarios and determine the "expected" quality attribute response levels that will result from them. Given that an architectural strategy may have effects on multiple scenarios, we must perform this calculation for each scenario affected.

- *Step 6: Determine the utility of the "expected" quality attribute response levels by interpolation.* Using the elicited utility values (that form a utility curve), determine the utility of the expected quality attribute response level for the architectural strategy. Do this for each relevant quality attribute enumerated in step 3.

- *Step 7: Calculate the total benefit obtained from an architectural strategy.* Subtract the utility value of the "current" level from the expected level and normalize it using the votes elicited in step 3. Sum the benefit due to a particular architectural strategy across all scenarios and across all relevant quality attributes.

- *Step 8: Choose architectural strategies based on ROI subject to cost and schedule constraints.* Determine the cost and schedule implications of each architectural strategy. Calculate the ROI value for each as a ratio of benefit to cost. Rank-order the architectural strategies according to the ROI value and choose the top ones until the budget or schedule is exhausted.

- *Step 9: Confirm results with intuition.* For the chosen architectural strategies, consider whether these seem to align with the organization's business goals. If not, consider issues that may have been overlooked while doing this analysis. If there are significant issues, perform another iteration of these steps.

12.4   Case Study: The NASA ECS Project

We now apply the CBAM to a real-world system as an example of the method in action.

The Earth Observing System is a constellation of NASA satellites that gathers data for the U.S. Global Change Research Program and other scientific communities worldwide. The Earth Observing System Data Information System (EOSDIS) Core System (ECS) collects data from various satellite downlink stations for further processing. ECS's mission is to process the data into higher-form information and make it available to scientists in searchable form. The goal is to provide both a common way to store (and hence process) data and a public mechanism to introduce new data formats and processing algorithms, thus making the information widely available.

The ECS processes an input stream of hundreds of gigabytes of raw environment-related data per day. The computation of 250 standard "products" results in thousands of gigabytes of information that is archived at eight data centers in the United States. The system has important performance and availability requirements. The long-term nature of the project also makes modifiability important.

The ECS project manager had a limited annual budget to maintain and enhance his current system. From a prior analysis, in this case an ATAM exercise, a large set of desirable changes to the system was elicited from the system stakeholders, resulting in a large set of architectural strategies. The problem was to choose a (much) smaller subset for implementation, as only 10% to 20% of what was being proposed could actually be funded. The manager used the CBAM to make a rational decision based on the economic criterion of return on investment.

In the execution of the CBAM described next, we concentrated on analyzing the Data Access Working Group (DAWG) portion of the ECS.

STEP 1: COLLATE SCENARIOS

Scenarios from the ATAM were collated with a set of new scenarios elicited from the assembled ECS stakeholders. Because the stakeholders had been through an ATAM exercise, this step was relatively straightforward.

A subset of the raw scenarios put forward by the DAWG team were as shown in Table 12.1. Note that they are not yet well formed and that some of them do not have defined responses. These issues are resolved in step 2, when the number of scenarios is reduced.[1]

STEP 2: REFINE SCENARIOS

The scenarios were refined, paying particular attention to precisely specifying their stimulus-response measures. The worst-case, current-case, desired-case,

---

[1] In the presentation of the DAWG case study, we only show the reduced set of scenarios.

TABLE 12.1 Collected Scenarios in Priority Order

Scenario	Scenario Description
1	Reduce data distribution failures that result in hung distribution requests requiring manual intervention.
2	Reduce data distribution failures that result in lost distribution requests.
3	Reduce the number of orders that fail on the order submission process.
4	Reduce order failures that result in hung orders that require manual intervention.
5	Reduce order failures that result in lost orders.
6	There is no good method of tracking ECSGuest failed/canceled orders without much manual intervention (e.g., spreadsheets).
7	Users need more information on why their orders for data failed.
8	Because of limitations, there is a need to artificially limit the size and number of orders.
9	Small orders result in too many notifications to users.
10	The system should process a 50-GB user request in one day, and a 1-TB user request in one week.

TABLE 12.2 Response Goals for Refined Scenarios

	Response Goals			
Scenario	Worst	Current	Desired	Best
1	10% hung	5% hung	1% hung	0% hung
2	> 5% lost	< 1% lost	0% lost	0% lost
3	10% fail	5% fail	1% fail	0% fail
4	10% hung	5% hung	1% hung	0% hung
5	10% lost	< 1% lost	0% lost	0% lost
6	50% need help	25% need help	0% need help	0% need help
7	10% get information	50% get information	100% get information	100% get information
8	50% limited	30% limited	0% limited	0% limited
9	1/granule	1/granule	1/100 granules	1/1,000 granules
10	< 50% meet goal	60% meet goal	80% meet goal	> 90% meet goal

and the best-case response goals for each scenario were elicited and recorded, as shown in Table 12.2.

STEP 3: PRIORITIZE SCENARIOS

In voting on the refined representation of the scenarios, the close-knit team deviated slightly from the method. Rather than vote individually, they chose to discuss each scenario and arrived at a determination of its weight via consensus. The votes allocated to the entire set of scenarios were constrained to 100, as shown in

TABLE 12.3   Refined Scenarios with Votes

Scenario	Votes	Response Goals			
		Worst	**Current**	**Desired**	**Best**
1	10	10% hung	5% hung	1% hung	0% hung
2	15	> 5% lost	< 1% lost	0% lost	0% lost
3	15	10% fail	5% fail	1% fail	0% fail
4	10	10% hung	5% hung	1% hung	0% hung
5	15	10% lost	< 1% lost	0% lost	0% lost
6	10	50% need help	25% need help	0% need help	0% need help
7	5	10% get information	50% get information	100% get information	100% get information
8	5	50% limited	30% limited	0% limited	0% limited
9	10	1/granule	1/granule	1/100 granules	1/1000 granules
10	5	< 50% meet goal	60% meet goal	80% meet goal	> 90% meet goal

Table 12.3. Although the stakeholders were not required to make the votes multiples of 5, they felt that this was a reasonable resolution and that more precision was neither needed nor justified.

STEP 4: ASSIGN UTILITY

In this step the utility for each scenario was determined by the stakeholders, again by consensus. A utility score of 0 represented no utility; a score of 100 represented the most utility possible. The results of this process are given in Table 12.4.

TABLE 12.4   Scenarios with Votes and Utility Scores

Scenario	Votes	Utility Scores			
		Worst	**Current**	**Desired**	**Best**
1	10	10	80	95	100
2	15	0	70	100	100
3	15	25	70	100	100
4	10	10	80	95	100
5	15	0	70	100	100
6	10	0	80	100	100
7	5	10	70	100	100
8	5	0	20	100	100
9	10	50	50	80	90
10	5	0	70	90	100

STEP 5: DEVELOP ARCHITECTURAL STRATEGIES FOR SCENARIOS AND DETERMINE THEIR EXPECTED QUALITY ATTRIBUTE RESPONSE LEVELS

Based on the requirements implied by the preceding scenarios, a set of 10 architectural strategies was developed by the ECS architects. Recall that an architectural strategy may affect more than one scenario. To account for these complex relationships, the expected quality attribute response level that each strategy is predicted to achieve had to be determined with respect to each relevant scenario.

The set of architectural strategies, along with the determination of the scenarios they address, is shown in Table 12.5. For each architectural strategy/scenario pair, the response levels expected to be achieved with respect to that scenario are shown (along with the current response, for comparison purposes).

TABLE 12.5   Architectural Strategies and Scenarios Addressed

Strategy	Name	Description	Scenarios Affected	Current Response	Expected Response
1	Order persistence on submission	Store an order as soon as it arrives in the system.	3	5% fail	2% Fail
			5	<1% lost	0% lost
			6	25% need help	0% need help
2	Order chunking	Allow operators to partition large orders into multiple small orders.	8	30% limited	15% limited
3	Order bundling	Combine multiple small orders into one large order.	9	1 per granule	1 per 100
			10	60% meet goal	55% meet goal
4	Order segmentation	Allow an operator to skip items that cannot be retrieved due to data quality or availability issues.	4	5% hung	2% hung
5	Order reassignment	Allow an operator to reassign the media type for items in an order.	1	5% hung	2% hung
6	Order retry	Allow an operator to retry an order or items in an order that may have failed due to temporary system or data problems.	4	5% hung	3% hung

TABLE 12.5 *Continued*

Strategy	Name	Description	Scenarios Affected	Current Response	Expected Response
7	Forced order completion	Allow an operator to override an item's unavailability due to data quality constraints.	1	5% hung	3% hung
8	Failed order notification	Ensure that users are notified only when part of their order has truly failed and provide detailed status of each item; user notification occurs only if operator okays notification; the operator may edit notification.	6	25% need help	20% need help
			7	50% get information	90% get information
9	Granule level-order tracking	An operator and user can determine the status for each item in their order.	6	25% need help	10% need help
			7	50% get nformation	95% get information
10	Links to user information	An operator can quickly locate a user's contact infor-mation. Server will access SDSRV infor-mation to determine any data restrictions that might apply and will route orders/order segments to appropri-ate distribution capa-bilities, including DDIST, PDS, external subsetters and data processing tools, etc.	7	50% get information	60% get information

STEP 6: DETERMINE THE UTILITY OF THE "EXPECTED" QUALITY ATTRIBUTE RESPONSE LEVELS BY INTERPOLATION

Once the expected response level of every architectural strategy has been charac-terized with respect to a set of scenarios, their utility can be calculated by con-sulting the utility scores for each scenario's current and desired responses for all of the affected attributes. Using these scores, we may calculate, via interpolation, the utility of the expected quality attribute response levels for the architectural strategy/scenario pair applied to the DAWG of ECS.

TABLE 12.6 Architectural Strategies and Their Expected Utility

Strategy	Strategy	Scenarios Affected	Current Utility	Expected Utility
1	Order persistence on submission	3	70	90
		5	70	100
		6	80	100
2	Order chunking	8	20	60
3	Order bundling	9	50	80
		10	70	65
4	Order segmentation	4	80	90
5	Order reassignment	1	80	92
6	Order retry	4	80	85
7	Forced order completion	1	80	87
8	Failed order notification	6	80	85
		7	70	90
9	Granule level order tracking	6	80	90
		7	70	95
10	Links to user information	7	70	75

The results of this calculation are shown in Table 12.6, for the architectural strategy/scenario pairs presented in Table 12.5.

STEP 7: CALCULATE THE TOTAL BENEFIT OBTAINED FROM AN ARCHITECTURAL STRATEGY

Based on the information collected, as represented in Table 12.6, the total benefit of each architectural strategy can now be calculated, following the equation on page 313. This equation calculates total benefit as the sum of the benefit that accrues to each scenario, normalized by the scenario's relative weight. The total benefit scores for each architectural strategy are given in Table 12.7.

TABLE 12.7 Total Benefit of Architectural Strategies

Strategy	Scenario Affected	Scenario Weight	Raw Architectural Strategy Benefit	Normalized Architectural Strategy Benefit	Total Architectural Strategy Benefit
1	3	15	20	300	
1	5	15	30	450	
1	6	10	20	200	950
2	8	5	40	200	200

TABLE 12.7   *Continued*

Strategy	Scenario Affected	Scenario Weight	Raw Architectural Strategy Benefit	Normalized Architectural Strategy Benefit	Total Architectural Strategy Benefit
3	9	10	30	300	
3	10	5	-5	-25	275
4	4	10	10	100	100
5	1	10	12	120	120
6	4	10	5	50	50
7	1	10	7	70	70
8	6	10	5	50	
8	7	5	20	100	150
9	6	10	10	100	
9	7	5	25	125	225
10	7	5	5	25	25

STEP 8: CHOOSE ARCHITECTURAL STRATEGIES BASED ON ROI VALUE SUBJECT TO COST CONSTRAINTS

To complete the analysis, the team estimated cost for each architectural strategy. The estimates were based on experience with the system, and a return on investment for each architectural strategy was calculated. Using the ROI, we were able to rank each strategy. This is shown in Table 12.8. Not surprisingly, the ranks roughly follow the ordering in which the strategies were proposed: strategy 1 has

TABLE 12.8   ROI of Architectural Strategies

Strategy	Cost	Total Strategy Benefit	Strategy ROI	Strategy Rank
1	1200	950	0.79	1
2	400	200	0.5	3
3	400	275	0.69	2
4	200	100	0.5	3
5	400	120	0.3	7
6	200	50	0.25	8
7	200	70	0.35	6
8	300	150	0.5	3
9	1000	225	0.22	10
10	100	25	0.25	8

the highest rank; strategy 3 the second highest. Strategy 9 has the lowest rank; strategy 8, the second lowest. This simply validates stakeholders' intuition about which architectural strategies were going to be of the greatest benefit. For the ECS these were the ones proposed first.

12.5 Results of the CBAM Exercise

The most obvious results of the CBAM are shown in Table 12.8: an ordering of architectural strategies based on their predicted ROI. However, just as for the ATAM method, the benefits of the CBAM extend beyond the qualitative outcomes. There are social and cultural benefits as well.

Just as important as the ranking of architectural strategies in CBAM is the discussion that accompanies the information-collecting and decision-making processes. The CBAM process provides a great deal of structure to what is always largely unstructured discussions, where requirements and architectural strategies are freely mixed and where stimuli and response goals are not clearly articulated. The CBAM process forces the stakeholders to make their scenarios clear in advance, to assign utility levels of specific response goals, and to prioritize these scenarios based on the resulting determination of utility. Finally, this process results in clarification of both scenarios and requirements, which by itself is a significant benefit.

12.6 Summary

The CBAM is an iterative elicitation process combined with a decision analysis framework. It incorporates scenarios to represent the various quality attributes. The stakeholders explore the decision space by eliciting utility-response curves to understand how the system's utility varies with changing attributes. The consensus basis of the method allows for active discussion and clarification amongst the stakeholders. The traceability of the design decision permits updating and continuous improvement of the design process over time.

Elicitation of information from real-world projects is difficult. As researchers, we are charged with creating methods that are usable by real-world engineers in real projects. These methods need to produce useful results quickly and at a reasonable "price," in terms of the stakeholders' time. As we have discovered in our experiences with the CBAM, solving a problem in theory and in practice are very different. We have already modified the CBAM considerably as a result of several applications of this method to NASA's ECS.

In spite of the practical difficulties, we believe that the application of economic techniques is inherently better than the ad hoc decision-making approaches that projects (even quite sophisticated ones) employ today. Our experience with the CBAM tells us that giving people the appropriate tools to frame and structure their discussions and decision making is an enormous benefit to the disciplined development of a complex software system.

12.7 For Further Reading

Early work on the CBAM can be found in [Kazman 01] and [Asundi 01]. Cost modeling is discussed in [Boehm 81] and [Jones 99]. The evaluation of the ECS architecture using the ATAM is described in [Clements 02a].

12.8 Discussion Questions

1. One of the novel aspects of the CBAM is the creation of utility-response curves. Consider the curve styles shown in Figure 12.2. What are the circumstances under which you can imagine each of those curves elicited from the stakeholders? What situations does each of these curves represent?

2. Determination of costs and benefits is fraught with uncertainty. What sources of uncertainty do you typically have to deal with and how would you go about characterizing, measuring, and minimizing them?

13

The World Wide Web
A Case Study in Interoperability
with Hong-Mei Chen

> *Flexibility was clearly a key goal. Every specification that was needed*
> *to ensure interoperability constrain[s] the Web's implementation.*
> *Therefore, there should be as few specifications as possible . . .*
> *and the necessary specifications should be made*
> *independently. . . . This would let you replace parts*
> *of the design while preserving the basic architecture.*
> — Tim Berners-Lee [Berners-Lee 96b]

> *In the not-too-distant future, anybody who doesn't have their*
> *own home page on the World Wide Web will probably*
> *qualify for a government subsidy for the home-pageless.*
> — Scott Adams, creator of *Dilbert*

Possibly the most dramatic example of the workings of the Architecture Business Cycle (ABC) can be found in the way in which the goals, business model, and architecture of the World Wide Web have changed since its introduction in 1990. No one—not the customers, the users, or the architect (Tim Berners-Lee)—could have foreseen the explosive growth and evolution of the Web. In this chapter, we interpret the Web from the point of view of the ABC and observe how changes in its architecture reflect the changing goals and business needs of the various players. We first look at the Web's origins in terms of its original requirements and players and then look at how its server-side architecture has changed as a result of the ABC.

Note: Hong-Mei Chen is an associate professor at the University of Hawaii's Department of Information Technology Management.

13.1   Relationship to the Architecture Business Cycle

The original proposal for the Web came from Tim Berners-Lee, a researcher with the European Laboratory for Particle Physics (CERN), who observed that the several thousand researchers at CERN formed an evolving human "web." People came and went, developed new research associations, lost old ones, shared papers, chatted in the hallways, and so on, and Berners-Lee wanted to support this informal web with a similar web of electronic information. In 1989, he created and circulated throughout CERN a document entitled *Information Management: A Proposal*. By October of 1990 a reformulated version of the project proposal was approved by management, the name World Wide Web was chosen, and development began.

Figure 13.1 shows the elements of the ABC as they applied to the initial proposal approved by CERN management. The system was intended to promote interaction among CERN researchers (the end users) within the constraints of a heterogeneous computing environment. The customer was CERN management, and the developing organization was a lone CERN researcher. The business case made by Berners-Lee was that the proposed system would increase communication among CERN staff. This was a very limited proposal with very limited (and speculative) objectives. There was no way of knowing whether such a system

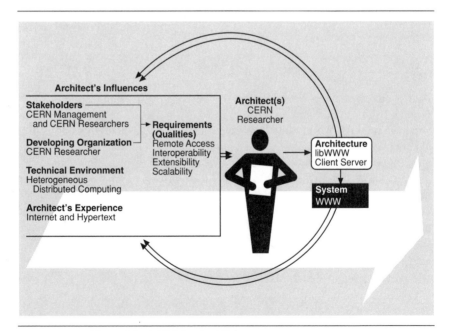

FIGURE 13.1   The original ABC for the Web

would, in fact, increase communication. On the other hand, the investment required by CERN to generate and test the system was also very limited: one researcher's time for a few months.

The technical environment was familiar to those in the research community, for which the Internet had been a mainstay since its introduction in the early 1970s. The net had weak notions of central control (volunteer committees whose responsibilities were to set protocols for communication among different nodes on the Internet and to charter new newsgroups) and an unregulated, "wild-west" style of interaction, primarily through specialized newsgroups.

Hypertext systems had had an even longer history, beginning with the vision of Vannevar Bush in the 1940s. Bush's vision had been explored throughout the 1960s and 1970s and into the 1980s, with hypertext conferences held regularly to bring researchers together. However, Bush's vision had not been achieved on a large scale by the 1980s: The uses of hypertext were primarily limited to small-scale documentation systems. That was to change.

CERN management approved Berners-Lee's proposal in October 1990. By November he had developed the first Web program on the NeXT platform, which meant he clearly had begun working on the implementation before receiving formal management approval. This loose coupling between management approval and researcher activity is quite common in research organizations in which small initial investments are required. By their nature, research organizations tend to generate projects from the bottom up more often than commercial organizations do, because they are dependent on the researchers' originality and creativity and allow far more freedom than is typical in a commercial organization.

The initial implementation of a Web system had many features that are still missing from more recent Web browsers. For example, it allowed users to create links from within the browser, and it allowed authors *and* readers to annotate information. Berners-Lee initially thought that no user would want to write HyperText Markup Language (HTML) or deal with uniform resource locators (URLs). He was wrong. Users have been willing to put up with these inconveniences to have the power of publishing on the Web.

13.2 Requirements and Qualities

The World Wide Web, as conceived and initially implemented at CERN, had several desirable qualities. It was portable, able to interoperate with other types of computers running the same software, and was scalable and extensible. The business goals of promoting interaction and allowing heterogeneous computing led to the quality goals of remote access, interoperability, extensibility, and scalability, which in turn led to libWWW, the original software library that supported Web-based development and a distributed client-server architecture. The realization of

TABLE 13.1 Web Growth Statistics

Date	Number of Web Sites	Percentage of .com Sites	Hosts per Web Server
6/93	130	1.5	13,000
12/93	623	4.6	3,475
6/94	2,738	13.5	1,095
12/94	10,022	18.3	451
6/95	23,500	31.3	270
1/96	100,000	50.0	94
6/96	252,000	68.0	41
1/97	646,162	62.6	40
1/98	1,834,710		16.2
1/99	4,062,280		10.6
1/00	9,950,491		7.3
1/01	27,585,719	54.68	4.0

Source: Used with permission of Matthew Gray of the Massachusetts Institute of Technology.

these properties in the original software architecture created an infrastructure that effectively supported the Web's tremendous growth (see Table 13.1). libWWW embodies strict separation of concerns and therefore works on virtually any hardware and readily accepts new protocols, new data formats, and new applications. Because it has no centralized control, the Web appears to be able to grow without bounds.

We will deal with these core requirements, and others, in more detail now, returning to the structure of libWWW later in Section 13.3. There is no explicit requirement for ease of use in the original requirements, and it was not until the development of point-and-click browsers that the Web began its tremendous growth. On the other hand, the requirement for portability and the heterogeneous computing environment led to the introduction of the browser as a separate element, thereby fostering the development of more sophisticated browsers.

THE ORIGINAL REQUIREMENTS

The initial set of requirements for the Web, as established in the original project proposals, were as follows:

- *Remote access across networks.* Any information had to be accessible from any machine on a CERN network.
- *Heterogeneity.* The system could not be limited to run on any specific hardware or software platform.

- *Noncentralization.* In the spirit of a human web and of the Internet, there could not be any single source of data or services. This requirement was in anticipation that the Web would grow. The operation of linking to a document, in particular, had to be decentralized.
- *Access to existing data.* Existing databases had to be accessible.
- *Ability for users to add data.* Users should be able to "publish" their own data on the Web, using the same interface used to read others' data.
- *Private links.* Links and nodes had to be capable of being privately annotated.
- *Bells and whistles.* The only form of data display originally planned was display on a 24 × 80 character ASCII terminal. Graphics were considered optional.
- *Data analysis.* Users should be able to search across the various databases and look for anomalies, regularities, irregularities, and so on. Berners-Lee gave, as examples, the ability to look for undocumented software and organizations with no people.
- *Live links.* Given that information changes all the time, there should be some way of updating a user's view of it. This could be by simply retrieving the information every time the link is accessed or (in a more sophisticated fashion) by notifying a user of a link whenever the information has changed.

In addition to these requirements, there were a number of nonrequirements identified. For example, copyright enforcement and data security were explicitly mentioned as requirements that the original project would *not* deal with. The Web, as initially conceived, was to be a public medium. Also, the original proposal explicitly noted that users should not have to use any particular markup format.

Other criteria and features that were common in proposals for hypertext systems at the time but that were missing from the Web proposal are as follows:

- Controlling topology
- Defining navigational techniques and user interface requirements, including keeping a visual history
- Having different types of links to express differing relationships among nodes

Although many of the original requirements formed the essence of what the Web is today, several were not realized, were only partially realized, or their impact was dramatically underestimated. For example, data analysis, live links, and private link capabilities are still relatively crude to this day. These requirements have gone largely unfulfilled.

Adaptation and selective postponement of requirements are characteristic of unprecedented systems. Requirements are often lists of desirable characteristics, and in unprecedented systems the tradeoffs required to realize these requirements are often unknown until a design exists. In the process of making the tradeoffs, some requirements become more important and others less so.

The effect of one of the requirements turned out to have been greatly *underestimated.* Namely, the "bells and whistles" of graphics dominate much of today's

Web traffic. Graphics today carry the bulk of the interest and consume the bulk of the Internet traffic generated by the Web. And yet Berners-Lee and CERN management did not concern themselves with graphics in the initial proposal, and the initial Web browser was line oriented. Similarly, the original proposal eschewed any interest in multimedia research for supporting sound and video.

Some nonrequirements, as the ABC has been traversed, have also become requirements. Security, for one, has proven to be a substantial issue, particularly as the Web has become increasingly dominated by commercial traffic. The security issue is large and complex, given the distributed, decentralized form of the Internet. Security is difficult to ensure when protected access to private data cannot be guaranteed—the Web opens a window onto your computer, and some uninvited guests are sure to crawl through.

This has become even more relevant in recent years as e-commerce has begun to drive the structure and direction of the Web and a large number of ad hoc mechanisms have been created to facilitate it. The most obvious is simple encryption of sensitive data, typically via SSL (Secure Sockets Layer), seen in Web browsers as HTTPS (HyperText Transfer Protocol Secure). But this protocol only decreases the likelihood of others snooping on your private data while it is being transmitted over a public network. Other solutions—such as Microsoft's Passport—have you prove that you are who you say you are. (Chapter 4 discussed the various aspects of security, and Chapter 5 presented a set of tactics to achieve it.)

REQUIREMENTS COME AND GO

No one could have foreseen the tremendous growth of the Web, or of the Internet, over the past few years. According to recent statistics, the Web has been doubling in size every three to six months, from about 130 sites in mid-1993 to more than 230,000 sites in mid-1996 to 27 million in early 2001 (see Table 13.1). Figure 13.2 shows how the base communication paths for the Internet blanket the United States. Similarly, the number of Internet hosts—at least as counted by registered Internet Protocol (IP) addresses—grew from 1.3 million in 1993 to 9.5 million in early 1996.

Both the Web and the Internet have grown, but the Web has grown much faster as a whole. This can be seen in the final column of Table 13.1, where we see that the ratio of Internet hosts to Web servers keeps decreasing. This means that an ever-greater proportion of Internet hosts are becoming Web servers.

In addition to its enormous growth, the nature of the Web has changed, as indicated by the third column of Table 13.1. Although its beginnings were in the research community, it is increasingly dominated by commercial traffic (as indicated by Internet hosts whose names end in ".com"). The percentage of .com sites has leveled out at around 55%, but this is due mainly to the rise of other domains, such as .net and .biz, rather than to any decline in commercial activity.

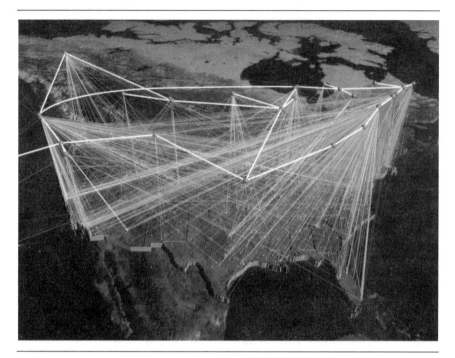

FIGURE 13.2   Internet backbones in the United States.   Copyright 1996 by Donna Cox and Robert Patterson; produced at the National Center for Supercomputing Applications, University of Illinois at Urbana-Champaign. Used with permission.

The advent of easy, widespread access to the Web has had an interesting side effect. Easy access to graphics in a distributed, largely uncontrolled fashion has spawned the "cyberporn" industry, which has led to a new requirement: that content be labeled and access to content be controllable. The result is the platform for Internet content selection (PICS) specification, an industry-wide set of principles, and vendor implementations of them, that allows the labeling of content and flexible selection criteria. In this way, content producers are not limited in what they provide, but content consumers can tailor what they view or what they permit others to view according to their own tastes and criteria. For example, a parent can prevent a child from viewing movies other than those suitably rated, and an employer can prevent an employee from accessing non-business-related sites during business hours.

To see how far and how fast the Web has diverged from its original concept, imagine that Berners-Lee had proposed a requirement for restriction of content to prevent children from accessing pornography. The management of CERN would have tossed out his proposal without discussion. We return to this point about changing stakeholder concerns when we revisit the ABC for the WWW in Section 13.5.

13.3   Architectural Solution

The basic architectural approach used for the Web, first at CERN and later at the World Wide Web Consortium (W3C), relied on clients and servers and a library (libWWW) that masks all hardware, operating system, and protocol dependencies. Figure 13.3 shows how the content producers and consumers interact through their respective servers and clients. The producer places content that is described in HTML on a server machine. The server communicates with a client using the HyperText Transfer Protocol (HTTP). The software on both the server and the client is based on libWWW, so the details of the protocol and the dependencies on the platforms are masked from it. One of the elements on the client side is a browser that knows how to display HTML so that the content consumer is presented with an understandable image.

We now go into more detail about both the libWWW and the client-server architecture used as the basis for the original Web and that still largely pervades Web-based software. Section 13.4 will discuss how the architecture of the Web and Web-based software have changed in response to the e-commerce revolution.

MEETING THE ORIGINAL REQUIREMENTS: libWWW

As stated earlier, libWWW is a library of software for creating applications that run on either the client or the server. It provides the generic functionality that is shared by most applications: the ability to connect with remote hosts, the ability to understand streams of HTML data, and so forth.

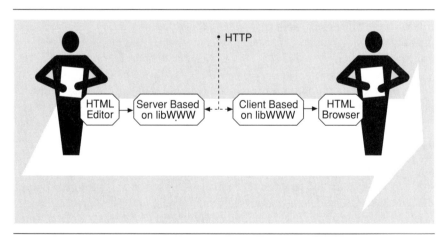

FIGURE 13.3   Content producers and consumers interact through clients and servers

libWWW is a compact, portable library that can be built on to create Web-based applications such as clients, servers, databases, and Web spiders. It is organized into five layers, as shown in Figure 13.4.

The generic utilities provide a portability layer on which the rest of the system rests. This layer includes basic building blocks for the system such as network management, data types such as container classes, and string manipulation utilities. Through the services provided by this layer, all higher levels can be made platform independent, and the task of porting to a new hardware or software platform can be almost entirely contained within the porting of the utilities layer, which needs to be done only once per platform.

The core layer contains the skeletal functionality of a Web application—network access, data management and parsing, logging, and the like. By itself, this layer does nothing. Rather, it provides a standard interface for a Web application to be built upon, with the actual functionality provided by plug-in modules and call-out functions that are registered by an application. *Plug-ins* are registered at runtime and do the actual work of the core layer—sending and manipulating data. They typically support protocols, handle low-level transport, and understand data formats. Plug-ins can be changed dynamically, making it easy to add new functionality or even to change the very nature of the Web application.

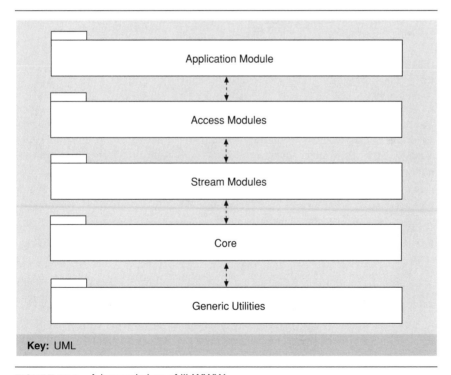

Key: UML

FIGURE 13.4   A layered view of libWWW

Call-out functions provide another way for applications to extend the functionality provided in the core layer. They are arbitrary application-specific functions that can be called before or after requests to protocol modules.

What is the relationship between the generic utilities and the core? The generic utilities provide platform-independent functions, but they can be used to build any networked application. The core layer, on the other hand, provides the abstractions specific to building a Web application.

The stream layer provides the abstraction of a stream of data used by all data transported between the application and the network.

The access layer provides a set of network-protocol-aware modules. The standard set of protocols that libWWW originally supported are HTTP—the underlying protocol of the World Wide Web; Network News Transport Protocol (NNTP)—the protocol for Usenet messages; Wide Area Information Server (WAIS)—a networked information retrieval system; File Transfer Protocol (FTP), TELNET, rlogin, Gopher, local file system, and TN3270. Many of these are becoming rare, but others, such as HTTPS (HTTP Secure) have been added. It is relatively simple to add new protocol modules because they are built upon the abstractions of the lower layers.

The uppermost layer, consisting of the Web application modules, is not an actual application but rather a set of functionality useful for writing applications. It includes modules for common functionality, such as caching, logging, and registering proxy servers (for protocol translation) and gateways (for dealing with security firewalls, for example); history maintenance, and so on.

LESSONS FROM libWWW

As a result of building libWWW and the many applications that rest on it, several lessons have been learned. These lessons have derived in part from the developers' experience in trying to meet the requirements that we listed in Section 13.2—that Web-based tools be heterogeneous, support remote access across networks, be noncentralized, and so forth. However, the requirement that turned out to be the most challenging was supplying unforeseen bells and whistles. That is, allowing the features of Web-based applications to grow has driven many decisions in libWWW and has led to the following lessons:

- *Formalized application programming interfaces (APIs) are required.* These are the interfaces that present the functionality of libWWW to the programs built on top of it. For this reason, APIs should be specified in a language-independent fashion because libWWW is meant to support application development on a wide variety of platforms and in many languages.
- *Functionality and the APIs that present it must be layered.* Different applications will need access to different levels of service abstraction, which are most naturally provided by layers.

- *The library must support a dynamic, open-ended set of features.* All of these features must be replaceable, and it must be possible to make replacements at runtime.
- *Processes built on the software must be thread safe.* Web-based applications must support the ability to perform several functions simultaneously, particularly because operations such as downloading large files over a slow communication link may take a considerable amount of real time. This requires the use of several simultaneous threads of control. Thus, the functionality exposed by the APIs must be safe to use in a threaded environment.

It turns out that libWWW does not support all of these goals as well as it might. For example, the libWWW core makes some assumptions about essential services, so not all features can be dynamically replaced. Furthermore, libWWW is meant to run on many different platforms, and so it can not depend on a single-thread model. Thus, it has implemented pseudothreads, which provide some, but not all, of the required functionality. Finally, most current Web applications do not support dynamic feature configuration; they require a restart before new services can be registered.

AN EARLY CLIENT-SERVER ARCHITECTURE USING libWWW

In Figure 13.5 we show a deployment view of a typical Web client-server that was built using libWWW services. A module decomposition view is also shown for the HTTP client and server components of the deployment view. The figure makes a few points about libWWW. First, not all parts of a client-server are built from it. For example, the user interface is independent. Second, the names of the managers do not directly correspond to the names of the layers: Although the access manager, protocol manager, and stream manager are clearly related to the access and stream layers, the cache manager uses the services of the application layer. The stream managers in the client-server pair manage the low-level communications, thus ensuring transparent communication across a network for the other parts of the system.

The user interface (UI) manager handles the look-and-feel of the client's user interface. However, given the open-ended set of resources that a WWW system can handle, another element, the presentation manager, can delegate information display to external programs (viewers) to view resources known by the system but that the UI manager does not directly support. For example, most Web viewers use an external program to view PostScript or .pdf files. This delegation is a compromise between the competing desires of user interface integration (which provides for a consistent look-and-feel and hence better usability) and extensibility.

The UI manager captures a user's request for information retrieval in the form of a URL and passes the information to the access manager. The access manager determines if the requested URL exists in cache and also interprets history-based

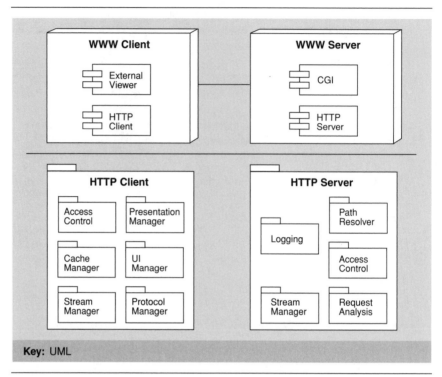

FIGURE 13.5   Deployment view of a Web client-server with a module
decomposition view of the HTTP client and server components

navigation (e.g., "back"). If the file is cached, it is retrieved from the cache manager and passed to the presentation manager for display to either the UI or an
external viewer. If it is not cached, the protocol manager determines the type of
request and invokes the appropriate protocol suite to service it. The client stream
manager uses this protocol for communicating the request to the server. Once it
receives a response from the server in the form of a document, this information is
passed to the presentation manager for appropriate display. The presentation
manager consults a static view control configuration file (mimerc, mailcap, etc.)
to help it map document types to external viewers.

The HTTP server ensures transparent access to the file system—the source
of the documents that the Web exists to transfer. It does this either by handling
the access directly (for known resource types) or through a proxy known as common gateway interface (CGI). CGI handles resource types that a native server
cannot handle and handles extension of server functionality, as will be discussed
next. Before these extensions, the available WWW servers implemented a subset of
defined HTTP requests, which allowed for the retrieval of documents, the retrieval
of document meta-information, and server-side program execution via CGI.

When a request is received by the server stream manager, its type is determined and the path of the URL is resolved via the path resolver. The HTTP server consults an access list to determine if the requesting client is authorized for access. It might initiate a password authentication session with the client to permit access to secured data. Assuming authentication, it accesses the file system (which is outside the server boundary) and writes the requested information to the output stream. If a program is to be executed, a process is made available (either new or polled) through CGI and the program is executed, with the output written by the server stream manager back to the client.

In either case, CGI is one of the primary means by which servers provide extensibility, which is one of the most important requirements driving the evolution of Web software. CGI became such an important aspect of Web-based applications that we now discuss this topic at greater length.

COMMON GATEWAY INTERFACE

Most information returned by a server is static, changing only when modified on its home file system. CGI scripts, on the other hand, allow dynamic, request-specific information to be returned. CGI has historically been used to augment server functionality: for input of information, for searches, for clickable images. The most common use of CGI, however, is to create *virtual documents*—documents that are dynamically synthesized in response to a user request. For example, when a user looks for something on the Internet, the search engine creates a reply to the user's search request; a CGI script creates a new HTML document from the reply and returns it to the user.

CGI scripts show the flexibility of early architectures which were based on libWWW. In Figure 13.5, CGI is shown as external to the HTTP server. CGI scripts are written in a variety of languages, some of which are compiled (C, C++, Fortran) and some of which are interpreted (perl, VisualBasic, AppleScript, etc.). These scripts allow a developer to extend a server's functionality arbitrarily and, in particular, to produce information that the server will return to the user.

However, because scripts may contain any functionality written in C, perl, and so on, they represent an enormous security hole for the system on which they are installed. For example, a script (which runs as a process separate from the server) might be "tricked" into executing an arbitrary command on the host system on behalf of a remote user. For this reason, server-side scripts such as CGI have led to a new requirement for increased security. The use of HTTPS to address this requirement will be described in the next section.

Probably the most important additional feature that CGI brought to the Web architecture is that it allows users to "put" information into the Web, in contrast to the "get" operation that servers normally provide. Although the requirement to put in information was listed in the original World Wide Web project requirements, it has not been fully achieved. CGI allows users to put information only in application-specific ways, such as adding it to a database by filling out a form.

Table 13.2 How the WWW Achieved Its Initial Quality Goals

Goal	How Achieved	Tactics Used
Remote Access	Build Web on top of Internet	Adherence to defined protocols
Interoperability	Use libWWW to mask platform details	Abstract common services Hide information
Extensibility of Software	Isolate protocol and data type extensions in libWWW; allow for plug-in components (applets and servlets)	Abstract common services Hide information Replace components Configuration files
Extensibility of Data	Make each data item independent except for references it controls	Limit possible options
Scalability	Use client-server architecture and keep references to other data local to referring data location	Introduce concurrency Reduce computational overhead

CGI solved many problems inherent in the original design of libWWW—principally because it provided much needed server extensibility to handle arbitrary resources, allowed users to put data in limited ways—it also had several substantial shortcomings. The security issue was one; another was portability. CGI scripts written in VisualBasic, AppleScript, and C Shell work on Windows, Macintosh, and UNIX, respectively. These scripts cannot be (easily) moved from one platform to another.

ACHIEVING INITIAL QUALITY GOALS

Table 13.2 describes how the Web achieved its initial quality goals of remote access, interoperability, extensibility, and scalability.

13.4 Another Cycle through the ABC: The Evolution of Web-Based E-Commerce Architectures

The incredible success of the Web has resulted in unprecedented interest from business and hence unprecedented pressure on the architecture, via the ABC. Business requirements have begun to dominate Web architecture. Business-to-business and business-to-consumer Web sites have fueled most of the innovation in Web-based software.

The original conception of the Web was as a web of documents, in keeping with its hypertext roots. E-commerce, however, views the Web as a web of data, and these different views have led to some tensions. For example, "pushing" data to a user is difficult; the most common technique for updating data is to reload it at specified periods rather than to rely on the change of data to force a screen update. Another is the back button on a browser, which in certain circumstances may result in stale data being displayed on a screen.

The new requirements of e-commerce are stringent and quite different from the original requirements presented in Section 13.2:

- *High performance.* A popular Web site will typically have tens of millions of "hits" per day, and users expect low latency from it. Customers will not tolerate the site simply refusing their requests.
- *High availability.* E-commerce sites are expected to be available "24/7." They never close, so must have minimal downtime—perhaps a few minutes per year.
- *Scalability.* As Web sites grow in popularity, their processing capacity must be able to similarly grow, to both expand the amount of data they can manage and maintain acceptable levels of customer service.
- *Security.* Users must be assured that any sensitive information they send across the Web is secure from snooping. Operators of Web sites must be assured that their system is secure from attack (stealing or modifying data, rendering data unusable by flooding it with requests, crashing it, etc.).
- *Modifiability.* E-commerce Web sites change frequently, in many cases daily, and so their content must be very simple to change.

The architectural solution to these requirements is more about *system* architecture than simply software architecture. The components that populate the system come from the commercial marketplace: Web servers and Web clients of course, but also databases, security servers, application servers, proxy servers, transaction servers, and so forth.

A typical reference architecture for a modern e-commerce system is shown in Figure 13.6. The browser/user interaction function is usually fulfilled by a Web browser (but it could be a kiosk, a legacy system with a Web connection, or some other Web-enabled device). The business rules and applications function is typically fulfilled by application servers and transaction servers. The data services layer is typically fulfilled by a modern database, although connections to legacy systems and legacy databases are also quite common. This scheme is often

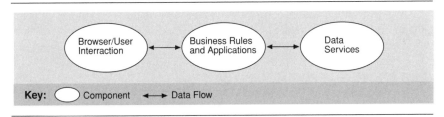

FIGURE 13.6 An e-commerce reference architecture

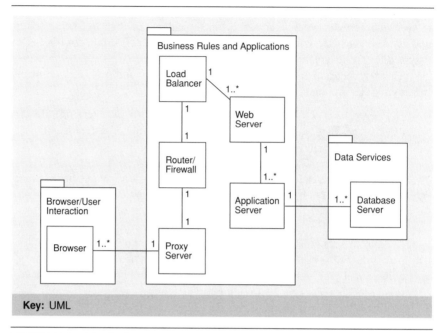

FIGURE 13.7 A typical e-commerce system

referred to as an *n*-tier architecture (here, $n = 3$). A *tier* is a partitioning of func-tionality that may be allocated to a separate physical machine.

A typical implementation of an e-commerce system architecture consists of a number of tiers, each consisting of a coherent grouping of software (typically customized commercial components) and hardware. Such a configuration is given in Figure 13.7, which shows how software is allocated to hardware.

The figure is annotated with the functional elements from Figure 13.6 to reinforce the notion that a single function in the reference architecture may map to multiple tiers in a typical e-commerce architecture. The two parts of Figure 13.5 occur here as elementary components: the Web browsers (clients) and the Web servers, respectively, reflecting the evolution toward component-based sys-tems in which the internal component structure is less relevant.

We will now discuss each of the elements in Figure 13.7, along with the qualities that each helps to achieve.

WEB BROWSERS FOR MODIFIABILITY

An end user typically initiates a request for information by interacting with a Web browser. Modern Web browsers support user interface modifiability in a wide variety of ways, the most obvious of which has not changed from the inception of the Web: The user interface that the browser supports is not hardwired but it is specified via HTML. At least, it used to be. Nowadays there are many other technologies for creating sophisticated user interfaces. XML, Flash, ActiveX, and Java applets are just a few of the methods by which the standard palette of Web interactors (graphics and hot spots) are widened to provide fully programmable interactive interfaces via browsers.

HTTPS FOR SECURITY

Once the user has submitted a request, it must be transmitted to a target Web site. This transmission may be via HTTP or, for sensitive information such as credit card or identification numbers, HTTPS (HTTP Secure). HTTPS uses Netscape's Secure Sockets Layer as a subprotocol underneath HTTP. It uses a different port (443 instead of the standard port 80 that HTTP uses) to request TCP/IP services in an encrypted form. SSL uses a 128-bit public/private key pair to encrypt the data, and this level of encryption is considered adequate for the exchange of small amounts of commercial information in short transactions.

PROXY SERVERS FOR PERFORMANCE

Requests from individual browsers may first arrive at a proxy server, which exists to improve the performance of the Web-based system. These servers cache frequently accessed Web pages so that users may retrieve them without having to access the Web site. (Caches carry out the tactic of "multiple copies.") They are typically located close to the users, often on the same network, so they save a tremendous amount of both communication and computation resources. Proxy servers are also used by companies that want to restrict their employees' access to certain Web sites. In this case the proxy server is acting somewhat like a firewall.

ROUTERS AND FIREWALLS FOR SECURITY

Requests from the browser (or proxy server) then arrive at a router, located on the e-commerce provider's network, that may include a firewall for security. (Alternately the router may pass HTTP requests on to a separate firewall.) The router may implement network address translation (NAT), which translates an externally visible IP address into an internal IP address. The IP address for any return traffic from the Web server is translated so that it appears to have originated from the externally visible site, not from the internal IP address. NAT is one of the techniques used in load balancing, as we will discuss shortly.

The purpose of the firewall is to prevent unauthorized information flows or accesses from the outside world, an example of the "limit access" tactic. There are several types of firewall, the most common being *packet filters* and *application proxies*. Packet filters examine the TCP and IP headers of each incoming packet and, if any bad behavior is detected (such as an attempt to connect via an unauthorized port or to send nonconforming file types), the packet is rejected. Packet filter firewalls are appropriate for Web-based communication because they examine each packet in isolation—there is no attempt to maintain a history of previous communication.

Application proxy firewalls are, as their name suggests, application specific. They typically understand application protocols and hence can filter traffic based on known patterns of behavior. An application proxy may, for example, refuse an HTTP response unless an HTTP request was recently sent to that site. These firewalls can be much slower than packet filter firewalls because they rely on keeping a certain amount of history information on hand and their processing tends to be more complex.

LOAD BALANCING FOR PERFORMANCE, SCALABILITY, AND AVAILABILITY

A load-balancing component is an integral part of any important e-commerce Web site, because it supports performance, scalability, and availability. The job of the load balancer is to distribute the "load"—incoming HTTP and HTTPS requests—among a pool of computers running Web servers. (Recall from Chapter 5 that load balancing follows from the tactic of "introducing physical concurrency.") The load balancer may simply (and transparently) redirect the request to another computer, or it may respond to the Web client and instruct it to redirect the request to a different server. While this redirection is transparent to the end user, it results in an additional roundtrip of communication.

In choosing which computer to redirect the traffic to, the load balancer may select in a round-robin fashion, or its choices may be based on known processing or load characteristics of each computer to which it is connected. Because the load balancer is acting as a proxy for the pool of computers, we can add to that pool without changing any external interface. In this way the load balancer supports performance scalability, known as horizontal scaling (adding more instances of a given resource).

In addition, the load balancer may monitor the liveness of each of its computers and, if one of them goes down, simply redirect traffic to the others in the pool. In this way it supports availability.

WEB SERVERS FOR PERFORMANCE

Next the HTTP or HTTPS request reaches the Web server. Early Web servers, such as those described in Figure 13.5, were typically single threaded. Modern versions are multithreaded, utilizing a pool of threads, each of which can be dispatched to handle an incoming request. A multithreaded server is less susceptible to bottlenecks (and hence long latency) when a number of long-running HTTP or

HTTPS requests (such as credit card validations) arrive because other threads in the pool are still available to serve incoming requests. This is the performance tactic of "introduce concurrency."

Vertical scaling (adding more powerful instances of a given resource) can be accomplished by replacing existing servers with more powerful machines that will run more threads simultaneously.

Upon analyzing the request, the Web server will send it to an application server that can respond, typically using the services of a database to do so.

Chapter 16 will discuss Enterprise JavaBeans, a modern implementation approach for Web servers.

APPLICATION SERVERS FOR MODIFIABILITY, PERFORMANCE, AND SCALABILITY

From the Web server the request is forwarded to an application server. "Application server" is a broad (some would say ill-defined) term for a class of applications that run in the "middle" of the *n*-tier architecture—business rules and applications. These servers implement business logic and connectivity, which dictate how clients and servers interact. The trend toward application servers has allowed significant portions of functionality to be moved from old-style "fat" clients into the middle tier. Also, they have allowed databases to concentrate on the storage, retrieval, and analysis of data without worrying about precisely how that data will be used.

Application servers at the low end typically offer an integrated development environment (IDE) and runtime server. IDEs support a programming model, such as COM (or, more recently, .NET), CORBA, or J2EE (discussed in Chapter 16). Many application servers also support a set of commonly used services for quickly creating business and e-commerce applications, such as billing, inventory, work flow, and customer relations management. At the upper end in terms of cost, complexity, and functionality are transaction processing and transaction monitoring. Transaction monitors and processors interact with databases and manage tasks like distributed transactions (including combining data from multiple sources), queuing, transaction integrity, and workload balancing (much like the load balancer mentioned earlier).

DATABASES FOR PERFORMANCE, SCALABILITY, AND AVAILABILITY

Finally, the request for service arrives at the database, where it is converted into an instruction to add, modify, or retrieve information. Modern database architectures share many of the qualities of the entire e-commerce system presented in Figure 13.7. They frequently use internal replication for performance, scalability, and high availability. They may use caching for faster performance.

TABLE 13.3   How the Web e-Commerce Architecture Achieves Its Quality Goals

Goal	How Achieved	Tactics
High Performance	Load balancing, network address translation, proxy servers	Introduce concurrency; increase resources; multiple copies
High Availability	Redundant processors, networks, databases, and software; load balancing	Active redundancy; transactions; introduce concurrency
Scalability	Allow for horizontal and vertical scaling; load balancing	Abstract common services; adherence to defined protocols; introduce concurrency
Security	Firewalls; public/private key encryption across public networks	Limit access; integrity; limit exposure
Modifiability	Separation of browser functionality, database design, and business logic into distinct tiers	Abstract common services; semantic coherence; intermediary; interface stability

13.5   Achieving Quality Goals

Together the elements we have described allow the Web-based e-commerce system to achieve its stringent quality goals of security, high availability, modifiability, scalability, and high performance. How they do this is shown in Table 13.3.

13.6   The Architecture Business Cycle Today

If we look at the current state of the Web after several cycles through the ABC, we see a number of phenomena.

- Several types of organizations provide the technical environment. They can be divided into service providers and content providers. Service providers produce the software that makes the Web—browsers, servers, databases, application servers, security technologies (such as firewalls), transaction servers, networks, and routers. Content providers produce the data for the Web. There is heavy competition in all of these areas.
- A number of open-source projects, aside from the W3C, have come to prominence in the development of the Web, particularly the Apache project.
- CERN has had no special role in the evolution of the Web.
- Web-enabled languages, particularly Java, are changing the way functionality is developed and delivered over the Web. (See Chapter 18 for an example of how Web-based applications are built using Enterprise JavaBeans.)

- The emergence of the Web as a distributed development environment has given rise to several new organizations and products. For example, UDDI (Universal Description, Discovery, and Integration) provides distributed Web-based registries of Web services. These services can be used as building blocks for distributed Web-based applications.

Figure 13.8 shows the ABC for the Web today.

The customers are the software server and browser providers and the service and content providers. The end users are the people of the world. The architect's role is provided by the W3C and other consortia such as UDDI, the Apache project, and several influential companies—Sun, Microsoft, and AOL/Netscape. The remainder of the ABC is the same except that the technical environment now includes the Web itself, which adds an upward compatibility requirement to the qualities.

We discussed the return cycle of the ABC in Section 1.1. The existence of a system creates new business opportunities for both the developing organization and its customers. In the World Wide Web case, the developing organization, CERN, decided that nuclear research, not Web activity, was its main business, so the business opportunities created by the return loop of the ABC were filled by other organizations.

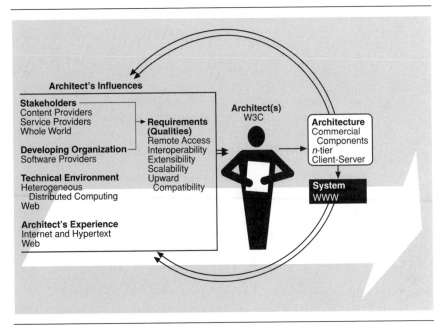

FIGURE 13.8   The current ABC for the Web

13.7 Summary

The Web has been so successful because of the manner in which the desired qualities were realized in its architectural structures, and in how these structures have
been reinvented in the face of dramatic new requirements. The success of the
Web has meant that the ABC has been traversed multiple times in just a few
years, with each traversal creating new business opportunities, new requirements,
and new technical challenges.

How the Web Has Changed the Business World: A Look at Amazon.com

When Amazon.com opened its virtual doors in 1995, it was already an order
of magnitude bigger than the average bookstore, carrying more than 1 million
titles. It was not like "brick-and-mortar" bookstores in other ways as well, and
these differences all stemmed from the fact that Amazon was an e-business,
delivering the message and products via the Web.

Being an e-store meant that Amazon could change the world (at least, the
business world). For example, it meant that Amazon could sell books created
by small, independent writers and publishers since it did not bear the costs of
publishing. It meant that it could change the ways in which people bought
books, with online user reviews, synopses, personal recommendation services, e-mail notifications of new books by a user's favorite author, and so
forth. It also meant that Amazon could keep its prices low since it avoided
most of the costs of traditional retail operations by outsourcing the majority of
its operations.

A shopper at Amazon.com receives customized, personalized service
such as suggestions for books similar to those the customer has browsed or
purchased. Amazon can do this only because of its enormous IT infrastructure and data-mining ability.

Rather than a simple purchaser and reseller of books, Amazon is a "middleman" and an information broker. It has succeeded in creating a loyal and
ever-growing community of sellers and buyers, not just of books. Amazon is a
hub, collecting a percentage of every sale made and receiving commissions
on referrals to other Web sites.

Ultimately Amazon's IT infrastructure has little to do with books. Amazon
realized this early on and was able to transform itself into a retailer of toys,
cell phones, drugs, cameras, software, car parts, pet supplies—virtually anything that could be sold to the public and shipped around the world. None of
this would have been possible without the Web's infrastructure.

Today, Amazon.com claims to be the world's largest online store serving
customers in more than 220 countries. It has five international Web sites and
approximately 20 million registered customers (almost the population of Can-
ada!). Repeat business is 70%, which is unheard of in retailing. At the time of

this writing, Amazon hasn't made an annual profit, but it expects to be profit-able in 2003 and beyond.

Although it is far from the only one, Amazon is perhaps the most dramatic example of how the Web has changed the world (at least the world of retailing).

— RK

13.8   For Further Reading

Readers interested in discovering more about hypertext should see [Bush 45] and the special issue of the CACM devoted to hypertext [CACM 88].

Information on the Web's history and growth can be found primarily on the Web. We used [Berners-Lee 96a], [Gray (*http://www.mit.edu/people/mkgray/net*)], and [Zakon (*http://www.zakon.com/robert/internet/timeline*)].

Much of the detail about libWWW comes from the W3C Reference Library at *http://www.w3.org/pub/WWW/Library*.

For a good general discussion of network security issues and cryptography, including all aspects of Web security, see [Stallings 99]. A good discussion of performance issues in e-commerce systems may be found in [Menasce 00].

The architectural style used in Web-based applications is treated in [Fielding 96]. A comparison of modern Web server patterns may be found in [Hassan 00], from which we adapted the client-server architecture shown in Figure 13.5.

Netcraft's May 2001 survey of Web server usage can be found at *http://www. netcraft.com/survey/*.

13.9   Discussion Questions

1.   We have identified a number of qualities that made the WWW successful:
     interoperability, portability, remote access, extensibility, and scalability.
     Which of these do you think contributed most substantially to the Web's suc-
     cess? If any of these qualities had been sacrificed, would the Web still have
     been successful? What tradeoffs did these quality goals entail in the architec-
     ture of applications based upon libWWW?

2.   The Web did not have performance as one of its early quality goals, which is
     unusual for a successful system. Why do you think the system was successful
     anyway? What, if anything, does this say about the future of computing?

3.   What patterns and tactics can you discern in the portions of the architecture
     shown in Figures 13.4, 13.5, and 13.7?

PART FOUR

MOVING FROM ONE SYSTEM TO MANY

Part Four continues our tour of the Architecture Business Cycle. Parts One, Two, and Three took us from the architect to a reviewed architecture. Part Four focuses on the construction of multiple systems from that architecture, discussing, and giving examples of system product lines. It does this from five perspectives: that of the technology underlying a product line, that of a single company that built a product line of naval vessel fire-control systems, that of an industry-wide architecture, that of a single company producing products based on the industry-wide architecture, and that of an organization building systems from commercial components.

Software product lines have the potential to re-use everything from requirements to test plans to personnel. The key to this re-use is architecture. Chapter 14 focuses on defining and developing an architecture for a product line. We deal with organizational issues here since, as you should be well aware of by now, there is a strong relationship between architecture and organizations.

Chapter 15 is our first case study. It is the story of a Swedish company, CelsiusTech, that constructed a product line of fire-control systems for naval vessels. We discuss the architecture here, but we also discuss in some detail how its organizational structure and culture changed as a result of adopting a product line.

CelsiusTech was a single organization building an architecture for multiple products. However, industries also have supporting architectures. For example, Java 2 Enterprise Edition/Enterprise JavaBeans (J2EE/EJB), an architectural specification designed for Web-based information systems, acts as a base architecture for products developed by many companies. Chapter 16 discusses J2EE/EJB's architectural decisions and the tradeoffs that are possible within it.

One of the companies building products based on J2EE/EJB is Inmedius, which produces solutions for frontline workers, such as maintenance technicians, who cannot sit in front of a desktop and rarely use a laptop but instead rely on a variety of mobile platforms. How Inmedius architected a solution based on wireless technology and wearable and handheld computers is the subject of Chapter 17.

Chapter 18 discusses constructing a single system when given an architecture and a collection of commercial components. We will see if there was anything left to design and build.

Finally, we end by engaging in our favorite pastime—predicting the future of software architecture. Chapter 19 presents our guesses (and they are no more than that) as to what might be in store.

14

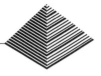

Software Product Lines
Re-using Architectural Assets

with Linda Northrop

> *In 1969, McIlroy first recognized the need for an industry of re-usable software components, but since then, this has continued to be an elusive goal for the software community. It is therefore fair to ask the question: If the benefits of re-usable software components are so overwhelming, why doesn't this practice already pervade the whole of computer science?*
> — Grady Booch [Booch 94]

14.1 Overview

A software architecture represents a significant investment of time and effort, usually by senior talent. So it is natural to want to maximize the return on this investment by re-using an architecture across multiple systems. Architecturally mature organizations tend to treat their architectures as valuable intellectual property and look for ways in which that property can be leveraged to produce additional revenue and reduce costs. Both are possible with architecture re-use.

This chapter is about the explicit, planned re-use of a software architecture (and other assets as well) across a family of related systems. When an organization is producing multiple similar systems and re-using the same architecture (and elements associated with that architecture), it enjoys substantial benefits that include reduced cost of construction and reduced time to market. This is the lure of the *software product line*, defined as

> a set of software-intensive systems sharing a common, managed set of features that satisfy the specific needs of a particular market segment or mission and that are developed from a common set of core assets in a prescribed way. [Clements 02b, 5]

Note: Linda Northrop is a member of the technical staff at the Software Engineering Institute.

The vision is of a set of re-usable assets that includes a base architecture and the common, perhaps tailorable, elements that populate it. It also includes designs and their documentation, user manuals, project management artifacts such as budgets and schedules, and software test plans and test cases. As we will see, achieving this vision depends critically on establishing the correct scope for the product line.

When a product line has been successfully established, each re-usable asset is saved in a *core asset base* because it can be applied to more than one system and because re-using it will be cheaper than re-inventing it. Core assets ideally are designed with variation points—that is, places where they can be quickly tailored in preplanned ways. Within a successful product line, system building becomes accessing the appropriate assets, tailoring them as required for the system at hand, and then assembling that system. Any software developed for an individual product, if needed at all, tends to account for less than 20% of the total software. Integration and testing replace design and coding as the predominant activities.

Product lines are, of course, nothing new in manufacturing. Many historians trace the concept to Eli Whitney's use of interchangeable parts to build rifles in the early 1800s, but earlier examples also exist. Today, Boeing has one, as do Ford, Dell, and even McDonald's. Each company exploits commonality in different ways. Boeing, for example, developed the 757 and 767 transports in tandem, and the parts lists of these two very different aircraft overlap by about 60%.

Software product lines based on inter-product commonality represent an innovative, growing concept in software engineering. Every customer has its own requirements, which demand flexibility on the part of the manufacturers. Software product lines simplify the creation of systems built specifically for particular customers or customer groups.

The improvements in cost, time to market, and productivity that come with a successful product line can be breathtaking. Consider:

- Nokia is able to produce 25 to 30 different phone models per year (up from 4 per year) because of the product line approach.
- Cummins, Inc., was able to reduce the time it takes to produce the software for a diesel engine from about a year to about a week.
- Motorola observed a 400% productivity improvement in a family of one-way pagers.
- Hewlett-Packard reported a time to market reduced by a factor of seven and a productivity increase of a factor of six in a family of printer systems.
- With a family of satellite ground control systems it commissioned, the U.S. National Reconnaissance Office reports the first product requiring 10% the expected number of developers and having 90% fewer defects.

Creating a successful product line depends on a coordinated strategy involving software engineering, technical management, and organization management. Since this is a book on software architecture, we focus on the software architectural aspects of software engineering, but all aspects must work together for an organization to successfully create a product line.

14.2   What Makes Software Product Lines Work?

The essence of a software product line is the disciplined, strategic re-use of assets in producing a family of products. What makes product lines succeed so spectacularly from the vendor or developer's point of view is that the commonalities shared by the products can be exploited through re-use to achieve production economies. The potential for re-use is broad and far-ranging, including:

- *Requirements.* Most of the requirements are common with those of earlier systems and so can be re-used. Requirements analysis is saved.

- *Architectural design.* An architecture for a software system represents a large investment of time from the organization's most talented engineers. As we have seen, the quality goals for a system—performance, reliability, modifiability, and so forth—are largely allowed or precluded once the architecture is in place. If the architecture is wrong, the system cannot be saved. For a new product, however, this most important design step is already done and need not be repeated.

- *Elements.* Software elements are applicable across individual products. Far and above mere code re-use, element re-use includes the (often difficult) initial design work. Design successes are captured and re-used; design dead ends are avoided, not repeated. This includes design of the element's interface, its documentation, its test plans and procedures, and any models (such as performance models) used to predict or measure its behavior. One re-usable set of elements is the system's user interface, which represents an enormous and vital set of design decisions.

- *Modeling and analysis.* Performance models, schedulability analysis, distributed system issues (such as proving absence of deadlock), allocation of processes to processors, fault tolerance schemes, and network load policies all carry over from product to product. CelsiusTech (as discussed in Chapter 15) reports that one of the major headaches associated with the real-time distributed systems it builds has all but vanished. When fielding a new product in the product line, it has extremely high confidence that the timing problems have been worked out and that the bugs associated with distributed computing—synchronization, network loading, deadlock—have been eliminated.

- *Testing.* Test plans, test processes, test cases, test data, test harnesses, and the communication paths required to report and fix problems are already in place.

- *Project planning.* Budgeting and scheduling are more predictable because experience is a high-fidelity indicator of future performance. Work breakdown structures need not be invented each time. Teams, team size, and team composition are all easily determined.

- *Processes, methods, and tools.* Configuration control procedures and facilities, documentation plans and approval processes, tool environments, system generation and distribution procedures, coding standards, and many other day-to-day engineering support activities can all be carried over from product to product. The overall software development process is in place and has been used before.

- *People.* Because of the commonality of applications, personnel can be fluidly transferred among projects as required. Their expertise is applicable across the entire line.

- *Exemplar systems.* Deployed products serve as high-quality demonstration prototypes as well as high-quality engineering models of performance, security, safety, and reliability.

- *Defect elimination.* Product lines enhance quality because each new system takes advantage of the defect elimination in its forebears. Developer and customer confidence both rise with each new instantiation. The more complicated the system, the higher the payoff for solving vexing performance, distribution, reliability, and other engineering issues once for the entire family.

Software product lines rely on re-use, but as revealed by this chapter's opening quotation, re-use has a long but less than stellar history in software engineering, with the promise almost always exceeding the payoff. One reason for this failure is that until now re-use has been predicated on the idea that "If you build it, they will come." A re-use library is stocked with snippets from previous projects, and developers are expected to check it first before coding new elements. Almost everything conspires against this model. If the library is too sparse, the developer will not find anything of use and will stop looking. If the library is too rich, it will be hard to search. If the elements are too small, it is easier to rewrite them than to find them and carry out whatever modifications they might need. If the elements are too large, it is very difficult to determine exactly what they do in detail, which in any case is not likely to be exactly right for the new application. In most re-use libraries, pedigree is hazy at best. The developer cannot be sure exactly what the element does, how reliable it is, or under what conditions it was tested. And there is almost never a match between the quality attributes needed for the new application and those provided by the elements in the library.

In any case, it is likely that the elements were written for a different architectural model than the one the developer of the new system is using. Even if you find something that does the right thing with the right quality attributes, it is doubtful that it will be the right kind of architectural element (if you need an object, you might find a process), that it will have the right interaction protocol, that it will comply with the new application's error-handling or failover policies, and so on.

Software product lines make re-use work by establishing a very strict context for it. The architecture is defined; the functionality is set; the quality attributes are known. Nothing is placed in the re-use library—or "core asset base" in product line terms—that was not built to be re-used in that product line. Product lines work by relying on strategic or planned, not opportunistic, re-use.

14.3 Scoping

The scope of a product line defines what systems are in it, and what systems are out. Put less bluntly, a product line's scope is a statement about what systems an organization is willing to build as part of its line and what systems it is not willing to build. Defining a product line's scope is like drawing a doughnut in the space of all possible systems, as shown in Figure 14.1. The doughnut's center represents the systems that the organization could build, would build, because they fall within its product line capability. Systems outside the doughnut are out of scope, ones that the product line is not well equipped to handle. Systems on the doughnut itself could be handled, but with some effort, and require case-by-case disposition as they arise. To illustrate, in a product line of office automation systems a conference room scheduler would be in; a flight simulator would be out. A specialized intranet search engine might be in if it could be produced in a reasonable time and if there were strategic reasons for doing so (such as the likelihood that future customers would want a similar product).

The scope represents the organization's best prediction about what products it will be asked to build in the foreseeable future. Input to the scoping process comes from the organization's strategic planners, marketing staff, domain analysts who can catalog similar systems (both existing and on the drawing board), and technology experts.

A product line scope is a critical factor in the success of the product line. Scope too narrowly (the products vary in a small number of features) and an insufficient number of products will be derived to justify the investment in development.

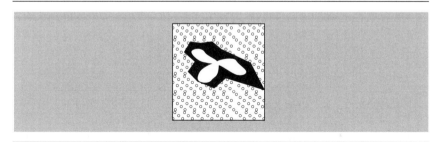

FIGURE 14.1   The space of all possible systems is divided into areas within scope (*white*), areas outside of scope (*speckled*), and areas that require case-by-case disposition (*black*).   Adapted from [Clements 02b].

Scope too broadly (the products vary in kind as well as in features) and the effort required to develop individual products from the core assets is too great to lead to great savings. Scope can be refined during the initial establishment of the product line or opportunistically depending on the product line adoption strategy (see the section Adoption Strategies).

The problem in defining the scope is not in finding commonality—a creative architect can find points of commonality between any two systems—but in finding commonality that can be exploited to substantially reduce the cost of constructing the systems that an organization intends to build.

When considering scope, more than just the systems being built should be considered. Market segmentation and types of customer interactions assumed will help determine the scope of any product line. For example, Philips, a Dutch manufacturer of consumer electronics, has distinct product lines for home video electronic systems and digital video communication. Video is the common thread, but one is a mass market, where the customer is assumed to have very little video sophistication, and the other is a much smaller market (in terms of number of customers), where the customer is assumed to be very knowledgeable. The products being developed reflect these assumptions about the sophistication of customers and the amount of care each customer will receive. These differences were sufficient to keep Philips from attempting to develop a single product line for both markets.

Narrowly scoped product lines offer opportunities to build specialized tools to support the specification of new products, for example:

- FAST is a process for product line development based on developing a domain-specific language and associated compiler. The compiler is one of the core assets. When product variations are captured in a domain-specific language, the runtime library for the code generated through the compiler becomes an additional core asset.
- GM Powertrain makes a product out of product line assets based on contracts stored in a database. Each element has well-defined interfaces and possible variation points. A tool searches the database based on desired features and assembles the product.

Broadly scoped product lines tend to be developed as frameworks or as collections of services, for example:

- An automotive supplier's product line of navigation systems is geared to automotive manufacturers, each of which insists on its own user interface and set of features. The supplier designed the architecture as a collection of frameworks. The development of each product consists of constructing the user interface and instantiating the frameworks for the specified features.
- The Luther system (see Chapter 17) is a product line constructed on top of J2EE (a framework). The development of each product consists of building the user interface and implementing some application support modules.

That Silver Lining Might Have A Cloud

The software product line paradigm is a powerful way to leverage an investment in architecture (and other core assets) into a family of related systems and thus see order-of-magnitude improvements in time to market, quality, and productivity.

These results are possible and have been demonstrated by companies large and small in many different domains. The effects are real. Further, data from many sources and companies confirms with astonishing consistency that to make the investment pay off, an organization needs to build only about three products. This is the minimum number we would expect to have in a product line anyway.

It must be pointed out, however, that other results are possible as well, and a spectacular crash-and-burn is not out of the question when trying to adopt this approach. Product line practice, like any new technology, needs careful thought given to its adoption, and a company's history, situation, and culture must be taken into account.

These factors can contribute to product line failure:

- Lack of a champion in a position of sufficient control and visibility
- Failure of management to provide sustained and unwavering support
- Reluctance of middle managers to relinquish autocratic control of projects
- Failure to clearly identify business goals for adopting the product line approach
- Abandoning the approach at the first sign of difficulty
- Failure to adequately train staff in the approach and failure to explain or justify the change adequately

Fortunately, there are strategies for overcoming most of these factors. One good strategy is to launch a small but visible pilot project to demonstrate the quantitative benefits of software product lines. The pilot can be staffed by those most willing to try something new while the skeptics go about their business. It can work out process issues, clarify roles and responsibilities, and in general work out the bugs before the approach is transitioned to a wider setting.

Joe Gahimer of Cummins, Inc. (the purveyor of a very successful software product line chronicled in [Clements 02b], tells the story of two features in his organization's products whose owners pleaded uniqueness. A tailshaft governor, they said, was nothing at all like a cruise control governor. Yes, they both controlled speed, but that was where the similarity ended. The core asset group patiently worked with both sides to capture the details of the two applications, and at the end of the exercise it turned out that the two features were not only similar but in fact functionally identical, modulo a numeric constant.

When adopting a product line approach, perseverance pays off. In fact, it is the best remedy for most of the failure causes enumerated here. The single most effective factor is often a champion who (by definition) perseveres in touting the product line approach, overcoming skepticism, and instilling the will to overcome hurdles.

— PCC

14.4   Architectures for Product Lines

Of all of the assets in a core asset repository, the software architecture plays the most central role. The essence of building a successful software product line is discriminating between what is expected to remain constant across all family members and what is expected to vary. Software architecture is ready-made for handling this duality, since all architectures are abstractions that admit a plurality of instances; a great source of their conceptual value is, after all, that they allow us to concentrate on design essentials within a number of different implementations. By its very nature an architecture is a statement about what we expect to remain constant and what we admit may vary. In a software product line, the architecture is an expression of the nonvarying aspects.

But a product line architecture goes beyond this simple dichotomy, concerning itself with a set of explicitly allowed variations, whereas with a conventional architecture almost any instance will do as long as the (single) system's behavioral and quality goals are met. Thus, identifying the allowable variations is part of the architecture's responsibility, as is providing built-in mechanisms for achieving them. Those variations may be substantial. Products in a software product line exist simultaneously and may vary in terms of their behavior, quality attributes, platform, network, physical configuration, middleware, scale factors, and so forth.

A product line architect needs to consider three things:

- Identifying variation points
- Supporting variation points
- Evaluating the architecture for product line suitability

IDENTIFYING VARIATION POINTS

Identifying variation is an ongoing activity. Because of the many ways a product can vary, variants can be identified at virtually any time during the development process. Some variations are identified during product line requirements elicitation; others, during architecture design; and still others, during implementation. Variations may also be identified during implementation of the second (and subsequent) products as well.

The variations discovered during the requirements process can include features, platforms, user interfaces, qualities, and target markets. Some are interdependent. For example, the user interface may be tied to the platform to be used, which may in turn be tied to a particular target market.

The variation points discovered during the architecture design process will be either options for implementing the variations identified during the requirements process or normal variations during design because particular decisions are deferred until more information is available. In any case, it is now appropriate to speak of "variation points" since there are places in the architecture that we can point to that capture the variation.

SUPPORTING VARIATION POINTS

In a conventional architecture, the mechanism for achieving different instances almost always comes down to modifying the code. But in a software product line, architectural support for variation can take many forms:

- Inclusion or omission of elements. This decision can be reflected in the build procedures for different products, or the implementation of an element can be conditionally compiled based on some parameter indicating its presence or absence.
- Inclusion of a different number of replicated elements. For instance, high-capacity variants might be produced by adding more servers—the actual number should be unspecified, as a point of variation. Again, a build file would select the number appropriate for a particular product.
- Selection of versions of elements that have the same interface but different behavioral or quality attribute characteristics. Selection can occur at compile or build time or, in some cases, even runtime. Two selection mechanisms are static libraries, which contain external functions linked to after compilation time, and dynamic link libraries, which have the flexibility of static libraries but defer the decision until runtime based on context and execution conditions. By changing the libraries, we can change the implementation of functions whose names and signatures are known.

These mechanisms produce wholesale changes at the architectural level. Other mechanisms can be introduced that change aspects of a particular element. Changing the source code falls into this category. More sophisticated techniques include the following:

- In object-oriented systems, specializing or generalizing particular classes can achieve variation. Classes can be written to admit a variety of specializations that can be written for various products as necessary.
- Building extension points into the element's implementation. This is a place where additional behavior or functionality can be safely added.
- Variation can be accomplished by introducing build-time parameters to an element, a subsystem, or a collection of subsystems, whereby a product is configured by setting a collection of values.
- Reflection is the ability of a program to manipulate data on itself or its execution environment or state. Reflective programs can adjust their behavior based on their context.
- Overloading is a means of re-using a named functionality to operate on different types. Overloading promotes code re-use, but at the cost of understandability and code complexity.

Of course, there must be documentation (see Chapter 9) for the product line architecture as it resides in the core asset base and for each product's architecture (to the extent that it varies from the product line architecture). The documentation for the product line architecture should clearly show its variation points and a rationale for each (probably using the scope definition as justification). It should also describe the architecture's instantiation process—that is, how its variation points are exercised. Theoretically, each variation point could be described separately, but in practice not all variations are allowed. Some combinations may be unused or (worse) result in an error, and so the documentation needs to explain valid and invalid variation bindings.

The documentation for an individual product's architecture can be written in terms of deltas from or binding of variation points. For example, the architecture for product #16 might require *three* servers, *sixty-four* client workstations, *two* databases, the *high-speed low-resolution version* of the graphics element, and *null* encryption in the message generator.

EVALUATING A PRODUCT LINE ARCHITECTURE

Like any other, the architecture for a software product line should be evaluated for fitness of purpose. In fact, given the number of systems that will rely on it, evaluation takes on an even more important role for a product line architecture.

The good news is that the evaluation techniques described earlier in this book work well for product line architectures. The architecture should be evaluated for its robustness and generality, to make sure it can serve as the basis for products in the product line's envisioned scope. It should also be evaluated to make sure it meets the specific behavioral and quality requirements of the product at hand. We begin by focusing on the what and how of the evaluation and then turn to when it should take place.

What and How to Evaluate.   The evaluation will have to focus on the variation points to make sure they are appropriate, that they offer sufficient flexibility to cover the product line's intended scope, that they allow products to be built quickly, and that they do not impose unacceptable runtime performance costs. If your evaluation is scenario based, expect to elicit scenarios that involve instantiating the architecture to support different products in the family. Also, different products in the product line may have different quality attribute requirements, and the architecture will have to be evaluated for its ability to provide all required combinations. Here again, try to elicit scenarios that capture the quality attributes required of family members.

Often, some of the hardware and other performance-affecting factors for a product line architecture are unknown to begin with. In this case, evaluation can establish bounds on the performance that the architecture is able to achieve, assuming bounds on hardware and other variables. The evaluation can identify potential contention so that you can put in place the policies and strategies to resolve it.

When to Evaluate.   An evaluation should be performed on an instance or variation of the architecture that will be used to build one or more products in the product line. The extent to which this is a separate, dedicated evaluation depends on the extent to which the product architecture differs in quality-attribute-affecting ways from the product line architecture. If it does not differ, the product line architecture evaluation can be abbreviated, since many of the issues normally be raised in a single product evaluation will have been dealt with in the product line evaluation. In fact, just as the product architecture is a variation of the product line architecture, the product architecture evaluation is a variation of the product line architecture evaluation. Therefore, depending on the evaluation method used, the evaluation artifacts (scenarios, checklists, etc.) will have re-use potential, and you should create them with that in mind. The results of evaluation of product architectures often provide useful feedback to the product line architects and fuel architectural improvements.

When a new product is proposed that falls outside the scope of the original product line (for which the architecture was presumably evaluated), the product line architecture can be re-evaluated to see if it will suffice for it. If it does, the product line's scope can be expanded to include the new product or to spawn a new product line. If it does not, the evaluation can determine how the architecture will have to be modified to accommodate the new product.

The product line and product architectures can be evaluated not only to determine architectural risks but also, using the CBAM (see Chapter 12), to determine which products will yield the most return.

14.5   What Makes Software Product Lines Difficult?

It takes a certain maturity in the developing organization to successfully field a product line. Technology is not the only barrier to this; organization, process, and business issues are equally vital to master to fully reap the benefits of the software product line approach.

The Software Engineering Institute has identified twenty-nine issues or "practice areas" that affect an organization's success in fielding a software product line. Most of these practice areas are applied during single-system development as well, but take on a new dimension in a product line context. Two examples are architecture definition and configuration management.

Architecture definition is an important activity for any project but, as we saw in the previous section, it needs to emphasize variation points in a software product line. Configuration management is also an important activity for any project but is more complex for a software product line because each product is the result of binding a large number of variations. The configuration management problem for product lines is to reproduce any version of any product delivered to any customer, where "product" means code and supporting artifacts ranging from requirement specs and test cases to user manuals and installation guides. This involves knowing what version of each core asset was used in a product's construction, how every asset was tailored, and what special-purpose code or documentation was added.

Examining every facet of product line production is outside the scope of this book, but the next section will examine a few of the key areas to give a flavor of the qualitative difference between product line and single-system development. These are issues that an organization will have to face when considering whether to adopt a product line approach for software development.

ADOPTION STRATEGIES

Getting an organization to adopt the product line approach is in many regards like any other technology insertion problem. How to solve it depends on the organization's culture and context.

Top-down adoption comes when a manager decrees that the organization will use the approach. The problem here is to get employees in the trenches to change the way they work. Bottom-up adoption happens when designers and developers working at the product level realize that they are needlessly duplicating each other's work and begin to share resources and develop generic core assets. The problem here is finding a manager willing to sponsor the work and spread the technique to other parts of the organization. Both approaches work; both are helped enormously by the presence of a strong *champion*—someone who has thoroughly internalized the product line vision and can share that compelling vision with others.

Orthogonal to the issue of in which direction the technology will grow is the question of how the product line itself grows. Here there are two primary models.[1]

In a *proactive* product line, an organization defines the family using a comprehensive definition of scope. They do this not with a crystal ball but by taking advantage of their experience in the application area, their knowledge about the market and technology trends, and their good business sense. The proactive model is the most powerful of the two product line growth models, because it allows the organization to make the most far-reaching strategic decisions. Explicitly scoping the product line allows you to look at areas that are underrepresented by products already in the marketplace, make small extensions to the product line, and move quickly to fill the gap. In short, proactive product line scope allows an organization to take charge of its own fate.

Sometimes an organization does not have the ability to forecast the needs of the market with the certainty suggested by the proactive model. Perhaps the domain is a new one. Perhaps the market is in flux. Or perhaps the organization cannot afford to build a core asset base that will cover the entire scope all at once. In this situation, a *reactive* model is more likely. Here an organization builds the

---

[1] These models were identified by Charles Krueger at a recent Dagstuhl workshop on software product lines (*www.dagstuhl.de*).

next member or members of the product family from earlier products. With each new product, the architecture and designs are extended as needed and the core asset base is built up from what has *turned out* to be common—instead of what was *preplanned* to be common. The reactive model puts much less emphasis on upfront planning and strategic direction setting. Rather, the organization lets itself be taken where the market dictates.

Knowing the various adoption models can help an organization choose the one that is right for it. The proactive model requires an initial investment but less rework than the reactive model. The reactive model relies exclusively on rework with little initial investment. Which model should act as a guide for a particular organization depends very much on the business situation.

CREATING PRODUCTS AND EVOLVING A PRODUCT LINE

An organization that has a product line will have an architecture and a collection of elements associated with it. From time to time, the organization will create a new member of the product line that will have features both in common with and different from those of other members.

One problem associated with a product line is managing its evolution. As time passes, the product line—or, in particualr, the set of core assets from which products are built—must evolve. That evolution will be driven by both external and internal sources:

1. *External sources*
   - New versions of elements in the line will be released by their vendors, and future products will need to be constructed from them.
   - Externally created elements may be added to the product line. Thus, for example, functions that were previously performed by internally developed elements may now be performed by elements acquired externally, or vice versa. Or future products will need to take advantage of new technology, as embodied in externally developed elements.
   - Features may be added to the product line to keep it responsive to user needs or competitive pressures.

2. *Internal sources*
   - It must be determined if new functions added to a product are within the product line's scope. If so, they can simply be built anew from the asset base. If not, a decision must be made: Either the enhanced product spins off from the product line, following its own evolutionary path, or the asset base must be expanded to include it. Updating the product line may be the wisest choice if the new functionality is likely to be used in future products, but this capability comes at the cost of the time necessary to update the core assets.
   - If the product line assets are changed, even if the organization is in a position to issue a "recall," replacing old products with ones built from the

most up-to-date version of the asset base does not mean that it should do so. Keeping products compatible with the product line takes time and effort. But not doing so may make future upgrades more time consuming, because either the product will need to be brought into compliance with the latest product line elements or it will not be able to take advantage of new functions added to the line.

ORGANIZATIONAL STRUCTURE

An asset base on which products depend, but which has its own evolutionary path, requires an organization to decide how to manage both it and product development. Jan Bosch [Bosch 00b] has studied product line organizational models and has identified four types.

1. *Development department.* All software development is concentrated in a single unit. Each unit member is expected to be a jack-of-all-trades in the product line, doing domain engineering or application engineering when and as appropriate. This model appears in small organizations and those that provide consulting services. Although it is simple, with short communication paths, having a single unit has a number of distinct drawbacks. Bosch wrote that it probably works only for units of up to 30 people (and that sounds high to us) but in very small organizations whose product lines are commensurately small, it can be a viable starting-out approach.

2. *Business units.* Each business unit is responsible for a subset of the systems in the product family, which are clustered by similarity. Shared assets are developed by the units that need them and made available to the community; collaboration across business units to develop new assets is possible. This model has variations depending on how flexible a business unit can be in developing (or modifying a shared asset). With no constraints, the products tend to diverge on their own evolutionary paths, negating the product line approach. Responsibility for particular assets is assigned to specific business units, which must maintain their assets for use by the entire product line. Other business units are required to make use of these assets. Bosch estimates that this model could apply to organizations with between 30 and 100 employees. It suffers from the obvious risk that a business unit will focus on its own product(s) first and the good of the product line will take a back seat.

3. *Domain engineering unit.* A special unit is given responsibility for the development and maintenance of the core asset base, from which business units build the products. Bosch writes that when organizations exceed 100 employees, communication channels among separate business units become untenable and a focusing channel to a central shared asset unit becomes necessary. In this model, a strong and disciplined process becomes much more important to manage the communication and to ensure that the overall health of the product line is the goal of all parties.

4. *Hierarchical domain engineering units.* It may pay to regard hierarchically a product line that is very large and/or very complex. That is, the product line may consist of subgroups that have more in common with each other than with other members of the product line. In this case, a domain engineering unit may turn out shared assets for the product line at large, and another domain engineering unit may turn out shared assets for the specialized subgroup. This example is of two levels, but the model could be extended indefinitely if the subgroups have specialized sub-subgroups, and so forth. Hierarchical domain units work for very large product lines, built by very large organizations. Their main disadvantage is the tendency to bloat, reducing the organization's responsiveness to new needs.

14.6 Summary

This chapter presented an architecture-based development paradigm known as software product lines. The product line approach is steadily climbing in popularity as more organizations see true order-of-magnitude improvements in cost, schedule, and quality from using it.

Like all new technologies, however, this one holds some surprises for the unaware. Architecturally, the key is identifying and managing commonalities and variations, but nontechnical issues must be addressed as well, including how the organization adopts the model, structures itself, and maintains its external interfaces.

14.7 For Further Reading

[Anastasopoulos 00] presents a nice list of variability techniques. [Jacobson 97] and [Svahnberg 00] also list these techniques.

[Clements 02a] is a comprehensive treatment of software product lines. It includes a number of case studies as well as a discussion of product line practice areas.

Organizational models are treated in [Bosch 00*b*].

The FAST process is from [Weiss 00]. The Philips example comes from [America 00]. Finally, the GM Powertrain example is taken from [Bass 00].

14.8 Discussion Question

1. Suppose a company builds two similar systems using a large set of common assets, including an architecture. Clearly these two systems form a product

line. If they shared only an architecture but no elements, would they still be a product line? Suppose they shared only a single element. Suppose that all they shared was the same operating system and programming language run-time libraries. Suppose that the shared asset was the team of developers. Would they be a product line then?

15

CelsiusTech
A Case Study in Product
Line Development
with Lisa Brownsword

> *We trained hard, but it seemed that every time we were beginning to form*
> *up into teams, we would be reorganized. I was to learn later in life that*
> *we tend to meet any new situation by reorganizing; and a wonderful*
> *method it can be for creating the illusion of progress while*
> *producing confusion, inefficiency, and demoralization.*
> — Petronius Arbiter, 210 B.C.

This chapter relates the experience of CelsiusTech AB, a Swedish naval defense contractor that successfully adopted a product line approach to building complex software-intensive systems. Called Ship System 2000 (SS2000), their product line consists of shipboard command-and-control systems for Scandinavian, Middle Eastern, and South Pacific navies.

This case study illustrates the entire Architecture Business Cycle (ABC), but especially shows how a product line architecture led CelsiusTech to new business opportunities. Figure 15.1 shows the roles of the ABC stakeholders in the CelsiusTech experience.

Note: Lisa Brownsword is a member of the technical staff at the Software Engineering Institute, Carnegie Mellon University.

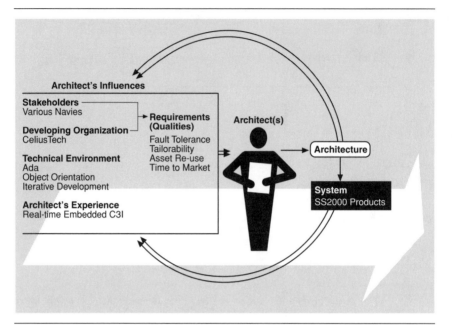

FIGURE 15.1   The ABC as applied to CelsiusTech

15.1   Relationship to the Architecture Business Cycle

CelsiusTech has long been known as a leading supplier of command-and-control systems within Sweden's largest, and one of Europe's leading, defense industry groups, which also includes Bofors, Kockums, FFV Aerotech, and Telub. At the time they developed the systems that are the subject of this chapter, CelsiusTech was composed of three companies: CelsiusTech Systems (advanced software systems), CelsiusTech Electronics (defense electronics), and CelsiusTech IT (information technology systems). It employed approximately 2,000 people and had annual sales of 300 million U.S. dollars. Their main site is near Stockholm, with subsidiaries located in Singapore, New Zealand, and Australia.

This study focuses on CelsiusTech Systems (CelsiusTech for short), whose focus includes command, control, and communication (C3) systems, fire control systems,[1] and electronic warfare systems for navy, army, and air force applications. The organization has undergone several changes in ownership and name since 1985 (see Figure 15.2). Originally Philips Elektronikindustrier AB, the division was sold to Bofors Electronics AB in 1989 and reorganized into NobelTech AB

---

[1] The term *fire control* refers to firing a gun at a moving target, from a platform that is itself moving with 6 degrees of freedom and flexing as well.

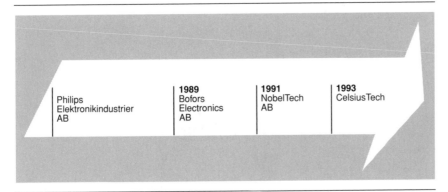

FIGURE 15.2   CelsiusTech Systems' corporate evolution

in 1991. It was purchased by CelsiusTech in 1993. Although senior management changed with each transaction, most of the mid- and lower-level management and the technical staff remained, thus providing continuity and stability.

THE SHIP SYSTEM 2000 NAVAL PRODUCT LINE

CelsiusTech's naval product line, known as Ship System 2000 (internally as Mk3), provides an integrated system that unifies all weapons, command-and-control, and communication systems on a warship. Typical system configurations include 1 million to 1.5 million lines of Ada code distributed on a local area network (LAN) with 30 to 70 microprocessors.

A wide variety of naval systems, both surface and submarine, have been or are being built from the same product line. These include the weapons, command-and-control, and communications portions of the following:

- Swedish Göteborg class coastal corvettes (KKV) (380 tons)
- Danish SF300 class multi-role patrol vessels (300 tons)
- Finnish Rauma class fast attack craft (FAC) (200 tons)
- Australian/New Zealand ANZAC frigates (3,225 tons)
- Danish Thetis class ocean patrol vessels (2,700 tons)
- Swedish Gotland class A19 submarines (1,330 tons)
- Pakistani Type 21 class frigates
- Republic of Oman patrol vessels
- Danish Niels Juel class corvettes

The Naval Systems division has sold more than 50 of its Mk3 naval systems to seven countries.

Figure 15.3 shows a Royal Swedish Navy multi-role corvette of the Göteborg class during a visit to Stockholm harbor. On top is the C/X-band antenna of the surveillance and target indication radar. Forward and aft of this, on top of the

FIGURE 15.3 Swedish multi-role Corvette of the Göteborg class featuring a CelsiusTech command-and-control system.   Photo from Studio FJK; reproduced with permission.

superstructure, are the two fully equipped fire control radar and optronic directors from CelsiusTech.

Systems built from the product line vary greatly in size, function, and armaments. Each country requires its own operator displays on different hardware and in different presentation languages. Sensors and weapons systems, and their interfaces to the software, also vary. Submarines have different requirements than surface vessels. Computers in the product line include 68020, 68040, RS/6000, and DEC Alpha platforms. Operating systems include OS2000 (a CelsiusTech product), IBM's AIX, POSIX, Digital's Ultrix, and others. The SS2000 product line supports this range of possible systems through a single architecture, a single core asset base, and a single organization.

ECONOMICS OF PRODUCT LINES: AN OVERVIEW OF CELSIUSTECH'S RESULTS

In this section we discuss CelsiusTech's results in building complex software-intense systems.

Shrinking Schedules.   Figure 15.4 shows the status and schedules for later systems under development from the CelsiusTech product line. Ships A and B were contracted for at the same time and, as we will see, caused CelsiusTech to move to a product line approach. System A is the basis of the product line. Customer project A ran almost nine years, although functional releases were running on the designated ship by late 1989. System B, the second of the two original projects, required approximately seven years to complete and is similar to the previous non-product-line Mk2.5 system. It was built in parallel with system A, validating the product line. While neither system individually showed greater

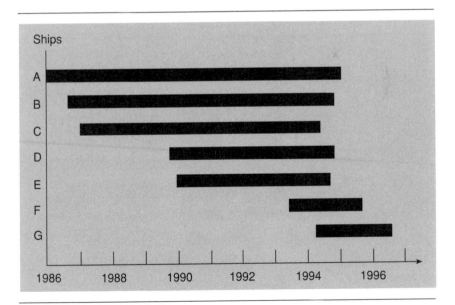

FIGURE 15.4   Product schedules

productivity, CelsiusTech was able to build both (and the product line) with roughly the same number of staff as for a single project.

Systems C and D were started after much of the product line existed, with a correspondingly shortened completion time. Systems E and F show a dramatic schedule reduction because they are fully leveraging the product line assets. Celsius-Tech reports that the last three ship systems were all *predictably* on schedule.

Code Re-use. While the production schedules show time to market for a product, they do not indicate how well the systems use a common asset base. Figure 15.5 shows the degree of commonality across the CelsiusTech naval systems. On average, 70% to 80% consist of elements used verbatim (i.e., checked out of a configuration control library and inserted without code modification).

Using Core Assets to Expand the Business Area. CelsiusTech has expanded its business into a related area that takes advantage of the architecture and other core assets that were originally developed for naval uses. STRIC, a new air defense system for the Swedish Air Force, embraces the abstraction that a ground platform is a ship whose location does not change very often and whose pitch and roll are constantly zero. Because of the flexibility (amenability to change) of the SS2000 architecture and product line, CelsiusTech was able to quickly build STRIC, lifting 40% of its elements directly from the SS2000 asset base. (See the sidebar Mastering Abstraction at CelsiusTech.) This demonstrates one of the feedback links in the ABC: The existence of the SS2000 product line and its architecture enabled new business opportunities.

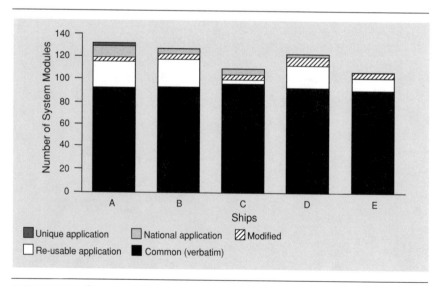

FIGURE 15.5 Commonality across CelsiusTech naval systems

Mastering Abstraction at CelsiusTech

Studying software product lines holds two particular fascinations for me. The first is discovering what all successful product line organizations have in common. Early in our study of product lines, the list of what I thought was required to be successful was fairly long. As we discovered and analyzed more examples, each brought with it a new dimension of experience and each seemed to whittle away at my list of organizational must-haves.

One common aspect still remains, however, and that is a product line mindset. A successful product line organization considers its business to be the care, nurturing, and growth of its software product line, *singular*, particularly its core asset base. This is in stark contrast to immature or unsuccessful product line organizations that see their enterprise as churning out a set of products, *plural*, that have some things in common.

The distinction is subtle but palpable. A product-based organization talks about its products and subjugates long-term product line goals to satisfy short-term product deadlines. Such an organization will, for example, reward workers for heroic measures to get a product out the door, even if it means performing a late night clone-and-own on a core asset. In contrast, a product-line-based organization talks about the product line and its health almost as if individual members of the family are coincidental byproducts. This singular mindset helps a product-line-based organization make strategic moves quickly and nimbly and as a unified whole.

The second fascination for me is what a successful product line organization can do, at the enterprise level, with this powerful capability. With an innate understanding of the product line's scope—that is, an articulated definition of what systems are within the product line's capability to build and what systems are not—an enterprise can make a conscious decision to "drive" its capability around the neighborhood and pick up business in nearby underutilized markets.

At CelsiusTech, both of these points were made eloquently by a cartoon I saw on a developer's bulletin board during our visit to gather information for this chapter. I wish I had asked for a photocopy of it, but it looked something like this:

> At about the time of our visit, CelsiusTech had announced a new project to build a product line of air defense systems—that is, ground-based anti-aircraft guns. The company estimated that on the day they made the announcement, fully 40% of the new product family was in place because it was based on Ship System 2000.
>
> The developer's cartoon made the point that an air defense system is just a simplified ship on land that does not pitch or roll much and stays stationary most of the time. It told me that the CelsiusTech staff had a firm grasp of the concept of abstraction, but it also told me that they had the product line mindset. This cartoon was not about the production of an air defense system but a celebration of what their beloved product line was about to become. It succinctly depicted the company's enterprise-level foray into a whole new business area via its product line capability. That cartoon was a magnificent exhibition of one organization's product line sophistication.
>
> *— PCC*

WHAT MOTIVATED CELSIUSTECH?

To understand why CelsiusTech made the decision to develop a product line and what actions were required, it is important to know where it began. Prior to 1986, the company developed more than 100 systems, in 25 configurations, ranging in size from 30,000 to 700,000 source lines of code (SLOC) in the fire control domain.

From 1975 to 1980, CelsiusTech shifted its technology base from analog to 16-bit digital, creating the so-called Mk2 systems. These tended to be small, real-time, and embedded. The company progressively expanded both system functionality and expertise with real-time applications in the course of building and delivering 15 systems.

From 1980 to 1985, customer requirements were shifting toward the integration of fire control and weapons with command and control, thus increasing the size and complexity of delivered systems. The Mk2 architecture was expanded to provide for multiple autonomous processing nodes on point-to-point links, resulting in Mk2.5. Mk2.5 systems were substantially larger, in both delivered code (up to 700,000 SLOC) and number of developers (300 engineer-years over 7 years).

Conventional development approaches were used for Mk2.5. These had served the company well on the smaller Mk2 systems, but difficulties in predictable and timely integration, cost overruns, and schedule slippage resulted. Such experiences were painful, but they were important lessons for CelsiusTech. The company gained useful experience in the elementary distribution of real-time processes onto autonomous links and in the use of a high-level, real-time programming language (in this case, the Pascal-like RTL/2). Figure 15.6 shows the systems built by CelsiusTech prior to 1985.

In 1985, a defining event for CelsiusTech (then Philips) occurred. The company was awarded two major contracts simultaneously—one for the Swedish Navy

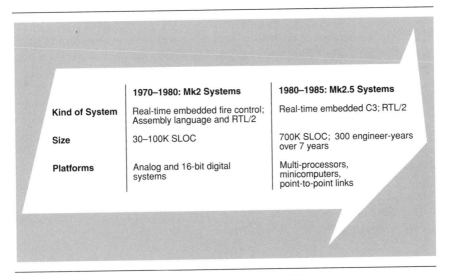

	1970–1980: Mk2 Systems	1980–1985: Mk2.5 Systems
Kind of System	Real-time embedded fire control; Assembly language and RTL/2	Real-time embedded C3; RTL/2
Size	30–100K SLOC	700K SLOC; 300 engineer-years over 7 years
Platforms	Analog and 16-bit digital systems	Multi-processors, minicomputers, point-to-point links

FIGURE 15.6   Systems built by CelsiusTech prior to 1985

and one for the Danish Navy. Requirements for both ships indicated the need for systems larger and more sophisticated than the Mk2.5s, which had suffered from schedule and budget difficulties. Having to build two even larger systems, let alone in parallel, presented management and senior technical staff with a severe dilemma. Clearly, the development technologies and practices applied on the Mk2.5 system would not be sufficient to produce the new systems with any reasonable certainty of schedule, cost, and required functionality. Staffing requirements alone would have been prohibitive.

This situation provided the genesis of a new business strategy that recognized the potential *business* opportunity of selling and building a series, or family, of related systems rather than some number of specific systems. Thus began the SS2000 product line. Another business driver was the recognition of a 20- to 30-year lifespan for naval systems. During that time, changes in threat requirements and in technology advances would have to be addressed. The more flexible and extensible the product line, the greater the business opportunities. These business drivers or requirements forged the technical strategy.

The technical strategy would need to provide a flexible and robust set of building blocks to populate the product line from which new systems could be assembled with relative ease. As new system requirements arose, new building blocks could be added to the product line to sustain its business viability.

In defining the technical strategy, an assessment of the Mk2.5 technology infrastructure indicated serious limitations. A strategic decision was made to create a new-generation system (the Mk3) that would include new hardware and software and a new supporting development approach. This would serve as the infrastructure for new systems development for the next decade or two.

EVERYTHING WAS NEW

CelsiusTech's decision to convert its business strategy to a product line approach coincided with a time of high technology flux. This meant that, to implement the technical strategy for the SS2000 product line, virtually all aspects of the hardware, the software, and development support would have to change. Thus, the hardware shifted from VAX/VMS minicomputers to Motorola 68000-series microcomputers. Whereas the Mk2.5 systems consisted of a small number of processors on point-to-point links, the SS2000 products have a large number of highly distributed processors with fault-tolerant requirements. The software life-cycle approach shifted from RTL/2-based structured analysis/design and waterfall development to Ada83 with more object-based and iterative development processes. Development support migrated from custom, locally created and maintained development tools to a large, commercially supplied environment. The major technical differences are summarized in Figure 15.7.

ANALYSIS OF THE BUSINESS CONTEXT

The CelsiusTech experience reveals several factors that played an important role in the establishment of the SS2000 product line, some of which were advantages, some inhibitors.

Ownership Changes. While it is routine to buy, sell, and restructure companies, the impact on an organization attempting to adopt significantly different

Prior to 1986 Previous Technical Infrastructure	1986 New Technical Infrastructure
• Minicomputers	• Microcomputers
• Few processors on point-to-point links	• Many processors on commercial LAN
• No fault tolerance	• Fault tolerant, redundant
• RTL/2	• Ada83
• Waterfall life cycle, early attempts at incremental development	• Prototyping, iterative, incremental development
• Structured analysis and design	• Domain analysis, object-based analysis and design
• Locally developed support tools	• Rational development environment

FIGURE 15.7 Changing technical infrastructures

business and technical strategies can be devastating. Typically, management changes associated with company ownership transactions are sufficient to stop any transition or improvement efforts under way (as observed by Petronius Arbiter over two millennia ago). That this did not happen at CelsiusTech can be attributed either to strong and far-sighted top management or to top management's preoccupation with the other issues. Since CelsiusTech changed hands several times during this period, the latter explanation is more likely. It is clear that middle management had a strong commitment to a product line and were allowed to proceed unfettered by top management, who might otherwise have been hesitant to approve the necessary upfront investments. Normally a reorganization disrupts the entire organization. In the CelsiusTech case, the effects of the reorganizations and changes of ownership were buffered by middle management.

Necessity.   The award of two major naval contracts in 1986, ostensibly a reason for celebration, was regarded as a crisis by CelsiusTech. Management immediately realized that they had neither the technical means nor the personnel resources to simultaneously pursue two large development efforts, each pioneering new technologies and application areas. Since all CelsiusTech contracts are fixed price, large-scale failure meant large-scale disaster. Indeed, less challenging systems had been over budget, past schedule, hard to integrate, and impossible to predict.

CelsiusTech was driven to the product line approach by circumstances; they were compelled to attempt it because their viability was clearly at stake. The fact that this period was also one of major technological change made it much more difficult to separate the costs associated with product line changes from those associated with adopting new technology.

Technology Changes.   In 1986, all the chosen technologies were immature, with limited use in large industrial settings. Big, real-time, distributed systems making extensive use of Ada tasks and generics were envisioned but at the time were unprecedented. Moreover, object-based development for Ada was still a theoretical discussion. From 1986 to 1989, then, CelsiusTech was coping with the following:

- The maturation of technologies, such as Ada and object technology
- The maturation of supporting technology, such as networking and distribution
- The maturation of infrastructure technology, such as development environments and tools to assist in the automation of development processes
- The learning curve of the company, both technical and managerial, in the use of new technologies and processes inherent in the product line approach
- The learning curve of customers, who did not fully understand the contractual, technical, and business approaches of product lines
- The management of similar requirements across several customers

These maturation issues significantly increased the time required to create the product line. An organization making the same development paradigm shift today would be in a much better position, with microcomputers, networks, portable operating systems, open systems standards, object-based development methods, Ada (or other programming languages appropriate to the domain and platforms), performance engineering, distributed systems technology, real-time operating systems, real-time analysis tools, large-project support environments, and large-project process assistants. These technologies are all either mature or at least usable and readily available. Also, much more is known about building and fielding software product lines (see Chapter 14). CelsiusTech estimates that up to one-third of its initial technology investment was spent building assets that can now be purchased commercially.

CELSIUSTECH'S ORGANIZATIONAL STRUCTURE

CelsiusTech's organizational structure and practices did not remain constant over the ten-year period covered here, but migrated through several distinct structures. The kind of knowledge and skills required of the staff also changed.

Project Organization Prior to 1986. The naval command-and-control system (Mk2.5) development was headed by a project manager who used the services of various functional areas, such as weapons or C3, to develop major segments of system capability. Figure 15.8 shows the organizational structure for the Mk2.5 project. Each functional area (command-and-control, tracking, etc.) was led by a project manager who had direct authority for staff resources and for all system development activities through release to system integration.

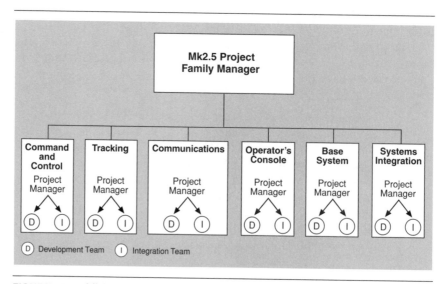

FIGURE 15.8 Mk2.5 project organization, 1980–1985

CelsiusTech found that this compartmentalized arrangement fostered a mode of development characterized by the following:

- Assignment of major system segments to their respective functional areas as part of system analysis
- Requirements and interfaces allocated and described in documents, with limited communication across functional area boundaries, resulting in individual interpretation of requirements and interfaces throughout design, implementation, and test
- Interface incompatibilities typically not discovered until system integration, resulting in time wasted in assigning responsibility and protracted, difficult integration and installation
- Functional area managers with little understanding of areas other than their own
- Functional area managers with limited incentives to work as a team to resolve program-level issues

SS2000 Organization Late 1986 to 1991.   With the introduction of the SS2000 product line in late 1986 came a number of organizational changes from the Mk2.5 project organization. Figure 15.9 shows the organizational structure CelsiusTech used from late 1986 until 1991. A general program manager designated to lead

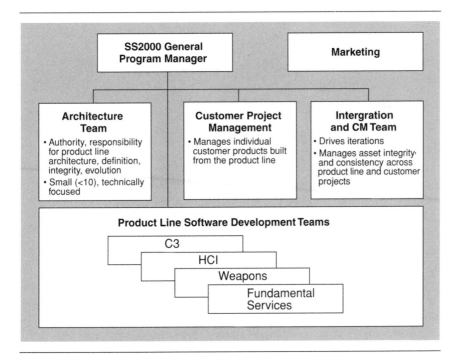

FIGURE 15.9   SS2000 organization, 1987–1991

the program was responsible for both creation of the product line and delivery of customer systems built from it. CelsiusTech sought to remedy the problems associated with the compartmentalized structure of the past by creating a strong management team focused on product line development as a company asset rather than on "empire building." To this end, functional area managers now reported directly to the general program manager. Developers were assigned to functional areas—weapons, C3, or human–computer interface (HCI), common services (used by the functional areas), and the interface to the various hardware and operating systems (called the Base System).

A small, technically focused architecture team with total ownership and control was created, reporting directly to the general program manager. CelsiusTech determined that the success of a product line hinged on a stable yet flexible architecture, one that was visible throughout the organization and vested with authority from the highest levels of management. In this way, the company reorganized itself to take advantage of the ABC: Architecture had to be at the heart of their new approach, and the architecture in turn changed important aspects of the organization.

The coordinated definition and management of multiple releases was central to the creation of a product line. To better support their release management, CelsiusTech combined software system integration and configuration management into a new group, reporting directly to the general program manager. Both the architecture team and the integration–configuration management group were novel approaches for CelsiusTech and were instrumental in the creation of the SS2000 product line.

The architecture team was responsible for the initial development and continued ownership and control of the product line architecture. This ensured design consistency and design interpretation across *all* functional areas. Specifically, the architecture team had responsibility and authority for the following:

- Creation of product line concepts and principles
- Identification of layers and their exported interfaces
- Interface definition, integrity, and controlled evolution
- Allocation of system functions to layers
- Identification of common mechanisms or services
- Definition, prototyping, and enforcement of common mechanisms such as error handling and interprocess communication protocols
- Communication to the project staff of the product line concepts and principles

The first iteration of the architecture was produced in two weeks by two senior engineers with extensive domain experience. It remains the framework for the existing product line, containing organizing concepts, layer definition, identification of approximately 125 system functions (out of the current 200 or so) and their allocation to specified layers, and the principal distribution and communication mechanisms. After completion of the first iteration, the architecture team took on the lead designers from each of the functional areas. The full team, now comprising ten senior engineers, continued to expand and refine the architecture. This was in sharp contrast to the past, when functional area leaders had autonomy for the design and interfaces for their respective areas.

The combined integration and configuration management team was responsible for the following:

- Development of test strategies, plans, and test cases beyond unit test
- Coordination of all test runs
- Development of incremental build schedules (in conjunction with the architecture team)
- Integration and release of valid subsystems
- Configuration management of development and release libraries
- Creation of the software delivery medium

SS2000 Organization 1992 to 1998.   From 1992 to 1994, CelsiusTech's emphasis increasingly shifted from the *development* of the architecture and product line elements to the *composition* of new customer systems from the product line. This trend increased the size and responsibilities of the customer project management group. CelsiusTech modified its organizational structure to assign the development staff to one of the following:

- *Component projects that develop, integrate, and manage product line elements.* The production was distributed across component project areas consisting of the functional areas (weapons, C3, and HCI), common services, and the operating system and network elements. Component project managers were rotated regularly, providing middle management with a broader understanding of the product line. The elements were provided to the customer projects.
- *Customer projects responsible for all financial, scheduling and planning, and requirements analysis through system integration/test/delivery.* Each customer system built from the product line was assigned a project manager responsible for all interactions and negotiations with the customer.

As CelsiusTech completed the basic product line and gained further experience using it, it looked for more efficient ways to produce systems and evolve the product line to take advantage of newer technology and changing customer needs. This was a feedback effect of the ABC, where the architecture caused the organization to continually reinvent itself, resulting in the organizational structure shown in Figure 15.10.

Each major application domain (naval and air defense) became its own business unit with its own manager. Each business unit had a marketing group, a proposal group, a customer projects group, and a systems definition group. The business unit was responsible for its software elements and its customer project managers. Each unit's operations were guided by a Marketing Plan, a Product Plan, and a Technical–Architecture Plan. The marketing group was responsible for the Marketing Plan that assessed the opportunities and value of each market

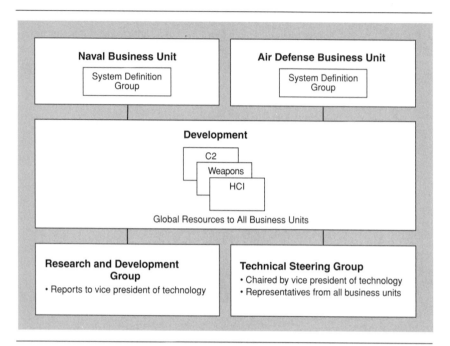

FIGURE 15.10   SS2000 organization, 1992–1998

segment. The Product Plan described the products the business unit sold and was owned by the proposal group. The Product Plan implemented the Marketing Plan. The system definition group was responsible for the Technical–Architecture Plan for their business unit. In turn the Technical–Architecture Plan implemented the Product Plan, outlining the evolution of the business unit's architecture. New project proposals took into account the business unit's Product and Technical–Architecture Plans. This approach kept the projects aligned with the product line.

Modules were supplied by the Development Group. Any customer-specific tailoring or development was managed from the business unit customer project using Development Group resources. The business unit's Systems Definition Group was responsible for the architecture. It owned and controlled the evolution of the architecture and major interfaces and mechanisms. For the Naval Business Unit, the Systems Definition Group was small (typically six members), consisting of senior engineers with extensive knowledge of the naval product line. It was responsible for overall arbitration of customer requirements and their impact on the product line.

The Naval Business Unit sponsored an SS2000 Product Line Users Group to serve as a forum for shared customer experiences with the product line and to provide direction for its evolution. The Users Group included representatives from all SS2000 customers.

The Development Group provided developer resources to all business units. Integration, configuration management, and quality assurance were also Development Group resources, matrixed to the business units as required. To further optimize creation of new systems from the product line, a Basic SS2000 Configuration Project was formed to create a basic, preintegrated core configuration of approximately 500K SLOC, complete with documentation and test cases that would become the nucleus of a new customer system.

The Technical Steering Group (TSG) was responsible for identifying, evaluating, and piloting potential new technology beneficial to any of CelsiusTech's business areas. It was headed by the vice president of technology and staffed by senior technical personnel from the naval and air defense business units, the Development Group, and the R&D Group. The TSG ensured that each Systems Definition Group created and evolved its architecture and technology plan.

Staffing Late 1986 to 1991.   As shown in Figure 15.11, the project staffing levels ranged from an initial 20 to 30 to a peak of more than 200, with an average of 150. During the early stages of the program, while product line concepts and architecture were being defined, CelsiusTech found the staff levels too high. There was confusion among developers because concepts and approaches were in a state of flux.

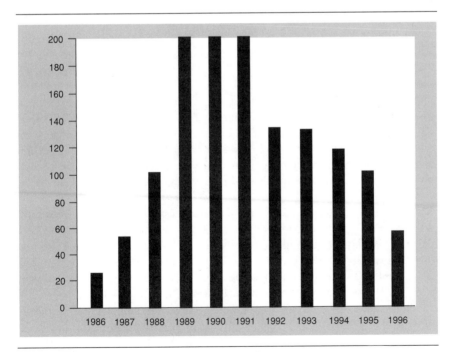

FIGURE 15.11   Approximate software staff profiles

The architecture team was responsible for creating the framework for the product line. Team members needed solid domain and customer knowledge combined with engineering skills and an ability to find relevant common mechanisms or product line elements. Communication and teaming skills were also mandatory. Developers needed to understand the framework, the building codes, and how their respective modules should fit. During the product line's formative period, the development staff required skills in the use of Ada, object-based design, and their software development environment, including the target testbed. In addition, they had to have broad knowledge of product line concepts, SS2000 architecture and mechanisms, creation of re-usable modules, incremental integration, and at least one functional area domain.

With much of the necessary technology immature, the management team (and senior technical staff) was operating largely on faith in the achievement of a shared ultimate capability. A key focus of their responsibilities included "selling" the business need and the desired future state to their teams.

Organizations that attempt to install immature technology encounter resistance as inevitable problems arise. Key to sustaining the early phases of such installations is strong, solutions-oriented management. At CelsiusTech, the general program manager focused on finding solutions rather than finding fault with the various immature technologies, their suppliers, or the development team. Managed experimentation was encouraged, not penalized, and technical innovations were supported. The general program manager thus became a role model for other managers.

During the formative years of the product line, managers were required to have extensive knowledge of product line concepts and business motivation. In addition, they needed strong skills in planning, communication, and innovative problem solving.

Management also had to cope with the inevitable discontent and resistance associated with a new business paradigm and its attendant technology. Substantial effort was made to help personnel understand the new business strategy and rationale. People who did not subscribe to or could not grasp the product line approach either left the company or found assignments on maintenance or other projects. This caused a loss of domain knowledge that took time to regain.

Staffing 1992 to 1998. By the end of 1991, four customer systems were under way, and a sufficient number of re-usable modules not only existed but had been delivered as part of the original two systems. The core of the product line was maturing rapidly so that, rather than all new modules, systems were now routinely composed from existing modules. Designers were needed less and were reassigned to other projects within the company. Howerer, with the increase in parallel customer projects, more integrators were needed, although the average of three to five per customer system remained steady. Because of the increasing number of projects during this period, the number of management staff did not decrease.

From 1994 to 1998, the staffing profile continued to change. As the product line and its use matured, CelsiusTech used fewer designers, developers, and integrators for the two latest customer systems in that period. Ever fewer designers were needed, potentially moving between business units. The downward trend was most notable in integration, given that CelsiusTech budgeted for an integration staff of one or two per system. Continuing system composition optimizations, such as the Basic SS2000 Configuration project, were expected to further reduce development-related staff levels. With the continued increase in parallel customer projects, the number of management staff remained constant.

With greater emphasis on the *composition* of systems from the product line, developers needed stronger domain and SS2000 knowledge than during product line creation. The use of Ada, object technology, and their development environment had become more routine. The integration group's focus turned to the integration and release management of many parallel systems. Increasing emphasis was placed on re-using test plans and data sets across customer systems.

The architecture team needed to maintain a solid knowledge of the product line and factor in growing current and approaching customer needs. Communication with customer project managers (for negotiation of multiple customer needs) and developers (desiring to optimize major interfaces and mechanisms) continued to be extremely important. Engineering skill to balance new needs yet preserve overall architectural integrity was vital for team members as they continually evolved the architecture and its major interfaces and mechanisms. The architecture team was involved in technical evaluations, prototype development of new interfaces (both for the external user and for application developers), and assessing the impact of the new technologies on the product line.

Less emphasis on technology maturation and training was required of management as more of the product line became available. With a larger set of customer systems existing, coordination of changing customer requirements across multiple customers emerged as a major management priority. Requirements negotiation involved not only customers but also other customer project managers and the product line architecture team. Customer project managers required increasing skill in negotiation and greater knowledge of the existing and anticipated future directions of the product line.

15.2 Requirements and Qualities

For new products to be derived from an organizational repository, they must be structured so that they can share modules. As we discussed in Chapter 14, this means that there must be a standard set of modules, with agreements about individual module's responsibility, behavior, performance, interface, locality of function, communication and coordination mechanisms, and other properties. This familywide structure, the modules it comprises, and the properties about each that are constant across all members of the product line constitute the *product line architecture*.

As we have seen throughout this book, the primary purpose of an architecture is to acheive a system that meets its behavioral and quality requirements. The architecture for each SS2000 product line member was no exception. The most important of these requirements were:

- *Performance*. Command-and-control systems must respond in real time to continuously arriving sensor inputs and be able to control weapons under tight deadlines.
- *Modifiability*. The architecture needs to be robust with respect to computing platforms, operating systems, addition or replacement of sensor and weapon systems, human–computer interface requirements, communication protocols, and the like.
- *Safety, reliability, and availability*. The system must be available when needed, provide the correct data and commands to weapon systems, and fire only under the correct conditions.
- *Testability*. Each system must be integrable and testable so that errors (if any) are quickly found, isolated, and corrected.

Besides these single-system requirements, the SS2000 architecture carried the additional burden of application to an entire class of systems. Thus its requirements included the ability to replace one module with another tailored to a particular system without disrupting the rest of the architecture.

OPERATING ENVIRONMENT AND PHYSICAL ARCHITECTURE

The requirements of modern shipboard systems influence design solutions in profound ways. Sensors and weapons systems are deployed all over the ship; crew members interact with them via a multitude of separately housed workstations. The HCI must be highly tuned to facilitate rapid information flow and command acceptance and must be tailored to the operational mission of the vessel and the cultural idiosyncrasies of its crew. The likelihood of component failure dictates a fault-tolerant design.

Figure 15.12 is a physical view of a typical system. A redundant LAN is the communications backbone, connecting from 30 to 70 different, cooperating processors. Nodes on the LAN can total around 30. A *node* is the end of a communication run and may correspond to a crew station, a weapons platform, or a sensor suite, all located in various parts of the ship and widely dispersed. It may host up to six processors. The LAN is a dual Ethernet. Device-interface modules send and receive data to and from the system's peripherals, primarily sensors, and the weapons systems being controlled.

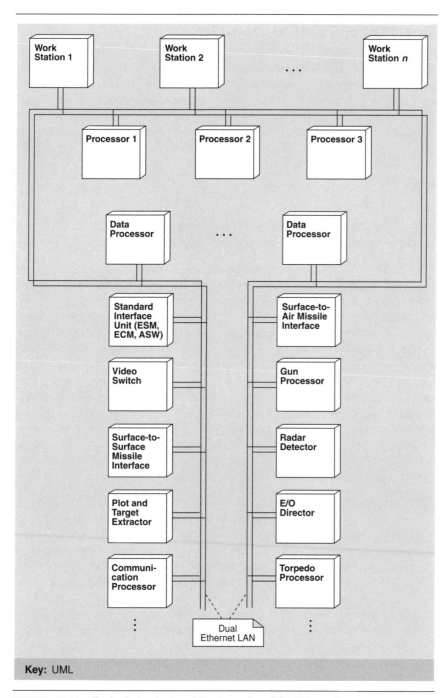

FIGURE 15.12   Typical physical architecture of an SS2000 product

15.3   Architectural Solution

We describe the architecture using three views—the process view so that we can explain how distribution was accomplished; the layered view as a basis for discussing how Ship System 2000 achieves a separation of concerns; and a module decomposition view to show assignment of responsibilities to different large-scale elements of the system, called *system functions* and *system function groups*. After presenting the architecture in terms of these three views, we discuss some of the issues that arose at CelsiusTech that are specific to the maintenance and use of a product line.

THE PROCESS VIEW: MEETING REQUIREMENTS
FOR DISTRIBUTION AND PRODUCT LINE SUPPORT

Each CPU runs a set of Ada programs; each Ada program runs on at most one processor. A program may consist of several Ada tasks. Systems in the SS2000 product line can consist of up to 300 Ada programs.

The requirement to run on a distributed computing platform has broad implications for the software architecture. First, it necessitates building the system as a set of communicating processes, bringing the process view into play. Having a process view at all means that the performance tactic "introduce concurrency" has been applied. Distributed systems also raise issues of deadlock avoidance, communication protocols, fault tolerance in the case of a failed processor or communications link, network management and saturation avoidance, and performance concerns for coordination among tasks. A number of conventions are used to support the distribution. These respond to the distributed requirements of the architecture as well as its product line aspects. The tasks and intercomponent conventions include the following:

- Communication among components is by the passing of strongly typed messages. The abstract data type and the manipulating programs are provided by the component passing the message. Strong typing allows compile-time elimination of whole classes of errors. The message as the primary interface mechanism between components allows components to be written independently of each other's (changeable) implementation details with respect to data representation.
- Inter-process communication is the protocol for data transport between Ada applications that supports location independence, allowing communication between applications regardless of their residence on particular processors. This "anonymity of processor assignment" allows processes to be migrated across processors, for pre-runtime performance tuning and runtime reconfiguration as an approach to fault tolerance, with no accompanying change in source code.
- Ada task facilities are used to implement the threading model.

A producer of data does its job without knowing who the consumer of that data is. Data maintenance and update are conceptually separate from data usage. This is an application of the tactic "introduce an intermediary" to achieve modifiability, which the designers accomplished using a blackboard pattern. The main consumer of the data is the HCI component. The component that contains the repository is called the common object manager (COOB).

Figure 15.13 illustrates the role of the COOB at runtime. It shows not only the data flow that uses the COOB but also the data flows that bypass the COOB for reasons of performance. Track information (the positional history of a target), carried in a large data structure, is passed directly between producer and consumer, as is trackball information because of its very high update frequency.

Data-producing conventions include the following:

- Data is sent only when altered. This prevents unnecessary message traffic from entering the network.
- Data is presented as object-oriented abstractions in order to insulate programs from changing implementations. Strong typing allows compile-time detection of variable misuse errors.
- Components own the data they alter and supply access procedures that act as monitors. This eliminates race conditions because each piece of data is accessed directly only by the component that owns it.
- Data is accessible to all interested parties at all nodes in a system. Assignment to a particular node does not affect the data a component can access.
- Data is distributed so that response time to a retrieval request is short.
- Data is kept consistent within the system over the long term. Short-term inconsistencies are tolerable.

Network-related conventions include the following:

- Network load is kept low by design—that is, considerable design effort goes into managing the data flow on the network, ensuring that only essential information is transmitted.

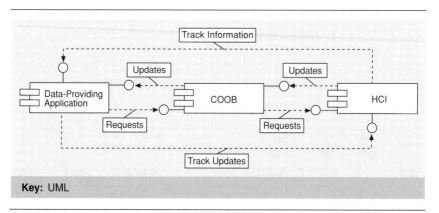

FIGURE 15.13   Using (and bypassing) the COOB

- Data channels are error resistant. Applications resolve errors internally as much as possible.
- It is acceptable for an application to "miss" an occasional data update. For instance, because a ship's position changes continuously, a position update may be missed but interpolated from surrounding updates.

Miscellaneous conventions include the following:

- Heavy use is made of Ada generics for re-usability.
- Ada standard exception protocols are used.

Many of these conventions (particularly those regarding abstract data types, IPC, message passing, and data ownership) allow a module to be written independently of many changeable aspects over which it has no control. In other words, the modules are more general and hence more directly usable in different systems.

THE LAYERED VIEW

The architecture for SS2000 is layered, as follows:

- The grouping of modules is roughly based on the type of information they encapsulate. Modules that must be modified if hardware platform, underlying LAN, or internode communication protocols are changed form one layer. Modules that implement functionality common to all members of the family form another. Modules specific to a particular customer product form a layer also.
- The layers are ordered, with hardware-dependent layers at one end of the relation and application-specific layers at the other.
- The layering is "strict," meaning that interactions among layers are restricted. A module residing in one layer can only access modules in its own or the next lower layer.

In SS2000, the bottom layer is known as Base System 2000; it provides an interface between operating system, hardware, and network on the one hand and application programs on the other. To applications programmers, Base System 2000 provides a programming interface with which they can perform intercomponent communication and interaction without being sensitive to the particular underlying computing platforms, network topologies, allocation of functions to processors, and so on. Figure 15.14 illustrates the architectural layers of SS2000.

THE MODULE DECOMPOSITION VIEW: SYSTEM FUNCTIONS AND SYSTEM FUNCTION GROUPS

As we mentioned in Chapter 2, an organization often has its own terms for the modules it introduces in a module decomposition view. CelsiusTech's modules were called system functions and system function groups.

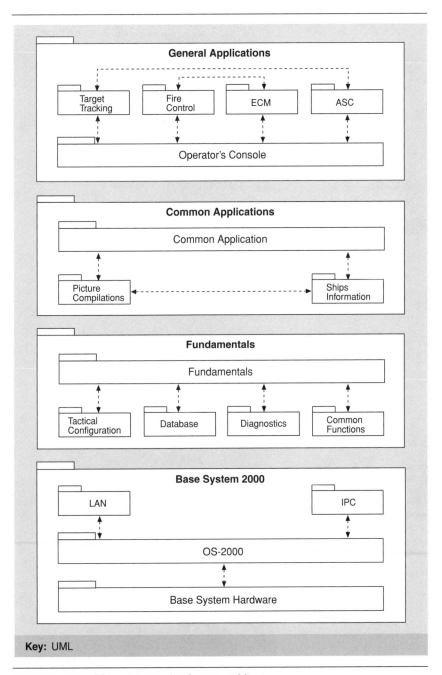

FIGURE 15.14 SS2000 layered software architecture

System functions are the primary element of module decomposition in SS2000. A system function is a collection of software that implements a logically connected set of requirements. It is composed of a number of Ada code units. A *system function group* comprises a set of system functions and forms the basic work assignment for a development team. SS2000 consists of about 30 system function groups, each comprising up to 20 or so system functions. They are clustered around major functional areas, including the following:

- Command, control, and communications
- Weapons control
- Fundamentals—facilities for intrasystem communication and interfacing with the computing environment
- Human–computer interface

Figure 15.15 illustrates the relationship between the various module types.

System function groups may (and do) contain system functions of more than one layer. They correspond to bigger pieces of functionality that are more appropriately developed by a large team. For example, a separate software requirements specification is written for each system function group.

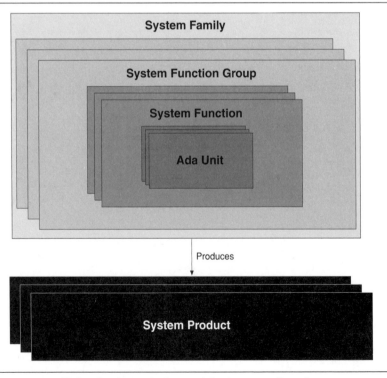

FIGURE 15.15   Units of software in the module decomposition view

System functions and system function groups, not the Ada code units, are the basic units of test and integration for the product line. This is crucial because it allows a new member of the product line to be treated as the composition of a few dozen high-quality, high-confidence modules that interact in controlled, predictable ways, as opposed to thousands of small units that must be regression-tested with each change. Assembly of large pretested elements was a key to making re-use work at CelsiusTech.

APPLYING THE SS2000 ARCHITECTURE

Table 15.2 summarizes the architectural goals for SS2000 and the approaches and tactics (from Chapter 5) used to achieve them. This section concludes the

TABLE 15.2   SS2000 Requirements and How the Architecture Achieved Them

Requirement	How Achieved	Related Tactic(s)
Performance	Strict network traffic protocols; software is written as a set of processes to maximize concurrency and written to be location independent, allowing for relocation to tune performance; COOB is by-passed for high-data-volume transactions; otherwise, data sent only when altered and distributed so response times are short	Introduce concurrency Reduce demand Multiple copies Increase resources
Reliability, Availability, and Safety	Redundant LAN; fault-tolerant software; standard Ada exception protocols; software written to be location independent and hence can be migrated in case of failure; strict ownership of data prevents multi-writer race conditions	Exceptions Active redundancy State resynchronization Transactions
Modifiability (including ability to produce new members of the SS2000 family)	Strict use of message-based communication provides interface isolated from implementation details; software written to be location independent; layering provides portability across platforms, network topologies, IPC protocols, etc.; data producers and consumers unaware of each other because of COOB; heavy use of Ada generics; heavy use of element parameterization; system functions and system function groups provide semantic coherence	Semantic coherence Anticipate expected changes Generalize modules Abstract common services Interface stability Intermediary Configuration files Component replacement Adherence to defined protocols
Testability	Interfaces using strongly typed messages push a whole class of errors to compile time; strict data ownership, semantic coherence of elements, and strong interface definitions simplify discovery of responsibility	Separate interface from implementation

presentation of the architecture by discussing four important issues that arose in building and maintaining the architecture and in building a family of systems from it.

Architecture as the Foundation. Although this case study emphasizes that technical solutions in a product line are insufficient without taking into account business and organizational issues as well, it remains a fact that the SS2000 architecture was the means for achieving a product line. Toward this end, abstraction and layering were vital. Abstraction allowed creation of modules that encapsulated changeable decisions within the boundaries of their interfaces. When a module is used in multiple products, the changeable decisions are instantiated whenever possible by parameterization. When the modules change across time as new requirements are accommodated, the changeable decisions held inside the module ensure that wholesale changes to the asset base are not needed.

The size and complexity of this architecture and the modules that populate it make clear that a thorough understanding of the application domain is required if a system is to be partitioned into modules that can be developed independently, are appropriate for a product line whose products are as widely varied as those in SS2000, and can accommodate evolution with ease.

Maintaining the Asset Base as New Systems Are Produced. As we discussed, the enduring product at CelsiusTech is not an individual ship for a specific customer, or even the set of systems deployed so far. Rather, the central task is viewed as maintaing the *product line itself*. Maintaining the product line means maintaining the re-usable assets in such a way that any previous member of the product line can be regenerated (they change and evolve and grow, after all, as their requirements change) and future members can be built. In a sense, maintaining the product line means maintaining a *capability*, the *capability* to produce products from the assets. Maintaining this capability means keeping re-usable modules up to date and general. No product is allowed to evolve in isolation from the product line. This is one approach to solving the problem, which we identified in Chapter 14, of keeping the evolution of the product line synchronized with the evolution of the variants.

Not every module is used in every member of the product line. Cryptologic and human interface requirements differ so widely across nationalities, for instance, that it makes more sense to build modules that are used in a few systems than to attempt a more general solution. In a sense, this yields product lines within the major product line: a Swedish set of products, a Danish set of products, and so on. Some modules are used only once but even these are maintained as product line assets, designed and built to be configurable and flexible, in case a new product is developed that can make use of them.

Externally, CelsiusTech builds ship systems. Internally, they evolve and grow a common asset base that provides the capability to turn out ship systems. This mentality—which is what it is—might sound subtle, but it manifests itself in the configuration control policies, the organization of the enterprise, and the way that new products are marketed.

Maintaining Large Pre-integrated Chunks.   In the classic literature on software re-use repositories, the unit of re-use is typically either a small fine-grained module (such as an Ada package, a subroutine, or an object) or a large-scale independently executing subsystem (such as a tool or a commercial standalone product). In the former case, the small modules must be assembled, integrated, configured, and tested after checking out; in the latter case, the subsystems are typically not very configurable or flexible.

CelsiusTech took an intermediate approach. Their unit of re-use is a system function, a thread of related functionality that comprises modules from different layers in the architecture. System functions are pre-integrated—that is, the modules they comprise have been assembled, compiled together, tested individually, and tested as a unit. When the system function is checked out of the asset repository, it is ready for use. In this way, CelsiusTech is not only re-using modules but also re-using the integration and test effort that would otherwise have to be repeated for each application.

Parameterized modules.   Although modules are re-used with no change in code in most cases, they are not always re-used entirely without change. Many of the elements are written with symbolic values in place of absolute quantities that may change from system to system. For example, a computation within some module may be a function of how many processors there are; however, that number need not be known when the module is written; therefore, the module may be written with the number of processors as a symbolic value—a parameter—the value of which is bound as the system is integrated. The module works correctly at runtime but can be used without code change in another version of the system that features a different number of processors.

Parameters are a simple, effective, and time-honored means to achieve module re-use. However, in practice they tend to multiply at an alarming rate. Almost any module can be made more general via parameterization. The modules for SS2000 feature 3,000 to 5,000 parameters that must be individually tuned for each customer system built from the product line. CelsiusTech had no way to tell that a certain combination of parameter values, when instantiated into a running system, would not lead to some sort of illegal operating state.

The fact that there were so many parameters undermined some of the benefits gained from treating large system functions and system function groups as the basic units of test and integration. As parameters are tuned for a new version of the system, they in fact produce a version that has never been tested. Moreover, each combination of parameter values may theoretically take the system into operating states that have never been experienced, let alone exhaustively tested.

Only a small proportion of the possible parameter combinations will ever occur. However, there is a danger that unwillingness to "try out" a new parameter combination could inhibit exploiting the built-in flexibility (configurability) of the elements.

In practice, the multitude of parameters seems to be mostly a bookkeeping worry; there has never been any incorrect operation that could be traced back solely to a set of parameter specifications. Often, a large module is imported with its parameter set unchanged from its previous utilization.

15.4 Summary

Between 1986 and 1998 CelsiusTech evolved from a defense contractor providing custom-engineered point solutions to essentially a vendor of commercial off-the-shelf naval systems. They found the old ways of organizational structure and management insufficient to support the emerging business model. They also found that achieving and sustaining an effective product line was not simply a matter of the right software and system architecture, development environment, hardware, or network. Organizational structure, management practices, and staffing characteristics were also dramatically affected.

The architecture served as the foundation of the approach, both technically and culturally. In some sense, it became the tangible thing whose creation and instantiation were the ultimate goal. Because of its importance, the architecture was highly visible. A small, elite architecture team had the authority as well as the responsibility for it. As a consequence, the architecture achieved the "conceptual integrity" cited by [Brooks 95] as the key to any quality software venture.

Defining the architecture was only the first step in building a foundation for a long-term development effort. Validation through prototyping and early use was also essential. When deficiencies were uncovered, the architecture had to evolve in a smooth, controlled manner throughout initial development and beyond. To manage this natural evolution, CelsiusTech's integration and architecture teams worked together to prevent any designer or design team from changing critical interfaces without the architecture team's explicit approval.

This approach had the full support of project management, and it worked because of the architecture team's authority. The team was a centralized design authority that could not be circumvented, which meant that conceptual integrity was maintained.

The organization necessary to create a product line is different from that needed to sustain and evolve it. Management needs to plan for changing personnel, management, training, and organizational needs. Architects with extensive domain knowledge and engineering skill are vital to the creation of viable product lines. Domain experts remain in demand as new products are envisioned and product line evolution is managed.

CelsiusTech's turnaround from one-at-a-time systems to a product line involved education and training on the part of management and technicians. All of these are what we mean by the return cycle of the ABC.

15.5 For Further Reading

There are two reports about CelsiusTech's conversion to a product line. One is from the Software Engineering Institute [Brownsword 96] and is the basis for this chapter. The other is a thesis from Sweden's Linkoping University [Cederling 92].

15.6 Discussion Questions

1. Could the CelsiusTech architecture have been used for the air traffic control system of Chapter 6? Could CelsiusTech have used that architecture? What are the essential differences?

2. CelsiusTech changed management structures several times during its development of the SS2000. Consider the implications of these changes, given our recommendation in Chapter 7 that product structure should mirror project structure.

16

J2EE/EJB

A Case Study of an Industry-Standard Computing Infrastructure

with Anna Liu

> *Write Once, Run Everywhere*
> —Sun Microsystems's mantra for Java

> *Write Once, Test Everywhere*
> —Cynical Java programmers

This chapter presents an overview of Sun Microsystems's Java 2 Enterprise Edition (J2EE) architecture specification, as well as an important portion of that specification, Enterprise JavaBeans (EJB). J2EE provides a standard description of how distributed object-oriented programs written in Java should be designed and developed and how the various Java components can communicate and interact. EJB describes a server-side component-based programming model. Taken as a whole, J2EE also describes various enterprise-wide services, including naming, transactions, component life cycle, and persistence, and how these services should be uniformly provided and accessed. Finally, it describes how vendors need to provide infrastructure services for application builders so that, as long as conformance to the standard is achieved, the resultant application will be portable to all J2EE platforms.

J2EE/EJB is one approach to building distributed object-oriented systems. There are, of course, others. People have been building distributed object-oriented systems using the Object Management Group's (OMG) Common Object Request

Note: Anna Liu is a senior research engineer at the Software Architecture and Technologies Group, CSIRO, Sydney, Australia. She is also an adjunct senior academic at the University of Sydney.

Broker Architecture (CORBA) during the last decade. In the CORBA model, an object request broker (ORB) allows objects to publish their interfaces and allows client programs (and perhaps other objects) to locate these remote objects anywhere on the computer network and to request services from them. Microsoft, too, has a technology, .NET, for building distributed systems. The .NET architecture has similar provisions for building distributed object systems for Windows-based platforms.

We will start the chapter by looking at the business drivers that led to the creation of an industry standard architecture for distributed systems. Then we will discuss how the J2EE/EJB architecture addresses such needs. We will look at the typical quality requirements of Web-based applications and see how the J2EE/EJB architecture fulfills them.

16.1   Relationship to the Architecture Business Cycle

In the 1980s, the price/performance ratio for personal computers was gradually dovetailing with that of high-end workstations and "servers." This newly available computing power and fast network technology enabled the widespread use of distributed computing.

However, rival computer vendors kept producing competing hardware, operating systems, and network protocols. To an end-user organization, such product differentiation presented problems in distributed computing. Typically, organizations invested in a variety of computing platforms and had difficulty building distributed systems on top of such a heterogeneous environment.

The Object Management Group's Common Object Request Broker Architecture was developed in the early 1990s to counter this problem. The CORBA model provided a standard software platform on which distributed objects could communicate and interact with each other seamlessly and transparently. In this case, an ORB allows objects to publish their interfaces, and it allows client programs to locate them anywhere on the computer network and to request services from them.

However, CORBA was not the only viable distributed object technology for very long. Sun Microsystems soon pushed the Java programming language, which supports remote method invocation (RMI) and so, in effect, builds Java-specific object request broker functionality into every Java Virtual Machine (JVM). Java has the appeal of portability. Once a Java application is developed, its code is portable across all JVMs, which have implementations on most major hardware platforms.

Sun Microsystems did not stop with Java. J2EE was developed in the late 1990s using Java RMI as an underlying communication infrastructure. It became an industry-standard specification for the software community to more easily build distributed object systems using the Java programming language. J2EE soon

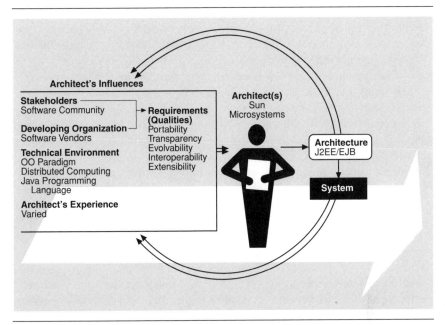

FIGURE 16.1 The ABC as it pertains to Sun Microsystems and J2EE/EJB

gathered momentum as software vendors rushed to implement it; Java programmers around the world showed great enthusiasm in developing e-commerce applications in "Internet time" using the J2EE framework. J2EE thus competed directly against CORBA as well as against the proprietary Microsoft technologies.

The ABC for J2EE/EJB is shown in Figure 16.1.

16.2   Requirements and Qualities

What are some of the goals of Sun Microsystems in developing the J2EE/EJB specification? How are these goals reflected in the qualities of the J2EE/EJB architecture?

THE WEB AND J2EE

In response to the increasing demands of Internet-enabled business systems, more and more enterprise information systems are constructed using distributed object technology. These systems require scalability, high performance, portability, and security. They need to handle large volumes of requests generated by the Internet community and must be able to respond to these requests in a timely fashion.

For many e-business organizations, the most challenging thing right now is a successful Web site. Successful sites attract large volumes of hits, and large volumes of hits stress the site software, as mentioned in Chapter 13. On the Internet, it is not uncommon for sites to receive millions or many millions of accesses daily. Such numbers might not be too frightening if user requests are spread out evenly during the day, but this is often not the case. Requests often arrive in bursts, which place greater demands on Web site software.

In fact, industry folklore is rife with stories of e-business sites failing under unexpected client surges. For example, the Wimbledon Tennis tournament experienced almost 1 billion Web accesses in 1999, with 420,000 hits per minute (7,000 per second) during one match. Bear in mind, that the Internet is currently used by only a small portion of the globe's population; things have just started.

In this sense, then, the Internet has forever changed the requirements for enterprise software systems. The very nature of the Internet brings new pressures to bear on applications that are not commonly experienced by traditional networked information systems. The impact of quality attribute requirements, such as manageability, scalability, security, and availability, are radically increased when applications are exposed to potentially limitless numbers of concurrent users. Table 16.1 describes the quality requirements that any Web-based application must fulfill.

Sun Microsystems, in developing J2EE, aimed to provide a basis for technology that supports the construction of such systems. In particular, as part of the J2EE specification, EJB aims to

- provide a component-based architecture for building distributed object-oriented business applications in Java. EJBs make it possible to build distributed applications by combining components developed with tools from different vendors.
- make it easier to write applications. Application developers do not have to deal with low-level details of transaction and state management, multithreading, and resource pooling.

TABLE 16.1   Typical Web-Based Application Quality Attribute Requirements

Quality	Requirement
Scalability	System should support variations in load without human intervention
Availability/ Reliability	System should provide 24/7 availability with very small downtime periods
Security	System should authenticate users and protect against unauthorized access to data
Usability	Different users should be able to access different content in different forms
Performance	Users should be provided with responsive systems

More specifically, the EJB architecture does the following:

- Addresses the development, deployment, and runtime aspects of an enterprise application's life cycle
- Defines the contracts that enable tools from multiple vendors to develop and deploy components that can interoperate at runtime
- Interoperates with other Java APIs
- Provides interoperability between enterprise beans and non-Java applications
- Interoperates with CORBA

J2EE makes it possible to re-use Java components in a server-side infrastructure. With appropriate component assembly and deployment tools, the aim is to bring the ease of programming associated with GUI-builder tools (like Visual Basic) to building server applications. And, by providing a standard framework for J2EE products based on a single language (Java), J2EE component-based solutions are, in theory at least, product independent and portable between the J2EE platforms provided by various vendors.

Thus, in addition to the core requirements given in Table 16.1, Sun added a set of requirements that address the activities of a programming team. These additional quality attribute requirements are listed in Table 16.2.

TABLE 16.2   Sun's Quality Attribute Requirements for J2EE

Quality Attribute	Requirement
Portability	J2EE should be able to be implemented with minimal work on a variety of computing platforms
Buildability	Application developers should be provided with facilities to manage common services such as transactions, name services, and security
Balanced Specificity	Detailed enough to provide meaningful standard for component developers, vendors, and integrators, but general enough to allow vendor-specific features and optimizations
Implementation Transparency	Provide complete transparency of implementation details so that client programs can be independent of object implementation details (server-side component location, operating system, vendor, etc.)
Interoperability	Support interoperation of server-side components implemented on different vendor implementations; allow bridges for interoperability of the J2EE platform to other technologies such as CORBA and Microsoft component technology
Evolvability	Allow developers to incrementally adopt different technologies
Extensibility	Allow incorporation of relevant new technologies as they are developed

16.3 Architectural Solution

Sun Microsystem's approach to satisfying the quality attributes discussed in the previous section is through the specification of two major architectures: J2EE and the EJB. J2EE describes the overall multi-tier architecture for designing, developing, and deploying component-based, enterprise-wide applications. EJB is a key part of J2EE technology, reflecting the deeper technical requirements of buildability, extensibility, and interoperability. Both J2EE and EJB reflect balanced specificity—that is, the ability for competitors to develop differentiation on the offerings while building them on a common base.

The major features of the J2EE platform are

- A multi-tiered distributed application model
- A server-side component model
- Built-in transaction control

A simple deployment view of the J2EE multi-tier model is given in Figure 16.2. The elements of this architecture are further described in Table 16.3.

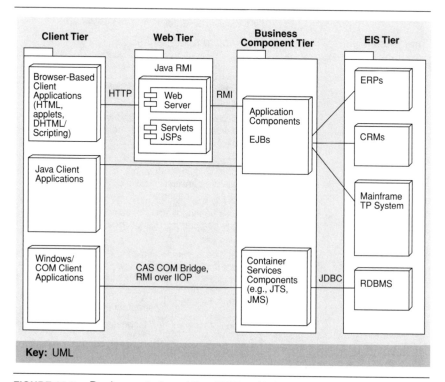

FIGURE 16.2   Deployment view of the J2EE multi-tier architecture

TABLE 16.3   Summary of J2EE Technology Components and Services

Component/Service	Description
Enterprise JavaBeans (EJB) Architecture	Specification defines an API that allows developers to create, deploy, and manage enterprise-strength server-side component-based applications
JavaServer Pages (JSP)	Provides a method for creating dynamic Web content
Java Servlet	Provides Web application developers with a mechanism for extending the functionality of a Web server
Java Messaging Service (JMS)	Provides J2EE applications with support for asynchronous messaging using either point-to-point (one-to-one) or publish-subscribe (many to many) styles of interaction; messages can be configured to have various qualities of service associated with them, ranging from best effort to transactional
Java Naming and Directory Interface (JNDI)	J2EE's directory service allows Java client and Web-tier servlets to retrieve references to user-defined objects such as EJBs and environment entries (e.g., location of a JDBC driver)
Java Transaction Service (JTS)	Makes it possible for EJBs and their clients to participate in transactions; updates can be made to a number of beans in an application, and JTS makes sure all changes commit or abort at the end of the transaction; relies on JDBC-2 drivers for support of the XA protocol and hence the ability to perform distributed transactions with one or more resource managers
J2EE Connector Architecture (JCA)	Defines a standard architecture for connecting the J2EE platform to heterogeneous Enterprise Information Systems, including packaged applications such as Enterprise Resource Planning (ERP) and Customer Relationship Management (CRM) systems
Client Access Services COM Bridge	Allows integration between COM and J2EE applications across a network; allows access to J2EE server-side components by COM-enabled client applications
RMI over IIOP	Provides developers with an implementation of Java RMI API over the OMG's industry-standard Internet Inter-ORB Protocol (IIOP); developers can write remote interfaces between clients and servers and implement them using Java technology and the Java RMI APIs
Java Database Connectivity (JDBC)	Provides programmers with a uniform interface to a wide range of relational databases and provides a common base on which higher-level tools and interfaces can be built

The role of each tier is as follows.

- *Client tier.* In a Web application, the client tier comprises an Internet browser that submits HTTP requests and downloads HTML pages from a Web server. In an application not deployed using a browser, standalone Java clients or applets can be used; these communicate directly with the business component tier. (See Chapter 17 for an example of using J2EE without a browser.)

- *Web tier.* The Web tier runs a Web server to handle client requests and responds to these requests by invoking J2EE servlets or JavaServer Pages

(JSPs). Servlets are invoked by the server depending on the type of user request. They query the business logic tier for the required information to satisfy the request and then format the information for return to the user via the server. JSPs are static HTML pages that contain snippets of servlet code. The code is invoked by the JSP mechanism and takes responsibility for formatting the dynamic portion of the page.

- *Business component tier.* The business components comprise the core business logic for the application. They are realized by EJBs (the software component model supported by J2EE). EJBs receive requests from servlets in the Web tier, satisfy them usually by accessing some data sources, and return the results to the servlet. EJB components are hosted by a J2EE environment known as the EJB container, which supplies a number of services to the EJBs it hosts including transaction and life-cycle management, state management, security, multi-threading, and resource pooling. EJBs simply specify the type of behavior they require from the container at runtime and then rely on the container to provide the services. This frees the application programmer from cluttering the business logic with code to handle system and environmental issues.

- *Enterprise information systems tier.* This typically consists of one or more databases and back-end applications like mainframes and other legacy systems, which EJBs must query to process requests. JDBC drivers are typically used for databases, which are most often Relational Database Management Systems (RDBMS).

THE EJB ARCHITECTURAL APPROACH

The remainder of this chapter focuses on the Enterprise JavaBeans architecture, which defines a standard programming model for constructing distributed object-oriented server-side Java applications. Because this programming model is standard, many beans that prepackage useful functionality can be (and have been) written. The EJB programmer's job is to bundle these packages with any application-specific functionality to create a complete application.

Not unlike J2EE, EJBs aim at realizing one of Java's major design principles—the oft-quoted "Write Once, Run Anywhere" mantra. The JVM allows a Java application to run on any operating system. However, server components require additional services that are not supplied directly by the JVM, such as transaction and security services. In J2EE and EJB, these services are supplied through a set of standard vendor-independent interfaces that provide access to the additional supporting infrastructure, which together form the services available in an application server.

A J2EE-compliant application server provides an EJB *container* to manage the execution of application components. In practical terms, a container provides an operating system process that hosts one or (usually) more EJB components.

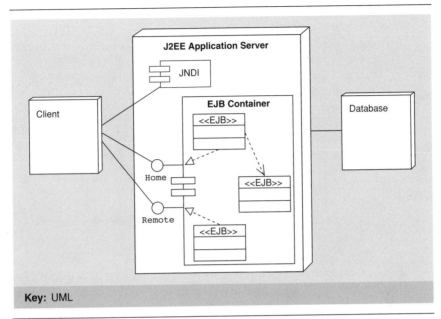

Key: UML

FIGURE 16.3   Example deployment view of the EJB architecture

Figure 16.3 shows the relationship between an application server, a container, and the services provided. In brief, when a client invokes a server component the container automatically allocates a thread and invokes an instance of the component. The container manages all resources on the component's behalf and manages all interactions between the component and the external systems.

The EJB component model defines the basic architecture of an EJB component, specifying the structure of its interfaces and the mechanisms by which it interacts with its container and other components. The model also provides guidelines for developing components that can work together to form a larger application.

The EJB version 1.1 specification defines two main types of components: *session beans* and *entity beans*.

- *Session beans* typically contain business logic and provide services for clients. The two types of session bean are known as *stateless* and *stateful*.
  - A *stateless session bean* is defined as not being *conversational* with respect to its calling process. This means that it does not keep any state information on behalf of any client. A client will get a reference to a stateless session bean in a container and can use it to make many calls on an instance of the bean. However, between each successive service invocation, a client is not guaranteed to bind to any particular stateless session bean instance. The EJB container delegates client calls to stateless session beans *as needed*, so the client can never be certain which bean instance it

will actually talk to. This makes it meaningless to store client-related state in a stateless session bean.

– A *stateful session bean* is said to be conversational with respect to its calling process and therefore can maintain state information about the conversation. Once a client gets a reference to a stateful session bean, all subsequent calls to the bean using this reference are guaranteed to go to the same bean instance. The container creates a new, dedicated stateful session bean for each client that creates a bean instance. Thus, clients can store any state information they wish in the bean and can be assured that it will still be there the next time they access that bean. EJB containers assume responsibility for managing the life cycle of stateful session beans. The container writes out a bean's state to disk if it has not been used for a while and automatically restores the state when the client makes a subsequent call on the bean. This mechanism is known as *passivation and activation* of the stateful bean. We will discuss passivation in more detail later.

- *Entity beans* are typically used for representing business data objects. The data members in an entity bean map directly to some data items stored in an associated database. Entity beans are usually accessed by a session bean that provides business-level client services. There are two types of entity bean, *container-managed persistence* and *bean-managed persistence*. Persistence in this context refers to the way in which a bean's data (usually a row in a relational database table) is read and written.

– With *container-managed persistence entity beans*, the data the bean represents is mapped automatically to the associated persistent data store (e.g., a database) by the container. The container is responsible for loading the data to the bean instance and writing changes back to the persistent data storage at appropriate times, such as the start and end of a transaction. Container-managed persistence relies on container-provided services and requires no application code—the container in fact generates the data access code so it is easy to implement.

– With *bean-managed persistence entity beans*, the bean code itself is responsible for accessing the persistent data it represents, typically using handcrafted JDBC calls. Bean-managed persistence gives the bean developer the flexibility to perform persistence operations that are too complicated for the container or to use a data source not supported by the container—for example, a custom or legacy database. While bean-managed persistence requires more programmer effort to implement, it can sometimes provide opportunities to optimize data access and, in such cases, may provide better performance than container-managed persistence.

Table 16.4 summarizes how the EJB architecture supports Sun's key quality attribute requirements for the overall J2EE architecture. An example deployment view of the J2EE/EJB architecture is illustrated in Figure 16.4.

TABLE 16.4 How EJB Supports Sun's J2EE Quality Attribute Requirements

Goal	How Achieved	Tactics Used
Availability/ Reliability	J2EE-compliant systems provide ready-to-use transaction services that enhance availability and reliability of the application by providing built-in failure recovery mechanisms	Heartbeat Transactions Passive redundancy
Balanced Specificity	EJB services specified in terms of Java APIs, effectively defer implementation decisions to EJB application server implementers; detailed enough to provide a meaningful standard for component developers, vendors and integrators, but general enough to allow vendor-specific features and optimizations	Anticipate expected changes Abstract common services Hide information
Buildability	EJB application servers provide many ready-to-use services for building server-side Java applications, including transactions, persistence, threading, and resource management; developer is thus freed from low-level distribution details; Sun Microsystems provides a reference J2EE implementation; application server vendors also participate in the J2EE specification process	Abstract common services Maintain interfaces Hide information
Evolvability	Specification partitioned into separately evolvable subcategories; the Java Community Process coordinates Java specification requests and responses	Semantic coherence Hide information
Extensibility	Component-based approach to the EJB specification allows for future extensions; message-driven beans are a feature introduced in later versions of the EJB specification and workable with existing EJB systems; J2EE describes stable core technologies, such as EJB, JMS, JNDI, JTS, etc., needed by most component developers; over time, extensions, such as JCA, are gradually incorporated	Anticipate expected changes
Implementation Transparency	`Home` and `Remote` interface specifications encourage decoupling of interface specification and implementation. Implementation decisions can thus be deferred, and are transparent to the client; provide complete transparency of implementation details so that client programs can be independent of object implementation details (server-side component location, operating system, vendor, etc.)	Maintain existing interfaces Semantic coherence
Interoperability	Supports interoperation of server-side components implemented on different vendor implementations; also allow bridges for interoperability of the J2EE platform to other technologies such as CORBA and Microsoft component technology	Adherence to defined protocols
Performance	Distributed-component approach to J2EE/EJB allows performance tuning across multiple systems	Configuration files Load balancing Maintain multiple copies

(Continued)

TABLE 16.4   *Continued*

Goal	How Achieved	Tactics Used
Portability	Contracts between EJBs and containers ensure application components are portable across different EJB containers; J2EE describes roles for application component providers, assemblers, deployers, EJB server providers, EJB container providers, and system administrators, as well as precise contracts between various J2EE components and application components; application component (in theory) is thus portable across different J2EE containers; J2EE is based on a language that contains its own virtual machine and is available on most major platforms	Maintain existing interfaces Generalize modules Abstract common services
Scalability	J2EE multi-tiered architecture and component-based EJB architecture has built-in mechanisms for expanding the number of servers available in a configuration and to load balance among servers	Load balancing
Security	J2EE-compliant systems provide declarative, role-based security mechanisms and programmatic security mechanisms that are ready to use	Authentication Authorization Data confidentiality
Usability	J2EE-compliant systems provide Java technologies, such as JSP and servlets, that enable the rendering of content to suit different users	Separate user interface

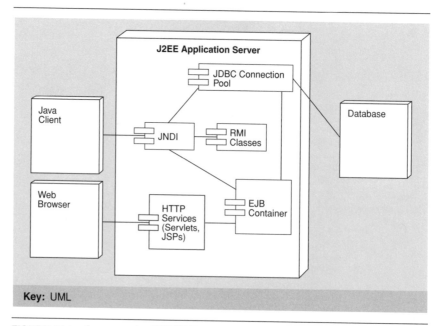

FIGURE 16.4   An example J2EE/EJB-compliant implementation

EJB PROGRAMMING

An EJB depends on its container for all external information. If an EJB needs to access a JDBC connection or another bean, it uses container services. Accessing the identity of its caller, obtaining a reference to itself, and accessing properties are all accomplished through container services. This is an example of an "intermediary" tactic. The bean interacts with its container through one of three mechanisms: callback methods, the EJBContext interface, and the Java Naming and Directory Interface (JNDI).

To create an EJB server-side component, the developer must provide two interfaces that define a bean's business methods, plus the actual bean implementation class. The two interfaces, remote and home, are shown in Figure 16.5. Clients use them to access a bean inside an EJB container. They expose the capabilities of the bean and provide all the methods needed to create the bean and update, interact with, or delete it.

The two interfaces have different purposes. Home contains the life-cycle methods of the EJB, which provide clients with services to create, destroy and find bean instances. In contrast, remote contains the business methods offered by the bean. These methods are application specific. To use them in the bean's remote interface, clients must use the bean's home interface to obtain a reference to the remote interface.

A simple home interface is shown in Figure 16.6. It must inherit from EJBHome and, in this example, contains a method to create an EJB of type Broker. Figure 16.7 shows the remote interface for the Broker EJB.

Remote interfaces must extend the EJBObject interface, which contains a number of methods that the container uses to manage an EJB's creation and life

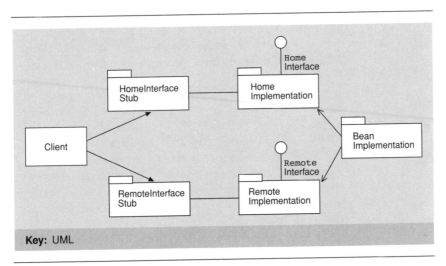

FIGURE 16.5 EJB package diagram

```
public interface BrokerHome extends EJBHome
{
  /*
   * This method creates the EJB Object.
   *
   * @return The newly created EJB Object.
   */
  Broker create() throws RemoteException, CreateException;
}
```

FIGURE 16.6   A simple home interface

```
public interface Broker extends EJBObject
{
  // Return the newly created account number
  public int newAccount(String sub_name, String sub_address, int
      sub_credit) throws RemoteException, SQLException;
  public QueryResult queryStockValueByID(int stock_id)
      throws RemoteException, SQLException;
  public void buyStock(int sub_accno, int stock_id, int amount)
      throws RemoteException, SQLException, TransDenyException;
  public void sellStock(int sub_accno, int stock_id, int amount)
      throws RemoteException, SQLException, TransDenyException;
  public void updateAccount(int sub_accno, int sub_credit)
      throws RemoteException, SQLException;
  public Vector getHoldingStatement(int sub_accno, int start_
      stock_id) throws RemoteException, SQLException;
}
```

FIGURE 16.7   The Broker `remote` interface

cycle. A programmer may wish to provide bean-specific behavior for the EJB, or may simply accept the default, inherited behavior. The client then uses `public` interfaces to create, manipulate, and remove beans from the EJB server. The implementation class, normally known as the bean class, is instantiated at runtime and becomes an accessible distributed object. Some sample client code, simplified, is shown in Figure 16.8.

EJB clients may be standalone applications, servlets, applets, or even other EJBs, as we will see shortly. All clients use the server bean's home interface to obtain a reference to an instance of the server bean. This reference is associated with the class type of the server bean's `remote` interface; so the client interacts with the server bean entirely through the methods defined in its `remote` interface.

In this next example, the `Broker` bean is acting as a stateless session bean that handles all client requests. Internally, it uses the services of a number of entity beans to perform the business logic. A sample of one of the `Broker` methods, `updateAccount`, is shown in Figure 16.9.

The `updateAccount` method uses an entity bean called `Account`, which encapsulates all of the detailed manipulation of the application's data—in this case, exactly how an account record is updated. The code in `updateAccount`

```
Broker broker = null;

// find the home interface
Object _h = ctx.lookup("EntityStock.BrokerHome");
BrokerHome home = (BrokerHome)
      javax.rmi.PortableRemoteObject.narrow(_h, BrokerHome.class);
// Use the home interface to create the Broker EJB Object
broker = home.create();
// execute requests at the broker EJB
broker.updateAccount(accountNo, 200000);
broker.buyStock(accountNo, stockID, 5000);

//we're finished...
broker.remove();
```

FIGURE 16.8   Simplified example EJB client code

```
public void updateAccount(int sub_accno, int sub_credit)
 throws RemoteException
{
 try {
     Account account = accountHome.findByPrimaryKey
        (new AccountPK(sub_accno));
     account.update(sub_credit);
 }
 catch (Exception e) {
     throw new RemoteException(e.toString());
 }
}
```

FIGURE 16.9   The Broker bean's updateAccount method

uses an entity bean finder method called findByPrimaryKey, which is provided by the Account bean in its home interface. This method takes the primary key for the account and accesses the underlying database. If an account record is found in the database with this primary key, the EJB container creates an Account entity bean. The entity bean methods—in this example update—can then be used to access the data in the account record. The home and remote interfaces for Account are shown in Figure 16.10.

The bean class for the entity bean implements the remote methods. The code for the update method is shown in Figure 16.11. It is very simple—in fact, a single line of executable Java code. This simplicity is due to the entity bean's use of *container-managed persistence*. The EJB container "knows" (we will see how soon) that there is a correspondence between the data members in the Account bean and the fields in an account table in the database the application is using.

Using this information, the container tools can generate the SQL queries needed to implement the finder method, and the queries needed to automatically read/write the data from/to the entity bean at the beginning/end of a transaction. In this example, at the end of the Broker session bean's updateAccount

```
public interface AccountHome extends EJBHome
{
 /*
  * This method creates the EJB Object.
  *
  * @param sub_name The name of the subscriber
  * @param sub_address The address of the subscriber
  * @param sub_credit The initial credit of the subscriber
  *
  * @return The newly created EJB Object.
  */
 public Account create(String sub_name, String sub_address,
     int sub_credit)  throws CreateException, RemoteException;
 /*
  * Finds an Account by its primary Key (Account ID)
  */
 public Account findByPrimaryKey(AccountPK key)
     throws FinderException, RemoteException;
}

public interface Account extends EJBObject
{
 public void update(int amount) throws RemoteException;
 public void deposit(int amount) throws RemoteException;
 public int withdraw(int amount) throws AccountException,
     RemoteException;
 // Getter/setter methods on Entity Bean fields
 public int getCredit() throws RemoteException;
 public String getSubName() throws RemoteException;
 public void setSubName(String name) throws RemoteException;
}
```

FIGURE 16.10   The Account bean's home and remote interfaces

```
public class AccountBean implements EntityBean
{
 // Container-managed state fields
 public int     sub_accno;
 public String sub_name;
 public String sub_address;
 public int     sub_credit;

 // lots missing ...
 public void update(int amount)
 {
     sub_credit = amount;
 }
}
```

FIGURE 16.11   The Account bean's update method

method, the data items in the Account entity bean are written back to the database, making the changes to the sub_credit field persistent. All of this is done without explicit control from the programmer, which contributes to the buildability of EJB-based systems.

DEPLOYMENT DESCRIPTORS

One of the major attractions of the EJB model is the way it achieves a separation of concerns between the business logic and the infrastructure code, an example of the "semantic coherence" tactic. This separation refers to the fact that EJBs are primarily concerned with pure business logic while the EJB container handles environmental and infrastructure issues such as transactions, bean life-cycle management, and security. This makes the bean components simpler—they are not littered with code to handle these additional complexities.

A bean tells the container which of the provided services it requires through a deployment descriptor. This is an XML document associated with an EJB. When a bean is deployed in a container, the container reads the deployment descriptor to find out how transactions, persistence (for entity beans), and access control should be handled. In this way the descriptor provides a declarative mechanism for how these issues are handled—an example of the "defer binding time" tactic.

The beauty of this mechanism is that the same EJB component can be deployed with different descriptors suited to different application environments. If security is an issue, the component can specify its access control needs. If security is not an issue, no access control is specified. In both cases the code in the EJB is identical.

A deployment descriptor has a predefined format that all EJB-compliant beans must use and that all EJB-compliant servers must know how to read. This format is specified in an XML Document Type Definition, or DTD. The deployment descriptor describes the type of bean (session or entity) and the classes used for `remote`, `home`, and the bean class. It also specifies the transactional attributes of every method in the bean, which security roles can access each method (access control), and whether persistence in the entity beans is handled automatically by the container or performed explicitly by the bean code.

The deployment descriptor for the `Broker` bean shown before is given in Figure 16.12. In addition to the attributes described, the deployment descriptor specifies that this is a stateless session bean and that a container-managed transaction is required to execute each of its methods (in the figure these attributes are in boldface for ease of reading). For example, if we simply change the `<session-type>` field in the XML to read `stateful`, the container will manage the bean very differently. Figure 16.13 shows the deployment descriptor for the `Account` entity bean. As well as the deployment attributes we have already seen, it tells the container the following:

- That it must manage persistence for beans of this type
- Where to find the JDBC data source for the database
- What primary key and data items must be mapped between the database and the entity bean

In Table 6.2, we presented Sun's quality attribute requirements for J2EE. In Table 16.5, we describe how some of these requirements are achieved by deployment descriptors.

```
<ejb-jar>
 <enterprise-beans>
    <session>
       <ejb-name>EntityStock.BrokerHome</ejb-name>
       <home>j2ee.entitystock.BrokerHome</home>
       <remote>j2ee.entitystock.Broker</remote>
       <ejb-class>j2ee.entitystock.BrokerBean</ejb-class>
       <session-type>Stateless</session-type>
       <transaction-type>Container</transaction-type>
    </session>
 </enterprise-beans>
 <assembly-descriptor>
    <container-transaction>
       <method>
          <ejb-name>EntityStock.BrokerHome</ejb-name>
          <method-intf>Remote</method-intf>
          <method-name>*</method-name>
       </method>
       <trans-attribute>Required</trans-attribute>
    </container-transaction>
 </assembly-descriptor>
</ejb-jar>
```

FIGURE 16.12   Deployment description for the `Broker` bean

TABLE 16.5   How Deployment Descriptors Support Sun's J2EE Quality
Attribute Requirements

Goal	How Achieved	Tactics Used
Portability	Common code base can be developed for multiple target platforms; multiple versions of deployment descriptor can be configured at deployment time to suit different target platforms, making the developed application component portable across multiple target environments	Semantic coherence, generalize modules, configuration files
Buildability	Deployment descriptors enable separation of concerns: development of code and deployment configuration options	Semantic coherence, configuration files, generalize module
Balanced Specificity	Deployment descriptors in XML format, providing a meaningful standard format for encoding configuration options, but general enough for vendors to extend deployment descriptors with vendor-specific features	Configuration files, generalize module
Implementation Transparency	Details of deployment descriptor used by server-side components are transparent to the clients of the components	Use an intermediary

```
<ejb-jar>
 <enterprise-beans>
    <entity>
       <ejb-name>EntityStock.AccountHome</ejb-name>
       <home>j2ee.entitystock.AccountHome</home>
       <remote>j2ee.entitystock.Account</remote>
       <ejb-class>j2ee.entitystock.AccountBean</ejb-class>
       <persistence-type>Container</persistence-type>
       <prim-key-class>j2ee.entitystock.AccountPK</prim-key-class>
       <reentrant>False</reentrant>
       <cmp-field>
          <field-name>sub_accno</field-name>
       </cmp-field>
       <cmp-field>
          <field-name>sub_name</field-name>
       </cmp-field>
       <cmp-field>
          <field-name>sub_address</field-name>
       </cmp-field>
       <cmp-field>
          <field-name>sub_credit</field-name>
       </cmp-field>
       <resource-ref>
          <res-ref-name>jdbc/sqlStock_nkPool</res-ref-name>
          <res-type>javax.sql.DataSource</res-type>
          <res-auth>Container</res-auth>
       </resource-ref>
    </entity>
 </enterprise-beans>
 <assembly-descriptor>
    <container-transaction>
       <method>
          <ejb-name>EntityStock.AccountHome</ejb-name>
          <method-intf>Remote</method-intf>
          <method-name>*</method-name>
       </method>
       <trans-attribute>Required</trans-attribute>
    </container-transaction>
 </assembly-descriptor>
</ejb-jar>
```

FIGURE 16.13 Deployment description for the `Account` entity bean

16.4 System Deployment Decisions

What we have described thus far is J2EE/EJB as it was created by Sun. However, when deploying a J2EE/EJB system, there are a number of implementation issues that the architect needs to consider. The EJB component model is a powerful way to construct server-side applications. And although the interactions between the different parts of the code are a little daunting at first, with some exposure and experience with the model, it becomes relatively straightforward to construct EJB applications. Still, while code construction is not difficult, a number of complexities remain, including the following.

- The EJB model makes it possible to combine components in an application in many different architectural patterns. Which are the best, and what does "best" mean in a given application?
- The way beans interact with the container is complex and has a significant effect on the performance of an application. In the same vein, all EJB server containers are not equal—product selection and product-specific configuration are important aspects of the application development life cycle.

In this final section, we present some of the key design issues involved in architecting and constructing highly scalable EJB applications.

STATE MANAGEMENT—AN OLD DESIGN ISSUE IN A NEW CONTEXT

There are two service models that can be adopted in developing the EJB server tier—stateless and stateful models, implemented by stateless and stateful session beans.

We will take an online bookshop as an example. In the stateful version, an EJB can be used to remember customer details and to manage the items the customer is placing in an online shopping cart. Hence, the EJB stores the state associated with the customer's visit to the site. By maintaining this conversational state in the bean, the client is relieved from the responsibility of keeping track of it. The EJB monitors potential purchases and processes them in a batch when a confirmation method is invoked.

To make better use of limited system memory, stateful session beans are passivated when not used by the client, meaning that a bean's conversational state is written to secondary storage (typically disk) and its instance is removed from memory. The client's reference to the bean is not affected by passivation, but remains alive and usable. When the client invokes a method on a bean that is passivated, the container activates the bean by instantiating a new instance and populating its state with the information written to secondary storage.

This passivation strategy has great implications for scalability. If there is a requirement for large numbers of stateful session bean instances to service individual clients, passivation and activation may prove to be too high an overhead in terms of application performance.

Alternatively, a stateless session bean does not maintain conversational state on behalf of the client. The client must inform the server of session information, such as customer details and shopping cart contents, with each service request, because, for each request, the container may assign a different stateless session bean instance. This is only possible because of the pure stateless service model. Figure 16.14 shows usage of both stateful and stateless session beans.

To summarize, the advantages of stateless session beans include the following:

- There is no performance overhead in passivating and activating session beans that involve expensive disk reads and writes.

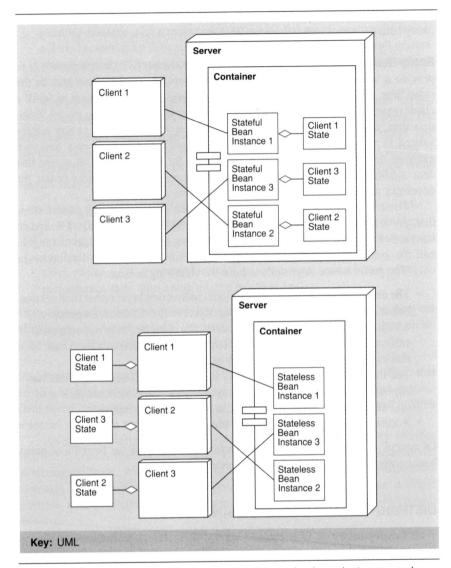

FIGURE 16.14   Clients' static bindings to stateful session bean instances and dynamic bindings to stateless session bean instances.

- Dynamic request routing means that requests can be routed to the least loaded server.
- If one session instance goes down, the request can be easily rerouted to another one.

The only disadvantage to the stateless approach is that more information needs to be passed between the client and the EJB on each request. Assuming that the

RESOURCE POOLING

Application resources, such as database connections and sockets, must be carefully managed in a distributed system. Resource pooling exploits the fact that not all clients need exclusive access to a resource at all times. With EJBs, not every bean needs a database connection for its exclusive use. It is much more efficient to configure a system so that database connections can be pooled and re-used for different client transactions.

When a database connection pool is used, the resulting connections required will be far less than the number of EJB components in a deployed system. Because database connections are expensive to create and manage, this architecture increases the overall application scalability. Furthermore, connections to the databases do not need to be reestablished continuously, thus improving application performance.

Resource pooling can be applied to other resources as well, such as socket connections and threads. Pooling of components simply means that a dedicated resource for each client is not necessary. Typical configurable parameters include container threads, session beans instances, entity bean cache size, and database connection pool size. All of these need to be configured appropriately to exhibit fast response times and high overall system throughput.

DEPENDENCE ON JAVA VIRTUAL MACHINE PERFORMANCE

In any Java application, the JVM is an important factor in performance tuning. Hence, to develop and deploy high-performing EJB server-side applications, several JVM configuration and performance tuning activities need to be considered.

JVM heap size is one important setting. The heap is a repository for Java objects and free memory. When the JVM runs out of memory in the heap, all execution in it ceases while a garbage collection algorithm goes through memory and frees space that is no longer required. This is an obvious performance hit because application code blocks during garbage collection. Thus, in an EJB application no server-side work can be done.

If heap size is huge, garbage collection will be infrequent; when it does kick in, however, it will take a much longer time, possibly long enough to disrupt normal system operations. Garbage collection can slow down (and sometime completely stop) server processing, giving the impression that the server is slow and unresponsive.

To appropriately set the JVM heap size, it is necessary to monitor the paging activities on the server machine. Paging is an expensive performance overhead and therefore should be avoided on application servers by increasing the JVM heap size to match the application's needs. Another way is to watch the garbage collector by using the `-gcverbose` compiler option. If incremental garbage collection is an option, it is almost always best to turn it on.

16.5   Summary

The creation of the J2EE multi-tier architecture was motivated by the business needs of Sun Microsystems. These business needs were influenced by the lessons of the CORBA model and by the competitive pressures of other proprietary distributed programming models, such as COM+ from Microsoft. J2EE features a server-side component framework for building enterprise-strength server-side Java applications, namely, Enterprise JavaBeans.

The J2EE/EJB specification is constantly expanding. Its ready-to-use services currently include transactions, security, naming, persistence, and resource management. These services enable the J2EE/EJB application programmer to focus on developing the business logic, thus removing the need to worry about low-level distribution details. J2EE/EJB achieves portability by using a common, portable language (Java) and by having precise contracts between components. It achieves performance and performance scalability via a number of mechanisms, including distributing applications across many processors (horizontal scaling), stateless session beans, and resource pools.

Despite the seeming simplicity of the J2EE/EJB programming model, there are many application-level architectural decisions that need to be carefully made. The various architectural tradeoffs must be analyzed and compared to derive an optimal design with respect to application quality requirements.

16.6   For Further Reading

There is an abundance of information about the J2EE/EJB architecture and specification. This includes Sun Microsystems's home page (*http://java.sun.com/j2ee*), which offers easy-to-follow tutorial material on J2EE, various white papers, and the J2EE/EJB specification itself. There are also numerous active forums focusing on the J2EE architecture and technology space, including one sponsored by The Middleware Company (*http://www.theserverside.com*).

16.7   Discussion Questions

1. An addition to the EJB component model version 2.0 is "message-driven beans." These are enterprise beans that allow J2EE applications to process messages asynchronously. What are some of the uses of such a component? What sort of new enterprise architecture possibilities do message-driven beans open up?

2. The J2EE/EJB specification uses many techniques that are actually just implementations of the "use an intermediary" tactic. Find as many distinct realizations of these instances as you can.

3. Consider the CelsiusTech case study presented in Chapter 15. Would J2EE/EJB be a good infrastructure choice for implementing this system? Justify your answer.

17

The Luther Architecture

A Case Study in Mobile Applications Using J2EE

with Tanya Bass, James Beck, Kelly Dolan, Cuiwei Li,
Andreas Löhr, Richard Martin, William Ross, Tobias
Weishäupl, and Gregory Zelesnik

> *God is in the details.*
> — Ludwig Mies van der Rohe

Workers involved in the maintenance or operation of large vehicles (such as tanks and aircraft) or portions of the industrial infrastructure (such as bridges and oil rigs) have great difficulty using computers to support their tasks. Because the object being maintained or operated is large, work on it must be in situ, outdoors or in special structures, neither of which is conducive to desktop computing. In particular, a computer solution usually involves a wireless infrastructure and either a handheld or a hands-free computing device.

Inmedius is a company that was established in 1995 as an outgrowth of Carnegie Mellon University's Wearable Project (see the sidebar History of Wearable Computing) to provide support for front-line maintenance and operation workers. Initially producing one-of-a-kind solutions for its customers, as the company grew it realized the necessity for general solutions that could be quickly tailored to a customer's needs.

The front-line worker does not work alone but requires a great deal of back-office support. Problem reports must be collected and work must be scheduled to enable repairs to be made, replacement parts must be taken from inventory and re-ordered, and maintenance records must be analyzed. All of this work-flow management requires integrating the front-line worker with the back-office worker who has access to a desktop computer.

Note: All of this chapter's contributors work for Inmedius Corporation in Pittsburgh.

427

The Luther architecture was designed to provide a general framework within which Inmedius could provide customized solutions for the maintenance problems of its customers. It is based on the Java 2 Enterprise Edition (J2EE) architecture, so becomes an application of the general J2EE/EJB framework (discussed in Chapter 16) to an environment where the end user is connected over a wireless network and has a device with limited input/output capabilities, limited computational capabilities, or both.

History of Wearable Computing

Arguably, the first wearable computer was the wristwatch. It was invented around 1900 and at first was unable to compete with the pocket watch. Why would someone wear a watch on his wrist when his existing pocket watch kept good time and could be accessed quite freely? However, during World War I, the British Army issued wristwatches to its troops so that they could synchronize attacks while keeping their hands free for weapons. Suddenly, it became fashionable in Britain to show support for the "boys in the trenches" by wearing wristwatches. Now, of course, you rarely see a pocket watch.

By the early 1990s, technology had begun to support the wearing of digital, full-function computing devices. One organization investigating the use of these devices was the Wearable Group of Carnegie Mellon University headed by Dan Siewiorek. They viewed a wearable computer as a tool to support workplace functions, with the workplace epitomized by locales where aircraft and other large vehicles were maintained—out of doors or within large buildings such as hangars or railroad roundhouses.

The focus on use in a workplace meant that ease of use and design sophistication were primary. The Wearable group conducted experiments with computers designed and constructed by students in actual workplaces. The success of these experiments created the demand that Inmedius was organized to exploit.

A second group, operating at the same time and centered at the Media Laboratory of the Massachusetts Institute of Technology, styled themselves "borgs." They viewed the wearable computer as a consumer product designed to change the lives of those who wore it. They wore their computers all of the time and were interested in innovative uses of them and in memory support applications. One example was using the conductivity of the skin as a network medium and having two computers exchange business cards when their wearers shook hands.

By the late 1990s, the two groups were collaborating to make wearable computers a viable academic discipline. Various commercial companies had begun to offer computers and head-mounted displays, and large commercial concerns had begun to show interest. Now, with the increasing miniaturization of hardware and the increasing sophistication of software (as evidenced by this chapter), wearable computing can only become more prevalent.

— LJB

17.1   Relationship to the Architecture Business Cycle

Figure 17.1 shows the Architecture Business Cycle (ABC) as it pertains to Inmedius and the Luther architecture. The quality goals of re-usability, performance, modifiability, flexibility of the end user device, and interoperability with standard commercial infrastructures are driven, as always, by the business goals of the customer and the end user.

INFLUENCES ON THE ARCHITECTURE

The next sections elaborate on the things that influence the Luther architecture.

End Users.   Inmedius's business is providing computer support for front-line workers. Figure 17.2 shows such a worker utilizing one of the hardware configurations supported by Luther applications. The worker is performing an industrial process, the steps of which are displayed on the head-mounted display apparatus that he is wearing. The computer is worn on the user's chest and uses a dial as its primary input device. The process is described in a manual stored on the back-office computers, and the manual pages are served to the worker as various steps of the process are completed, which can number more than 500. The worker

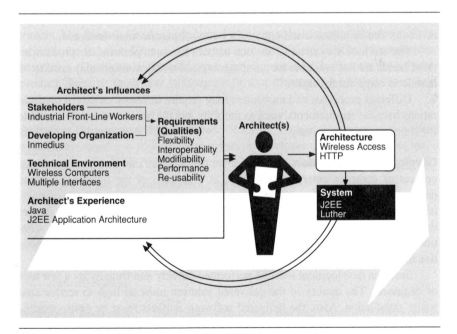

FIGURE 17.1   The ABC as it pertains to Inmedius and Luther

mentality associated with single system development inhibits global thinking. The move to a product line based on Luther enabled Inmedius to begin thinking about product lines instead of focusing on individual systems. Furthermore, as we saw with CelsiusTech, new markets became available to Inmedius that could be seen as generalizations of existing markets, not only in a business sense but also in a technical sense.

17.2 Requirements and Qualities

The Luther architecture was designed to meet two sets of complementary requirements. The first set governs the applications to be built—namely, enterprise applications for field service workers. These requirements are directly visible to customers, since failure to meet them results in applications that do not perform according to expectations—for instance, an application that may work correctly but perform poorly over a wireless network. The second set of requirements involves introducing a common architecture across products. This reduces integration time, brings products to market faster, increases product quality, eases introduction of new technologies, and brings consistency across products.

Overall, the requirements can be separated into six categories:

- Wireless access
- User interface
- Device type
- Existing procedures, business processes, and systems
- Building applications
- Distributed computing

Wireless Access.   Field service workers must move about while performing their tasks. Furthermore, they must move about in an environment rich in machines, hazards, and other people. In order to interact with back-office systems, the devices used by workers must access remote servers and data sources without being tethered by a landline to a local area network. Because of the variety of Inmedius customers, these wireless networks may need to be of varying capacity and availability.

User Interface.   Part of the Inmedius competitive advantage is its high-fidelity user interfaces, which allow a worker to focus on the task at hand without being hindered by the interface or the access device. Different devices have different screen footprints, and the Luther architecture must facilitate the display of meaningful information on each of them. This does not mean constructing a single user interface and adapting it to all device types. Instead, Luther must support the rapid construction of interfaces that filter, synthesize, and fuse information in ways that are displayable on a particular device and useful to its user.

Variety of Devices.   Field service workers use a variety of computing devices in the field. No one device will suffice for all field applications, and each has limitations that must be addressed by the Luther architecture. Inmedius must engineer performance-enhancing solutions to run on all of these devices, which include:

- Personal data assistant (PDA) devices such as Palm Pilot, Handspring Visor, vTech Helio, IBM WorkPad, and Apple's Newton and MessagePad 2000
- Pocket PC devices such as Compaq iPAQ, Casio EM500, HP Jornada, and Phillips Nino
- Handheld, pen-based tablets running Windows CE such as Fujitsu Stylistic and PenCentra and Siemens SIMpad SL4
- Handheld Windows CE PC devices with pen and keyboard such as Vadem Clio, HP Jornada 700 series, NEC MobilePro, Intermec 6651 Pen Tablet Computer, and Melard Sidearm
- Wearable computing devices such as Xybernaut MA-IV, Via family of products, and Pittsburgh Digital Greenhouse's Spot

Different classes of device have different memory footprints, processor speeds, and user input devices that can radically affect a user's interaction style from one class to another. For example, a wearable computer can bring the power of the desktop computer into the field, making client applications as sophisticated there as they are in the office. Users in this case also have a plethora of input devices to choose from, including keyboard, voice, pen, and custom devices.

On the other hand, the processor speeds, memory footprints, and available input devices for the PDA class are severely limited, which means that user interactions that can be engineered for these devices are also constrained. Still, PDAs are extremely important in the various contexts in which field service workers perform their tasks. The Luther architecture must address the variability of the users' interaction styles, which are limited by differences in hardware capability among the device classes.

Existing Procedures, Business Processes, and Systems.   Field service workers are only one part of most enterprises. Information gathered by them must be stored in the back office; instructions for them come, partially, from outside the field; and many applications already support existing business processes.

To respond to these needs, the Luther architecture must intergrate its functions with a worker's existing procedures and processes, enable applications to be hosted on servers and databases from many vendors, and simplify the integration of applications with legacy systems

Building Applications.   Enabling faster construction of applications is one of the main motivations for Luther. There are a number of aspects to this goal, including:

- Encouraging software re-use and making it easier for applications to work together. This avoids wasting valuable resources to "re-invent the wheel."
- Enabling a build-first, buy-later strategy for enterprise functions (e.g., work flow).

- Providing a stable platform for adoption of new features and emerging technologies that span applications, such as location sensing, automatic detection and identification of nearby physical objects and services, and advanced user interface features like synthetic interviewing.

Distributed Computing. The Luther architecture must provide enterprise application developers with a framework and infrastructure that even out the differences in client device capabilities and provide application servers with the following distributed application features.

- *Scalability.* The Luther server framework must facilitate scalability with no impact on performance. That is, the addition of any number of domain-specific components over time must have no impact on the performance of the application software, nor must it cause the re-engineering of client applications. In addition, client applications must be easily reconfigurable to make use of added capability. The framework must also support the ability of applications to discover new capability and to dynamically reconfigure themselves to make use of it.

- *Load balancing.* The Luther architecture must support load balancing in a distributed environment. Most of the computation in its applications will be performed on the server side, with the results sent to the client. As more and more clients access the capability from a given server, the application server infrastructure will have to detect heavy loads on a given server and offload processing to application server components located on different server nodes within the enterprise. Similarly, the enterprise environment application must be able to detect a node failure and shift to another application server in the enterprise to continue execution. In both cases, load balancing must be transparent to the user, and in the first case it must also be transparent to the client application.

- *Location independence.* To support load balancing, domain-specific application capability must be distributed, and the Luther architecture must support this. To be able to change locations dynamically, applications must be location independent.

- *Portability.* Enterprise application environments invariably comprise a set of heterogeneous server hardware platforms. The Luther architecture framework will have to allow the software to run on myriad platforms in order for enterprise applications to work.

17.3 Architectural Solution

The main architectural decision made in response to requirements was that Luther would be constructed on top of J2EE, which has the following advantages:

- It is commercially available from a variety of vendors. Components, such as work-flow management, that may be useful in Luther are being widely developed.

- HTTP becomes the basis of communication because it is layered on top of the TCP/IP protocol, which in turn is supported by a variety of commercial wireless standards, such as the IEEE 802.11b. Any Web-based client can be made mobile given the appropriate wireless LAN infrastructure. Most of the devices that must be supported by Luther can support HTTP.

- It separates the user interface and allows the *user experience* paradigm to be implemented. This paradigm proposes that the computer and its application be another, noninvasive, tool for the field service worker. It must be a natural extension of the way that tasks are performed, yet provide performance-enhancing benefits for both the field service worker and the organization.

  The paradigm goes on to say that multiple views of an enterprise application should be developed, each for a particular field service worker's role. A view is tailored to that role to enhance performance and job satisfaction, and filters, fuses, synthesizes, and displays the appropriate information for it. The view includes the use of role-appropriate input devices.

  For example, if a keyboard is not appropriate, perhaps voice input can be used. If the environment is too noisy, perhaps a custom input device like a *dial* is used, which a user can turn (the dial is mounted on the user's uniform as shown in Figure 17.2) to navigate through links, buttons, radio buttons, and other similar UI widgets in the client application to make them hot. In the middle of the device, the user can tap an "enter" key to select the link, click the button, and so forth. This device can be used in the most rugged environments, for example, even when a worker is wearing thick gloves.

  "Separating the user interface" is a tactic we saw for usability in Chapter 5. In Luther it brings the flexibility to change the user interface and adapt it to different devices and needs as well, which is a kind of modifiability. Again we see that some tactics apply to achieving more than one kind of quality attribute.

- It supports the separation and abstraction of data sources. The user experiences require the filtering, fusion, synthesis, and display of data that comes from multiple, disparate data sources. Some of these data sources are database management systems, others are legacy applications built on enterprise resource planning systems that encapsulate corporate data. Inmedius realized that by abstracting and separating data sources from the applications that use them and by providing them with well-defined, standard interfaces, the applications remain true to their defined abstractions and thus are re-usable. Additionally, some interfaces are industry standards, such as JDBC/ODBC, which allow the data sources themselves to be treated as abstract components that can be swapped in and out of the enterprise application at will.

Figure 17. 3 shows how a Luther application interacts with its environment. (It does not show the J2EE elements; we will discuss the mapping of the application to J2EE shortly.) First, note the (n:1:m) relationship among user interfaces,

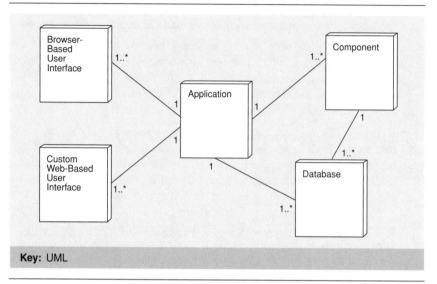

FIGURE 17.3   Deployment view of a Luther application

applications, and what Inmedius calls "components," that is, building blocks for application functionality. A Luther application is thin; much of its business logic is assembled from existing components, and it is not tied to any specific user interface. Essentially, the application code contains these three things:

- Session state definition and management
- Application-specific (i.e., nonreusable) business logic
- Logic that delegates business requests to an appropriate sequence of component method invocations

The application does not have a main method; it has an application programming interface (API), which represents the features and functions available from the application to its user interfaces. The user interface is independent of the application. It may expose any subset of features appropriate for the target interface device. For instance, if a user interface is created for a device with a microphone and speaker but no display, it does not expose features of the application that require graphics.

Now we turn to an in-depth discussion of the three main elements shown in Figure 17.3: the user interface (UI), the application, and the components.

USER INTERFACE

The strategy for developing user interfaces in the Luther architecture is as follows. First, a combination of domain experts, cognitive psychologists, and graphic artists work with a client to understand the various workers' tasks and roles, the work environments, and the necessary interface characteristics of the desired access devices. Next, they craft the user experience based on these constraints, with the result being a storyboard, screen shots, and a prototype. The point is that the result of the design process must be a high-quality, high-fidelity user experience, as described before. This is essential, since the application is meant to augment the user's existing work procedures and be a natural extension of the work environment. Consequently, the task of developing the user experience is delegated to the people best suited for it—domain experts who understand the task and the work environment; cognitive psychologists who understand how people think, reason, and absorb information; and graphic artists who are skilled at presenting information in an effective and appealing manner.

The next step is to take the output of the design process—the storyboard, screen shots, and prototype—and quickly convert this to a working user interface on real devices. Here, the architecture must support the integration of custom user experiences. Integration must be rapid, and it should enable creation of common portions and re-use of software to the greatest extent possible, all the while preserving the integrity and fidelity of the original user experience design.

Turning a user experience design into a working user interface is complicated by many factors. First, a variety of client devices must be supported. This includes an assortment of mobile devices with varying screen sizes, operating systems, and input devices. A user interface that performs well on a desktop PC is severely limited by the smaller screen, less memory, and less functional support on a mobile device. Some mobile devices, for example, have no keyboard or mouse support, rendering user interfaces that require them useless. A second factor is the limitations introduced by technology. For instance, certain types of user interaction or information display are cumbersome over HTTP and may lead to poor performance.

In the end, there may be multiple client devices and user interfaces for any given application. The software architecture must be flexible enough to deal with multiple clients that differ greatly from one another. In Figures 17.4 and 17.5, the two types of user interface implementation supported by Luther are shown—namely, browser-based clients (Figure 17.4) and custom, Web-based clients (Figure 17.5). Figure 17.6 refines the view given in Figure 17.3 and illustrates the structure of each type.

Browser-Based Clients.   Browser-based user interface clients correspond simply to browser-based clients in J2EE. They are not restricted to Web browsers, however, but equally support other forms of markup such as a Wireless Markup Language (WML) over a Wireless Application Protocol (WAP) for cellular phones. While the markup language is different in this case (i.e., WML), the same mechanisms for delivering the content can still be employed—that is, a combination of servlets and JavaServer Pages (JSPs).

Browser-based clients use standardized methods for the exchange of information (i.e., commercial Web browsers on the client side, HTTP over TCP/IP as the network protocol, and JSPs and Java servlets on the server side), and use common data formats (i.e., hypertext documents and style sheets). To make the

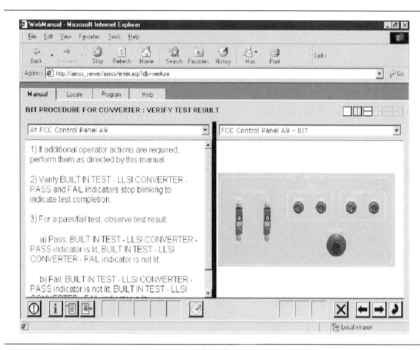

FIGURE 17.4 Browser interface for maintenance procedure

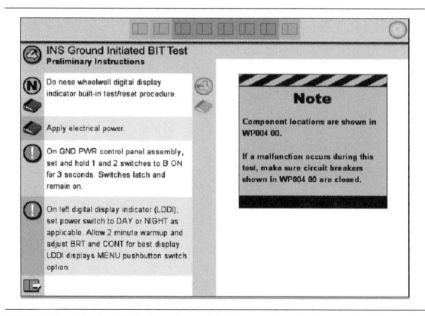

FIGURE 17.5 Custom Web-based user interface

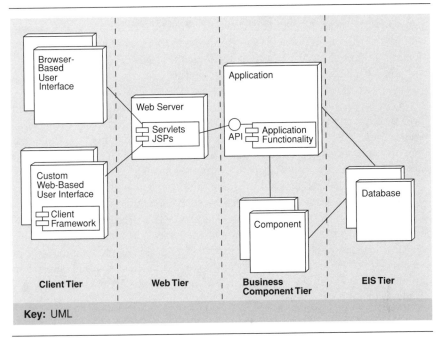

FIGURE 17.6   User interface as a C&C view overlaid onto a deployment view

client thin, most of the presentation logic is implemented on the server, which increases the chance of creating an interface that is portable across browser vendors and versions.

Browser-based clients are primarily intended for

- devices that support browsers and have traditional input devices such as pens, keyboards, and mice.
- applications that display content easily representable with markup languages and renderable by a browser, perhaps augmented with plug-ins.

Browsers were originally designed for desktop computers—making PCs their optimum target device—but today's mobile devices also support them.

Certain restrictions limit the use of browser-based interfaces. In design, for instance, they do not always make the best use of valuable resources, such as the available screen real estate, and the browser model supports only limited types of user interactions built around the HTTP request/response cycle. Also, browser-based interfaces are not suitable for all mobile devices because no browsers exist for certain ones; when they do, they may lack support for essential features such as frames, graphics, and JavaScript.

Custom Web-Based Clients.   Custom Web-based user interfaces are more complex. This type is different from a custom client, which in J2EE is a standalone program that implements all of the presentation logic and uses the remote invocation method (RMI) over the Internet Inter-ORB Protocol (IIOP) to interact directly with the business logic (i.e., EJBs). A custom Web-based client is also a stand-alone program but, unlike a custom J2EE client, it uses HTTP to communicate with the server and interacts with Web-tier entities, such as servlets and JSPs, in the same way as a browser-based client does.

Custom Web-based clients are written in a native development environment for a specific device or class of devices. Since the user interface is a standalone program, this gives the UI designers the most freedom in terms of user interactions that can be supported, and can lead to the best use of resources such as screen real estate. The downside is higher cost of development.

The Luther architecture has tried to minimize the amount of native code that must be written to create a custom, Web-based client, with a client framework that supports interfaces of this type, as shown in Figure 17.6. Basically, the framework standardizes elements that are needed across applications, including session management, authentication, and support for creating and sequencing presentation logic on the client, the Web container, or both. In essence, the client is a thin, standalone program that creates and lays out the native UI widgets. It also implements a small portion of the presentation logic such as input validation and sorting of tabular displays. Just as with browser-based clients, the bulk of the presentation logic is implemented on the Web tier in components managed by the client framework.

Custom, Web-based clients have advantages over other types of custom user interfaces. First, they are thin. In other words, compared to a fat client (i.e., a custom program where all of the presentation logic is implemented in the client tier), they are smaller, easier to maintain, and easier to port across devices. Second, they use HTTP to interact with the Web tier, unlike J2EE custom clients that use RMI over IIOP. This makes them more appropriate for non-Java implementations and simpler to implement over wireless networks.

Creating a custom, native user interface for each application on each device is too costly, even for a small number of devices. This is avoided by sorting interface devices into classes by characteristics. For each device class, a high-fidelity interface is designed and implemented as described previously. The client framework eases the burden of implementing this interface across a device class. Likewise, by implementing a significant portion of the presentation logic in the Web tier, client devices in the same class can use this software and thus share a significant portion of their implementation. Finally, the client framework introduces features that allow a device to advertise its interface characteristics. This information is made available to the presentation logic on the Web tier so that small adaptations can be made to the content before it is delivered to the client.

APPLICATIONS

In the Luther architecture, the application is responsible for uniting the system into a single functional entity and exposing an API for interacting with it. The user interfaces call into this API to provide these features to an end user.

Applications reside between any number of user interfaces and any number of components. An application ties together *m* components and exposes the aggregated "application" functionality to *n* user interfaces. The applications are "user interface agnostic," meaning that they expose functionality that any user interface can use. Each interface can expose all or a subset of this functionality as appropriate. For example, a user interface running on a mobile client like a Windows CE device cannot expose the administrative features you would expect to find in a desktop version. The idea is to expose all functions that can be performed in the system; each user interface decides which of these functions to expose to the user and how to expose them.

The requirement for rapid development and deployment leads to designing the application to be as thin as possible. This is achieved by delegating the bulk of the business work to components (discussed in the next section). The criterion for moving application code into a component is simple: Is the functionality re-usable? If so, it should be generalized (to increase re-usability) and implemented as a component. On the other hand, if a piece of functionality is not likely to be re-used, it is incorporated into the application.

The essential elements of an application include the following:

- *Application programming interface.* A façade for the functions exposed by the system to the user interfaces. Note that data passed through the API is generic (e.g., XML) rather than presentation specific (e.g., HTML).

- *Session state.* Initialized when a user authenticates, a session state exists until the client program terminates. J2EE simplifies state management, since the containers support authentication and authorization along with storage and retrieval of the session state. The application simply determines what data needs to be persisted across requests and makes the appropriate calls to store and to retrieve it.

- *Application-specific business logic.* Any logic that is unique to this application and that cannot be re-used in other applications.

- *Delegation to components.* Code for delegating work to components. In general, this is achieved via the *Business Delegate* design pattern.[1]

---

[1] A business delegate acts as a façade for a component—it locates the component and makes its functions available to the rest of the application. In this way, only the business delegate need be concerned with how to locate and access the component, hiding these details from the rest of the application. For instance, if a component is implemented as an EJB, the business delegate performs the necessary Java Naming Directory Interface (JNDI) look-ups and narrows the EJB remote interface; the fact that the component is implemented as an EJB remains hidden. The application is *not* responsible for component life-cycle management because the J2EE containers perform this function. However, since it does the delegating, it has to choose which component(s) to use. The application also includes logic that manages component interactions and inter-relationships. Clearly such logic belongs in the application. Following this rule simplifies the implementation of the components and minimizes inter-dependencies.

These elements result from application of the "anticipate expected changes" tactic and the associated "separate user interface" tactic for modifiability.

A new user interface can be created without changing the application layer or components at all. A new implementation of a component can be integrated into the system without affecting the application layer or the user interfaces. New functionality can be added to the system by incorporating another component, adding the necessary API methods to the application layer, and adding (or not) new features to each user interface to expose the new functions.

COMPONENTS

The intention behind a component is that it represent an element for re-use. The strategy is therefore to create a library of components from which applications can be easily and quickly synthesized to create specialized solutions for customers. The library contains *core* components related to the client and server frameworks; *domain-specific* components for domains, such as maintenance, repair, and overhaul; and *generalized capability* (i.e., utility) components that applications might need to round out functionality, such as security, authorization, and user management.

Inmedius's strategy is to evolve a large library of core, domain-specific, and generalized capability components for the Luther architecture framework and for specific customer domains. Application development therefore becomes an exercise in creating business logic that composes the necessary set of capability components into a customized solution for the customer.

Crafting common components is a central theme in the construction of software product lines and represents an intense application of the "abstract common services" tactic for modifiability—in this case, the ability to produce new solutions.

Component Design.   The strategy for designing components is to use design standards, wherever possible, for the component's API and behaviors. For example, the Inmedius work-flow component (described later) is an instantiation of the Workflow Management Coalition's specification for work-flow functionality and behavior. This design strategy allows Inmedius to replace its own components with any other vendor's components that adhere to the same capability specifications. It facilitates the expansion of the Inmedius component library to include such components.

Capability Partitioning.   It may be that the library does not contain a capability component required by a given application under development. A decision must be made as to whether to design and implement the capability as part of the application itself or as a new, re-usable component.

The key design heuristic is whether the capability is a part of the application's business logic for this specific solution or an instance of a more general capability that might be used in other applications.

Component Packaging. Any application in Luther uses the J2EE environment and its services. Given this constraint, components in that environment can be packaged as EJBs; Java bean components; individual Java class libraries, applets, servlets, or some combinations of these. In other words, a component is *not* synomous with an EJB, but rather can be packaged in a variety of ways.

The strategy for packaging a given capability depends on the J2EE services used as well as the tradeoffs among a number of key factors (e.g., frequency of inter-object communication, location of object instances, and need for J2EE services such as transactions and persistence of object state over multiple user sessions). For example, communication with an EJB is via RMI, a heavyweight communication mechanism. In some J2EE containers, communication with EJBs is optimized (into local method calls) if the communication is within the same Java Virtual Machine (JVM). However, since optimization is not required of a J2EE container, communication between EJBs always has the potential of being costly, so must not be taken lightly if performance is an issue. An alternative is to create a Java class library to avoid the need (and overhead) for RMI. However, this also forces the component to take on additional responsibilities previously handled by the container, such as creation and deletion of component instances.

Objects associated with a component must be made accessible to a user for the extent of a session. They may change during that time but the data must persist and be consistent across sessions. Consequently, components often require transactions. Multiple users may be accessing the same objects simultaneously, potentially for the same purpose, and this has to be handled gracefully. Supporting transactions also makes graceful recovery from failure easier by leaving the database in a consistent state.

As described in Chapter 16, the EJBs model supports several bean types, including entity beans, session beans, and stateless session beans. The different types are intended to support different forms of business logic, and they are handled differently by the container. For instance, an entity bean allows the choice of managing persistence yourself via callbacks supported by the container (i.e., bean-managed persistence) or having the container do it for you (i.e., container-managed persistence). In either case, a significant amount of overhead is involved, which limits the practical use of an entity bean to long-lived business entities characterized by coarse-grained data accesses.

What the J2EE Container Provides. There are several capabilities that applications require, such as transaction support, security, and load balancing. These capabilities are very complex (indeed, many corporations organize their entire business around offering them) and are outside the scope of a given application or application domain. One of the main drivers in Inmedius's decision to build Luther using J2EE was the fact that commercially available J2EE-compliant containers provide these features, so Inmedius does not have to implement them.

Many of these capabilities can be configured for an individual EJB at application deployment time, or they are provided to the EJB transparently by the

J2EE container. In either case, the EJB developer does not have to embed calls to them directly into the code, so they can be easily configured for a given customer. This not only facilitates the creation of application-independent EJB components but also guarantees that the components will successfully run within all J2EE-compliant containers.

- The EJB container provides transaction support both declaratively and programmatically. The component developer can programmatically interact with the container to provide fine-grained, hard-coded EJB transaction support. The developer may also declaratively specify, via the deployment descriptor, how EJB methods should behave within transactions. This allows transactions to behave differently in different applications without the EJB having to implement or configure them directly in the code.

- J2EE provides an integrated security model that spans both Web and EJB containers. Like transaction support, security features can be used either declaratively or programmatically. If methods are written to include definitions of the permissions required to execute them, the developer can specify which users (or groups of users) are allowed method access in the deployment descriptor. Otherwise, entries in the deployment descriptor can be used to declaratively associate access rights with methods. Again, this allows the component methods to have arbitrary permissions determined by the application, without having to rewrite the component.

- The EJB container also provides transparent load balancing. EJB instances are created and managed by the container at runtime; that is, they are created, activated, passivated, and removed, as necessary. If an EJB has not been accessed recently, it may be passivated, meaning that its data will be saved to persistent storage and the instance removed from memory. In this way, the container effectively performs load balancing across all of the instances in the container to manage resource consumption and to optimize system performance.

What the Component Developer Provides. The component developer provides the client view, or API, of the component, as well as the component implementation. With a simple EJB, this amounts to writing only three classes: the home interface, the remote interface, and the implementation class.

The component developer also provides definitions of the data types exposed to clients through the API. These are implemented as additional classes, and often take the form of value objects that are passed back and forth to an EJB through the API.

EXAMPLE OF A RE-USABLE COMPONENT: WORK FLOW

In this section, we will look at one of the re-usable capability components developed for the Inmedius component library, the issues it raised, and the decisions made. The work-flow component, the largest of the capability components thus far created, is an example of the how a generalized capability is engineered and packaged for inclusion in the Luther architecture.

Design Rationale.   The primary responsibility of the work-flow component is to allow a client to model a work flow and then move digital artifacts through it. The component must also allow clients to define resources and assign them to work-flow activities. Naturally, the component must be highly re-usable and extendable, which means that it should provide general work-flow capabilities; provide a clear but generic model of operation to the applications that will use it; and be agnostic with respect to the digital artifacts that may move through a particular work-flow instance. The creation of a full-functionality work-flow component requires complex idioms such as branching, merging, and looping. Generally implementing a work-flow capability is a very large, complex task.

Inmedius faced a dilemma in that there was a legitimate need for work-flow capabilities in its applications but many factors, such as the following, prevented their complete implementation:

- The size and complexity of a complete work-flow capability was beyond Inmedius's resources.
- Complete work-flow capability was not a core business objective or a core competency.
- Other companies had built far more complete solutions.

The long-term solution was to form alliances with organizations that provide componentized work-flow capability for J2EE applications. Until that happened, however, Inmedius had to implement a subset of capability in order to deploy solutions.

Thus, the strategy was to design a component that could be easily swapped with a more complete one from another organization at a later time. This created the need for a standardized work-flow component interface. Notice how the ABC works in this case. The design of the Luther architecture opened up a new business opportunity (work-flow management) and Inmedius had to make an explicit business decision to enter this market. Inmedius decided that it was outside its core competence.

The Workflow Management Coalition has developed of a set of functional and behavioral work-flow specifications that have been recognized by the work-flow community. Inmedius architects built its component to those specifications, yet implemented only the functionality that is necessary for use by the current applications.

This strategy leveraged the knowledge and experience of the work-flow community and all of its activities. The community had already defined business objects and relationships between objects, so Inmedius did not have to reinvent them. Second, by adhering to Workflow Management Coalition specifications, Inmedius could now replace its work-flow component with that of another vendor, with

minimal effort if a customer required a certain degree of functionality not provided in the Inmedius component.

Two Workflow Management Coalition specifications describe the two primary
elements: the definition of a work-flow model and the representation of its runtime instances (see Figure 17.7). The work-flow model definition is made up of
one or more process definitions, each of which consists of activity definitions and
transitions between those activities and all participating resources. In each process
definition, a process manager oversees all runtime instances of a specific process
definition; each runtime instance maintains state as to which activities have been
completed, which are active and who is assigned them, and context data that the
work-flow component needs to make decisions while the process is active.

One issue of concern to Inmedius was concurrency. Should more than one user
be permitted to modify a work-flow model definition at one time? If active runtime instances exist, should a user be permitted to modify a work-flow model definition? Should a user be permitted to start a new work flow if its definition is
being modified? Given the implementation, a yes answer to any of these questions posed a significant problem because of the relationship between a definition

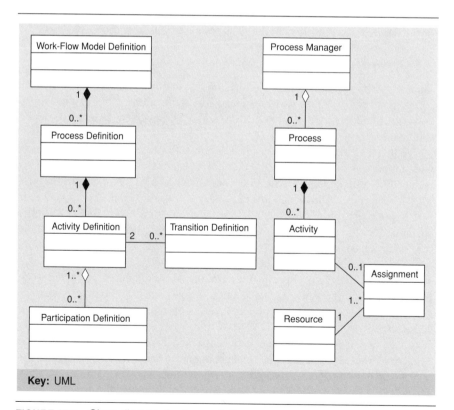

FIGURE 17.7   Class diagram for the work-flow component

and its runtime instances. As a result, any solution would have to prohibit these situations from occurring.

Because the underlying problem in each of the situations described before revolved around modifying the work-flow model definition, the solution was to associate a lock with it. In order to modify a definition, a user must obtain a lock. Only one lock can exist for a given definition and it cannot be obtained if the definition has any associated active runtime instances. In addition, a new runtime instance cannot be started if the work-flow model definition is locked.

Packaging. The work-flow component is packaged as two EJBs: a stateless session bean for managing instances of work-flow model definitions and a single entity bean for managing the definition itself (see Figure 17.8). The decision to package the component this way was based strongly on the characteristics of the different EJBs.

Entity EJBs implement abstractions in an application that represent shared resources, where persistent object data is shared among many components and users. The work-flow model definition represents just such a single shared resource—namely, a definition of a process that can be instantiated many times. In Inmedius applications, any user in any location can start a new process based on this single work-flow model definition and participate in its activities.

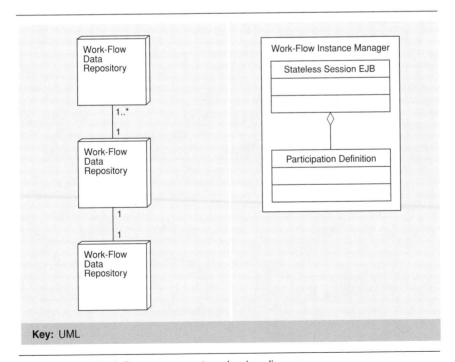

FIGURE 17.8 *Work-flow component packaging diagram*

Session EJBs model state and behavior. The definition of new work-flow models, the creation of work-flow model instances, the creation of activities, the assignment of resources to activities, and the completion of activities, for example, are all services provided to users over the course of a work-flow instance life cycle or session. Therefore, work-flow instances are most naturally implemented by session EJBs.

Once it was decided to make the work-flow instance manager a session EJB, a decision had to be made as to whether to make the session EJB stateful or stateless. This depended on the characteristics of the state to be maintained. Typically, a stateful session EJB maintains state for a single client with whom it is having a dialog. However, the state of a runtime work-flow instance is not manipulated by just a single client but is updated by many clients, including those who participate in the actual work-flow process and managers who want to monitor the process and analyze its results. As a result, the work-flow instance manager was implemented as a stateless session EJB, which is more lightweight and scalable than a stateful session EJB and which persists the state in a database on behalf of a given client, where all the other clients have access to it.

Another design tradeoff concerned how to package the individual objects within a work-flow model definition. Should they be packaged as entity EJBs, or should they comprise Java classes packaged using some other structure, such as a library? Because these objects interact with and are dependent on each other, to package them as entity EJBs would constantly require locating and retaining multiple EJB handles in the application, creating much overhead. In addition, recall that any method invocation on an EJB is essentially an RMI call and can be quite costly. While most J2EE containers can determine if the method invocation is in the same Java Virtual Machine and therefore optimize it into a local method call, this is not guaranteed. For these reasons, the design decision was to create entity EJBs for coarse-grained abstractions in the application, such as the work-flow model definition, and to implement the finer-grained abstractions in the entity EJB itself as libraries of Java classes—all to reduce the overhead associated with the heavyweight entity EJB relationships.

An example of this type of design decision in the work-flow component was deciding where to locate the logic that determines whether to grant a request for a lock on the work-flow model definition. Originally, that logic was placed inside the entity EJB implementing the work-flow model definition. A request to lock the definition would be made directly to the entity EJB, which would determine if the lock could be granted (and, if so, lock it).

A problem became apparent when it came time to enhance the business logic so that a lock could be granted only if no active runtime work-flow instances existed. The methods that provided runtime work-flow instance information were defined on the stateless session EJB, the object interacting with the entity EJB. It did not seem right to pass a reference to the stateless session EJB into the entity EJB—first, because the entity EJB would be aware of the environment in which it exists (thus, hampering re-use); second, because any method invocations made by the entity EJB on the stateless session EJB would be RMI calls.

Another option was to use the data access objects of the entity EJB directly in order to retrieve the necessary information from the database. However, this would break the abstraction implemented by the entity EJB, forcing it to be responsible for something that it should not be responsible for and that is already the responsibility of another object. Lastly, there would be a duplication of code that would create maintainability problems.

The solution was to place the logic (i.e., that determines whether a request for a lock on the work-flow model definition is granted) in the stateless session EJB. The entity EJB now simply knows how to persist and retrieve locks to and from the database. When a request for a lock is received, the stateless session EJB determines if it can be granted and, if so, instructs the entity EJB to lock the work-flow model definition. This solution maintains the integrity of the abstractions implemented by the objects and eliminates unnecessary inter-EJB relationships.

Distributed and Detached Operations. When designing the component to support distributed and detached operations, a number of interesting issues arose, primarily about whether to support distributed concurrency of work-flow activities. Consider a scenario in which a work-flow model definition and its runtime instances are located across multiple servers. While J2EE transaction support can guarantee that no two users can violate work-flow rules if they access the same data in the same database, it cannot guarantee that rules will not be violated if two users access replicated data for the same work flow in different databases.

In this scenario, one user could lock a work-flow model definition in one location for the purpose of modifying it while another user was creating a new runtime instance of the same definition in another location. During data replication and synchronization among the distributed servers, conflicts might arise that could corrupt the work-flow data in the enterprise environment if not resolvable. To guarantee that work-flow rules would not be violated across multiple databases, additional functionality would be needed to resolve every type of conflict. Implementing this level of functionality was outside the scope of Inmedius's initial release. To meet the requirement, distributed and detailed operation scenarios had to be supported.

The system architecture and environment dictated the two scenarios of distributed and detached operations initially supported. In a distributed operation, a common repository is shared that itself supports transactions (e.g., a database). In other words, multiple instances of the application server may exist in several locations but each must access the same data repository that contains the work-flow model definitions and runtime instances. This is because the information used by the application server to determine whether work-flow rules have been violated is stored in the data repository. In detached operations, one installation (i.e., application server and data repository) is designated as the master installation and all others as subordinate instances. The work-flow model definition must be created and defined via the master and then replicated to all subordinates. Once a definition is distributed, it cannot change other than specifying who can participate in the defined activities. As runtime work-flow instances at the subordinate installations are created and eventually closed, these are replicated back to the master for historical purposes.

RAMIFICATIONS OF USING J2EE

This section discusses the rationale for several Luther decisions regarding the use of J2EE.

Decisions Made by Design versus Those Dictated by J2EE.   When designing a system using the J2EE runtime environment, some decisions are left up to the designer and others are constrained by the J2EE rules and structure. For example, J2EE mandates where servlets, JSPs, and EJBs reside within a container—servlets and JSPs in the Web tier and EJBs in the EJB tier.

However, the Java 2 Enterprise Edition environment also provides the designer with some flexibility—for example, in implementing security (declarative versus programmatic), transaction support (declarative versus programmatic), and data access (container-managed versus bean-managed).

When designing a component, the designer has total control over functionality to allocate to a servlet, JSP, or EJB, and here the obvious choices might not always be the best. For instance, one of Inmedius's components supports collaboration between two or more users. Since this component represents re-usable business logic, the rules of component selection specify that it should be packaged as an EJB. Unfortunately, further analysis proved that this was not the correct design. Additional factors must be considered when determining how to map a component design onto the four logical tiers provided by J2EE, as shown in Figure 16.2.

Issues Introduced by the Multiple Tiers in the J2EE.   One issue is performance. A major contributor to poor performance is the number of calls made from one J2EE entity (e.g., servlet, EJB) to another within a given transaction. Technically, each EJB method call is an RMI call, which can be very expensive. The implementation of coarse-grained EJBs and the elimination of inter-entity EJB relationships are two ways to address this issue and thereby ensure good component performance.

Another issue is transactions, which may be managed programmatically or declaratively. Obviously, managing transactions declaratively is somewhat easier because code does not have to contain begin and end transaction statements. However, developers must be mindful of how their J2EE entity will be used. The easy course is to require transactions for all methods. Unfortunately, this creates unnecessary runtime overhead if transactions are not truly needed. Another problem arises when methods on a J2EE entity do not require transaction support and the deployment descriptor enforces this. If another container involved in a transaction uses the J2EE entity, the transaction it has created will fail. Instead, the deployment descriptor should declare that the method supports transactions. Careful thought must be given to what aspects of a component require transactions to ensure correct operation, and these decisions must be mapped to a combination of the declarative and programmatic mechanisms supported by J2EE.

17.4   How Luther Achieved Its Quality Goals

All but one of Luther's quality requirements came from its customers: wireless access; flexibile user interfaces and devices; support for existing procedures, business processes, and systems; and for distributed computing. The only one that came from Inmedius was ease of building applications.

The primary decision in achieving these requirements was to use J2EE, but only in a particular fashion. The user interface was clearly and cleanly separated from the applications, standards were used whenever possible, and a re-usable library of components was to be constructed opportunistically. Table 17.1 shows the strategies and tactics used in this effort.

TABLE 17.1   How Strategy Achieves Goals

Goal	Strategy	Tactics
Wireless Access	Use standard wireless protocols	Adherence to defined protocols
Flexible User Interface	Support both browser-based and custom interfaces through HTTP	Semantic coherence; separate user interface; user model
Support Multiple Devices	Use standard protocols	Anticipate expected changes; adherence to defined protocols
Integration with Existing Business Processes	Use J2EE as an integration mechanism	Abstract common services; component replacement
Rapid Building of Applications	Use J2EE as a basis for Luther and construct re-usable components	Abstract common services; generalize module (in this case, J2EE represents the generalized module)
Distributed Infrastructure	Use J2EE and standard protocols	Generalize module; runtime registration

17.5   Summary

Inmedius develops solutions for field service workers. Such workers require high mobility with untethered access to computers. These computers are typically highly portable—sometimes with hands-free operation. In each case, systems require integration with back-office operations.

Luther is a solution that Inmedius constructed to support the rapid building of customer support systems. It is based on J2EE. A great deal of attention has been given to developing re-usable components and frameworks that simplify the addition of various portions, and its user interface is designed to enable customer- as well as browser-based solutions.

Reliance on J2EE furthered the business goals of Inmedius but also introduced the necessity for additional design decisions in terms of what was packaged as which kind of bean (or not). This is an example of the backward flow of the ABC, emphasizing the movement away from stovepipe solutions toward common solutions.

17.6   For Further Reading

The reader interested in wearable computers is referred to [Barfield 01] as well as the proceedings of the annual IEEE-sponsored International Symposium on Wearable Computers (*http://iswc.gatech.edu/*).

The business delegate pattern used in Luther can be found in [Alur 01]. The Workflow Management Coalition reports its activities on *http://www.wfmc.org*.

17.7   Discussion Questions

1. Many of the case studies in this book feature architectures that separate the producers of data within a system from the consumers of data. Why is that important? What kind of tactic is it? Compile a list of the tactics or design approaches used to achieve separation, beginning with the ones shown in this chapter.

2. A great deal of attention has been given to separating the user interface from the remainder of the application both in Luther and in our other case studies. Why is this such a pervasive tactic?

18

Building Systems from Off-the-Shelf Components

with Robert C. Seacord and Matthew Bass

> *It's so beautifully arranged on the plate—you just know someone's fingers have been all over it.*
> — Julia Child, on nouvelle cuisine

Throughout this book we have emphasized the connection between desired quality attributes and architecture. Our underlying assumption has been that control over system design means control over the qualities achieved. Increasingly this is not true. Systems are being constructed with more and more off-the-shelf components, for economic reasons and because the expertise needed in many technical areas is so specialized. Components change the design process; they can also constrain the architecture. Although typically chosen to achieve some set of functionality, components also embody architectural (and hence quality) assumptions. The architect must ensure that these assumptions are the right ones and that they are compatible.

Operating systems impose certain solutions and have since the 1960s. Database management systems have been around since the early 1970s. Because of the ubiquity of computers the possibility of using externally developed components to achieve some system goals has been increasing dramatically. Even the availability of components may not cause you to use or keep them (see the sidebar Quack.com), but you certainly need to understand how to incorporate them into your system.

Note: Robert C. Seacord is a senior member of the technical staff at the Software Engineering Institute; Matthew Bass is a member of the technical staff at the Software Engineering Institute.

For systems built from off-the-shelf (OTS) components, component selection involves a discovery process, which seeks to identify *assemblies* of compatible components, understanding how they can achieve the desired quality attributes, and deciding whether they can be integrated into the system being built.

Quack.com

The beginning:
The Quack.com company was founded in late 1998 by two former SEI colleagues (Jeromy Carriére and Steve Woods), as well as University of Hawaii professor Alex Quilici. Their goal was to make only commerce and content available over the telephone. They built a demo, and by late summer 1999 had convinced a few "angels" and venture capitalists to give them funding. They understood the importance of a sound architecture and built their "real" system as a voice portal on top of a speech-application publishing platform and toolkit. This allowed them to quickly build and maintain a wide variety of applications and potentially be the underlying platform for a whole new industry. Nine months after acquiring their first funding, they released a preliminary Web-based consumer voice portal. It allowed people to access information about weather, movies, stocks, and so forth using a telephone. On August 31, 2000, America Online acquired Quack. A short time later, October 25, 2000, AOL released AOLbyPhone, which had been built by Quack's team; it used their platform and toolkit.

The story of Quack.com is instructive in terms of the roles and limitations of off-the-shelf components. As can be inferred, Quack was under severe time-to-market pressure to demonstrate a voice portal. Other startups were also active in this space, some of them better funded. Quack searched for as many available components as they could locate, and constructed their architecture to accommodate them. This played a significant part in their ability to get to market nine months after they first acquired external funding.

Quack's first portal was important to their success and useful in its own right, but they never had a broad user base for it. Once they were acquired by AOL, however, their business focus changed. With its 34,000,000 subscribers, AOL quickly elevated availability and performance as primary business drivers. Quack.com was now subject to much more intense use and more stringent availability requirements.

Their response was to rewrite the components. Their architecture was flexible enough to allow scaling up to the expected number of users and to support the required availability, but they did not know how the components would respond. By rewriting them (in the order of their criticality), they gained control of the performance and availability of the whole system.

This experience is echoed in other systems we have seen. We recently visited a small startup company launching a software product line. The people there knew that there is no second chance to make a first impression, and so reliability and scalability led their list of architectural concerns. As their architect told us, "If the function is unimportant, COTS will do. If there's an actual or de facto standard for some aspect of the system, then COTS will do, as there is likely to be a choice of more than one vendor that meets the standard. But when in doubt, with no practical workarounds available, we will not hesitate to build the components in-house." Before coming to this small start-up, this architect helped build a major Web search engine and content provider. In four years, he watched usage go from 45,000 to 45,000,000 page views per day. With millions of people using the system, he learned very quickly to do what it takes to avoid being awakened in the middle of the night with a business-threatening problem.

Off-the-shelf components fill an important role in providing large amounts of functionality in quickly available packaging. However, they also can prevent the architect from having total control over the quality attributes that the system displays. Like so much in software engineering, components are extremely useful but they are not the silver bullet that they are sometimes portrayed to be.

— LJB and PCC

This chapter describes a lightweight, common-sense process that can guide component selection. The process begins by hypothesizing what it means for the components you have chosen to "work," building some simple prototypes to test those hypotheses, evolving what works, and keeping a backup plan in case your guess is wrong. The key insight here is that choosing and selecting single components is not enough. You need to choose and test assemblies of components that will work in concert.

The chapter includes a demonstration of the process that was applied to a recently fielded system.

18.1   Impact of Components on Architecture

Consider the following situation. You are producing software to control a chemical plant. Within chemical plants, specialized displays keep the operator informed as to the state of the reactions being controlled. A large portion of the software you are constructing is used to draw those displays. A vendor sells user interface controls that produce them. Because it is easier to buy than build, you decide to purchase the controls—which, by the way, are only available for Visual Basic.

What impact does this decision have on your architecture? Either the whole system must be written in Visual Basic with its built-in callback-centered style or the operator portion must be isolated from the rest of the system in some fashion.

This is a fundamental structural decision, driven by the choice of a single component for a single portion of the system.

The use of off-the-shelf components in software development, while essential in many cases, also introduces new challenges. In particular, component capabilities and liabilities are a principle architectural constraint.

All but the simplest components have a presumed architectural pattern that is difficult to violate. For example, an HTTP server assumes a client-server architectural pattern with defined interfaces and mechanisms for integrating back-end functionality. If the architecture you design conflicts with the architecture assumed by an HTTP server component, you may find yourself with an exceptionally difficult integration task.

The fact that components assume an architectural pattern makes it difficult to select an architecture prior to understanding the component assembly that has been selected (or is under consideration) for the system under design. The architectural assumptions inherent in these components, and the mechanisms for successfully integrating them, are often dictated or at least strongly influenced by component selections. This means that an understanding of components and their interactions must be established before an architecture can be finalized.

18.2 Architectural Mismatch

Not all components work together—even if they are commercial products that claim compatibility. Components are often "almost compatible," where "almost" is a euphemism for "not." More insidious is the case where components appear to work together—the assembled code compiles and even executes—but the system produces the wrong answer because the components do not work together quite as expected. The errors can be subtle, especially in real-time or parallel systems in which the components might rely on seemingly innocuous assumptions about the timing or relative ordering of each other's operations.

In short, components that were not developed specifically for *your* system may not meet all of *your* requirements—they may not even work with the components you pair them with. Worse, you may not know if they are suitable or not until you buy them and try them because component interfaces are notoriously poor at specifying their quality attributes: How secure is the compiler you are using right now? How reliable is the mail system on your desktop? How accurate is the math library that your applications depend on? And what happens when you discover that the answer to any of these questions is "not enough"?

Garlan, Allen, and Ockerbloom coined the term *architectural mismatch* to describe this impediment to successfully integrating component-based systems. They state the problem as a mismatch between assumptions embodied in separately developed components, which often manifests itself architecturally, such as when two components disagree about which one invokes the other. Architectural mismatch usually shows up at system integration time—the system will not compile, will not link, or will not run.

Architectural mismatch is a special case of *interface mismatch*, where the interface is as Parnas defined it: the assumptions that components can make about each other. This definition goes beyond what has, unfortunately, become the standard concept of interface in current practice: a component's API (for example, a Java interface specification). An API names the programs and their parameters and may say something about their behavior, but this is only a small part of the information needed to correctly use a component. Side effects, consumption of global resources, coordination requirements, and the like, are a necessary part of an interface and are included in a complete interface specification. Interface mismatch can appear at integration time, just like architectural mismatch, but it can also precipitate the insidious runtime errors mentioned before.

These assumptions can take two forms. *Provides* assumptions describe the services a component provides to its users or clients. *Requires* assumptions detail the services or resources that a component must have in order to correctly function. Mismatch between two components occurs when their provides and requires assumptions do not match up.

What can you do about interface mismatch? Besides changing your requirements so that yesterday's bug is today's feature (which is often a viable option), there are three things:

- Avoid it by carefully *specifying* and inspecting the components for your system.
- Detect those cases you have not avoided by careful *qualification* of the components.
- Repair those cases you have detected by *adapting* the components.

The rest of this section will deal with techniques for avoiding, detecting, and repairing mismatch. We begin with repair.

TECHNIQUES FOR REPAIRING INTERFACE MISMATCH

To date, mismatch correction (or "component/interface repair") has received little systematic attention. Terms such as "component glue" are evocative of the character of the integration code and reflect the second-class status we assign to its development. Often repairing interface mismatches is seen as a job for hackers (or sometimes junior programmers) whose sense of aesthetics is not offended by the myriad "hacks" involved in integrating off-the-shelf components. However, as is often the case, the weak link in a chain defines the chain's strength. Thus, the quality of component repair may be directly responsible for achieving—or failing to achieve—system-wide quality attributes such as availability and modifiability.

A first step toward a more disciplined approach to interface repair is to categorize the basic techniques and their qualities. One obvious repair method is to change the code of the offending component. However, this is often not possible, given that commercial products seldom arrive with their source code, an old component's source code may be lost, or the only person who understood it may be lost. Even if possible, changing a component is often not desirable. If it is used in more than one system—the whole premise of component use—it must now be maintained in multiple versions if the change to make it work renders it unusable for some of the old systems.

The alternative to changing the code of one or both mismatched components is to insert code that reconciles their interaction in a way that fixes the mismatch. There are three classes of repair code: wrappers, bridges, and mediators.

Wrappers.   The term *wrapper* implies a form of encapsulation whereby some component is encased within an alternative abstraction. It simply means that clients access the wrapped component services only through an alternative interface provided by the wrapper. Wrapping can be thought of as yielding an alternative interface to the component. We can interpret interface translation as including:

- Translating an element of a component interface into an alternative element
- Hiding an element of a component interface
- Preserving an element of a component's base interface without change

As an illustration, assume that we have a legacy component that provides programmatic access to graphics-rendering services, where the programmatic services are made available as Fortran libraries and the graphics rendering is done in terms of custom graphics primitives. We wish to make the component available to clients via CORBA, and we wish to replace the custom graphics primitives with X Window System graphics.

CORBA's interface description language (IDL) can be used to specify the new interface that makes the component services available to CORBA clients rather than through linking with Fortran libraries. The repair code for the "provides assumptions" interface is the C++ skeleton code automatically generated by an IDL compiler. Also included in the repair code is hand-written code to tie the skeleton into component functionality.

There are various options for wrapping the component's "requires assumptions" interface to accomplish the switch from custom graphics to the X system. One is to write a translator library layer whose API corresponds to the API for the custom graphics primitives; the implementation of this library translates custom graphics calls to X Window calls.

Bridges.   A *bridge* translates some requires assumptions of one arbitrary component to some provides assumptions of another. The key difference between a bridge and a wrapper is that the repair code constituting a bridge is independent of any particular component. Also, the bridge must be explicitly invoked by some external agent—possibly but not necessarily by one of the components the bridge spans. This last point should convey the idea that bridges are usually transient and that the specific translation is defined at the time of bridge construction (e.g., bridge compile time). The significance of both of these distinctions will be made clear in the discussion of mediators.

Bridges typically focus on a narrower range of interface translations than do wrappers because bridges address specific assumptions. The more assumptions a bridge tries to address, the fewer components it applies to.

Assume that we have two legacy components, one that produces PostScript output for design documents and another that displays PDF (Portable Document Format) documents. We wish to integrate these components so that the display component can be invoked on design documents.

In this scenario, a straightforward interface repair technique is a simple bridge that translates PostScript to PDF. The bridge can be written independently of specific features of the two hypothetical components—for example, the mechanisms used to extract data from one component and feed it to another. This brings to mind the use of UNIX filters, although this is not the only mechanism that can be used.

A script could be written to execute the bridge. It would need to address component-specific interface peculiarities for both integrated components. Thus, the external agent/shell script would not be a wrapper, by our definition, since it would address the interfaces of both end points of the integration relation. Alternatively, either component could launch the filter. In this case, the repair mechanism would include a hybrid wrapper and filter: The wrapper would involve the repair code necessary to detect the need to launch the bridge and to initiate the launch.

Mediators. Mediators exhibit properties of both bridges and wrappers. The major distinction between bridges and mediators, however, is that mediators incorporate a *planning* function that in effect results in runtime determination of the translation (recall that bridges establish this translation at bridge construction time).

A mediator is also similar to a wrapper insofar as it becomes a more explicit component in the overall system architecture. That is, semantically primitive, often transient bridges can be thought of as incidental repair mechanisms whose role in a design can remain implicit; in contrast, mediators have sufficient semantic complexity and runtime autonomy (persistence) to play more of a first-class role in a software architecture. To illustrate mediators, we focus on their runtime planning function since this is the key distinction between mediators and bridges.

One scenario that illustrates mediation is intelligent data fusion. Consider a sensor that generates a high volume of high-fidelity data. At runtime, different information consumers may arise that have different operating assumptions about data fidelity. Perhaps a low-fidelity consumer requires that some information be "stripped" from the data stream. Another consumer may have similar fidelity requirements but different throughput characteristics that require temporary buffering of data. In each case, a mediator can accommodate the differences between the sensor and its consumers.

Another scenario involves the runtime assembly of sequences of bridges to integrate components whose integration requirements arise at runtime. For example, one component may produce data in format D^0, while another may consume data in format D^2. It may be that there is no direct $D^0{\rightarrow}D^2$ bridge, but there are separate $D^0{\rightarrow}D^1$ and $D^1{\rightarrow}D^2$ bridges that can be chained. The mediator would thus assemble the bridges to complete the $D^0{\rightarrow}D^2$ translation. This scenario covers the mundane notion of desktop integration and the more exotic runtime adaptive systems.

TECHNIQUES FOR DETECTING INTERFACE MISMATCH

In order to repair mismatches, we must first detect or identify them. We present the process of identifying mismatches as an enhanced form of component qualification.

The term *component qualification* has been used to describe the process of determining whether a commercial component satisfies various "fitness for use" criteria. Some component qualification processes include prototype integration of candidate components as an essential step in qualifying a component. This integration step discovers subtle forms of interface mismatch that are difficult to detect, such as resource contention. The need for this step is a tacit acknowledgment of our poor understanding of component interfaces.

Carrying out this evaluation starts with the observation that, for each service offered by a component, a set of requires assumptions must be satisfied in order to provide that service. A service is just a convenient way of describing how component functionality is packaged for use by clients. Qualification, then, is the process of

- discovering all of the requires assumptions of the component for each of the services that will be used by the system.
- making sure that each requires assumption is satisfied by some provides assumption in the system.

To illustrate these ideas more concretely, consider the qualification of a component that provides primitive data management services for multi-threaded applications. One service it provides is the ability to write a data value into a specified location (possibly specified by a key). In order to provide a multi-threaded storage service, the component might require various resources from an operating system—for example, a file system and locking primitives. This listing of the component's requires assumptions might be documented by a component provider, or it might need to be discovered by the component evaluator. In either case, this particular mapping would be useful for determining whether an upgrade of the operating system will have any impact on this particular integration relation. That is, did the new operating system change the semantics of `fwrite` or `flock`?

The list may include additional assumptions; for example, a provides assumption may stipulate that a CORBA interface be provided to the storage service. Depending on which implementation of the object request broker is used, this may or may not imply an additional provides assumption concerning the existence of a running object request broker process on the host machine that executes the storage service.

The assumptions list may reveal more interesting dependencies. For example, the same hypothetical component may allow a variable, but defined, number of clients to share a single data manager front-end process, with new processes created to accommodate overflow clients. This form of assumption can be crucial in predicting whether a component will satisfy system resource constraints.

TECHNIQUES FOR AVOIDING INTERFACE MISMATCH

One technique for avoiding interface mismatch is to undertake, from the earliest phases of design, a disciplined approach to specifying as many assumptions about a component's interface as feasible. Is it feasible or even possible to specify all of the assumptions a component makes about its environment, or that the components used are allowed to make about it? Of course not. Is there any evidence that it is practical to specify an important subset of assumptions, and that it pays to do so? Yes. The A-7E software design presented in Chapter 3 partitioned the system into a hierarchical tree of modules, with three modules at the highest level, decomposed into about 120 modules at the leaves. An interface specification was written for each leaf module that included the access programs (what would now be called methods in an object-based design), the parameters they required and returned, the visible effects of calling the program, the system generation parameters that allowed compile-time tailoring of the module, and a set of assumptions (about a dozen for each module).

Assumptions stated assertions about the *sufficiency* of the services provided by each module and the *implementability* of each service by identifying resources necessary to the module. Specific subject areas included the use of shared resources, effects of multiple threads of control through a module's facilities, and performance. These assumptions were meant to remain constant over the lifetime of the system, whose main design goal was modifiability. They were used by module designers to reassure themselves that they had appropriately encapsulated all areas of change within each module, by domain and application experts as a medium for evaluation, and by users of the modules to ensure suitability. Participants on the A-7 project felt that careful attention to module interfaces effectively eliminated integration as a step in the life cycle of the software. Why? Because architectural mismatch was avoided by careful specification, including the explicit assumptions lists that were reviewed for veracity by application and domain experts.

The notion of an interface as a set of assumptions, not just an API, can lead to a richer understanding of how to specify interfaces for components that work together in a variety of contexts. *Private interfaces* make visible only those provides and requires assumptions from a component's base interface that are relevant to its integration requirements in a particular system, or even to particular components in it. The idea is to suppress information about facilities that are not needed and whose presence may needlessly complicate the system.

There are advantages to different interfaces for the same component rather than a single omnibus base interface. The finer control over inter-component dependencies makes certain kinds of system evolution more tractable—for example, predicting the impact of upgrading a commercial component to a new version. Wrappers can be thought of as a repair strategy for introducing privacy. Additionally, architectural patterns can provide canonical forms that satisfy the provides and requires assumptions for the interface so that the number of distinct derivatives of a base interface may be relatively small in a system based on an architectural pattern that defines a small set of component types.

A *parameterized interface* is one whose provides and requires assumptions can be changed by changing the value of a variable before the component service is invoked. Programming languages have long possessed semantically rich parameterization techniques (e.g., Ada generics, ML polymorphism) that tailor a component's interface between the time it was designed and coded and the time its services are invoked. Commercial products also frequently provide some degree of customization via product parameterization (e.g., resource files or environment variables). Parameterized interfaces result in adaptation code that is both external to the component, where the values of the parameters are set, and within the component (to accommodate different parameter values).

Just as a mediator is a bridge with planning logic, a *negotiated interface* is a parameterized interface with self-repair logic. It may auto-parameterize itself, or it may be parameterized by an external agent. Self-configuring software can be thought of as involving negotiated interfaces, where the negotiation is a one-way "take-it-or-leave-it" dialog between component-building software and a host platform. Alternatively, products, such as modems, routinely use protocols to establish mutually acceptable communication parameters at runtime (rather than at install time).

Like wrappers, which can be used as a repair strategy to introduce translucency, mediators can be used as a repair strategy to introduce negotiated interfaces into a nonnegotiating component.

18.3   Component-Based Design as Search

Since component capabilities and liabilities are a principle source of architectural constraint in system development, and since systems use multiple components, component-based system design becomes a search for compatible *ensembles* of off-the-shelf components that come the closest to meeting system objectives. The architect must determine if it is feasible to integrate the components in each ensemble and, in particular, to evaluate whether an ensemble can live in the architecture and support system requirements.

In effect, each possible ensemble amounts to a continued path of exploration. This exploration should initially focus on the feasibility of the path to make sure there are no significant architectural mismatches that cannot be reasonably adapted. It must also take into account the feasibility of the repair and the residual risk remaining once the repair is completed.

Of course, the simultaneous exploration of multiple paths is expensive. As we show in our example, it is more likely that the focus will be on a primary path with additional paths treated as secondary. The important point is to view the selection of components in terms of ensembles rather than singly and to keep in mind that a particular path constitutes a hypothesis to be verified rather than a definitive design.

"How is it possible for one to achieve system quality attributes when dealing with component-dominated architectures?" The first answer may be that one does not. In many cases, the ability to use an existing off-the-shelf package to deploy greater functionality in a short time may outweigh performance, security, or other system requirements. Using OTS components sometimes blurs the line between requirements and system design. Evaluating components often causes modification of system requirements, adding to expectations about capabilities that may be deployed while forcing other "requirements" to be reconsidered.

Some flexibility in system requirements is beneficial in the integration of component-based systems, but it is also important to recognize when a requirement is essential to the success of the system and to not allow these requirements to be compromised. How, then, do we ensure that essential qualities are maintained in our component-dominated architecture?

In the previous section, we mentioned that component integration was a principal risk area and that the system architect must determine the feasibility of integrating a component ensemble such that the system is functionally complete and meets its quality attribute requirements. Ensembles then, must be evaluated to ensure not only that the components can be successfully integrated but also that they can support quality attribute objectives. To evaluate the feasibility of a component ensemble, including its ability to support the system's desired quality attributes, we use model problems.

Narrowly defined, a *model problem* is a description of the design context, which defines the constraints on the implementation. For example, if the software under development must provide a Web-based interface that is usable by both Netscape's Navigator and Microsoft's Internet Explorer, this part of the design context constrains the solution space. Any required quality attributes are also included in the design context.

A prototype situated in a specific design context is called a *model solution*. A model problem may have any number of model solutions, depending on the severity of risk inherent in the design context and on the success of the model solutions in addressing it.

Model problems are normally used by design teams. Optimally, the design team consists of an architect who is the technical lead on the project and makes the principal design decisions, as well as a number of designers/engineers who may implement a model solution for the model problem.

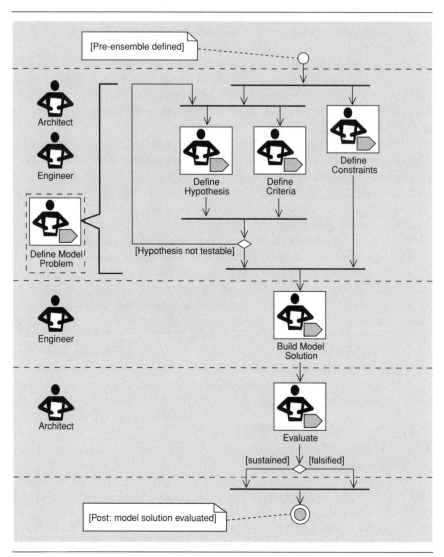

FIGURE 18.1 Model problem work flow

An illustration of the model problem work flow is shown in Figure 18.1. The process consists of the following six steps that can be executed in sequence:

1. The architect and the engineers identify a *design question*. The design question initiates the model problem, referring to an unknown that is expressed as a hypothesis.

2. The architect and the engineers define the *starting evaluation criteria*. These criteria describe how the model solution will support or contradict the hypothesis.

3. The architect and the engineers define the *implementation constraints*. The implementation constraints specify the fixed (inflexible) part of the design context that governs the implementation of the model solution. These constraints might include such things as platform requirements, component versions, and business rules.

4. The engineers produce a *model solution* situated in the design context. The model solution is a minimal application that uses only the features of a component (or components) necessary to support or contradict the hypothesis.

5. The engineers identify *ending evaluation criteria*. Ending evaluation criteria include the starting set plus criteria that are discovered as a by-product of implementing the model solution.

6. The architect performs an *evaluation* of the model solution against the ending criteria. The evaluation may result in the design solution being rejected or adopted, but often leads to new design questions that must be resolved in similar fashion.

In the remainder of this chapter we introduce an example and illustrate the application of these steps in the development of a Web-based application called ASEILM.

"O ATAM, Where Art Thou?"

This chapter is about finding out if a chosen ensemble of components can meet the quality and behavioral requirements of a system in which they are to be used. This is clearly an architectural question. Why, then, are we not using an architecture evaluation method, such as the ATAM, to answer it? After all, the ATAM's whole purpose is to evaluate architectural decisions (such as the decision to use certain components "wired" together in particular ways) in light of a system's quality and behavioral requirements. Why not simply say, "Perform an ATAM-based evaluation here" and be done with it?

The answer is that the process we describe in this chapter is less about evaluating the results of a packaged set of architectural decisions, and more about activities to help you make those decisions in the first place. The activities more resemble prototyping than analytical evaluation.

The ASEILM example shows how many very detailed issues of compatibility have to be resolved before developers can even begin to think about how the resulting ensemble provides various quality attributes. Just putting the ensemble together is a challenge. And while we are dealing with one ensemble, another one is waiting in the wings in case the first one does not work out. The process lets us manage the juggling act between candidate ensembles, and it lets us make a choice among them in a reasoned way by laying out small, practical, common-sense steps.

Each candidate ensemble implies several hypotheses that assert that you know what you are doing. You proceed in semi-parallel, wiring ensembles to each other and to the rest of your system until you discover that you *do not* know what you are doing. Then you try to wire them together differently, or you jump to plan B (the next ensemble). Typically, the quality attributes come in because you discover that what you do not know is how the ensembles manage quality attributes.

In order to do an ATAM evaluation you need to know something about the components you are using. The point of the process we describe here is that it is not yet clear what you know.

We have wrapped the process in a method's clothing to make it more repeatable and learnable, but it is pretty much just common sense. You make an informed guess at what components you want to use, build prototypes to test them and their interactions, evolve what works, and keep a backup plan in case your guess is wrong. The key insight is that you want to do this with an ensemble, not one component at a time.

Once an ensemble has been validated in this way, can it (and its encompassing system's architecture) still be the subject of an ATAM-based or other architecture evaluation? Absolutely.

— LJB and PCC

18.4 ASEILM Example

Our example centers around a Web-based information system developed at the Software Engineering Institute (SEI) for automating administrative interactions between SEI and its transition partners. The Automated SEI Licensee Management (ASEILM) system was created with the following objectives:

- To support the distribution of SEI-licensed materials, such as courses and assessment kits, to authorized individuals
- To collect administrative information for assessments
- To graphically present revenue, attendance, and other information about SEI licensed materials
- To track course attendance and royalties due to SEI

ASEILM must support the following multiple user types, each with varying authorization to perform system functions:

- Course instructors can input course attendee lists, maintain contact information, and download course materials.
- Lead assessors can set up assessments, input assessment information, and download assessment kits.
- SEI administrators can maintain lists of authorized instructors and lead assessors, as well as view or edit any information maintained by the system.

TABLE 18-1 Quality Attribute Requirements

Quality Attribute	Requirement
Functionality	Provide Web-based access to a geographically dispersed customer base
Performance	Provide adequate performance to users running overseas on low-bandwidth connections (i.e., download times in tens of minutes, not hours)
Compatibility	Support older versions of Web browsers including Netscape 3.0 and Internet Explorer 3.0
Security	Support multiple classes of users and provide an identification and authorization scheme to allow users to identify themselves
Security	Provide commercial-grade secure transfer of data over the Internet

Based on an initial analysis, the developers were able to generate a list of system requirements, many of which mapped directly to the qualities of the system being developed (see Table 18.1).

The normal give and take of requirements negotiation is different with off-the-shelf components. You may expect both more and less from them—more in the sense that more functionality is provided by these components "for free," less in the sense that this functionality may not precisely meet your organization's needs, and changing it may be difficult or impossible.

MIVA EMPRESSA ENSEMBLE

Building systems from off-the-shelf components is viewed by management as a simplification of the development process, requiring less experienced programmers than standard custom development. In fact, the opposite is almost always true: Development is typically *more* difficult, at least new development, with a new set of components. Extensive experience is often necessary to identify components that can be used to achieve a design; to understand compatibilities between these components and others; and to determine the tradeoffs between requirements, the use of specific components, and the overall costs. In the absence of this experience, a time-consuming search and qualification process must be undertaken.

In our example, the development team already had some familiarity with the Miva Empressa application server and preferred to use it as part of their initial hypothesis. *Miva Empressa* is an extension of Microsoft's Internet Information Server (IIS) that runs XML-based Miva Script. Miva Script applications running under Miva Empressa execute within IIS and can carry out complex computations, including database access. They are embodied in the "custom component" shown in Figure 18.2. Note that this was the *only* component developed from scratch by the ASEILM team.

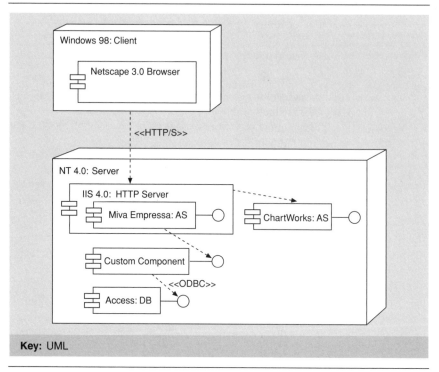

FIGURE 18.2 Miva Empressa ensemble

The ASEILM ensemble used several off-the-shelf components in addition to the Miva Empressa application server:

- Microsoft Access as a database management system
- Visual Mining's ChartWorks product to graph revenue, attendance, and other related information
- Microsoft IIS as an HTTP server
- Windows NT 4.0 as the operating system on the server platform

A client could be represented by any number of potential platforms and browsers. The initial ensemble included the Netscape 3.0 browser and the Windows 98 operating system. Netscape 3.0 represented an older browser version, with limited capabilities, but it was used by many lead assessors (one kind of ASEILM user). Windows 98 was used extensively in the ASEILM user base.

The definition of an ensemble is a pre-condition to the model-process work flow. This ensemble then, served as the basis for the initial model solution illustrated in Figure 18.2. In the following sections, we illustrate the model problem process using as the primary hypothesis that the Miva Empressa ensemble would be a satisfactory solution.

Step 1: Identify a Design Question.   The first step in the model problem process is to formulate one or more hypotheses, as use cases or scenarios, that test the design to see if the ensemble is a feasible solution. The following hypotheses were derived from the system quality attributes given in Table 18.1:

- *Hypothesis 1.* The ensemble can provide Web-based access to data maintained within the Access database, and display this data graphically using bar charts and other business graphics.
- *Hypothesis 2.* Communication between the Web browser and the HTTP server can be encrypted using HTTPS.

Hypothesis 1 was established primarily to test the functionality of the system and the ability to integrate the required components. Hypothesis 2 was established to prove the feasibility of meeting one of the stated security quality objectives for ASEILM: providing secure transfer of data over the Internet.

Proving both hypotheses does not, in this case, prove the feasibility of the overall ensemble, but it does allow progress toward a demonstration of feasibility by evaluating its additional required qualities. At the same time, evaluation of these hypotheses allows increased understanding of the components and their interactions within the ensemble.

Step 2: Define the Starting Evaluation Criteria.   Evaluation criteria are necessary to determine if the model solution supports or disproves the initial hypotheses.

- *Criterion 1.* The model solution can display a chart in the browser using data stored in the Access database.
- *Criterion 2.* Secure data can be transferred between the HTTP server and the Web browser over an HTTPS connection.

It is important that the success of the evaluation criteria be verifiable. For example, in the case of criterion 2, the security of data transfer can usually be established by observing the presence of the lock icon in the Web browser. Proper testing procedures must be used, however, to ensure that data being displayed in the Web browser actually originated in the database and was not "cached" somewhere along the route.

Step 3: Identify Implementation Constraints.   The constraints define inflexible elements in the design context. They make sure that the design solution is valid for the system under development. In this example, there were no implementation constraints other than those already identified.

Step 4: Produce a Model Solution.   After the model problem had been fully defined, the development team began implementing the model solution—that is, the minimal application necessary to support or contradict the hypothesis. During implementation, it is permissible and beneficial to identify additional criteria that must be satisfied to demonstrate the feasibility of the ensemble.

In the model solution for this example, ChartWorks is used to graph revenue, attendance, and other related information. The developers first attempted a straightforward solution that had the browser sending IIS an HTML statement to be forwarded to ChartWorks. The statement contained a query that identified the data to be graphed. They discovered two problems, however: coupling the labels of the graph to the data in it and maintaining a secure connection.

Coupling labels and data – ChartWorks uses the chart description language (CDL) to describe the chart, including how information would be extracted from the database (in this case, Access) and integrated into it. In this ensemble, chart labels and chart data needed to be extracted from the Access database, which required two different CDL statements. Unfortunately, CDL does not provide any mechanisms that could be used to pair the information generated as a result of different statements. This prevented its use to query the database directly. Instead, Miva was used to query the Access database and to create a text file that combined the label and the data information. A CDL statement was created to retrieve data from this file instead of communicating directly with the database.

Although this approach worked, it introduced significant complexity. For example, it was necessary to keep track of multiple intermediate files for different user sessions and to make sure these were not confused.

Secure communication – The HTML statement processed by IIS specifies the retrieval of an image generated by ChartWorks. Thus, IIS is constrained to use the ChartWorks APIs. ChartWorks provides an API for HTTP but not for HTTPS. This prevents a secure connection from being established between ChartWorks and the browser. To work around this problem, the team experimented with removing the HTTPS connection between IIS and ChartWorks. Since they are located on the same processor, security is enforced through access to the processor, not through the communication protocol. Unfortunately, this did not work either because there were both secure and insecure elements in a single Web page and the browser either did not allow the display of the page or informed the user of an insecure portion of a transmission. Neither option was acceptable.

To repair these problems, the team created a perl proxy server that sits between IIS and ChartWorks. They were then able to establish a secure connection between IIS and the proxy server so that the proxy server could communicate with ChartWorks using an HTTP connection. This solution is illustrated in Figure 18.3. The HTML statement was modified to invoke the perl proxy server.

Step 5: Identify Ending Evaluation Criteria. Additional evaluation criteria were identified during implementation of the Miva model solution; in particular, new quality attribute requirements were identified. During implementation, it was observed that the graphical presentation elements of the solution were highly intertwined with back-end logic. This made it difficult for graphic designers to help develop the system's user interface because they were unfamiliar with general-

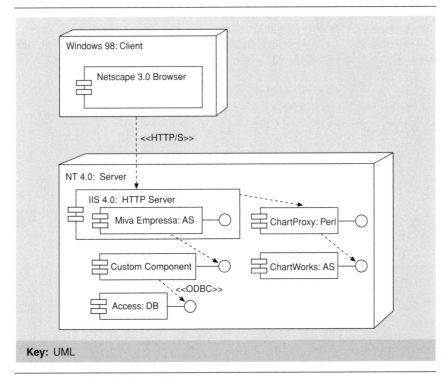

FIGURE 18.3   Introduction of Proxy server

purpose programming. The following evaluation criterion thus joined the model problem:

- *Criterion 3.* Presentation logic must be maintained separately from back-end business and database logic, and communicated through well-defined interfaces.

It was also discovered that the Access database did not support remote connections. Although communication with the database from the Miva application server through the ODBC interface was possible, the database had to be co-located on the same platform as the IIS server. Since IIS had to be located outside the SEI firewall to be available to the user community, the database had to be outside as well. This constraint was unacceptable, leading to the addition of a fourth criterion:

- *Criterion 4.* The database must be located in a secure location, behind the firewall.

Step 6: Evaluate the Model Solution.   Once the model solution had been implemented, and the additional evaluation criteria identified, the architect could evaluate the solution against the criteria.

Through the use of repair mechanisms, both of the initial criteria could have been satisfied. Not surprisingly, however, neither of the new criteria could have been satisfied. Because there were no obvious remedies for either problem, this ensemble was judged to be infeasible.

JAVA SERVLET ENSEMBLE

In addition to the primary ensemble based on Miva Empressa, an alternative, based on Java servlets, was identified. Miva Empressa was selected as the primary ensemble to investigate because of the existence of component expertise within the ASEILM development team; therefore, it received the most project resources. However, a limited effort was also devoted to evaluating the Java servlet ensemble. This exploration was the second time through the model problem work flow, so three steps could be saved:

- Step 1—The design question was unchanged.
- Step 2—The beginning evaluation criteria included all four criteria.
- Step 3—The constraints were unchanged.

The new evaluation was able to start with step 4, which involves building a model solution, as pictured in Figure 18.4.

This solution was able to satisfy the first two criteria using the same processes implemented in the Miva Empressa ensemble. As ChartWorks was a part of the Java ensemble, the developers continued using adapters to repair the HTTP/S mismatch.

The use of Java servlets allows separation of the presentation aspects of the system from the business and database logic. The presentation logic was restricted to HTML pages while the business and database logic was moved to servlets and Java beans executing in the Tomcat application server, satisfying criterion 3. Also, by replacing the Access database with SQL Server, the developers were able to use a remote connection to host the database behind the firewall, satisfying criterion 4.

In the process of developing a model solution for the new ensemble, the following four things happened:

- The initial criteria were shown to be insufficient, as already discussed.
- Portions of the design did not meet the initial criteria. In particular,
  - *Criterion 2.* Secure data can be transferred between the HTTP server and Web browser over an HTTPS connection.

  was insufficient to ensure the security of the system for reasons to be discussed shortly.
- Additional requirements surfaced from the stakeholders.
- The new Java ensemble introduced additional concerns.

We now discuss the last three items.

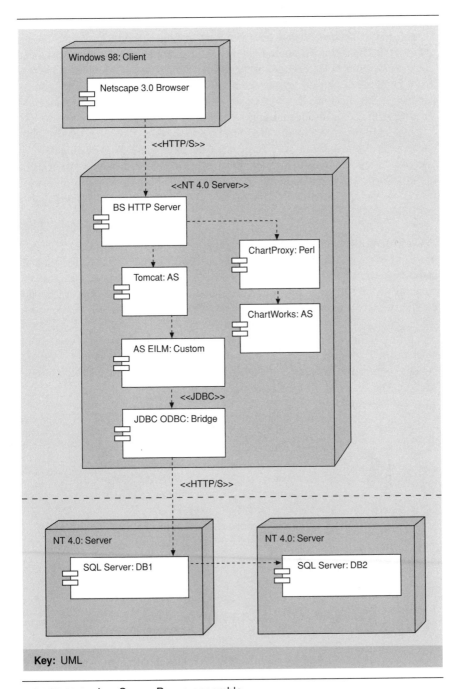

FIGURE 18.4   JavaServer Pages ensemble

Security – In addition to securing the transfer of data over the wire, the authentication model needed revisiting. Users were authenticated by placing a unique identifier, in the form of a cookie, on the client machine and mapping it to a session. The developers learned that, if the client machine was compromised, the user could be spoofed and the system compromised. To protect against this, the IP address of the machine that logged on was mapped to a unique identifier and checked with each subsequent request.

An additional technique, called "cross-side scripting," is sometimes used by hackers. In this case, the Web form is saved on the hacker's machine and is altered in some malicious way. The form is then submitted, potentially causing the server to crash and displaying code or some other unintended information to the client machine. ASEILM's solution was to define exceptions to guard against this kind of attack.

Additional requirements – During development, another group became aware of ASEILM and wished to integrate their data with its data. It was not immediately clear what data needed to be integrated or for what purpose. Nor was the structure of the data to be integrated clear. During investigation, it became apparent that many people kept their own copy of data that pertained in some way to the data that ASEILM was meant to track. To minimize the effect on ASEILM of supporting additional data types, the team needed to separate the data abstraction layer in the custom components from the business logic. This would allow the system to function without knowledge of the source or structure of the data store(s). The layers of the custom component are shown in Figure 18.5.

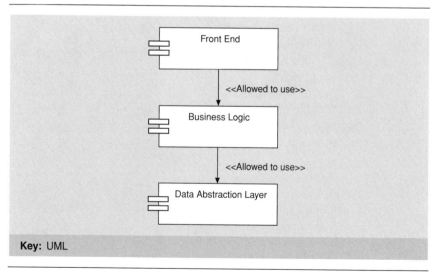

FIGURE 18.5 Layers of custom component

Concurrency – While the Java ensemble satisfied criteria that the Miva ensemble was unable to, it also introduced new concerns about concurrency management. Through the development of the model solution the team realized that (unlike the Miva ensemble) the Java ensemble did not manage concurrency.

Tomcat documentation did not discuss concurrency. To determine whether this was in fact a concern, the team had to discover the thread model for this ensemble. In particular, they had to learn how IIS and Tomcat related to each other and what effect this would have on the system. They analyzed the thread model and hypothesized that every user login created a distinct thread. This suggested three cases:

- *Two users access the system simultaneously and use different data.* When the custom component was divided into business logic and data abstraction layers, the decision was made to cache the appropriate data within the data abstraction layer. That is, on initialization the data is retrieved by the business logic from the database through the data abstraction layer and maintained within the business logic. The developers took no special actions to make the business logic thread safe. Thus, in the case of two users simultaneously accessing the business logic, they chose to treat the business logic as a critical section and to make access to all of it sequential by user. Since all relevant data is memory resident, satisfying each request is a fast operation and the wait for each user becomes intolerable only if there are many simultaneous users. In the environment of use, only a few simultaneous users are expected.

- *Two users access the system simultaneously and use the same data.* One aspect of this case—ensuring consistent data within the database—is a by-product of the solution for case 1. Since access to the business logic is kept sequential, each update is based on consistent data. A second aspect of this case— that a user may be viewing and operating on stale data—is a manifestation of the problem of "pushing" data to the user using HTTP. The team decided to build periodic reloading of the current Web page into the generated HTML, and thus the data being viewed and operated on is guaranteed to be current within a set tolerance. This is not an optimal solution, but it was easy to implement and, based on expectations of user load, probably adequate.

- *A single user with two simultaneous sessions.* The team simply disallowed this option.

The team evaluated this solution against the ending evaluation criteria, which were unchanged from the initial experiment with Miva. The Java servlet ensemble met the criteria, and implementation was continued.

The Java servlet ensemble solution turned out to be suitable for the project's needs, and the ASEILM system was fielded early in 2002. It is still too early to know if the assumptions about usage patterns with respect to concurrency are correct, but early indications are positive. Note, however, that this solution is not expected to scale well.

18.5 Summary

Quality attributes can be maintained in a system, even if that system is largely integrated from off-the-shelf components whose design and interaction mechanisms are not under the architect's control. However, achieving quality attributes in this type of system requires significantly different practices than for custom-developed code. The requirements process needs to be more flexible, allowing what is available in the marketplace to modify requirements to provide a better overall business solution. Essential requirements need to be identified and introduced as a critical constraint in the evaluation of feasible component ensembles. Multiple contingencies need to be considered, and as essential requirements increase in number and difficulty, custom development must be considered as a fallback.

18.6 Further Reading

This chapter contained techniques and processes excerpted from [Wallnau 02]. Issues in COTS adoption, including qualification, risk, and migration are covered at *http://www.sei.cmu.edu/cbs/*.

Architectural mismatch and techniques for recovering from it are explained in more detail in [Garlan 95].

19

Software Architecture in the Future

Prediction is very difficult, especially about the future.
— Niels Bohr

The history of programming can be viewed as a succession of ever-increasing facilities for expressing complex functionality. In the beginning, assembly language offered the most elementary of abstractions: exactly where in physical memory things resided (relative to the address in some base register) and the machine code necessary to perform primitive arithmetic and move operations. Even in this primitive environment programs exhibited architectures: Elements were blocks of code connected by physical proximity to one another or knitted together by branching statements or perhaps subroutines whose connectors were of branch-and-return construction. Early programming languages institutionalized these constructs with connectors being the semicolon, the goto statement, and the parameterized function call. The 1960s was the decade of the subroutine.

The 1970s saw a concern with the structuring of programs to achieve qualities beyond correct function. Data-flow analysis, entity-relation diagrams, information hiding, and other principles or techniques formed the bases of myriad design methodologies, each of which led to the creation of subroutines or collections of them whose functionality could be rationalized in terms of developmental qualities. These elements were usually called modules. The connectors remained the same, but some module-based programming languages became available to enhance the programmer's ability to create them. Abstractions embedded in these modules became more sophisticated and substantial, and for the first time reusable modules were packaged in a way so that their inner workings could theoretically be ignored. The 1970s was the decade of the module.

In the 1980s, module-based programming languages, information hiding, and associated methodologies crystallized into the concept of objects. Objects became the components du jour, with inheritance adding a new kind of (non-runtime) connector.

In the 1990s, standard object-based architectures, in the form of frameworks, started appearing. Objects have given us a standard vocabulary for elements and have led to new infrastructures for wiring collections of elements together. Abstractions have grown more powerful along the way; we now have computing platforms in our homes that let us treat complex entities, such as spreadsheets, documents, graphical images, audio clips, and databases, as interchangeable black-box objects that can be blithely inserted into instances of each other.

Architecture places the emphasis above individual elements and on the arrangement of the elements and their interaction. It is this kind of abstraction, away from the focus on individual elements, that makes such breathtaking interoperability possible.

In the current decade, we see the rise of middleware and IT architecture as a standard platform. Purchased elements have security, reliability, and performance support services that a decade ago had to be added by individual project developers. We summarize this discussion in Figure 19.1.

This is where we are today. There is no reason to think that the trend toward larger and more powerful abstractions will not continue. Already there are early *generators* for systems as complex and demanding as database management and avionics, and a generator for a domain is the first sign that the spiral of programming language power for that domain is about to start another upward cycle. The phrase *systems of systems* is starting to be heard more commonly, suggesting an emphasis on system interoperability and signaling another jump in abstraction power.

In this chapter, we will revisit the topics covered in the book. Heeding Niels Bohr, our vision will be not so much predictive as hopeful: We will examine areas of software architecture where things are not as we would wish and point out areas where the research community has some work to do.

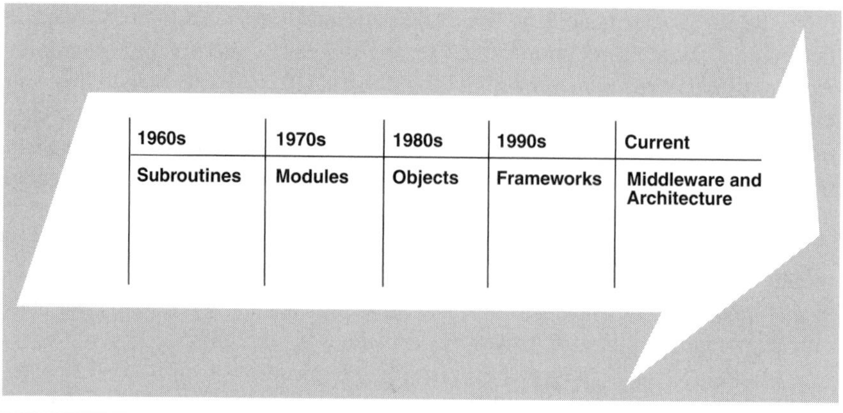

1960s	1970s	1980s	1990s	Current
Subroutines	Modules	Objects	Frameworks	Middleware and Architecture

FIGURE 19.1   Growth in the types of abstraction available over time

We begin by recapping what we have learned about the Architecture Business Cycle (ABC) and then discuss the process of creating an architecture, how architecture fits within the life cycle, and how we see components and component frameworks changing the tasks of an architect.

19.1   The Architecture Business Cycle Revisited

In Chapter 1, we introduced the ABC as the unifying theme of this book. We exemplified and elaborated this cycle throughout the book and have tried to convey some of the principles of architectural creation, representation, evaluation, and development along the way. If the study of software architecture is to have stamina, there must be areas of research that create a more mature field, with results that can be transitioned into practice. In this context, we can now identify and discuss four different versions of the ABC that appear to have particular promise in terms of future research:

- The simplest case, in which a single organization creates a single architecture for a single system
- One in which a business creates not just a single system from an architecture but an entire product line of systems that are related by a common architecture and a common asset base
- One in which, through a community-wide effort, a standard architecture or reference architecture is created from which large numbers of systems flow
- One in which the architecture becomes so pervasive that the developing organization effectively becomes the world, as in the case of the World Wide Web

Each of these ABCs contains the same elements as the original: stakeholders, a technical environment, an existing experience base, a set of requirements to be achieved, an architect or architects, an architecture or architectures, and a system or systems. Different versions of the ABC result from the business environment, the size of the market, and the goals pursued.

We believe that future software cost and benefit models, of which CBAM is an early version, will incorporate all of these versions of the ABC. In particular, they will take into account the upfront cost that architecture-based development usually entails, and they will be able to predict the quantitative benefits that architectures yield.

19.2   Creating an Architecture

In all of our case studies, we emphasized the quality requirements for the system being built, the tactics used by the architect, and how these tactics were manifested in the architecture. Yet this process of moving from quality requirements to architectural designs remains an area where much fruitful research can be done. The design process remains an art, and introducing more science into the process will yield large results.

Answers to the following questions will improve the design process:

- *Are the lists of quality attribute scenarios and tactics complete?* We presented lists for six different quality attributes. Almost certainly they should be augmented with additional tactics and scenarios. Also, additional attributes should have scenarios and tactics created for them. Interoperability and buildability are two quality attributes that may be as important as the six we wrote about.

- *How are scenarios and tactics coupled?* With what we have presented, the coupling is at the attribute level. That is, a scenario is generated according to the generation table for a particular attribute—performance, say. Then the tactics are examined to determine those most likely to yield the desired result. Surely, we can do better. Consider the performance scenario from our garage door opener example in Chapter 7: *Halt the door in 0.1 second when an obstacle is detected.* A series of questions can be asked that yield more insight into the choice of tactics. Can the obstacle be detected and the door halted in 0.1 second if there is nothing else going on in the system? If the answer is no, the tactic "increase computational efficiency" should be applied to the obstacle-detection algorithm. If the answer is yes, other questions regarding contention can be asked that should lead to the type of scheduler we choose in our design. Finding a systematic method for coupling scenarios and possible tactics would be an important research result.

- *How can the results of applying a tactic be predicted?* A holy grail of the software engineering community is to be able to predict the qualities of a system prior to its construction. One approach to this problem is to predict the effect of applying a tactic. Tactics are motivated by analytic models (formal and informal) of various attributes. For some, it is possible to predict the results of applying them. For example, a modifiability tactic is to use a configuration file managed by the end user. From a modifiability perspective, the result of applying that tactic is to reduce the time of changing and deploying a configuration item from (essentially) the deployment time if the modification is performed by a developer to near zero (in the worst case, the time to reboot a system). This is a predictable result. Developing the same type of predictions (and understanding the parameters to which a prediction applies) is a large step toward constructing systems with predictable qualities.

- *How are tactics combined into patterns?* In our garage door example, tactics were chosen and then, almost magically, combined into a pattern. Again, there should be a systematic method for this combination that maintains the predictability of quality responses as well. Since each tactic is associated with a predictable change in a quality attribute, tradeoffs in quality attributes can be considered within patterns. How these predictions are represented and combined becomes an open research question once tactics become combined into patterns.

- *What kind of tool support can assist in the design process?* We are forecasting a world with larger building blocks having progressively more functionality and associated quality attributes. What are its implications on tool support? Can tactics and their combination into patterns be embedded into an expert design assistant, for example?

- *Can tactics be "woven" into systems?* Aspect-oriented software development is an effort to develop methods and tools to deal with so-called "cross-cutting" requirements. A cross-cutting requirement applies to a variety of objects. Supporting diagnosis in an automobile, for example, is a requirement that applies to all of the automobile components and thus cross-cuts the requirements for the individual components. Quality attributes provide cross-cutting requirements, and tactics are methods for achieving particular responses. Can tactics, then, be treated as other cross-cutting requirements, and will the methods and tools developed by the aspect-oriented community apply?

19.3 Architecture within the Life Cycle

Although we have argued that architecture is *the* central artifact within the life cycle, the fact remains that a life cycle for a particular system comprises far more than architecture development. We see several areas ripe for research about architecture within the life cycle:

- *Documentation within a tool environment.* In Chapter 9, we discussed architecture documentation but not how this documentation is generated. Ideally, knowledge of a system's architecture is embedded in a tool, from which documentation can be generated automatically or semi-automatically. The generation of documentation from a tool assumes that the tool has knowledge of architectural constructs. Not only does it have this knowledge, but it provides a method for moving from one view to another. This, in turn, assumes that there is a method for specifying the mapping between views.

  The mapping between views comes with problems of its own: maintaining consistency across views—a change that is made in one view is automatically reflected in other views—and maintaining constraints both within and across views. For example, you should be able to specify that a process has no more than three threads (constraint within a view) and that particular modules should be bound into the same process (constraint across views).

- *Software architecture within configuration management systems.* One reason software architecture reconstruction exists is to determine whether the as-built architecture conforms to the as-designed architecture. Suppose a configuration management system knows about the designed architecture and can verify that consistency when a new or revised code module is checked in. In that case, there is no need for architecture conformance testing since conformance is guaranteed by the configuration management system. In that way, one motivation for architectural reconstruction disappears.

- *Moving from architecture to code.* Whenever there are multiple representations of a system, there is the problem of keeping these representations consistent, whether they are design models or architecture or code. The representation maintained becomes the correct one and the other representation degrades over time. If there is no tight coupling between the architecture and the code within some tool environment, then two problems exist. The first is moving from an architectural specification to code, since architecture design precedes coding. The second is maintaining the architecture in the face of system evolution, since code, not architecture, typically becomes the representation kept up to date.

19.4 The Impact of Commercial Components

As we said in Chapter 18, the capabilities and availability of commercial components are growing rapidly. So too are the availability of domain-specific architectures and the frameworks to support them, including the J2EE for information technology architectures. The day is coming when domain-specific architectures and frameworks will be available for many of today's common domains. As a result, architects will be concerned as much with constraints caused by the chosen framework as by green-field design.

Not even the availability of components with extensive functionality will free the architect from the problems of design, however. The first thing the architect must do is determine the properties of the used components. Components reflect architectural assumptions, and it becomes the job of the architect to identify them and assess their impact on the system being designed. This requires either a rich collection of attribute models or extensive laboratory work, or both. Consumers of components will want a trusted validation agency, such as Underwriters Laboratories, to stand behind the predictions.

Determination of the quality characteristics of components and the associated framework is important for design using externally constructed components. We discussed a number of options with J2EE/EJB in Chapter 16 and the performance impact of each. How will the architect know the effect of options that the framework provides, and, even more difficult, the qualities achieved when the architect has no options? We need a method of enumerating the architectural assumptions of components and understanding the consequences of a particular choice.

Software Architecture in Education

In this chapter, we focused on the technical future of software architecture and how we believe it is going to evolve. But what about the future of architecture in software engineering education? The discerning reader will have noticed that three members of the Bass family contributed to this book. I received a BA in mathematics in 1964, Tanya received a BS in computer science in 1991, and Matt received a BS in computer science in 2000. I will use our experiences to draw some general conclusions.

When I received my degree, I had seen one computer (we took a tour just to see it) and had absolutely no knowledge of programming or how computers worked. Of course, I was immediately hired as a programmer. The world was different then.

Given that you are going to spend thirty or forty years in your career, the clear message is that what you learn in school ages quickly and you need to keep current in order to remain on the leading edge of the field.

Tanya graduated having learned a variety of programming languages, including C but not C++, without being exposed to object-oriented concepts. Matt graduated having learned a different set of programming languages, including C++ and Java. He also learned about object-oriented design.

Within nine years, curricula evolved to include object-oriented languages and techniques. Although Matt did not take a course in architecture, by the time he graduated software architecture courses were common in graduate programs and in existence in undergraduate programs.

The education that Matt received included more elements of abstraction and design than the education that Tanya received, and this trend is only going to continue. Thus, my prediction for the year 2010 is that undergraduate curricula will routinely include courses in software architecture with some universities offering more than one course at that level. At the graduate level, software architecture as an area of specialization should be common.

We hope that this book foreshadows what will be in curricula in 2010 and that it leads the way for the other courses in software architecture that will be appearing.

— LJB

Finally, components and their associated frameworks must be produced and the production must be designed to achieve desired qualities. Their designers must consider an industry-wide set of stakeholders rather than those for a single company. Furthermore, the quality attribute requirements that come from the many stakeholders in an industry will likely vary more widely than the requirements that come from the stakeholders of a single company.

19.5 Summary

Where are the study and practices of software architecture going? Our clairvoyance is no more powerful than anyone else's, but, as with everyone else, that does not prevent us from indulging in some predictions. In addition to more powerful design techniques, an evolution of life-cycle tools to include more architectural information, and more sophisticated component building blocks for systems, we offer a prediction for the future where architecture is concerned.

Fred Brooks was once asked what made his book, *The Mythical Man-Month,* so timeless. He replied that it was not a book about computers but rather a book about people. Software engineering is like that. Dave Parnas says that the difference between programming and software engineering is that programming is all you need for single-person, single-version software, but if you expect other people to ever look at your system (or expect to look at it yourself later on), you need to employ the discipline of software engineering. Architecture is like that, as well. If all we cared about was computing the right answer, a trivial monolithic architecture would suffice. Architecture is brought to bear when the people issues are exposed: making the system perform well, building the system within cost constraints, achieving desired benefits, letting teams work cooperatively to build the system, helping the maintainers succeed, letting all the stakeholders understand the system.

With this in mind, we can offer our safest prediction. Architecture will continue to be important as long as people are involved in the design and development of software.

Acronyms

AAS	Advanced Automation System, the name given to the planned complete overhaul of the U.S. air traffic control system
ABC	Architecture Business Cycle
ABM	Atomic Broadcast Manager
ADD	Attribute Driven Design method
API	application programming interface
ASEILM	Automated SEI Licensee Management
AST	Abstract syntax tree
ATAM	Architecture Tradeoff Analysis Method
ATC	air traffic control
BCN	Backup Communications Network
CBAM	Cost Benefit Analysis Method
C&C	component-and-connector, a category of views
CDL	Chart description language
CERN	European Laboratory for Particle Physics
CGI	common gateway interface
COCOMO	constructive cost modeling
COOB	common object manager
CORBA	Common Object Request Broker Architecture
COSE	common operating system environment
COTS	commercial off-the-shelf, referring to software or other components that can be readily purchased
CPU	central processing unit
CSC	Computer Software Components
CSCI	Computer Software Configuration Item, a component of software
CSCW	Computer Supported Cooperative Work
C3	command, control, and communications
DAWG	Data Access Working Group
DBMS	database management systems
DMZ	demilitarized zone
DSRGM	Decision Support and Report Generation Manager
ECS	Earth Core System
EDARC	Enhanced Direct Access Radar Channel within the ISSS
EFC	EDARC format conversion, an application within Display Management
EIS	EDARC interface software, an application within Common System Services

EJB	Enterprise JavaBeans
EOS	Earth Observing System
EOSDIS	Earth Observing System Data System Information System
ESI	External System Interface
ESIP	ESI processor
FAA	Federal Aviation Administration, the customer for ISSS
FAR	Federal Acquisition Regulations
FG	functional group, an application that is not fault tolerant (i.e., is not an operational unit) for the ISSS
FIFO	first-in/first-out
FTP	File Transfer Protocol
GIOP	General Inter-ORB Protocol
GUI	graphical user interface
HCI	human-computer interface
HCIS	Host computer interface software, an application within Common System Services of the ISSS
HCS	Host Computer System, the central ATC computer
HTML	HyperText Markup Language
HTTP	HyperText Transfer Protocol
HTTPS	HyperText Transfer Protocol Secure
I/O	input/output
IAPR	interactive architecture pattern recognition
IDE	integrated development environment
IDL	Interface Definition Language
IEEE	Institute of Electrical and Electronics Engineers
IIOP	Internet Inter-ORB Protocol
IMS	inertial measurement system
IP	Internet Protocol
ISO	International Organization for Standardization
ISSS	Initial Sector Suite System, the system intended to be installed in the en route air traffic control centers, and the subject of the case study in Chapter 6
ISV	independent software vendor
IT	information technology
JDBC	Java Database Connectivity
JMS	Java Messaging Service
JNDI	Java Naming and Directory Interface
JSP	JavaServer Pages
J2EE	Java 2 Enterprise Edition
JTS	Java Transaction Service
JVM	Java Virtual Machine

KSLOC	thousands of source lines of code, a standard measure of a computer program's static size
KWIC	keyword in context
LAN	local area network
LCN	Local Communications Network
LGSM	local/group SMMM, an application within Common System Services
LIU	LCN interface unit
M&C	Monitor and Control, a type of console in ISSS
MIFT	manage internal facility time, an application within Common System Services for the ISSS
MIPS	million instructions per second
MODN	Noise Model
MODP	Prop Loss Model
MODR	Reverb Model
MRI	magnetic resonance imaging
MVC	Model-View-Controller
NASA	National Aeronautics and Space Administration
NASM	national airspace system modification, one of the CSCIs of ISSS
NAT	network address translation
NISL	network interface sublayer within the ISSS
NIST	National Institute of Standards and Technology
NNTP	Network News Transport Protocol
NRL	Naval Research Laboratory
OLE	object linking and embedding
OLTM	OnLine Transaction Manager
OMA	object management architecture
OMG	Object Management Group
ORB	object request broker
PAC	Presentation-Abstraction-Control pattern
PAS	primary address space, the copy of an application that does actual work for the ISSS; *see also* SAS
PCTE	portable common tools environment
PDF	Portable Document Format
PICS	platform for Internet content selection
PMS	prepare messages, an application within Common System Services for the ISSS
RCS	Revision Control System
RISC	reduced instruction set chip
RMI	Remote Method Invocation
ROOM	real-time object-oriented modeling
RPC	remote procedure call
RUP	Rational Unified Process

SAAM	Software Architecture Analysis Method
SAR	system analysis and recording, a function of ISSS; also an application within the recording, analysis, and playback function
SAS	standby, or secondary, address space, a backup copy of an application ready to take over if the corresponding PAS fails within the ISSS
SCR	Software Cost Reduction
SEI	Software Engineering Institute
SIMD	single instruction, multiple data
SLOC	source lines of code
SMMM	system monitor and mode management
SQL	Structured Query Language
SSL	Secure Sockets Layer
TAFIM	Technical Architecture for Information Management
TARGET	Theater-Level Analysis, Replanning and Graphical Execution Toolbox
TCA	Terminal Control Area
TCP	Transmission Control Protocol
TCP/IP	Transmission Control Protocol/Internet Protocol
UDDI	Universal Description, Discovery, and Integration
UI	user interface
UML	Unified Modeling Language
URL	Uniform Resource Locator
VPN	virtual private network
W3C	World Wide Web Consortium
WAIS	Wide Area Information Service
WAP	Wireless Application Protocol
WIMP	window, icon, mouse, pointer
WWW	World Wide Web
XML	eXtensible Markup Language

References

[Abowd 93] Abowd, G., Bass, L., Howard, L., Northrop, L. "Structured Modeling: An O-O Framework and Development Process for Flight Simulators," CMU/SEI-1993-TR-14. Software Engineering Institute, Carnegie Mellon University, 1993.

[Abowd 96] Abowd, G., Bass, L., Clements, P., Kazman, R., Northrop, L., Zaremski, A. "Recommended Best Industrial Practice for Software Architecture Evaluation," Technical Report CMU/SEI-96-TR-025. Software Engineering Institute, Carnegie Mellon University, 1996.

[Alur 01] Alur, D., Crupi, J., Malks, D. *Core J2EE Patterns: Best Practices and Design Strategies.* Sun Microsystems Press, 2001.

[Alexander 77] Alexander, C., Ishikawa, S., Silverstein, M., Jacobson, M., Fiksdahl-King, I., Angel, S. *A Pattern Language.* Oxford University Press, 1977.

[America 00] America, P., Obbink, H., van Ommering, R., van der Linden, F. "CoPAM: A Component-Oriented Platform Architecture Method Family for Product Family Engineering," in *Software Product Lines: Experience and Research Directions* (P. Donohoe, ed.). Kluwer, 2000.

[Anastasopoulos 00] Anastasopoulos, M., Gacek, C. "Implementing Product Line Variability," IESE report 89.00/E, v. 1.0. Fraunhofer Institut Experimentelles Software Engineering, 2000.

[ASCYW 94] ASCYW. *Structural Modeling Handbook.* Air Force Aeronautical Systems Command, 1994.

[Asundi 01] Asundi, J., Kazman, R., Klein, M. "Using Economic Considerations to Choose amongst Architecture Design Alternatives, CMU/SEI-2001-TR 035. Software Engineering Institute, Carnegie Mellon University, 2001.

[AT&T 93] AT&T. "Best Current Practices: Software Architecture Validation." Internal report, copyright 1991. AT&T, 1993.

[Bachmann 02] Bachmann, F., Bass, L., Klein, M. "Illuminating the Fundamental Contributors to Software Architecture Quality," SEI/CMU-2002-TR-025. Software Engineering Institute, Carnegie Mellon University, 2002.

[Barfield 01] Barfield, W., Caudell, T. (eds.). *Fundamentals of Wearable Computers and Augmented Reality.* Lawrence Erlbaum Associates, 2001.

[Bass 00] Bass, L., Clements, P., Donohoe, P., McGregor, J., Northrop, L. "Fourth Product Line Practice Workshop Report," CMU/SEI-2000-TR-002. Software Engineering Institute, Carnegie Mellon University, 2000.

[Bass 01a] Bass, L., John, B., Kates, J. "Achieving Usability through Software Architecture," CMU/SEI-2001-TR-005. Software Engineering Institute, Carnegie Mellon University, 2001.

[Bass 01b] Bass, L., Klein, M., Moreno, G. "Applicability of General Scenarios to the Architecture Tradeoff Analysis Method," CMU/SEI-2001-TR-014. Software Engineering Institute, Carnegie Mellon University, 2001.

[Berners-Lee 1996a] Berners-Lee, T. *WWW Journal* 3 (*http://www.w3.org/pub/WWW/Journal*), 1996.

[Berners-Lee 1996b] Berners-Lee, T. "WWW: Past, Present, Future," *IEEE Computer*, October 1996.

[Boehm 76] Boehm, B., Brown, J., Lipow, M. "Quantitative Evaluation of Software Quality," *Proceedings of the Second International Conference on Software Engineering.* IEEE Computer Society, 1976.

[Boehm 81] Boehm, B. *Software Engineering Economics.* Prentice Hall, 1981.

[Boehm 95] Boehm, B. "Engineering Context," *Proceedings of the First International Workshop on Architectures for Software Systems.* Available as CMU-CS-TR-95-151 from the School of Computer Science, Carnegie Mellon University, April 1995.

[Booch 94] Booch, G. *Object-Oriented Design with Applications, Second Edition.* Benjamin-Cummings, 1994.

[Bosch 00a] Bosch, J. *Design and Use of Software Architectures: Adopting and Evolving a Product Line Approach.* Addison-Wesley, 2000.

[Bosch 00b] Bosch, J. "Organizing for Software Product Lines," *Proceedings of the Third International Workshop on Software Architectures for Product Families.* Springer LNCS, 2000.

[Bowman 99] Bowman, T., Holt, R., Brewster, N. "Linux as a Case Study: Its Extracted Software Architecture," *Proceedings of the Second International Conference on Software Engineering.* ACM Press, 1999.

[Brand 97] van den Brand, M., Sellink, M., Verhoef, C. "Generation of Components for Software Renovation Factories from Context-Free Grammars," *Proceedings of the Fourth Working Conference on Reverse Engineering.* ACM Press, 1997.

[Briand 99] Briand, L., Daly, J., Wust, J. "A Unified Framework for Coupling Measurements in Object-Oriented Systems," *IEEE Transactions of Software Engineering* 25(1), 1999.

[Britton 81] Britton, K., Parnas, D. "A-7E Software Module Guide," NRL Memorandum Report 4702, December 1981.

[Brooks 69] Brooks, F., Iverson, K. *Automatic Data Processing (System 360 Edition).* John Wiley, 1969.

[Brooks 75] Brooks, F. *The Mythical Man-Month: Essays on Software Engineering.* Addison-Wesley, 1975.

[Brooks 95] Brooks, F. *The Mythical Man-Month: Essays on Software Engineering (Anniversary Edition).* Addison-Wesley, 1995.

[Brown 95] Brown A., Carney, D., Clements, P. "A Case study in Assessing the Maintainability of a Large, Software-Intensive System," *Proceedings of the International Symposium on Software Engineering of Computer-Based Systems.* IEEE Computer Society, 1995.

[Brownsword 96] Brownsword, L., Clements, P. "A Case Study in Successful Product Line Development," CMU/SEI-96-TR-016. Software Engineering Institute, Carnegie Mellon University, 1996.

[Buschmann 96] Buschmann, F., Meunier, R., Rohnert, H., Sommerlad, P., Stal, M. *Pattern-Oriented Software Architecture: A System of Patterns.* John Wiley, 1996.

[Bush 45] Bush, V. "As We May Think," *Atlantic Monthly,* July 1945.

[CACM 88] Special Issue: HyperText Systems. *Communications of the ACM,* July 1988.

[Cederling 92] Cederling, U. "Industrial Software Development: A Case Study," thesis. Linkoping University (Linkoping, Sweden), 1992.

[Chastek 96] Chastek, G., Brownsword, L. "A Case Study in Structural Modeling," CMU/SEI-1996-TR-35, ESC-1996-TR-025. Software Engineering Institute, Carnegie Mellon University, 1996.

[Chretienne 95] Chretienne, P., Lenstra, J., Coffman, E. (eds.). *Scheduling Theory and Its Applications.* John Wiley, 1995.

[Chung 00] Chung, L., Nixon, B., Yu, E., Mylopoulos, J. *Non-Functional Requirements in Software Engineering.* Kluwer, 2000.

[Clements 02*a*] Clements, P., Kazman, R., Klein, M. *Evaluating Software Architectures: Methods and Case Studies.* Addison-Wesley, 2002.

[Clements 02*b*] Clements, P., Northrop, L. *Software Product Lines: Practices and Patterns.* Addison-Wesley, 2002.

[Clements 03] Clements, P., Bachmann, F., Bass, L., Garlan, D., Ivers, J., Little, R., Nord, R., Stafford, J. *Documenting Software Architectures: Views and Beyond.* Addison-Wesley, 2003.

[Conway 68] Conway, M. "How Do Committees Invent?" *Datamation* 14(4), 1968.

[Cristian 93] Cristian, F. "Understanding Fault-Tolerant Distributed Systems" (*ftp. cs.ucsd.edu/pub/tech-reports/understandingftsystems.ps.Z*), 1993.

[Cusumano 95] Cusumano, R., Selby, R. *Microsoft Secrets: How the World's Most Powerful Software Company Creates Technology, Shapes Markets, and Manages People.* The Free Press, 1995.

[Dijkstra 68] Dijkstra, E. "The Structure of the 'T.H.E.' Multiprogramming System," *Communications of the ACM* 18(8), 1968.

[Fielding 96] Fielding, R., Whitehead, E., Anderson, K., Bolcer, G., Oreizy, P., Taylor, R. "Software Engineering and the WWW: The Cobbler's Barefoot Children, Revisited," Technical Report 96-53. Department of Information and Computer Science, University of California, Irvine, November, 1996.

[Fogarty 67] Fogarty, L. "Survey of Flight Simulation Computation Methods," *Proceedings of the Third International Simulation and Training Conference.* Society for Computer Simulation, 1967.

[Gamma 95] Gamma, E., Helm, R., Johnson, R., Vlissides, J. *Design Patterns: Elements of Reusable Object-Oriented Software.* Addison-Wesley, 1995.

[Garlan 95] Garlan, D., Allen, R., Ockerbloom, J. "Architectural Mismatch: Or Why It's Hard to Build Systems out of Existing Parts," *Proceedings of the Seventeenth International Conference on Software Engineering.* ACM Press , 1995.

[Gibbs 94] Gibbs, W. "Software's Chronic Crisis," *Scientific American*, September 1994.

[Glass 98] Glass, R, "Editorial," *Journal of Systems and Software* (Elsevier Science) 43(3): 161-163, 1998.

[Gram 96] Gram, C., Cockton, G. *Design Principles for Interactive Software.* Chapman & Hall, 1996.

[Guo 99] Guo, G., Atlee, J., Kazman, R. "A Software Architecture Reconstruction Method," Report No. WICSA1. *Proceedings of the First Working IFIP Conference on Software Architecture.* Kluwer, 1999.

[Hager 89] Hager, J. "Software Cost Reduction Methods in Practice," *IEEE Transaction on Software Engineering* 15, 1989.

[Hager 91] Hager, J. "Software Cost Reduction Methods in Practice: A Post-Mortem Analysis," *Journal of Systems Software* 14, 1991.

[Harris 95] Harris, D., Reubenstein, H., Yeh, A. "Reverse Engineering to the Architectural Level," *Proceedings of the Seventeenth International Conference on Software Engineering.* ACM Press, 1995.

[Hassan 00] Hassan, A., Holt, R. "A Reference Architecture for Web Servers," *Proceedings of the Working Conference on Reverse Engineering.* IEEE Computer Society, 2000.

[Hoffman 00] Hoffman, D., Weiss, D. (eds). *Software Fundamentals: Collected Papers by David L. Parnas.* Addison-Wesley, 2001.

[Hofmeister 00] Hofmeister, C., Nord, R., Soni, D. *Applied Software Architecture.* Addison-Wesley, 2000.

[IEEE 00] The Institute of Electrical and Electronics Engineers Standards Board. *Recommended Practice for Architectural Description of Software-Intensive Systems,* IEEE-Std-1471- 2000, September 2000.

[ISO 91] *International Standard ISO/IEC 9126. Information Technology: Software Product Evaluation—Quality Characteristics and Guidelines for Their Use.* International Organization for Standardization/International Electrotechnical Commission, Geneva, 1991.

[Jacobson 97] Jacobson, I., Griss, M., Jonsson, P. *Software Reuse: Architecture, Process, and Organization for Business Success.* Addison-Wesley, 1997.

[Jalote 94] Jalote, P. *Fault Tolerance in Distributed Systems.* Prentice Hall, 1994.

[Jones 99] Jones, T. Capers. *Estimating Software Costs.* McGraw-Hill, 1999.

[Kazman 94] Kazman, R., Bass, L., Abowd, G., Webb, M. "SAAM: A Method for Analyzing the Properties of Software Architectures," *Proceedings of the Sixteenth International Conference on Software Engineering.* ACM Press, 1994.

[Kazman 99*a*] Kazman, R., Carrière, S. "Playing Detective: Reconstructing Software Architecture from Available Evidence," *Journal of Automated Software Engineering* 6(2), April 1999.

[Kazman 99*b*] Kazman, R., Barbacci, M., Klein, M., Carrière, S., Woods, S. "Experience with Performing Architecture Tradeoff Analysis," *Proceedings of the Twenty-First International Conference on Software Engineering.* ACM Press, 1999.

[Kazman 01] Kazman, R., Asundi, J., Klein, M. "Quantifying the Costs and Benefits of Architectural Decisions," *Proceedings of the Twenty-Third International Conference on Software Engineering.* IEEE Computer Society, 2001.

[Krikhaar 99] Krikhaar, R. *Software Architecture Reconstruction.* Ph.D. thesis, University of Amsterdam, 1999.

[Kruchten 95] Kruchten, P. "The 4+1 View Model of Architecture," *IEEE Software* 12(6), 1995.

[Kruchten 00] Kruchten, P. *The Rational Unified Process: An Introduction, Second Edition.* Addison-Wesley, 2000.

[Laprie 89] Laprie, J. *Dependability: A Unifying Concept for Reliable Computing and Fault Tolerance* (T. Anderson, ed.). Blackwell Scientific, 1989.

[Lee 88] Lee, K., Rissman, M., D'Ippolito, R., Plinta, C., van Scoy, R. *An OOD Paradigm for Flight Simulators, Second Edition,* CMU/SEI-1988-TR-30. Software Engineering Institute, Carnegie Mellon University, 1988.

[Marsman 85] Marsman, A. "Flexible and High-Quality Software on a Multi-Processor Computer System Controlling a Research Flight Simulator," *AGARD Conference Proceedings No. 408: Flight Simulation* 9(1), 1985.

[McCabe 00] McCabe & Associates. "IQ2" (an integrated set of products and processes), *http://www.mccabe.com*, 1996.

[McConnell 96] McConnell, S. *Rapid Development: Taming Wild Software Schedules.* Microsoft Press, 1996.

[McGregor 01] McGregor, J., Sykes, D. *A Practical Guide for Testing Object-Oriented Software.* Addison-Wesley, 2001.

[Menasce 00] Menasce, D., Almeida, V. *Scaling for E-Business: Technologies, Models, Performance, and Capacity Planning.* Prentice Hall, 2000.

[Morris 93] Morris, C., Fergubor, C. "How Architecture Wins Technology Wars," *Harvard Business Review*, 71(March-April): 86-96, 1993.

[Müller 93] Müller, H., Mehmet, O., Tilley, S., Uhl, J. "A Reverse Engineering Approach to System Identification," *Journal of Software Maintenance: Research and Practice* 5(4), 1993.

[Parnas 71] Parnas, D. "Information Distribution Aspects of Design Methodology," *Proceedings of the 1971 IFIP Congress*, North Holland, 1971.

[Parnas 72] Parnas, D. "On the Criteria for Decomposing Systems into Modules," *Communications of the ACM* 15(12), 1972.

[Parnas 74] Parnas, D. "On a 'Buzzword': Hierarchical Structure," *Proceedings of the 1974 IFIP Congress.* Kluwer, 1974.

[Parnas 76] Parnas, D. "On the Design and Development of Program Families," *IEEE Transactions on Software Engineering,* SE-2(1), 1976.

[Parnas 79] Parnas, D. "Designing Software for Ease of Extension and Contraction," *IEEE Transactions on Software Engineering* SE-5(2), 1979.

[Parnas 85*a*] Parnas, D., Clements, P., Weiss, D. "The Modular Structure of Complex Systems," *Proceedings of the Seventh International Conference on Software Engineering.* Reprinted in *IEEE Transactions on Software Engineering* SE-11, 1985.

[Parnas 85*b*] Parnas D., Weiss, D. "Active Design Reviews: Principles and Practices," *Proceedings of the Eighth International Conference on Software Engineering,* 1985.

[Paulish 02] Paulish, D. *Architecture-Centric Software Project Management.* Addison-Wesley, 2002.

[Perry 66] Perry, D., Warton, L., Welbourn, C. "A Flight Simulator for Research into Aircraft Handling Characteristics," Report No. 3566. Aeronautical Research Council Reports and Memoranda, 1966.

[Pfaff 85] Pfaff, G. (ed.). *User Interface Systems.* Eurographics Seminars, Springer-Verlag, 1985.

[Ramachandran 02] Ramachandran, J. *Designing Security Architecture Solutions.* John Wiley, 2002.

[Rissman 90] Rissman, M., D'Ippolito, R., Lee, K., Steward, J. "Definition of Engineering Requirements for AFECO: Lessons from Flight Simulators," CMU/SEI-1990-TR-25. Software Engineering Institute, Carnegie Mellon University, 1990.

[Rumbaugh 99] Rumbaugh, J., Jacobson, I., Booch, G. *The Unified Modeling Language Reference Manual.* Addison-Wesley, 1999.

[Schmidt 00] Schmidt, D., Stal, M., Rohnert, H., Buschmann, F. *Pattern-Oriented Software Architecture, Volume 2: Patterns for Concurrent and Networked Objects.* John Wiley, 2000.

[Seacord 99] Seacord, R., Wallnau, K., Robert, J., Comella-Dorda, S., Hissam, S. "Custom vs. Off-the-Shelf Architecture," *Proceedings of the Third International Enterprise Distributed Object Computing Conference,* 1999.

[SEI ATA] See *http://www.sei.cmu.edu/ata/ata_init.html.*

[Shaw 96] Shaw, M., Garlan, D. *Software Architecture: Perspectives on an Emerging Discipline.* Prentice Hall, 1996.

[Sneed 98] Sneed, H. "Architecture and Functions of a Commercial Software Reengineering Workbench," *Proceedings of the Second Euromicro Conference on Maintenance and Reengineering.* IEEE Computer Society, 1998.

[Soni 95] Soni, D., Nord, R., Hofmeister, C. "Software Architecture in Industrial Applications," *Proceedings of the Seventeenth International Conference on Software Engineering.* ACM Press, 1995.

[Stallings 99] Stallings, W. *Cryptography and Network Security: Principles and Practice, Third Edition.* Prentice Hall, 1999.

[Stonebraker 90] Stonebraker, M., Rowe, L., Hirohama, M. "The Implementation of POSTGRES," *IEEE Transactions on Knowledge and Data Engineering* 2(1), 1990.

[Svahnberg 00] Svahnberg, M., Bosch, J. "Issues Concerning Variability in Software Product Lines," *Proceedings of the Third International Workshop on Software Architectures for Product Families.* Springer LNCS, 2000.

[UIMS 92] UIMS Tool Developers Workshop. "A Metamodel for the Runtime Architecture of an Interactive System," *SIGCHI Bulletin* 24(1), 1992.

[Wallnau 02] Wallnau, K., Hissam, S., Seacord, R. *Building Systems from Commercial Components.* Addison-Wesley, 2002.

[Weiss 00] Weiss, D., Lai, C. *Software Product Line Engineering: A Family-Based Software Development Process.* Addison-Wesley, 2000.

[Witt 94] Witt, B., Baker, F., Merritt, E. *Software Architecture and Design.* Van Nostrand Reinhold, 1994.

[Wong 94] Wong, K., Tilley, S., Muller, H., Storey, M. "Programmable Reverse Engineering," *International Journal of Software Engineering and Knowledge Engineering* 4(4), December 1994.

Index

ABC. *See* Architecture Business Cycle
ABM. *See* Atomic Broadcast Manager
"Abstract common services" tactic, 106, 135, 138, 148–149, 442
Abstraction, 21, 37, 43, 210, 477, *478*
  mastering at CelsiusTech, 375–376
  and packaging, 142
  and SS2000, 396
Abstract syntax tree, for information extraction, 235, 236
Access control, 117, 118
Accessibility, and the Web, 331
Access layer, for libWWW, 336
Access (Microsoft), 468, 470
Access procedures, 54, 64
access_read relationship, 235
access_write relationship, 235
Account bean, 414, 415, *416, 419*
Acronyms, 218, 485
Activation, of stateful bean, 410
Activation list, in Active Object design pattern, 124
Active design review, 268
Active Object design pattern, 124
"Active redundancy" tactic, 103, 141
ActiveX, 343
Activity control problems, 162
actually_calls relation, 240
Ada, 132, 139, 144, 371, 380, 387, 462
Ada package specification, and signature specification, 212
Ada programs, 142, 147, 378, 390
Adaptation data, 147–148
Adapters, 109
ADD. *See* Attribute-Driven Design
Address spaces, 139, *140*
"Adherence to defined protocols" tactic, 111
  and client-server view, 142
  and code templates, 149
  and integrability, 175
Ad hoc tools, for information extraction, 236
Advanced Automation System (AAS), 129, 131
Aerodynamics, and flight simulator, 181, 182
Aggregate, 122
Aggregation, in UML, 219–221
Aircraft structure, unclear mapping between software structure and, 181

Aircraft systems, and airframe, 193, 195
Air traffic control case study, 129–151
  architectural solution in, 135–149
  requirements and qualities in, 132–135
Air traffic controllers, 132, 133, *134*
Air traffic control system, *132, 150*
  ABC applied to, *132*
  availability requirements for architecture of, 155
Air vehicle model, 182, 183
  application modules, 187–192
  executive modules, 185–187
  n-square chart for, 194, *195*
AIX (IBM), operating system, 144
  Ada tasks mapped onto processes, 142
  and SS2000, 373
Algorithms, voting, 102
"Allocated-to" relation, 38
Allocation structures, 36, 38–39
Allocation views, 41, 206
  options in, 208–209
  in UML, 227–229
Allowed-to-use structure, 60, *61*, 62, 63
Amazon.com, 348–349
Analysis results, in architecture background, 209
Analyze architectural approaches
  in ATAM evaluation phases, 282–284, 285
  in Nightingale system evaluation phases, 297–299, 302
"And" states, 210
Annotations, interfaces as, 224
Anomaly detection, 118
"Anonymity of processor assignment," and SS2000, 390
"Anticipate expected changes" tactic, 107, 138, 148, 442
AOLbyPhone, 454
AOL/Netscape, 347
Apache project, 346, 347
Aperiodic operations, 187, 191
Aperiodic processing, and flight simulator, 183
AppleScript, CGI scripts in, 339, 340
Application constituent, of Structural Model architectural pattern, 185
Application Data Type Module, 57, 62
Application module layer, for libWWW, 336

495

Fault-tolerant ISSS applications, code structure template for, *149*
Federal Aviation Administration, 70, 129, 130, 132
Fidelity, range of and flight simulators, 179
File containment, code segments for, *254*
Files, 234
  in UCMEdit model, 250
File Transfer Protocol, 336
Filter architectural type, 227
Filter Behavior Module, 58
Filter class, 223
Filtering, 118
Filters, and bridges, 459
Financial benefits, from architectural inspections, 263
findByPrimaryKey method, 415
finder method, 415
Finite-state-machine models, 13
Fire control systems, 370, 372
Firewalls, 87, 117, 336, 343–344, 471, 472
First-in/First-out (FIFO), 115
First-order effects, and flight simulator, 193
"Fitness for use" criteria, and component qualification, 460
Fitness of purpose, evaluating software product line for, 362
Fixed-priority scheduling, 115
Flight controls system, in air vehicle model, 195
Flight data, and ISSS physical view, 136
Flight simulation case study, 175–199
  architectural solution, 182–196
  relationship to ABC, 176–177
  requirements and qualities, 177–181
Flight simulators, 70
  and ABC, 176–*177*
  design challenges with, 175
  execution states with, 179–181, 189
  geographically distributed areas, 180
  properties of, 179–181
  purpose of, 177
  reference model for, *182*
  roles in, 177–178
Flight simulator software, 155
Flight strips, 136, 151
Follow-up (phase 3)
  and ATAM, 276
  in Nightingale system, 303
Formal specification languages, 13
Fortran, CGI scripts in, 339
Fortran libraries, 458
Forward-looking radar, 50, 51
"Four Plus One" approach, 41

Frame rates
  for flight simulators, 179–180
  and periodic time management, 183
Frameworks, 478, 482
Front-line workers, computer support for, 427, 429
FTP. *See* File Transfer Protocol
Fuel system, in air vehicle model, 196
Functional group (FG), 139, *140*
Functionality, 72
  allocating in example, 160, 161
  and architecture, 72
  for controller children, 192–193
  and market share, 95
Functional requirements, for child modules in ADD, 164–165
Functional subsets, rapid identification of, 60
Function calls, disambiguating, 241
function_calls_function, 239
Function Driver modules, 58, 62, 65, 66
Function pointers, 236
Functions, 234, 253
Function type, 244
Fused views, items, *240*
Future, in Active Object design pattern, 124

Garage door opener example, 156–166, 480
Garbage collection, and heap size, 424
Gateways, 336
-gcverbose compiler option, 424
Gen++, 235
Generalization, in UML, *221*–222
Generalized capability components, 442
"Generalize the module" tactic, 107, 147
  and code templates, 149
  and module decomposition view, 138
General quality scenarios, generation of, 78
General scenarios, 75, 97
  availability, *76*
  communicating concepts and use of, 93–94
Generate quality attribute utility tree
  in ATAM evaluation phase 1, 279–282
  in Nightingale system evaluation phase 1, 294–295, 297
Generators for systems, 478
Generic utilities, for libWWW, 335, 336
get method, 422
get_outbound_msg operation, 187
Global Availability Management, 144
Global variables, in UCMEdit model, 250
GNU make utility, 248
Good design, promotion of, 265
Gopher, 336

Carnegie Mellon
Software Engineering Institute

SEI^{SM} Classroom Training

Based on decades of experience and supported by four widely acclaimed practitioner books in the SEI Addison-Wesley Series, the SEI offers the Software Architecture Curriculum and the Software Product Lines Curriculum.

Software Architecture Curriculum

Collection of six courses, three certificate programs, and a field exercise that equip software professionals with state-of-the-art practices so they can efficiently design software-intensive systems that meet their intended business and quality goals.

Courses:

Software Architecture: Principles and Practices

Documenting Software Architectures

Software Architecture Design and Analysis

Software Product Lines

Architecture Tradeoff Analysis Method (ATAM) Evaluator Training

ATAM Facilitator Training

ATAM Coaching and Observation

Certificate Programs:

Software Architecture Professional Certificate Program

ATAM Evaluator Certificate Program

ATAM Lead Evaluator Certificate Program

Software Product Lines Curriculum

Collection of five courses and three certificate programs that equip software professionals with state-of-the-art practices so they can efficiently use proven product lien practices to achieve their strategic reuse and other business goals.

Courses:

Software Product Lines

Adopting Software Product Lines

Product Line Technical Probe Training

Developing Software Product Lines

Product Line Technical Probe Facilitator Training

Certificate Programs:

Software Product Lines Professional Certificate

Product Line Technical Probe Team Member Certificate

Product Line Technical Probe Leader Certificate

For current course information visit: *www.sei.cmu.edu/products/courses/*
To register for courses call: **412.268.7388**
or email: *courseregistration@sei.cmu.edu*

In addition to the curricula and certificate programs, the SEI has developed software architecture and product line methods and approaches to assist organizations in achieving their technical and business objectives.

To learn more, visit: *www.sei.cmu.edu/programs/pls/*

Software Engineering Institute
4500 Fifth Avenue
Pittsburgh, PA 15213

412.268.5800 **www.sei.cmu.edu**

^{SM} SEI is a service mark of Carnegie Mellon University

The SEI Series in Software Engineering

ISBN 0-201-73500-8

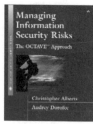

ISBN 0-321-11886-3

ISBN 0-201-73723-X

ISBN 0-201-54664-7

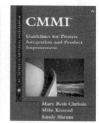

ISBN 0-321-15496-7

ISBN 0-201-70372-6

ISBN 0-201-70482-X

ISBN 0-201-70332-7

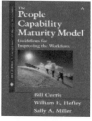

ISBN 0-201-60445-0

ISBN 0-201-60444-2

ISBN 0-201-25592-8

ISBN 0-201-54597-7

ISBN 0-201-54809-7

ISBN 0-201-18095-2

ISBN 0-201-54610-8

ISBN 0-201-47719-X

ISBN 0-201-77639-1

ISBN 0-201-61626-2

ISBN 0-201-70454-4

ISBN 0-201-73409-5

ISBN 0-201-85480-5

ISBN 0-321-11884-7

ISBN 0-201-70064-6

ISBN 0-201-17782-X

ISBN 0-201-52577-1

Please see our Web site at http://www.awprofessional.com for more information on these titles.

Additional Software Architecture Titles

Documenting Software Architectures
Views and Beyond
Paul Clements, Felix Bachmann, Len Bass, David Garlan, James Ivers, Reed Little, Robert Nord, and Judith Stafford

Although architecture is now widely recognized as a critical element in software development, there has been little guidance independent of language or notation on how to capture it. Based on the authors' extensive experience, this book helps you decide what information to document, and then, with guidelines and examples, shows you how to express an architecture in a form that all project stakeholders can understand.

0-201-70372-6 • Hardcover • 560 Pages • ©2003

Evaluating Software Architectures
Methods and Case Studies
Paul Clements, Rick Kazman, and Mark Klein

This book is a comprehensive, step-by-step guide to software architecture evaluation, describing specific methods that can quickly and inexpensively mitigate enormous risk in software projects. The methods are illustrated both by case studies and by sample artifacts put into play during an evaluation: view-graphs, scenarios, final reports—everything you need to evaluate an architecture in your own organization.

0-201-70482-X • Hardcover • 240 Pages • ©2002

Software Product Lines
Practices and Patterns
Paul Clements and Linda Northrop

Building product lines from common assets can yield remarkable improvements in productivity, time to market, product quality, and customer satisfaction. This book provides a framework of specific practices, with detailed case studies, to guide the implementation of product lines in your own organization.

0-201-70332-7 • Hardcover • 608 Pages • ©2002